The **BIG** Book of Big Secrets

William Poundstone

The BIG Book of Big Secrets

The Uncensored Truth About All Sorts of Stuff You Are Never Supposed to Know

BARNES
&NOBLE
B O O K S
NEW YORK

2001 Barnes & Noble Books

ISBN 0-7607-2707-4

Printed and bound in the United States of America

04 05 M 9 8 7 6

Contents

I: People

II: Merchandise

III: Codes

IV: Illusion

V. Performance

VI: Ritual

Big Secrets

William Poundstone

BIG SECRETS

The Uncensored Truth
About All Sorts of Stuff
You Are Never
Supposed to Know

The following recipes are used with permission of The AVI Publishing Company, Inc., 250 Post Road East, Westport, CT 06881: Cola Flavor Base (MF 238), Cola Flavor (MF 241), Benedictine-Type Cordial Flavor (MF 297), and Grand "M"-Type Flavor from pages 332–333, 333–334, 392–393, and 405, respectively, of *Food Flavorings* by Joseph Merory, 1968; Angostura Essence (MF 296A) and Italian Bitter Essence (MF 314A) from pages 806 and 817 of *Source Book of Flavors* by Henry B. Heath, 1981.

The recipe for Chartreuse flavor is reprinted with permission from page 625 of *Fenaroli's Handbook of Flavor Ingredients,* edited, translated, and revised by Thomas E. Furia and Nicolo Bellanca. Copyright © 1971 by CRC Press, Inc., Boca Raton, FL.

The outlines of the Rorschach blots are reproduced courtesy of Verlag Hans Huber, Bern, Switzerland.

The excerpts from *The Amazing World of Kreskin* by Kreskin are reprinted with permission of Random House, Inc. Copyright © 1973 by Kreskin.

The initiation stunts from *Initiation Stunts* by Lieutenant Beale Cormack are described by permission of the publisher, Baker's Plays, Boston. Copyright 1922 by Fitzgerald Publishing Corporation. Copyright in renewal 1950 by Walter Ben Hare.

Library of Congress Cataloging in Publication Data

Poundstone, William.
  Big secrets.

  Includes index.
  1. Trade secrets. I. Title.
HD38.7.P68 1985   031'.02   85-3603
ISBN 0-688-04830-7 (pbk.)

Printed in the United States of America

    33 34 35 36 37 38 39 40

BOOK DESIGN BY VICTORIA HARTMAN

To Judith Schnerk

Preface

The subject matter of this book ought not to exist at all. This is a book about institutional secrets—big secrets, secrets that affect the masses. It may seem incredible that something like a club handshake or a franchised fried chicken recipe can remain a secret. Surely too many insiders know the secret (and might talk). Surely too many outsiders are exposed to the secret (and might surmise it). Yet, by and large, institutional secrets remain secrets.

No harm is done by most institutional secrets. But it is only natural to be curious about them. The best gossip, after all, is gossip somebody doesn't want you to hear. Would anyone other than a chemist care what is in Coca-Cola if the Coca-Cola Company were not so loath to discuss the ingredients? Would the reversed message in Pink Floyd's *The Wall* be as intriguing if you could play it on an ordinary stereo? Would you puzzle over Doug Henning's magic if not for his smug assurance that you really don't want to know how it is done? Here, then, is a whole book about what people don't want you to know.

Few secrets are imponderable mysteries. The knack of doing a book such as this is to find out whom to talk to. I have been aided by all those who suggested topics or lines of research, directed me to friends of friends, revealed secrets, and provided advice and assistance. Thanks to Benton Arnovitz, Nicholas Bakalar, James S. Bradbury, Michael Chellel, Karon Corley, the staff of the Cornell University libraries, Paul Crouch, Jr., Mitch Douglas, Norman Farnsworth, Charles P. Grier, Cynthia Hayes, Luis Herrero, E. J. Kahn, Jr., Valerie Battle Kienzle, Gerry Kroll, Stuart C. Lerner and the staff of Associated Analytical Laboratories, James Mastroberti, Russell D. Meltzer, Cheryl Messemer, Julia F. Morton, Ric Myers, Gloria and Paul Pitzer, George A. Pollak, Stefan Rudolf and the staff of High Rise Sound, Daniel Schindler, Beverly Smith, Stewart Stogel, Barry Streims, Theresa Sullivan, and Rosalie Muller Wright.

And thanks especially to those who asked that their names not be mentioned.

Contents

PART ONE

Going to Hell in a Shopping Basket

I t's really your parents' fault. But how were they supposed to know that the Gee-Whiz ElectroShock Toilet Trainer wasn't the latest scientific development? Now you've got the cleanest apartment in town and a five-dollar-a-day Bon Ami habit. You're on a first-name basis with *E. coli*. And you know it's a none-too-spic-'n'-span world out there, chock full of lax personal hygiene and shrimp somebody forgot to devein. Given the propensity of hairnets for finding their way into corn dogs, you probably like to know exactly what's in food before you eat it. Well, *tough*. The processed-food industry isn't a restaurant, and you'll have to take what everyone else is eating. Food is not enough; most people want mystery. Secret recipes, secret sauces, secret spices. Millions of hearty eaters like postindustrial *je ne sais quoi* and are willing to pay for it. If there's a life beyond Dr Pepper, it's as welcome at the Safeway as a wet cleanup in aisle nine. Mom was right: Don't play with your food; you never know where it's been.

But how can big companies keep their secret recipes secret from the hundreds of employees who prepare the stuff? They can't. As the following pages demonstrate, the corporate grapevines have plenty to say.

1·

Kentucky Fried Chicken

As far as anyone knows, Colonel Harland Sanders revealed his recipe for Kentucky Fried Chicken to just two living souls. One was his wife, Claudia. The other was Jack C. Massey, head of the three-man syndicate that purchased the Kentucky Fried Chicken Corporation from Sanders in 1964.

Apparently, none of the five thousand Kentucky Fried Chicken franchisees has ever been told the full recipe. New restaurant operators attend "KFC University," a company-owned outlet in Louisville. There they are initiated into the special cooking method. They aren't told what is in the seasoning mix, however. Franchisees must buy the seasonings premixed from the Kentucky Fried Chicken Corporation. Some outlets buy ten-ounce packets of seasonings that are to be mixed with twenty-five pounds of flour. Others buy a preseasoned coating mix that contains the flour.

No Platinum in There

Ever since the Kentucky Fried Chicken chain mushroomed in the mid-1960s, the secret recipe has been the object of speculation. Examination of the chicken shows that the coating is a thin, almost soggy layer (in the "original recipe"; there is also a "spicy-crispy" version) adhering to the skin. The meat is notably moist, allegedly because of the special pressure-cooking process. There is little popular conviction as to what seasonings figure in the "secret blend of eleven herbs and spices." The chicken is flavorful, but no herb or spice predominates. *The New York Times* quoted Sanders as maintaining that the herbs and spices "stand on everybody's shelf."

The presumption that the seasonings in Kentucky Fried Chicken are in fact perfectly ordinary ones has long been a bone of contention between franchisees and Kentucky Fried Chicken management. Restaurateurs are charged a steep price for the seasonings—more than any conceivable combination of herbs and spices ought to cost, say franchisees. In a 1976 book on McDonald's (*Big Mac: The Unauthorized Story of McDonald's* by Max Boas and Steven Chain), McDonald's founder Ray Kroc observed: "Kentucky Fried Chicken licensees claimed that they were paying three to four to five times for the same herbs and for the same chicken, and that they could get it from Durkee's or Kraft or any big company in the United States. And Kentucky Fried Chicken said, no, you couldn't because the formula was a secret. You know that was a lot of crap. Any laboratory can tell you what's in it. There's no platinum in there. There's no gold in there."

That there isn't platinum or eye of passenger pigeon in the mix is supported by the fact that the colonel occasionally whipped up the seasoning mixture impromptu. In Sanders' autobiography, *Life as I Have Known It Has Been Finger Lickin' Good,* he tells of selling his first franchisee, Leon "Pete" Harmon, on the chicken. Sanders concocted a batch of the seasoning mix from the pantry of Harmon's Salt Lake City restaurant.

Granting that all of the colonel's seasonings could be found at any well-stocked A&P, the task of identifying them remains formidable. There are approximately forty herbs, spices, and other seasonings available in American supermarkets and gourmet stores. Of these, perhaps twenty or thirty are common enough to "stand on everybody's shelf," figuratively speaking, and to have been in use at Sanders' roadside cafe. The use of eleven different seasonings is not remarkable. The standard "poultry seasoning" of the food industry has ten herbs and spices: pepper, ginger, mace, allspice, cloves, marjoram, nutmeg, thyme, savory, and sage.

In 1974 *Esquire* magazine asked four food writers to try Kentucky Fried Chicken and offer their analyses. There was little consensus.

James Beard found the chicken "well seasoned with salt"; with less assurance, he thought he detected monosodium glutamate, cayenne pepper, and cinnamon. Roy Andries de Groot was "reasonably sure of minuscule amounts" of rosemary, savory, tarragon, thyme, pepper, turmeric, and cinnamon. He also noted salt, monosodium glutamate, "tiny globules of what might be honey or brown sugar," and "the faintest touch of both almond and mint." Waverly Root concluded that the chicken was "dunked in some sort of batter" containing flour, milk, and perhaps egg. Root was certain only of salt and pepper in the seasoning; he guessed that celery salt, caraway, chili powder, and/or horseradish might be present. James Villas doubted that any milk or egg was used in the coating and further doubted that there were eleven herbs and spices. He detected only cinnamon and cloves. Villas argued that the secret of Kentucky Fried Chicken is sugar: "Real fried chicken is not sweet; this is." The sugar, he suspected, was added to the "very light and very safe and very healthy cooking oil."

Another analysis comes from Gloria Pitzer, a St. Clair, Michigan, homemaker and newsletter publisher. Pitzer's *Secret Recipe Report* attempts to duplicate the recipes of popular processed foods for home use. In the late 1970s, Pitzer devised three recipes for facsimile Kentucky Fried Chicken.

The recipes call for the chicken pieces to be fried in a pan or deep fryer until brown and then transferred to an oven for thirty to thirty-five minutes' additional cooking. One-fourth to one-half inch of water in the baking pan keeps the chicken moist in the oven. In Pitzer's first recipe, the chicken is seasoned with a marinade made from commercial Italian salad dressing mix, flour, salt, lemon juice, and oil.

Pitzer's second and third recipes use eleven herbs and spices each. The second, said to simulate spicy-crispy Kentucky Fried Chicken, requires garlic salt, onion powder, paprika, black pepper, allspice, sweet basil, oregano, sage, summer savory (substitution: parsley flakes), ginger, and rosemary. All are mixed with flour and salt. Chicken pieces are dampened with beer or club soda, dredged in the flour/seasoning mix, and fried.

The third recipe uses a modified list of herbs and spices: rosemary, oregano, sage, ginger, marjoram, thyme, parsley, pepper, paprika, garlic salt, and onion salt. Three additional flavorings— brown sugar, powdered chicken bouillon, and Lipton Tomato Cup-a-Soup mix—supplement the herbs and spices. Pitzer's recipes are the result of her own experimentation; she disavows any special knowledge of Kentucky Fried Chicken's actual recipe.

Does Phyllis George Know the Colonel's Recipe?

As late as June 1967, *Business Week* magazine could claim that "only Sanders, Massey [then chairman of the board of the corporation], and the company's food engineer know the recipe." This was not strictly correct. Sanders' wife, Claudia, certainly knew the recipe. It may be conjectured that other spouses, children, and business associates were told too.

Who Told Whom?
The Kentucky Fried Chicken Recipe

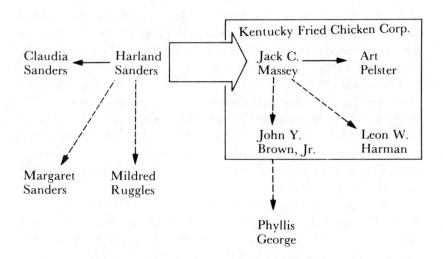

Claudia Sanders was a former employee at the Sanders Café in Corbin, Kentucky. In 1948 she became Sanders' second wife. Interstate 75 diverted the tourist traffic from the Sanders' motel/restaurant operation, forcing them to sell. The colonel took to the road at age sixty-six to promote his chicken franchise business. He had twenty-five white suits, always traveled with a pressure cooker and a bag of seasonings in the back seat of his Packard, and ate his chicken three to five times a week. Claudia stayed at home, mixed the secret seasonings, and sent them to franchisees. The colonel sold the business—too soon, too cheaply—in 1964, retaining the Canadian operation. He spent his last years praising the Lord and cursing the Heublein Corporation, which purchased the business from Sanders' buyers. Harland Sanders died in 1980 at the age of ninety. Claudia is proprietor of Claudia Sanders' Dinner House in Shelbyville, Kentucky.

It is hard to believe that the children weren't let in on the secret recipe. Sanders had two, both by his first marriage. At least one, Margaret, played a crucial role in the business by coming up with the idea of take-out service. For this Sanders gave her the franchise to the state of Florida. Margaret Sanders now lives in Palm Springs; sister Mildred Ruggles lives in Lexington, Kentucky.

The secret passed out of the family in 1964, when Sanders sold Kentucky Fried Chicken to a three-man syndicate for $2 million. Heading the syndicate was Jack C. Massey, a Nashville financier who had become bored with early retirement in Florida. Massey knew the secret, and so did food engineer Art Pelster. Pelster, originally an aerospace engineer, was in charge of mixing up the seasonings and refining the cooking method. He invented and patented several new types of frying and heating equipment for Kentucky Fried Chicken. Seven years after Massey's group bought the company, it was sold to Heublein, Inc.—purveyors of Smirnoff vodka, A.1 steak sauce, Snap-E-Tom tomato cocktail, Beaulieu Vineyard wines, Ortega Mexican food, and Arrow liqueurs—for a reported $287 million.

It is uncertain if Massey's two partners knew the recipe. One, Utah franchisee Leon "Pete" Harmon, seems to have had little role in day-to-day management. The other partner was attorney John Y. Brown, Jr. Brown helped convince Sanders to sell. After the sale, Massey groomed Brown to succeed him, and it seems a reasonable conjecture that Massey told Brown the secret recipe. Brown replaced Massey as chief executive officer and served as chairman of the board after the Heublein acquisition. (Massey left the company, reportedly after a tiff with Brown.) Profits from the sale to Heublein helped finance Brown's late, successful entry in the 1979 Kentucky gubernatorial race. Young, bright, and skillful at answering charges that he swindled an old man out of a chicken business, Brown is said to have higher political ambitions. ("Hell, governing Kentucky is easier than running Kentucky Fried Chicken," he told the press. "There's no competition.")

So the chain of initiates grew. If Brown knows the secret recipe, wouldn't he have told his wife, Phyllis George? Perhaps. A much-touted secret recipe might be more interesting to spouses, relatives, and friends than the average trade secret. A dozen or more people may now know the secret recipe, many of them not directly connected with the Kentucky Fried Chicken Corporation.

If so, they've been circumspect. No one has come forward to reveal the secret recipe.

Laboratory Analysis

Big Secrets selected a large college near a Kentucky Fried Chicken outlet. Advertisements asking that Kentucky Fried Chicken employees respond were placed in a student newspaper and on campus bulletin boards. Interviews with respondents revealed how the chicken is prepared. In essence, the descriptions agreed with Sanders' 1966 patent for a "process of producing fried chicken under pressure" (no. 3,245,800; copies available from the U.S. Patent Office).

The patent, of course, does not tell what seasonings are used. None of the respondents to the ads knew what seasonings are in the coating mix. Nor had they heard any rumors. But one respondent supplied a sample of the coating mix: a pungent-smelling white powder with black and tan flecks.

On the basis of Kroc's contention that any laboratory could tell what's in the mix, a food laboratory was consulted. It refused to do an analysis after hearing where the sample had come from. A second laboratory agreed to do an analysis. Approximately one cup of coating mix was sent for testing. The laboratory was asked to do a qualitative analysis—to identify everything in the sample, but not to worry about determining exact proportions. A list of likely herbs and spices compiled from Pitzer's recipes, the *Esquire* article, and the ingredients of the standard poultry seasoning was supplied as a starting point.

Based on the interviews, Sanders' patent, and the lab results, the secret recipe goes roughly like this:

Chickens weighing between 2¼ and 2½ pounds are preferred. They are cut into eight to ten pieces. What makes the Kentucky Fried Chicken recipe different from most others is that the quantity of chicken must be geared to the amount and temperature of the oil. If you try cooking just one piece of chicken in the usual amount of oil at the usual temperature, you get a cinder. This is why Sanders' method has not been duplicated widely at home.

For the typical five-pound batch cited in the patent, about eight quarts of oil at 400 ° F is needed. Sanders reasons in the patent description as follows: Chicken cooked by ordinary means tends to lose its natural moisture before the meat is fully done. Chicken tends to be undercooked or dried out. The obvious remedy is to cook the chicken in a watery liquid. Then the chicken looks and tastes "boiled." Furthermore, if a browned coating is desired, it often requires higher temperatures or longer cooking times than is appropriate for the chicken proper.

Sanders' solution is to start the cooking process at about 400 ° F—a high temperature that quickly browns the coating. A pressure cooker supplied with an air hose and pump is used. Continued cooking at 400 ° would incinerate the chicken, but the cold chicken and the generation of steam from the moisture in the coating lower the temperature of the cooking fat to about 250 ° F in a minute or two. The heating elements are then turned down to maintain a 250 ° F temperature throughout the remainder of the cooking cycle.

Meanwhile, the moisture boiling out of the chicken builds up the pressure in the closed vessel. If the various quantities have been measured correctly, a pressure of about fifteen pounds per square inch (above atmospheric pressure) is created. This raises the boiling point of water, and thus the actual cooking temperature of the moist chicken meat, to about 250 ° F. Under these conditions, chicken cooks two to ten times faster than in conventional cooking. The steam pressure prevents any further loss of moisture. If for some reason the steam pressure is not quite fifteen pounds per square inch, the air pump attached to the cooker makes up the difference. The total cooking time, including the browning phase, is about ten minutes. Then the pressure is released and the chicken is drained and stored in a warming oven (at about 160 ° F) until purchase.

There is no batter as such. The chicken pieces are "immersed in a dip made of skimmed or reconstituted skimmed milk and whole eggs (approximately eight per gallon of milk)," explains Sanders in his patent. "The dipped pieces are then rolled in flour to which has been added salt and other seasoning ingredients" and fried.

The seasonings, the most carefully guarded part of the Kentucky Fried Chicken recipe, yielded a surprise. The sample of coating mix was found to contain four and only four ingredients: flour, salt, monosodium glutamate, and black pepper. There were no eleven herbs and spices—no herbs at all, in fact. There was no sugar.

All the common herbs and spices can be identified unequivocally by trained personnel. Had there been so much as a good-sized grain or two of basil or nutmeg anywhere in the cup's worth of mix tested, it should have been detected, according to the director of the laboratory. Nothing was found in the sample that couldn't be identified.

The Kentucky Fried Chicken employees interviewed denied that anything was added to the chicken at any other stage in the cooking process—the seasonings in the coating mix are the only seasonings. This agrees with Sanders' own description of the cooking process in his patent. If the sample of coating mix tested was representative (and the company prides itself on the uniformity of its product), there seems to be no escaping the conclusion that there are no eleven herbs and spices. The real secret of Kentucky Fried Chicken, it seems, is simple and aimed dead center at the American palate: pepper and MSG.

Who's Killing the Herbs and Spices of Kentucky Fried Chicken?

It is possible that someone throws a pinch of each of the "missing" herbs and spices into the company seasoning vat every now and then. But if so, it seems that not a grain of anything other than pepper and MSG found its way into the sample tested, nor would it have found its way into any chicken made from the sample. (The sample should have been enough to coat a dozen or more pieces.) It seems presumptuous to claim eleven herbs and spices if the average piece of chicken does not contain a trace of each.

Maybe the colonel's original recipe had an honest eleven herbs and spices and the recipe was changed after he sold the company. There is certainly precedent for such tinkering. Prior to 1964, the

Kentucky Fried Chicken: An Ingredients List

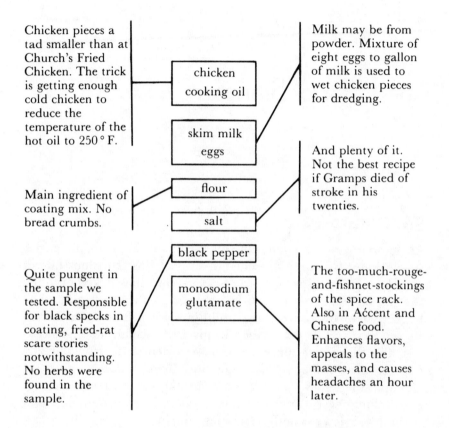

Chicken pieces a tad smaller than at Church's Fried Chicken. The trick is getting enough cold chicken to reduce the temperature of the hot oil to 250° F.

Main ingredient of coating mix. No bread crumbs.

Quite pungent in the sample we tested. Responsible for black specks in coating, fried-rat scare stories notwithstanding. No herbs were found in the sample.

chicken cooking oil

skim milk eggs

flour

salt

black pepper

monosodium glutamate

Milk may be from powder. Mixture of eight eggs to gallon of milk is used to wet chicken pieces for dredging.

And plenty of it. Not the best recipe if Gramps died of stroke in his twenties.

The too-much-rouge-and-fishnet-stockings of the spice rack. Also in Accent and Chinese food. Enhances flavors, appeals to the masses, and causes headaches an hour later.

Kentucky Fried Chicken gravy was pure ambrosia—"so good you can throw the chicken away and eat the gravy," boasted the colonel. But the new owners decided the gravy recipe was too labor-intensive for a fast-food operation and changed it. The result, charged Sanders, was "wallpaper paste." Kentucky Fried Chicken gravy remains a mediocre product, while the colonel's gravy recipe is presumably locked away, unused, in a company vault.

In all fairness, a chicken recipe with eleven seasonings probably has deadwood. If there was much pepper and MSG in the original recipe, they may have drowned out any subtler seasonings anyway.

2.

Food Horror Stories

Sex on Ritz Crackers

Little does Aunt Dagmar, who even clipped the recipe for Mock Apple Pie ("No Apples Needed"), suspect this scurrilous tale of prefab gastronomy. The word "SEX" is somehow baked onto the surface of Nabisco's Ritz Crackers—or so the story goes. The SEXes were "discovered" by subliminal advertising guru Wilson Bryan Key and first described in his 1976 book, *Media Sexploitation*. The SEXes are supposed to be scrawled in the irregular surface mottling of the crackers. Key finds about a dozen SEXes (in all-capital letters) on both the top and bottom surfaces. He suggests taking several crackers, placing them face up, and gazing at them for a few seconds. Provided you are relaxed, the secret SEXes are supposed to be visible. Key thinks the SEXes are created by special molds and that they are there to be perceived subliminally and thus to link subconsciously the eating of Ritz Crackers with sex. A lot of people think Key is nuts.

Is the Big Mac Secret Sauce
Just Thousand Island Dressing?

A few definitions are in order. To the processed-food biz, French dressing is a thin, pourable mayonnaise with a little tomato paste thrown in for color. Add chopped pickle to French dressing, and you have Thousand Island dressing. Add chopped bell pepper instead, and you have a bland incarnation of Russian dressing.

The Big Mac Secret Sauce plainly has a mayonnaise-type base. That is to say, it probably contains vegetable oil, water, vinegar, and egg yolk. Most mayonnaise also contains sugar. The Secret Sauce is the color of French dressing, but it contains chopped solids. If you scoop up a glob of the Secret Sauce and wash off the mayonnaise part, what is left? It seems to be chopped pickle, recognizable by the thin green skins adhering to white interiors. McDonald's may claim the exact composition of the sauce to be a secret, but it appears to be well within the conventional definition of Thousand Island dressing. In fact, the color of the Secret Sauce is a dead ringer for Kraft Thousand Island Dressing. For what it's worth, Kraft's list of ingredients reads: "Soybean oil, water, sugar, tomato paste, chopped pickle, vinegar, egg yolk, salt, mustard, flour, propylene glycol alginate, dehydrated onion, spice, calcium disodium EDTA to protect flavor, natural flavor."

According to McDonald's employees, corporate policy dictates exactly where the sauce is glopped onto the sandwich. There are thirteen layers in a Big Mac, two of them being dollops of Secret Sauce. The stacking order runs as follows: top bun, onions, meat, pickles, lettuce, Secret Sauce, middle bun, onions, meat, cheese, lettuce, Secret Sauce, bottom bun.

Sugar on Burger King French Fries

There may be no ice cream in fast-food "shakes," but there is sugar on the french fries. In an interview, Burger King president Donald Smith said that his chain's fries are sprayed with a sugar solution shortly before being packaged and shipped to individual outlets. The sugar carmelizes in the cooking fat, producing the golden color customers expect. Without it, the fries would be nearly the same color outside as inside: pasty white. Smith believes that McDonald's also sugar-coats its fries.

Is There Eggshell in Orange Julius?

It has been rumored that the secret behind this frothy mall fare is whole eggs—shells and all. Orange Julius is made by mixing orange juice with a mysterious white powder supplied by the company headquarters in Santa Monica, California. Thus the average Orange Julius employee has little idea what is in the drink.

If there are eggshells in the drink, they would have to be a component of that white powder.

The drink has an egglike smell. A recipe for a simulated "Orange Julius" has long been circulating. It calls for eight ounces of orange juice, one tablespoon of sugar syrup (mix sugar with just enough boiling water to dissolve), an egg, and about half a cup of crushed ice. All ingredients are mixed in a blender. Some people use the fluid part of the egg only; others throw the shell in too.

No bits of eggshell are apparent in a real Orange Julius. *Big Secrets* tried the above recipe, with the eggshells, to see if the shell fragments could be pulverized into invisibility. A whole, unbroken egg was plopped into eight ounces of orange juice, some syrup, and crushed ice in an Osterizer Galaxie blender. The blender was set on "Liquefy," the highest setting. After five minutes—far longer than the mixture would normally be blended—the liquid was poured out to check for shell fragments. The shell was still visible as a fine powder settled on the bottom of the blending chamber.

A letter asking about the eggshell story was sent to Orange Julius' headquarters. Orange Julius' reply: "There are no eggshells in an Orange Julius unless specifically requested by the customer."

Regular vs. Dry-Roasted Peanuts

Are dry-roasted peanuts less fattening? Just look at the labels. Vendors have managed to sell the idea of dry-roasted nuts as a diet aid, but they can't lie outright on the packages. Planter's Cocktail Peanuts have 170 calories an ounce. Planter's Dry-Roasted have 160 calories—scarcely enough of a difference to bother with. You do even worse with Planter's Salt-Free Dry-Roasted Peanuts, which contain not a calorie less per ounce (170) than the regular peanuts.

Two-Year-Old Fish in Worcestershire Sauce

Lea & Perrins' secret formula for Worcestershire sauce has been imitated widely. The label lists "water, vinegar, molasses, sugar, anchovies, tamarinds, hydrolyzed soy protein, onions, salt, garlic, eschalots, spices & flavorings" as ingredients—the only mystery being the "spices and flavorings."

Some conjecture that there must be dissolved anchovy bones in Worcestershire sauce. Whole anchovies go into the sauce; the sauce digests the fish as it ages. *People* magazine described the process in a 1982 profile of Worcestershire sauce heir Ransom Duncan: "Worcestershire [sauce] in various stages of aging sits in 35 6,000-gallon fir vats (which impart no flavor). 'That's been there quite a while,' notes Duncan, peering into a lumpy brown liquid. 'You can see onions, and you can see garlic. By this time you won't find fish; you might find skeletons. The meat begins to fall off and get absorbed.' "

The skeletons probably meet the same fate. Chicken bones dissolve in vinegar after a few weeks; Lea & Perrins' sauce is aged for a total of two years. Most of the water content is not added until shortly before bottling, so the liquid is largely vinegar.

The layer of crud at the bottom of a bottle of Worcestershire sauce has inspired its own speculation. The usual explanation is that it consists of tiny grains of the spices used. According to various standard recipes for Worcestershire sauce, common flavorings are Cayenne and black pepper, allspice, coriander, cloves, mace, crushed pickled walnuts, mushrooms, brandy, and sherry. The salient spice of Worcestershire sauce is something called asafetida or devil's dung—which may explain why it is never mentioned on the label.

Asafetida has a fetid odor and a bitter garlic/onion taste. It comes from a six-foot-tall carrotlike plant of Asia. When the top of the "carrot" is cut, a gummy resin—the asafetida—oozes out and dries as "tears" an inch across. At first a translucent pale yellow, the tears turn purple-streaked pink as they dry. Fully cured tears are opaque reddish-brown outside, milky-white inside. In the pure state, asafetida is used as a laxative; in Worcestershire sauce, a little goes a long way. According to a 1965 article in the *Journal of Food Technology,* the asafetida content of condiments runs from 5 to 160 parts per million.

Some Worcestershire sauces contain meat. Boiled pork liver is most frequently cited as an ingredient (some recipes demand it be cooked for eight to ten hours). Some recipes use beef extract.

None of the familiar commercial Worcestershire sauces list pork or beef on their labels. All, however, admit unspecified spices and flavorings. Pork is not a spice, but it could be a flavoring. French's, Crosse and Blackwell, and Ann Page Worcestershire sauces display the circled-U parve symbol. Parve food may contain fish (the anchovies), but it must not contain the meat of any mammal. Lea & Perrins and Heinz Worcestershire sauces do not have the parve symbol.

Big Secrets wrote the major Worcestershire sauce producers, asking if there is pork in their products. Lea & Perrins and French's denied any pork. Heinz and Crosse and Blackwell did not respond. But if Crosse and Blackwell is truly parve, it cannot contain pork. That leaves only Heinz as a possible pork-formula sauce.

What keeps the anchovies—and maybe pork—from spoiling without refrigeration? The vinegar and sugar keep them embalmed.

Stag's Leap vs. Stags' Leap

Every pop oenologist has heard of Stag's Leap, the Napa Valley *Wunderkind* that beat out several first growths of Bordeaux at a 1976 blind tasting in Paris. But before you shell out for a bottle, watch that apostrophe. Not to be confused with Stag's Leap Wine Cellars is Stags' Leap Winery, also of Napa Valley. A vinous knock-off? Not exactly. Each winery disputes the other's right to the name. Of course, only Stag's Leap won the Paris tasting. Restaurant wine lists are not above capitalizing on the confusion—and price differential.

Are Pink Peppercorns a Fraud?

Despite a thumbs-down from the Food and Drug Administration, hard-core *nouvelle cuisine* buffs still pay five to ten dollars an ounce for pink peppercorns. That's about what garden-variety caviar fetches; about ten times the cost of wild rice. Pink peppercorns are scarlet, about the size of regular peppercorns, and impart a bitter-pungent flavor to meat and fish. And pink peppercorns are slightly poisonous. They are suspected of causing headaches, chest congestion, nausea, intestinal inflammation, and hemorrhoids.

The extravagant price has always been justified by the source—the far-off isle of Réunion in the Indian Ocean. Pink peppercorns are harvested in Réunion by French firms, shipped to the mother country for processing, and then imported to the United States. They are sold in bulk, freeze-dried, or bottled in brine or vinegar.

Black pepper is the fruit of a vine. White pepper is black pepper with the skins removed. Pink peppercorns, however, are the fruit of an unrelated tree, *Schinus terebinthifolius. Schinus* is related to poison ivy, which explains its toxic potential.

Schinus is not found in Réunion only. The pink peppercorn tree is native to Brazil. It was introduced to Réunion long ago and has run wild there. *S. terebinthifolius* was also introduced into the southern half of Florida. There it goes by the names "Brazilian Pepper Tree" and "Florida Holly." It was brought to Florida as a sort of tropical holly for homesick transplants. During the Christmas season it fruits heavily, the boughs and red berries sometimes being used for Christmas decorations. *S. terebinthifolius* grows so rapidly in Florida that it has become a weed. Dotting roadsides, the tree and its berries are considered worse than useless. By one estimate, the tree now covers several thousand acres in Florida.

No one seems to have gotten the idea of selling the berries as pink peppercorns. A very similar tree, also with red berries, grows in Southern California (*Schinus molle*). The same *S. terebinthifolius* also grows in Hawaii. Anyone who orders salmon with *trois*-color peppercorns is paying over a hundred dollars a pound for a Fort Lauderdale weed.

3.

Coca-Cola

It is claimed that only two persons know the complete formula for Coca-Cola syrup. Company policy forbids them from traveling in the same plane. When one dies, the other is to choose a successor and impart the secret to that person. So secret is Coca-Cola's formula that the identity of the two initiates is itself a secret. Coca-Cola chairman Roberto Goizueta—a likely candidate because his background is in research and quality control—refused comment when *Fortune* magazine asked him in 1981 if he knew the formula. The written recipe is in a safe-deposit vault at the Trust Company of Georgia. The vault, it's claimed, can be opened only with the approval of the Coca-Cola board of directors. Clearly, the syrup recipe is perceived as the heart and soul of the Coca-Cola organization. Said the 1981 Coca-Cola annual report, commenting on the Columbia Pictures acquisition, "Programming is to the communications and entertainment businesses what syrup is to the beverage business."

Does Pepsi Know Coke's Secret?

Security was not always so tight. Coke's inventor, Atlanta pharmacist John Styth Pemberton, seems to have taken a casual attitude toward the recipe's secrecy.

In 1885 Pemberton mixed up a pirated version of a popular drink of the time, Vin Mariani. Vin Mariani was a wine spiked with coca leaves. It was both an aperitif and a stimulant—something on the order of Dubonnet, only with cocaine in it. According to a promotional book, Ulysses S. Grant, Jules Verne, Emile

Zola, Henrik Ibsen, the Russian Czar, and Pope Leo XIII drank Vin Mariani. (Some historians think it was responsible for Thomas Edison's insomnia.) Pemberton called his drink French Wine of Coca. Sales were disappointing.

The following year, Pemberton overhauled the formula. The wine was taken out. Still envisioning a stimulant product, he retained the coca leaf extract and added an extract of the African "hell seed" or kola nut. Kola nut contains caffeine, the same stimulant in coffee and tea.

Both coca and kola extracts are bitter. So Pemberton added sugar and flavorings to kill the unpleasant taste. The result was a syrup, not a beverage. The name "Coca-Cola" was adopted when Pemberton's partner, Frank M. Robinson, decided that two Cs would work well in the Spencerian-script logo he was designing.

During its first years in Atlanta, Coca-Cola was sold at pharmacies as a syrup that could be taken as is or diluted with water. Nothing on the market today is a counterpart of the early Coca-Cola. Coca-Cola was promoted as a stimulant—more the 1880s equivalent of No-Doz or Vivarin than just a drink. But No-Doz and Vivarin are not seen as particularly healthful products; Coca-Cola was. Coke was stimulant, health tonic, and beverage.

Pemberton is known to have revealed the Coca-Cola formula to at least four persons. He told his partner/ bookkeeper, Frank M. Robinson. Apparently Pemberton told his son, Charles. (Later, at the behest of the Coca-Cola Company founder Asa G. Candler, Charles signed a document renouncing his right to use the formula.) And Pemberton told Willis E. Venable and George S. Lowndes, the two men who purchased the formula in July 1887.

A scarce five months later, Venable and Lowndes themselves sold out. They transmitted the formula and rights to Coca-Cola to Woolfolk Walker and Mrs. M. C. Dozier. Then in two separate transactions in 1888, Walker and Dozier sold their rights and the formula to Asa G. Candler. The same year saw the death of John Pemberton and a new marketing angle: mixing the syrup with carbonated water.

Candler was the first to recognize the potential of Coke. He equally recognized the importance of keeping the formula a secret. Unfortunately, at least seven people knew the Coke formula by the time Candler got it. At least some of them no longer had any particular incentive to preserve the secret.

Candler tied up one loose end by taking on Pemberton's old

Who Told Whom?
The Coca-Cola Formula

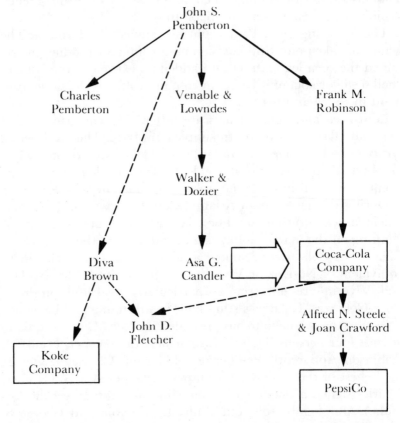

partner and one of the initiates, Frank Robinson, as his partner. Candler, evidently a more knowledgeable flavorist than Pemberton, soon revised the formula. By most accounts, Candler's changes were improvements. They also entitled Candler to claim that the increasing circle of outsiders who knew Pemberton's formula no longer knew the real Coca-Cola formula. In 1892, Candler, Robinson, and three others incorporated their operations as the Coca-Cola Company.

Candler instituted the shroud of secrecy that has since enveloped the formula. Candler and Robinson formed the first pair of initiates. Not until 1903 was anyone else allowed to make the syrup. The syrup was prepared in a locked laboratory, only Candler and Robinson having the combination to the door.

Shipments of ingredients were promptly deposited in the laboratory. There Candler or Robinson tore or scratched off the labels. They identified the ingredients by sight and smell. Lest a mail clerk learn the ingredients from the suppliers' bills, Candler opened all the company's mail himself. Likewise, Candler paid the bills himself to keep the accounting department from surmising any part of the secret. The invoices were kept in a locked file, and the only key to the file was kept on Candler's key ring, recounts Candler's son, Charles, in a 1950 biography, *Asa Griggs Candler*.

As the company got larger, Candler no longer could prepare all the syrup himself. In 1894 the first branch syrup plant was started in Dallas. Rather than relinquish the secret, Candler hit upon a scheme whereby people in other cities could prepare Coca-Cola syrup without knowing what was in it. The ingredients were numbered from 1 to 9, inclusive. Branch factory managers were told the relative proportions of the ingredients and the mixing procedure, but not the identities of the numbered ingredients. If the Dallas plant was running low on ingredient no. 6, it would order "merchandise no. 6" from Atlanta headquarters. Further to defy ready analysis, some of the merchandises were themselves mixtures of more basic ingredients.

To an extent, Candler was locking the barn after the horse had been stolen. It isn't clear who among the early initiates talked, but it seems someone must have.

For instance, there was Diva Brown, a woman who claimed that John Pemberton had sold her the Coca-Cola formula shortly before he died. True or not, Brown had somehow gleaned enough information about Coke's recipe to mix up passable imitations. She marketed Better Cola, Celery-Cola, Lime Cola, My-Coca, Vera-Coca, Vera Cola, and Yum-Yum in the southern states, claiming they were based on Pemberton's formula.

The Koke Company claimed to have gotten hold of Brown's formula upon her death in 1914 and thereby produced Koke, still another ersatz Coca-Cola. (For a long time, Coca-Cola neglected to trademark "Coke," fearing the nickname would encourage substitution. So the Koke Company was able to call its product Koke until stopped by a U.S. Supreme Court ruling in 1920.)

Meanwhile, John D. Fletcher, proprietor of a drink called "Coca and Cola," also claimed to have learned the Coke formula from Brown. He further claimed to have seen the formula in a Coca-Cola lawyer's briefcase during a protracted trial beginning in 1909, *United States* v. *Forty Barrels and Twenty Kegs of Coca-Cola.* Fletcher likewise was put out of business by a Coca-Cola lawsuit.

More problematic in the long run has been Pepsi-Cola, created by Caleb Bradham of New Bern, North Carolina, in 1898. The resemblance of the two drinks is all the more striking in view of the fact that kola nuts have little or nothing to do with the taste of either beverage (as we will see). Bradham did not have gas chromatography or other sophisticated analytic techniques. That he was able to produce such a convincing imitation of Coca-Cola suggests that he had heard something too.

In 1949 a top Coca-Cola Company executive, Alfred N. Steele, defected to PepsiCo. Steele's actress/wife, Joan Crawford, defected as well; Crawford had done endorsements for Coca-Cola. Steele was followed by several colleagues from Coca-Cola. After joining Pepsi, Steele boasted, "Their [Coca-Cola's] chemists know what's in our product, and our chemists know what's in theirs. Hell, I know both formulas."

Steele had been in Coca-Cola's marketing division, not in quality control. Whether Steele was one of the few formally initiated into knowledge of the full formula is questionable. But there can be little doubt about the contention that Pepsi knows Coke's formula (or most of it) and vice versa. There are ways of analyzing soft-drink flavorings, and it is hard to believe that both Coke and Pepsi haven't been thoroughly scrutinized by their competitors.

If Pepsi really knows Coke's secret, why hasn't it become a clone of the more popular drink? Most likely, Pepsi has considered the economics of duplicating Coke and decided against it. Being a larger company, Coca-Cola can produce its beverage at a lower unit cost than Pepsi could. In head-on competition with indistinguishable products, Pepsi would have to charge a higher price and eventually lose out. Instead, Pepsi produces a drink different enough from Coke that a segment of the public prefers it to Coke.

Secret Ingredient 7X

Today the Coca-Cola Company is nearly mute about Coke's flavoring ingredients. It no longer even mentions kola nuts in promotional literature. A short brochure, *You asked about soft drinks . . .* is bold enough to deny cocoa as an ingredient. (Some people confuse cocoa with coca.) If you write to ask if there is something truly repugnant in Coca-Cola, the company will, of course, deny it. Coca-Cola denies, for instance, pig blood, a rumored ingredient that has hurt sales to African Moslems. In E. J. Kahn, Jr.'s study of Coca-Cola, *The Big Drink*, he mentions the equally dubious rumor of peanuts as an ingredient—from former Coke president Robert W. Woodruff's peanut plantation.

Coke's label discloses, "Carbonated water, sugar, caramel color, phosphoric acid, natural flavorings, caffeine." Everything that makes Coke unique is subsumed under "natural flavorings."

The known ingredients can all be squared with Candler's system of numbered "merchandises." It is known that sugar is merchandise no. 1, caramel is no. 2, caffeine is no. 3, and phosphoric acid is no. 4. The water and carbonation apparently don't rate a merchandise number.

Coke's sugar used to be pure sucrose. Since 1980, syrup producers have been permitted to substitute high-fructose corn syrup for as much as 50 percent of the sugar. Some purists think the Coke with corn syrup doesn't taste as good. Before the change, former Coke Chairman J. Paul Austin knocked corn syrup: "It produces a chemical reaction with the Coca-Cola that throws the flavor off," he said in *Fortune*. Pepsi still uses sugar only. Not everyone notices the difference between sugar and corn syrup, but those who do apparently favor sugar. By one hypothesis, this slight tipping of the flavor scales in favor of Pepsi recently made it possible, for the first time, for Pepsi to gather "evidence" that most people favor Pepsi over Coke and use it in ads.

Coke's caramel is intended only as coloring. Virtually all Coke's brown color comes from the caramel. Coke's caramel is burnt cane or corn sugar.

Caffeine is the stimulant principle. Though it was Pemberton's idea to use natural extracts of kola nuts (containing caffeine) and coca leaves (containing cocaine) for stimulant effect, the amount of these ingredients in Coke is far too small to be significant. Nearly all the caffeine in Coke is chemically pure caffeine, a white powder.

Caffeine has a strong, bitter taste. The bitterness is largely covered up by the massive amounts of sugar used and the other flavorings. At the time of the *United States* v. *Forty Barrels and Twenty Kegs of Coca-Cola* trial, the caffeine used in Coke was refined from tea dust. During World War II, caffeine was scarce, and Coke's chemists toyed with the idea of synthesizing caffeine from bat guano. Coca-Cola executives rejected the plan on the grounds that the possible discovery of bat droppings as an "ingredient" of Coke would be too damaging. Coke may now be getting its caffeine from the guarana shrub of the Amazon basin; the seeds of these shrubs contain 5 percent caffeine.

The phosphoric acid provides a flat acidity. Other acids commonly used in soft drinks, such as citric or tartaric, suggest the acidity of specific fruits. Phosphoric acid doesn't. Pepsi lists both phosphoric and citric acids on its label, reflecting a more lemony acidity.

So much for merchandises 1 through 4. Several clues to the other ingredients come from the writings of Charles Howard Candler, son of the Coca-Cola Company's founder and an initiate. In his biography of his father, Candler tells of the merchandises: "The ingredients of Coca-Cola, throughout its early history, were categorized and referred to by numbers from one to nine inclusive . . ."

At another point, Candler tells where they bought the ingredients: "Among the suppliers of essential ingredients in the period under discussion were the E. Berghausen Chemical Company of Cincinnati; the Maywood Chemical Works, of Maywood, N. J.; the Monsanto Chemical Company of St. Louis; the Mallinckrodt Chemical Works, also of St. Louis; Harshaw, Fuller and Goodwin Company of Elyria, Ohio; and Procter & Gamble of Cincinnati."

In 1953, the younger Candler published another cola memoir, *Coca-Cola & Emory College.* In it he provides some cagey hints about the changes his father made in the Coca-Cola formula:

> Some of the very same people to whom he [Asa G. Candler] had paid hard-earned cash for what was then generally considered of little value, constantly plagued him by making and selling to unscrupulous dealers imitations of and for Coca-Cola, asserting that their concoctions were made from or based upon the original Coca-Cola formula. These unfair competitors may have had some knowledge of the Pemberton formula, but they knew absolutely nothing of the composition of *the* formula with which Asa G. Candler made Coca-

Cola. The Pemberton product did not have an altogether agreeable taste, it was unstable, it contained too many things, too much of some ingredients and too little of others.

Father's pharmaceutical knowledge convinced him that the formula had to be changed in certain particulars to improve the taste of the product, to insure its uniformity and its stability. Some of the ingredients were incompatible with others in the formula; the bouquet of several of the volatile essential oils previously used was adversely affected by some ingredients. Several needed materials, one notable for its preservative virtue, were added. The first thing he did was to discontinue the use of tin can containers for shipping. On account of the inclusion of a very desirable constituent in the formula, the use of tin cans was dangerous.

Here the "people to whom he had paid hard-earned cash" would include Walker, Dozier, and also the Pembertons, who retained an interest in Coca-Cola for several years. The second ingredient Candler hints at, the one that doesn't go with tin cans, is easy to guess. It's phosphoric acid. Phosphoric acid eats through tin, forming poisonous tin phosphate. (Currently, Coke uses stainless-steel containers.)

That means that the phosphoric acid was Candler's innovation and wasn't in the original formula. But Charles Candler says in the same book that the Pemberton formula included "an acid for zest." Perhaps this acid was one of the ingredients Candler took out of the formula. Or it could have been lime juice.

Lime juice is one of the ingredients that has been reported in chemical analyses of Coke. Several analyses of Coke were offered as evidence in the *United States* v. *Forty Barrels and Twenty Kegs of Coca-Cola* trial. In 1909 the federal government seized the latter quantity of Coca-Cola syrup en route from Atlanta to a bottling plant in Chattanooga and charged Coca-Cola with violation of the Pure Food Act. Trial and appeals ran about a decade. One analysis of the syrup claimed:

Caffein (grains per fluid ounce)	0.92–1.30
Phosphoric acid (H_3PO_4) (percent)	0.26–0.30
Sugar, total (percent)	48.86–58.00
Alcohol (percent by volume)	0.90–1.27
Caramel, glycerin, lime juice, essential oils, and plant extractives	Present
Water (percent)	34.00–41.00

Another analysis from the trial ran:

> Caffeine 0.20 per cent or 1.19 grains per ounce.
> Phos. Acid 0.19 per cent.
> Sugar 48.86 per cent.
> Alcohol 1.27 per cent.
> Caramel, glycerine,
> Lime Juice, oil of cassia
> Water about 41 per cent.

There seems little doubt that Coca-Cola contained lime juice circa 1909. To confirm its presence in Coke today, *Big Secrets* wrote the Coca-Cola Company asking about lime juice. Bonita Holder of Coca-Cola replied: "While we are unable to comment specifically on the various flavors utilized in Coca-Cola, I can nonetheless confirm for you that Coca-Cola contains no lime juice, or any fruit juice."

Lime juice is perishable and somewhat cloudy; it varies with each season's crop. Coke therefore might have wanted to replace it with a more stable substitute. A mixture of citric acid and some of the flavoring principles of lime juice (which are distinct from those found in the oil of lime peel) might have been substituted for the original lime juice without anyone noticing much of a change in the taste of Coca-Cola. Citrus juices are easy to fake. Coca-Cola produces such soft drinks as Hi-C Orange, Hi-C Lemonade, Hi-C Punch, and Hi-C Grape, which don't contain any fruit juice either.

The analyses mention three other ingredients: alcohol, glycerin, and oil of cassia. Evidently glycerin is the preservative Candler described. It is a customary ingredient in soft-drink syrups. It is believed to prevent separation of essential oils on standing.

Coke syrup is about 2 proof. The alcohol probably only enters in as a solvent for the "plant extractives." Oil of cassia seems to be one of the essential oils that provide Coke's flavoring. Cassia is a form of cinnamon, sometimes called Chinese cinnamon to distinguish it from true or Ceylon cinnamon. Most of the stick cinnamon sold in supermarkets is Ceylon cinnamon. Most of the cinnamon used in commercial baked goods such as coffee cakes is cassia.

Conspicuously absent from the above analyses is any mention of coca or kola. This was one of the main issues of the *United States*

v. *Forty Barrels and Twenty Kegs of Coca-Cola* trial. Coca leaves contain cocaine; ergo, it was claimed that Coca-Cola must either contain that recently outlawed drug, or the coca must have been dropped from the formula. In the latter case, the government charged, it was mislabeling to use "Coca" in the name. Further, it was charged the kola in Coca-Cola was an imposition—a trace ingredient added only so that the company could claim it was there. Thus the "Cola" part of the name was misleading, too.

Indeed, there is precious little coca or kola in Coca-Cola. None of the chemical analysts consulted at the trial were able to detect coca or kola. But there are traces of coca and kola present, in what Coca-Cola calls merchandise no. 5. At the time of the trial, merchandise no. 5 was manufactured by a contractor, the Schaeffer Alkaloid Works of Maywood, New Jersey. Its president, Dr. L. Schaeffer, described the manufacture of Coke's fifth ingredient:

Q. Now, Doctor, do you make Merchandise No. 5 for the Coca-Cola Co.?

A. Yes, sir.

Q. From what substance do you make that Merchandise No. 5?

A. Of the Coca leaf and the Cola nut, and of dilute alcohol sir.

Q. What do you use the alcohol for, what is the purpose of putting in the alcohol?

A. To extract from the bodies mentioned the extractive matter.

Q. Do you use anything else in that compound except the extracts from the coca leaves and cola nuts and dilute alcohol?

A. No, I do not use anything to speak of, or essentially.

Q. Now just state the process, Dr. Schaeffer, by which you manufacture this Merchandise No. 5?

A. The process consists of two parts. The first part is to decocanize the coca leaf, the second part is to use the decocanized coca leaf and cola nut, both of which are in powdered form, to make the infusion, that is, the same extract made by percolation with dilute alcohol.... The proportions which are used in the process are as follows: 380 lbs. of coca leaf, 125 lbs. of cola nuts and 900 gallons of dilute alcohol of about twenty per cent strength ...

The cocaine was removed from the coca leaves by rinsing with toluol, a solvent. Cocaine dissolves in toluol; repeated rinsing leaches away the cocaine.

According to Dr. Schaeffer's testimony, there was wine in Coca-Cola. The alcohol used in making merchandise no. 5 was usually a mixture of California white wine and 95 percent commercial alcohol. But Dr. Schaeffer sometimes used an alcohol-water mixture "if California wine is too high in price. It is altogether a matter of price of the wine or of the alcohol."

Merchandise no. 5, according to testimony, was a dark, winey liquid. Several of the witnesses were given samples of merchandise no. 5. One thought it tasted and smelled no different from the wine it was made from. One Coca-Cola witness claimed it had the characteristic odor of coca but proved unable to describe the odor. Another witness said it smelled like toluol, the toxic solvent that isn't supposed to be present in the final product at all.

An experiment was performed for the benefit of the court. Coca-Cola made up a special batch of syrup containing no merchandise no. 5. Witnesses thought it tasted the same as the regular syrup.

In short, neither coca nor kola has much, if anything, to do with the taste of Coca-Cola. Both substances, in fact, have unpleasant, bitter flavors wholly unlike that of Coca-Cola.

Pemberton, remember, was concocting a medicinal syrup. Because his two active ingredients had unpleasant flavors, he masked them with other flavors—the way a codeine cough syrup might be cherry-flavored.

As it happened, Coca-Cola became successful for its flavor rather than for any medicinal value. Dozens of imitations sprang up, most with "Cola" in their name. Thus "cola" became the generic term for soft drinks similar to Coca-Cola. Most—though not all—of these imitations contained kola nuts. But as with Coke, the kola really didn't contribute to the flavor.

Cherry cough syrup tastes like cherries. The "cola" flavor tastes like . . . nothing familiar. That raises two possibilities. Cola flavor may come from an exotic substance, otherwise unknown to Western taste buds. Or it may be what the soft-drink industry calls a "fantasia" flavor, a new flavor created by the artful combination of other flavors.

The basics of cola flavor are no mystery. Pepsi, Royal Crown, and every supermarket chain know enough about the Coca-Cola formula to make good imitations. The cola flavor is a fantasia blend of three familiar flavors: citrus, cinnamon, and vanilla.

The prevailing philosophy, and certainly the philosophy behind Coca-Cola, is that these flavors should be blended so that none predominates and becomes identifiable in its own right. To the average palate, Coke does not taste like citrus, cinnamon, or vanilla.

But some of the cheaper, supermarket house-brand colas taste slightly of cinnamon or vanilla. Pepsi has a more lemony taste than Coke—and Pepsi Light advertises its lemon flavor.

Here citrus means the oils pressed from the peels. The oils are responsible for most of the smell of citrus fruits but taste nothing like the juice. All citrus oils are very bitter by themselves. Diluted in a soft-drink emulsion, they acquire a more pleasant taste.

All three familiar citrus fruits—oranges, lemons, and limes—are probably used in Coca-Cola. At any rate, Pepsi-Cola, which is more candid about its formula, admits to orange, lemon, and lime oils (as well as vanilla and kola nuts) in a brochure, *Pepsi-Cola: Quality in Every Drop.* The theory always has been that Coke has relatively more orange and less lemon than Pepsi. Food writer Roy Andries de Groot tells of plying a Coca-Cola Company executive with rum-and-Cokes to get an admission. According to de Groot, the executive uh-huhed the Coke:orange/Pepsi:lemon analysis.

How are these ingredients combined? The sources *Big Secrets* consulted pointed to a book, *Food Flavorings: Composition, Manufacture, and Use,* by Joseph Merory (second edition, 1968). Merory was the founder and president of Merory Food Flavors, a small flavoring supplier in Fairfield, New Jersey. To the horror of many of his colleagues, Merory published dozens of standard flavoring formulations in the book, drawing on his own experience and what was common knowledge in the flavoring industry. One of his recipes, designated MF 241, is a "cola flavor" that seems to be Merory's version of Coca-Cola. Another recipe, "Cola Syrup" MF 234, suggests Pepsi.

The seeming Coca-Cola recipe, MF 241, is for a cola flavor, which must be mixed with sugar syrup and phosphoric acid to produce cola syrup. Cola syrup in turn must be mixed with carbonated water to produce the finished drink. Merory's recipe specifies these ingredients:

> Caramel (32 fluid ounces)
> Lime juice (32 fluid ounces)
> Glycerin (16 fluid ounces)
> Alcohol (95 percent) (12 fluid ounces)
> Cola flavor base (12 fluid ounces)
> Kola nut extract (12 fluid ounces)
> Caffeine solution (2 ounces of caffeine in
>   10 fluid ounces of water)
> Vanilla extract (2 fluid ounces)

These are mixed to produce 128 ounces (1 gallon) of cola flavor. Four ounces of this cola flavor, plus .5 fluid ounce of diluted phosphoric acid (one part 85 percent phosphoric acid to seven parts water), are used to flavor a gallon of sugar syrup. The composition of the cola flavor base and the kola nut extract are given in accompanying recipes.

This recipe suggests the identities of the unknown merchandises. Merchandise no. 1, sugar, is the syrup to which the cola flavor is added. Nos. 2 and 3, caramel and caffeine, are in the recipe, caffeine in a water solution. No. 4, phosphoric acid, is added to the sugar syrup. No. 5, in Coca-Cola's recipe, is coca and kola extract in an alcohol-water solution. This corresponds to two ingredients in the Merory recipe: the kola nut extract and the 95 percent alcohol. The kola nut extract is to be prepared according to another Merory recipe, MF 237. This requires that kola nuts be extracted with a solvent, propylene glycol, most of which is then distilled off. Water is added, so the result is a water-based extract of kola. Were alcohol added to this extract, you'd have a sort of merchandise no. 5 (without the coca, though). Of course, the alcohol and kola extract can be treated as separate ingredients—which is how Merory lists them.

There are four remaining ingredients in Merory's list—and four remaining merchandises of the nine Candler claimed. Merory's four are lime juice, glycerin, a cola flavor base, and vanilla extract. Of these, the first two were reported in lab analyses of Coke (though Coke now denies lime juice). The last, vanilla extract, is a generally acknowledged component of the cola flavor.

It is tempting if not compelling to identify these four with merchandises nos. 6 through 9. We can't be sure that Coca-Cola doesn't mix together glycerin and vanilla extract, say, and call it merchandise no. 6. But since glycerin and vanilla extract must be prepared or purchased separately, it makes sense to consider them as separate merchandises. The cola flavor base is a composite product—a mixture of citrus and spice oils in alcohol. It includes all the essential oils used in the cola. Because essential oils are powerful flavorings and must be diluted, it makes sense to mix them up in a large batch (to ensure a uniform product) and to draw from this premixed batch as needed. The oil mixture would then be regarded as a single ingredient.

The oil mixture may be the mysterious ingredient 7X of Coke lore. Merchandise 7X is the most secret of Coke's secret ingredients. The "X" has never been explained; 7X seems to be simply merchandise no. 7. It might make sense if there was a merchandise no. 7 composed of many ingredients, all given letters: 7A, 7B, 7C . . . 7X. But no one associated with Coke has ever alluded to any of the other members of this hypothetical series. What's more, we know that 7X is itself a composite ingredient. Charles Candler writes of making "a batch of merchandise 7X" while his father supervised the measuring and mixing.

Certainly the essential oil mixture is the most important component of a cola's flavor. The "cola flavor base" referred to above is given in another Merory recipe, MF 238. It is made from the following:

Cold-pressed California lemon oil (46.80 grams)
Orange oil (24.84 grams)
Distilled lime oil (14.20 grams)
Cassia or cinnamon oil (10.65 grams)
Nutmeg oil (3.50 grams)
Neroli oil ["can be omitted," says Merory] (0.01 gram)

If the aforementioned analysis presented at the *United States* v. *Forty Barrels and Twenty Kegs of Coca-Cola* trial was correct, it is cassia rather than true cinnamon oil that is used in Coca-Cola. Nutmeg is a likely minor component of the Coca-Cola flavor base, for aside from Merory's equivocal endorsement of it here, it has been claimed detected in outside chemical analyses. Neroli is an oil distilled from the blossoms of the bitter orange tree. It forms only one part in ten thousand of Merory's oil mixture, though. That and the difficulty of distinguishing citrus oil in chemical analysis make it hard to say if neroli oil is in Coca-Cola. According to the Merory recipe for flavor base, the above mixture of oils (100 grams) is mixed with 11 fluid ounces of 95 percent alcohol and shaken. Five ounces of water are added, and the mixture is left to stand for twenty-four hours. A cloudy layer of terpenes will develop; only the clear part of the mixture is taken off and used in recipe MF 241.

There may be other ingredients in the Coca-Cola oil mixture. In *The Big Drink,* E. J. Kahn, Jr., mentions the possibility of lavender as an ingredient. The alternate Merory cola recipe, which uses citric acid and less orange oil, suggesting a Pepsi-like product, includes coriander in lieu of nutmeg. (Coriander is a spice found in Danish pastries.) Perhaps there is a trace of coriander in Coca-Cola. In another of the occasional breaches of industry close-mouthedness, flavorist A. W. Noling published a pamphlet on colas in 1952. The *Hurty Peck Pamphlet on Cola* attributed the secret of cola flavor to extracts of decocanized coca leaves and kola nuts, oils of lime, lemon, orange, cassia, nutmeg, neroli, cinnamon, and coriander, and lime juice and vanilla. Noling's analysis seems to have been directed specifically at Coca-Cola. Among modern cola drinks, only Coca-Cola is known to use the coca leaves.

The proportions in the accompanying recipe are based on the analyses of Coke quoted above and Merory's recipes. The amount of caffeine agrees with that stated in Coca-Cola's *So you asked about soft drinks . . .* pamphlet; this is about a third of the caffeine found in the trial analyses.

The following recipe produces a gallon of syrup very similar to Coca-Cola's. Mix 2,400 grams of sugar with just enough water to dissolve (high-fructose corn syrup may be substituted for half the sugar). Add 37 grams of caramel, 3.1 grams of caffeine, and 11 grams of phosphoric acid. Extract the cocaine from 1.1 grams of coca leaf (*Truxillo* growth of coca preferred) with toluol; discard the cocaine extract. Soak the coca leaves and kola nuts (both finely powdered; 0.37 gram of kola nuts) in 22 grams of 20 percent alcohol. California white wine fortified to 20 percent strength was used as the soaking solution circa 1909, but Coca-Cola may have switched to a simple water/alcohol mixture. After soaking, discard the coca and the kola and add the liquid to the syrup. Add 30 grams of lime juice (a former ingredient, evidently, that Coca-Cola now denies) or a substitute such as a water solution of citric acid and sodium citrate at lime-juice strength. Mix together 0.88 gram of lemon oil, 0.47 gram of

Coca-Cola: The Real Things?

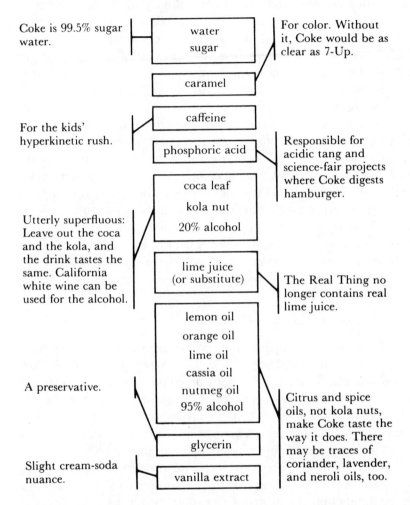

Coke is 99.5% sugar water.

water
sugar

For color. Without it, Coke would be as clear as 7-Up.

caramel

For the kids' hyperkinetic rush.

caffeine

phosphoric acid

Responsible for acidic tang and science-fair projects where Coke digests hamburger.

coca leaf

kola nut

Utterly superfluous: Leave out the coca and the kola, and the drink tastes the same. California white wine can be used for the alcohol.

20% alcohol

lime juice (or substitute)

The Real Thing no longer contains real lime juice.

lemon oil

orange oil

lime oil

cassia oil

A preservative.

nutmeg oil

95% alcohol

Citrus and spice oils, not kola nuts, make Coke taste the way it does. There may be traces of coriander, lavender, and neroli oils, too.

glycerin

Slight cream-soda nuance.

vanilla extract

orange oil, 0.27 gram of lime oil, 0.20 gram of cassia (Chinese cinnamon) oil, 0.07 gram of nutmeg oil, and if desired, traces of coriander, lavender, and neroli oils, and add to 4.9 grams of 95 percent alcohol. Shake. Add 2.7 grams of water to the alcohol/oil mixture and let stand for twenty-four hours at about 60° F. A cloudy layer will separate. Take off the clear part of the liquid only and add to the syrup. Add 19 grams of glycerin (from vegetable sources, not hog fat, so the drink can be sold to Orthodox Jews and Moslems) and 1.5 grams of vanilla extract. Add water (treated with chlorine) to make 1 gallon of syrup.

Yield (used to flavor carbonated water): 128 6.5-ounce bottles.

The amount of kola in this recipe—or in any cola—is tiny. Some colas are reported to contain none at all. By this recipe, a gallon of cola syrup is made from 0.37 gram of kola nut. But a gallon is 128 fluid ounces, and each ounce can flavor a bottle of finished, carbonated beverage. So the amount of kola nut used in making a bottle of cola drink is about 3 milligrams. That tiny speck is merely soaked in alcohol and then discarded, only the alcohol going into the cola syrup.

Many Coca-Cola drinkers swear that the drink tastes different in various parts of the country. Coke's standard answer is to blame the mineral content of the water used by the bottling plants. (Now that the syrup plants have the option of using corn syrup for part of the sugar, the Coke in regions where they do use corn syrup ought to taste different from—probably not as good as—the Coke where only cane sugar is used.) Where soda fountains still make Coke from syrup, another variable is the "throw"—the amount of carbonated water added to the syrup. Southerners tend to like Coke on the syrupy side.

Is There Cocaine in Coca-Cola?

Coca-Cola was not always alone in its use of coca. There were coca elixirs and beverages before there were colas. Until 1903, Coca-Cola contained the full cocaine content of its coca extract. Since then, Coca-Cola has taken great pains to remove the cocaine from the coca leaves before they go into merchandise no. 5. According to one source, there were sixty-nine imitations of Coca-Cola still containing measurable cocaine in 1909.

One version of the chestnut about putting an aspirin in Coca-Cola says that the cocaine is thus precipitated. (The more usual version holds that the aspirin-Coke mixture acts as a Mickey, the opposite of what would be expected from cocaine.) Of course, the Coca-Cola Company bristles at any suggestion that there might still be cocaine in the drink.

Even before 1903, the amount of cocaine in Coca-Cola was trifling. One analysis put the cocaine content of an ounce of Coca-Cola syrup—in the pre-extraction days—at 0.04 grain (2.6 milligrams).

That's not much. In small doses, cocaine has roughly the stimulant effect of a dose of caffeine ten times larger. A milligram of cocaine might have the effect of 10 milligrams of caffeine, and so forth. So the cocaine in an ounce of the old syrup had the stimulant effect of about 26 milligrams of caffeine. In comparison, a cup of tea contains about 60 milligrams of caffeine.

By the same analysis, the old Coke syrup contained about 1.21 grains (78 milligrams) of caffeine. Even when Coke contained measurable amounts of cocaine, most of its stimulant effect must have been from the caffeine.

Figure that a line of uncut cocaine is about 50 milligrams. Then it would have taken nearly 20 ounces of the old Coca-Cola syrup (or 20 of the 6.5-ounce bottles of carbonated beverage) to represent an equivalent amount of cocaine. Anyone trying to consume that much would have gotten sick from the caffeine, phosphoric acid, or sugar.

From time to time, various chemists and government agencies have wondered if there is any residual cocaine in Coca-Cola even yet. In 1912, nine years after the switch to decocanized coca leaves, a Canadian government study found no cocaine in Coca-Cola syrup.

In 1972 Dr. Norman Farnsworth of the University of Illinois, Chicago, had graduate students test Coke and other colas for cocaine. A gas-chromatography "peak" near that expected for cocaine was found. To confirm the apparent finding, Farnsworth's group added cocaine to a sample of Coca-Cola and retested. This time there were two peaks—meaning that something other than cocaine was causing the first peak. A scientific paper reporting the original finding was hastily shelved.

So jittery was the Coca-Cola Company on hearing of the results that it funded further research to find the cause of the spurious peak—lest a less careful researcher might report the "cocaine." Farnsworth finally concluded the peak was due to a polymer formed from the ammonia used in the gas chromatography.

You can make a strong argument that there must be *some* cocaine in Coca-Cola nonetheless. The decocanization process used on the coca leaves that go into Coke is similar to the decaffeination of coffee. A solvent is passed through the leaves repeatedly, leaching away a little more cocaine each time. So it is with the caffeine in decaffeinated coffee. But no coffee producer claims its decaffeinated coffee is entirely free from caffeine. A brand that advertises itself as 98 percent caffeine-free contains only 2 percent of the caffeine of regular coffee. For all practical purposes, that's good enough.

Coke's decocanization is good enough, too, as far as the drug laws are concerned. No one suggests that there is enough cocaine in a bottle of Coke to have any physiological effect whatsoever. But it's quite another thing to assert that there is no cocaine in Coca-Cola. A molecule of cocaine, the smallest possible amount, weighs 0.000000000000000000504 milligram. If an ounce of the old syrup contained 2.6 milligrams of cocaine, then it must have contained about 5 quintillion (5,000,000,000,000,000,000) molecules of cocaine.

Does Coke's decocanization process catch every last one of those 5 quintillion molecules? Surely not. If it removed 99 percent of them—which would be pretty good—there would still be a whopping 50 quadrillion molecules left.

Even if the Coca-Cola Company invested in a hypothetical superdecocanizer capable of removing 99.99999999 percent of the cocaine (a pointless waste of money, given the insignificant role of coca extract in the finished beverage), there would still be millions and millions of molecules of cocaine left in every bottle of Coke. As long as Coca-Cola is made from coca leaves, it can hardly avoid containing cocaine.

4·

Uncolas

Dr Pepper

It's easier to say what isn't in Dr Pepper than what is. Though Dr Pepper is sometimes categorized as a cherry cola, the Dr Pepper Company denies both cherry and kola flavorings. Likewise, almost everything that has been rumored to be in Dr Pepper isn't in it. There is no black pepper, chili pepper, bell pepper, or peppermint. And no prune juice.

The formula contains twenty-three ingredients and is locked in two bank vaults. Four persons know it. Company CEO W. W. Clements said he saw the formula once but didn't understand it. The only surprise on the label ingredient panel is lactic acid. This is what gives sour milk its bite. If you hold some Dr Pepper in your mouth a few minutes before swallowing, there is a slight yogurtlike note.

Dr Pepper smells. The honeysuckle-sweet odor is prominent when the drink is served cold, overpowering when served hot. Industry opinion holds that vanilla or vanillin is a prime ingredient in Dr Pepper, responsible in part for that smell. In reply to a query from *Big Secrets*, a Dr Pepper Company vice president confirmed that synthetic vanillin is an ingredient. Synthetics figure prominently in Dr Pepper's fantasia blend. The label credits "artificial and natural flavoring," the word order implying that there are more artificial than natural flavors in Dr Pepper. At any rate, Dr Pepper is the only soft drink of the big four to be artificially flavored.

In 1981 W. W. Clements told a *Los Angeles Times* reporter that he used to fear theft of the Dr Pepper formula. "Then I got to thinking," recalled Clements. "Why would anyone go to all that trouble just to produce another Dr Pepper? Then I quit worrying."

Hires Root Beer

Root beer used to be a fermented, slightly alcoholic brew flavored with bruised sassafras bark, wintergreen bark, and sarsaparilla root. Hires bears but a faint resemblance to the original product. It is made like a cola—lots of sugar, caramel for the brown color, artificial carbonation. Its flavor comes mainly from a secret flavoring extract that may not contain any of the traditional trio of root beer flavorings. Predominant in most modern root beer formulations is methyl salicylate, an oily synthetic compound also present naturally in wintergreen. Much cheaper than natural oil of wintergreen—and by most accounts, an agreeable substitute—methyl salicylate is a likely component of Hires. A typical modern-type recipe for root beer flavoring in Merory's *Food Flavorings* calls for methyl salicylate along with oil of northern birch, oil or star anise (or synthetic anethol as a substitute), ginger oleoresin, cold-pressed lemon oil, ginger oil, citral (a synthetic also present in lemons), and coriander. How does Hires create its foam? If it's like most root beer producers, it uses the sap of the desert yucca tree. Root beer is no more highly carbonated than a cola, but something in the yucca sap keeps the bubbles from breaking.

Moxie

Moxie's secret formula once overshadowed Coca-Cola's. In the 1920s Moxie outsold Coke and may have been the biggest-selling trademarked soft drink in the world. Then sugar prices went up, and the company decided to use its advertising budget to buy sugar instead. Bad decision. People forgot about Moxie except in its New England stronghold. Now the syrup is made in Doraville, Georgia, strangely enough, though the drink is rarely seen except in Maine and Massachusetts. Moxie looks like a cola; it tastes (and smells) like root beer heavily laced with Angostura Bitters.

The one flavoring credited on Moxie's label, gentian root extract, is in Angostura Bitters as well. The Moxie Company once claimed twenty other flavorings besides the gentian. Cinchona alkaloids, responsible for the bitterness of tonic water, used to be listed as an ingredient on the fountain syrup label. Sassafras was another alleged ingredient.

Never identified is the mysterious "simple sugarcane-like plant grown near the equator and farther south" touted in Moxie's early advertising. The plant, "discovered accidentally by Lieut. Moxie," according to the old label, was claimed to be a remedy for "brain and nervous exhaustion; loss of manhood, imbecility and . . . softening of the brain." Neither gentian, cinchona, nor sassafras is anything like sugarcane. A 1903 book, *The Secrets of the Specialists,* claimed the secret ingredient was oats. Author Dr. Dale Covey found Moxie to be a "decoction of oats made into a syrup and flavored with sassafras and wintergreen." But oats are hardly sugarcane-like or equatorial. Be that as it may, old Moxie labels depicted a woman carrying grain (oats?) on her shoulder.

7-Up

This is the only major soft drink with no secrets. 7-Up has six ingredients and reveals them to anyone who cares to know. They are carbonated water, sugar (corn syrup substitution allowed), citric acid, sodium citrate, lemon oil, and lime oil.

Vernors

You either think Vernors is the champagne of ginger ales, or you think it has a weird, off taste and wish you'd bought the regular stuff. The company notes sales are exceptionally strong during the Christmas and Easter seasons, when the drink is used to glaze turkeys and hams. The first batch of Vernors was prepared in 1865. Vernors is thus older than Coca-Cola (1886), Dr Pepper (1885), and Moxie (1876). Inventor James Vernor flavored his drink with the contents of a wooden keg of secret ingredients he had left stewing in Detroit before joining the Union army in 1861. Ever since, ingredients have been aged for four years in forty-seven-gallon oak barrels. Vernors contains three types of ginger and seventeen other ingredients, according to the company. Presumably, part of the taste seeps in from the oak. Even regular ginger ales contain flavorings other than ginger. A Merory recipe for ginger ale flavoring calls for lime, lemon, and orange oil. Though never confirmed, citrus oils likely figure in the recipe for Vernors too. The "hot" taste of Vernors may be due to hot peppers, another sometime ingredient of ginger ales.

Yoo-Hoo

Yoo-Hoo is not a chocolated nondairy creamer; the label claims milk and whey. The chocolate flavor is from natural cocoa, synthetic vanillin, and some unspecified natural flavorings. Yoo-Hoo is made in part from seaweed (the "carrageenan gum" they hope you won't notice on the label). Coconut oil replaces the fat lost by watering down the whey-milk mixture. Whatever's in Yoo-Hoo, a lot of it precipitates out to form a three-tone layer of sediment at the bottom of the bottle or can. From bottom to top, the layers are dark brown, light brown, and burnt sienna.

Industry sources say Yoo-Hoo owes its open-ended shelf life to a special steam sterilization process. Sterilization takes place after the bottles are filled and capped but before labels are applied. Unopened Yoo-Hoo is as sterile as a Band-Aid; as long as it's sealed, it can't go sour.

5.

Liqueurs and Bitters

Formulas for many aperitifs, bitters, and liqueurs are still family affairs. Secrets are handed down on deathbeds, with the curtains drawn and the servants in town on errands. The longevity of these arcane elixirs has given outsiders plenty of time to puzzle out the recipes. Outside chemists' best guesses follow.

Angostura Bitters
Port of Spain, Trinidad
90 proof

Angostura Bitters are the family secret of the Siegerts of Trinidad, descendents of Dr. J.G.B. Siegert. The family is said to eat their food heavily laced with the bitters. The German Dr. Siegert served in the army of Simón Bolívar on the South American mainland. In 1824 Dr. Siegert invented the bitters as a tonic for Bolívar's army. The bitters proved a success, and Siegert secretly moved the family business to the more stable political turf of Trinidad. For a long time after its creation, the recipe was communicated only by word of mouth. At last report, the recipe has been written down, the paper torn in two, and the halves locked in separate bank vaults.

Although Angostura Bitters enter into recipes for Manhattans, Old-Fashioneds, Rob Roys, and countless other mixed-drink recipes, few have any idea what's in Angostura Bitters. In *Islands in the Stream*, Ernest Hemingway likens the flavor to varnish. The odor suggests plum pudding. Taken straight up (as the label suggests to stimulate the appetite or relieve flatulence), Angostura Bitters are thoroughly unpleasant. The taste is so bad that Angostura Bitters are exempted from the alcoholic-beverage tax. The reasoning is that no one could down enough of the 90-proof bitters to get drunk.

The label admits only three ingredients: water, alcohol, and gentian. Gentian is a wild flower with a bitter root. The rest is "harmless vegetable flavoring extractives and vegetable coloring matter." There seems not to be any sugar.

Angostura bark is to Angostura Bitters what cocaine is to Coca-Cola. The label eagerly denies angostura bark as an ingredient. According to the label, the bitters aren't named after angostura bark, but rather after the town of Angostura, Venezuela (since renamed Ciudad Bolívar). Yet the *Encyclopaedia Britannica* and other older sources claim angostura bark is—or was—the bitters' principal flavoring.

What's wrong with angostura bark? Angostura is a small tree from northern Brazil and adjacent Venezuela. Its bark is spicy-bitter and was used medicinally. Then scandal erupted when someone discovered that the "angostura bark" of commerce was often adulterated with the poisonous bark of the strychnine tree. Presumably, Angostura Bitters were made from this same contaminated angostura bark. The family has always refused to discuss ingredients, but apparently Angostura Bitters were hastily reformulated to exclude angostura bark.

Now gentian is mostly responsible for the bitter-Moxie flavor of the bitters. According to economic botanist Julia F. Morton, Sc.D., of the University of Miami (Fla.), two other flavorings are bitter orange peel and galangal. Citrus peel enters into many other bitter drinks, such as Campari. Galangal is a pungent root spice, related to ginger, that otherwise turns up in Indonesian cooking. Another widely suspected ingredient is cloves.

The most complete published breakdown of Angostura Bitters appears in the *Source Book of Flavors* by Henry B. Heath (Westport, Conn.: AVI Publishing Co., 1981). Heath's Angostura recipe is not a complete chemical analysis, but it is an expert guess, based on the best available information, about what goes into Angostura Bitters. Heath's recipe uses angostura bark rather than gentian and thus seems to simulate the old-style bitters. In order of declining quantity, it calls for:

10 parts	Angostura Bark
4 parts	Bitter Orange Fruit
4 parts	Bitter Orange Peel
4 parts	Cinnamon Bark
4 parts	Tonka Beans
3 parts	Cloves
2 parts	Calisaya Bark
2 parts	Cardamon
2 parts	Carob
2 parts	Ginger
2 parts	Lemon Peel
1 part	Galangal
1 part	Zedoary

According to Heath, all ingredients are percolated with 50 percent alcohol. Two ounces of the resulting concentrated extract are used to flavor a gallon of the finished product.

What about the bright pink color Angostura Bitters impart to gin? It must come from a vegetable dye. None of the flavoring ingredients have much color when diluted to final strength.

Benedictine
Fécamp, France
80 proof

Benedictine boasts the oldest secret recipe of any popular food or drink. It was invented at the Benedictine Abbey of Fécamp by Dom Bernardo Vincelli in 1510. For centuries the recipe was concocted only by monks. Now the formula is in the more secular hands of a family-owned corporation. It is still made at Fécamp, though in a replica of the original monastery. According to *Grossman's Guide*, only three people are ever permitted to know the complete recipe.

Benedictine fairly taunts its imitators with a Salon de Contrefaçons (Hall of Counterfeits) at its distillery. The Salon is a massive collection of the hundreds of imitation "Benedictines" produced around the globe.

The taste of true Benedictine is agreeable, sweet, and distinctive. The alcohol base is brandy. It is known that there are many ingredients; that they mixed in more than one step; and that the liqueur is aged for four years before bottling.

Fenaroli's Handbook of Flavor Ingredients, an industry bible, argues knowingly that the gist of Benedictine flavor is three ingredients: citrus, angelica, and juniper berries. Angelica is a sweet, licorice-flavored herb of northern Europe; juniper berries, from the common shrub, are also used to flavor gin. Most flavor chemists agree with the *Fenaroli* assessment, but no one doubts that many other trace ingredients are used as well. Peppermint, cloves, and balm (sold in health-food stores for brewing a lemon-scented herb tea) are widely suspected.

In *Food Flavorings*, Joseph Merory gave a recipe for imitation Benedictine with twenty flavorings. The ingredients in the left-hand column below are soaked in thirty-three gallons of 40 percent alcohol for four days. Twenty gallons are removed for later use. The ingredients in the right-hand column are added to the remaining mixture. A day later, this entire mixture is distilled. The first ten gallons of distillate are mixed with the twenty gallons of filtered extract set aside on the fourth day. The result, a 100-proof flavoring, is mixed with sugar syrup, water, and brandy to yield the correct flavor intensity, sweetness, and proof.

lbs.		*lbs.*	
7.5	Angelica Root	4.5	Angelica Root
2.5	Balm	4.5	Calamus
2.5	Mugwort	4.5	Gentian
2.5	Peppermint	4.5	Mace
2.25	Valencia Orange Peel	2.25	Spanish Orange Peel
2.0	Coriander	1.875	Cardamon Seeds
1.5	Calamus	1.875	Cloves
1.25	Hyssop (Herbs)	1.875	Roman Chamomile
1.25	Hyssop (Leaves)	1.25	Thyme
1.25	Thyme		
1.0	Arnica Blossom		
0.875	Musk Seed		
0.5	Cardamon Seeds		
0.5	Cassia		
0.25	Cloves		
0.15	Nutmeg		

Campari
Milan, Italy
48 proof

Gaspare Campari's crimson aperitif is sold as a bottled carbonated beverage in Europe. The product sold in the United States is the "syrup" from which Campari soda can be made. Chemical analysis shows that syrup is the right word. By weight, about 23 percent of Campari is sugar—a sucrose megadose for a drink that does not, to the first-time drinker, taste sweet at all. Whatever is in Campari, it is bitter enough to mask a cloying base. An even sweeter version of Campari is sold as an after-dinner cordial.

There is no question that citrus oils are the primary flavorings. They are probably bitter orange, with some lemon and possibly some sweet orange. There is less agreement on the other flavorings. According to Guido Zamarini, a flavor chemist who produced a Campari imitation in Mexico, Campari's chiaroscuro undertones come from rhubarb and cocoa. Zamarini's formula used rhubarb, quinine, oils of bitter orange, sweet orange, and lemon, cocoa, and gentian.

Heath's *Source Book of Flavors* includes an "Italian Bitters" recipe—evidently intended as an approximation to Campari—in which angelica and other herbs back up the citrus. The recipe uses:

1¼ lb.	Bitter Orange Peel	12 oz.	Wormwood Leaves
1 lb.	Angelica Root	8 oz.	Cinnamon
1 lb.	Buckbean Leaves	7 oz.	Cloves
1 lb.	Lemon Peel	5 oz.	Marjoram
12 oz.	Anise	5 oz.	Sage
12 oz.	Calamus	5 oz.	Thyme
12 oz.	Fennel	2 oz.	Rosemary
12 oz.	Orris Root		

All are percolated with 50 percent alcohol; 2 ounces flavor a gallon of sweetened alcohol/water mixture. Campari's color apparently is a combination of red carmine and brown caramel.

Chartreuse
Voiron, France
80 proof (yellow) and 110 proof (green)

The secret formula for Chartreuse was a gift from the Maréchal d'Estrées to the monastery of the Grande Chartreuse near Grenoble in 1607. It is still produced by Carthusian monks. It was slightly reformulated once—in 1757, by Brother Gérome Manbec. The secret almost fell out of the order's control in the early part of this century. Legal problems forced the Carthusian fathers to flee France in 1901. All the order's property, including the recipe, was to have been sold at auction. No copy of the recipe remained in France, however. The exiled fathers produced Chartreuse in Tarragona, Spain. After protracted litigation in France, the Carthusians were able to return to Voiron and resume production in France.

Green, yellow, and white (colorless) Chartreuse is produced. The green and yellow colors, it's suspected, are as artificial as those of lemon and lime Kool-Aid. Green Chartreuse is more alcoholic than the yellow form. Some tasters claim slight flavor differences as well. Others think the "differences" are nothing more than the suggestive power of the two colors. Taste as well as chemical analysis show that both forms are ungodly sweet: about 28 percent sugar by weight in the yellow variety. A 750-milliliter bottle of yellow Chartreuse contains about half a pound of sugar.

Is Chartreuse a rip-off of Benedictine? Connoisseurs charge the two liqueurs are similar. (Presumably Chartreuse has been spared display in the Salon de Contrefaçons.) The comparison is more striking if you close your eyes and have someone give you sips of Benedictine and yellow Chartreuse. No one knows exactly how the Maréchal d'Estrées came by his recipe, but his gift came a century after the invention of Benedictine.

Like Benedictine, Chartreuse has a brandy base. *Fenaroli's Handbook* contends that the basic Chartreuse flavor is a mélange of citrus, angelica, juniper berries, anise, and wormwood. Three of these five were listed as the primary flavorings of Benedictine. Anise provides a second, licoricelike note, not unlike angelica; wormwood, a constituent of vermouth, provides bitterness. The *Fenaroli's Handbook* recipe for Chartreuse flavoring uses essential oils rather than raw spices and herbs:

60 parts	Lemon Oil
20 parts	Anethol (main component of anise oil)
15 parts	Juniper Oil
7.1 parts	Clary Sage Oil
4 parts	Hyssop Oil
3 parts	Bitter Orange Oil
3 parts	Mint Oil
3 parts	Petitgrain Oil
2.5 parts	Coriander Oil
2.1 parts	Angelica Oil
2.1 parts	Mace Oil
2.1 parts	Wormwood Oil
2 parts	Sweet Orange Oil
1 part	Caraway Oil
1 part	Cinnamon Oil
Trace	Lavender Oil

One part of this oil mixture flavors about five thousand parts of liqueur. This is a "compound" Chartreuse flavor. *Fenaroli's Handbook* suggests that the anise note should be more pronounced in the yellow form and subdued in the green.

Fernet Branca
New York
78 proof

Fernet Branca is a hangover cure and sometime ingredient of mixed drinks. It was devised by a Dr. Fernet, a Swede, as a tonic against cholera. The biting, medicinal taste gives no clue to its composition. The color is a murky sepia-black.

The label lists nine ingredients: aloes, gentian, zedoary, cinchona, calumba, rhubarb, angelica, chamomile, and saffron. This sounds like enough ingredients, but some authorities suspect there are others, not mentioned. For one thing, Fernet Branca smells like mint. None of the label ingredients smell much like mint, and it is questionable if their odors could combine to simulate mint. *Fenaroli's Handbook* maintains that mint essential oil is an ingredient. *Fenaroli's* further claims calamus, centaury, imperatoria, larch agaric (a mushroom growing around larch trees), St. Johnswort, and myrrh (as in the Bible, a hardened, pungent sap from an African tree) as ingredients of Fernet Branca or Fernet imitations. No citrus is used, says *Fenaroli's*.

Priciest of Fernet's ingredients is saffron. Better known for its color than flavor, saffron has a pungent, bitter taste. It sells for over a hundred dollars a pound. But according to a recipe in Merory's *Food Flavorings*, a scant 50 grams of saffron suffice for a 100-liter batch of imitation Fernet. If this approximates the proportion of saffron in genuine Fernet Branca, the cost of saffron per bottle is on the order of ten cents.

Fernet's inky color comes from a larger-than-usual dose of caramel coloring.

Grand Marnier
Paris, France
80 proof

Grand Marnier is an orange liqueur, yet it tastes different from generic orange Curaçao-type liqueurs. Part of the reason is the cognac base. Cheaper brands use flavorless "neutral spirits." The other difference is a secret list of background flavorings. According to a recipe in *Food Flavorings*, the principal secret ingredient is peppermint. Merory's recipe for "Grand 'M'-Type Flavor" uses more noncitrus than citrus flavorings:

4750 gm.	Bitter Orange Peel
2500 gm.	Peppermint
2250 gm.	Sweet Orange Peel
1750 gm.	Lemon Peel
1500 gm.	Coriander Seed
1500 gm.	Curaçao Orange Peel
1500 gm.	Ginger
1500 gm.	Orange Blossoms
1075 gm.	Cloves
875 gm.	Angelica Seed
875 gm.	Cinnamon
250 gm.	Cardamon
100 gm.	Saffron
100 gm.	Tonka Beans

Cointreau is believed to use many of the same ingredients but is prepared less sweet.

PART TWO

Everything You Owe Is Wrong

F ace it: Of healthy, wealthy, and wise, only one is going to get you a good seat at a restaurant. Now that everyone has finally sold out for a life of materialist depravity, it is time to face some hard economic facts. The free marketplace has seen us coming. Prices are pure sadism, and no one knows the safe word. We've become a nation of MBAs with hot plates and a standard of living you can't dress up and take anywhere. But there is something you should know before heading back to the commune you glossed over on your résumé. To keep things honest through the coming bad years, the issuers of money, checks, and credit cards are keeping secrets from us. Take a five-dollar bill out of your wallet and look carefully at the back. . . .

6·

Weird Stuff on Money

The Five-Dollar Bill

The U.S. Treasury Department denies that there are any secret anticounterfeiting gimmicks in currency artwork. Many people think otherwise. For some reason, the most popular hunting ground for anticounterfeiting devices—or clues to some unspecified conspiracy—is the picture of the Lincoln Memorial on the back of the five-dollar bill.

For instance, there's the "secret number." Look in the bushes to the left of the steps leading up to the Memorial. The pattern of shading seems to spell out a three-digit number: 372. The numerals are dark against a lighter background. The 3 has an exaggerated lower stroke; the 7 has a strong downward serif at the left end of the horizontal stroke. The shadows in the bushes on the right form no coherent pattern.

Once you see the 372, it's hard not to see it. Persistent rumors allege that the number must have some significance—but stop short of explaining just what purpose a barely legible, unchanging three-digit number could serve. The number is too coarse to be a useful anticounterfeiting device. A counterfeit bill so grainy as to smear the secret number would certainly have a funny-looking Lincoln on the other side. The Treasury Department doggedly maintains the number is a mere accident of engraving.

No accident are the near-invisible names of twenty-six U.S. states in the same engraving. Sucker bet: Get someone to wager five dollars that North Dakota is not mentioned on U.S. currency. You will need a magnifying glass to collect.

The state names are in two rows. The larger, bottom row of names is on the frieze above the tops of the twelve columns. Directly above each column is a roundish ornament suggesting two intersecting circles. These ornaments separate the eleven state names in this row. From left to right the names read (in order of admission to the union): DELAWARE PENNSYLVANIA NEW JERSEY GEORGIA CONNECTICUT MASSACHU-SETTS MARYLAND CAROLINA HAMPSHIRE VIR-GINIA NEW YORK. Each letter is less than half a millimeter high. With good lighting and a fresh bill, persons of excellent eyesight can just read the names. The outlines of the letters are incomplete because of the small scale.

An even finer row of fifteen states appears on the frieze on the upper, indented part of the Memorial. These names are on the lower, less ornamented section of the upper part, just below the smooth horizontal molding. They read: ARKANSAS MICHIGAN FLORIDA TEXAS IOWA WISCONSIN CALIFORNIA MINNESOTA OREGON KANSAS WEST VIRGINIA NEVADA NEBRASKA COLORADO NORTH DAKOTA. These names are virtually impossible to read unless you use a magnifying glass and follow the list. Depending on bill wear, some states may be illegible even with magnification.

The names appear on the Lincoln Memorial in Washington; any detailed picture of the Memorial must contain them. It is not clear if the engraver realized that they could be used as a check against counterfeiting. Because the names are almost invisible on a legitimate bill, they aren't likely to show up well on a photographically reproduced counterfeit. Of course, the checker must realize how faint the names can be on a real bill.

Still another object of suspicion is the funny shadow on the Memorial steps. It draws attention even though it could hardly serve any anticounterfeiting purpose. The peculiar shadow—that of the left stair guard and its torchlike ornament—seems to be much longer than it should be. The angle of sunlight can be judged from the shadow of the top of the Memorial, behind the leftmost columns. If a line parallel to this line of shadow is drawn from the top of the bowl or torch on the left stair guard, it intersects the steps much closer than the far end of the engraved shadow. Furthermore, the right stair guard doesn't cast any shadow on the bushes. Geometrically correct or not, the shadow would be easily duplicated in any counterfeiting process.

What do Treasury agents really look for on a suspected counterfeit? Most published sources say the eyes of the portrait are the best places to look. The eyes may not be any more susceptible to poor printing, but the right portion of the brain is quick to pick up on any slight modification in a familiar face. Another trick uses a hair-thin line that appears on the front but not the back of the five-dollar bill. (It is also on the front and back of one-, ten-, and twenty-dollar bills.)

Look at the large 5s in the upper right and upper left corners of the front of the five-dollar bill. Just inside the margin of the 5s is a fine dark line. Normally the line is sharp and entire. The fineness of the line makes it difficult to reproduce. It almost always comes out with parts of the line faded or missing. This scarcely changes the basic look of the bill, but if you know the line should be entire, it is a simple check. A faded line on a bill that otherwise seems unworn is particularly suspicious.

The One-Dollar Bill

The remarkable part of the one-dollar bill is the Great Seal of the United States (the two circular emblems on the back). Some see in the seal evidence of a Masonic conspiracy. At any rate, the pyramid with the eye above it is an obvious nod to Freemasonry. (The truncated pyramid represents the unfinished Temple of Solomon; the eye represents the Grand Architect of the Universe.)

In 1954 University of Texas doctoral candidate James David Carter wrote a dissertation (*Freemasonry in Texas: Background, History, and Influence to 1846*) that summarized further rumored significance of the Great Seal. It is claimed that the eagle on the seal has thirty-two feathers in its right wing and thirty-three feathers in its left. The thirty-two feathers symbolize the thirty-two Scottish Rite degrees (earned titles) of Freemasonry. There is also a thirty-third honorary degree, which accounts for the thirty-three feathers. The eagle's nine tail feathers correspond to the nine degrees of the York Rite. "E Pluribus Unum," on the eagle's banner, is a Masonic motto. Above the eagle's head are thirteen stars, representing the thirteen colonies but arranged to suggest a Star of David. King David figures into Masonic legend. The glory around the thirteen stars is calibrated with alternating long and short marks, suggesting the twenty-four divisions of the Masonic gauge (ruler).

Not all these claims check out. The thirty-third feather is elusive. There are three rows of feathers on each wing. The outer row on each wing has seventeen feathers. The middle row seems to have fifteen feathers on each wing. Together, that makes thirty-two feathers for each wing. The feathers in the inner row are lighter and hard to count. There seem to be about twelve inner feathers on each wing, which would not help achieve thirty-three in any case.

There are indeed nine tail feathers, and the stars do form a Star of David. But there are twenty-eight, not twenty-four, divisions of the glory.

Another Masonic symbol of sorts is on the front of the one-dollar bill. George Washington was a Mason and is venerated by American lodges—as are fellow Masons (and Presidents) Monroe, Jackson, Polk, Buchanan, Andrew Johnson, Garfield, McKinley, both Roosevelts, Taft, Harding, Truman, and Ford.

Other People's Money

U.S. greenbacks are a cinch to counterfeit compared to many foreign currencies. Not only do foreign currencies carry watermarks (a valuable anticounterfeiting device the U.S. Treasury has declined to use), but they also sport various high-tech gimmicks.

Buried inside the Scottish pound note is a strip of microfilm. Across the top of the front of the one-pound note is written "The Royal Bank of Scotland Limited." The microfilm runs vertically through the "n" in the word "Bank." If you hold the note up to a light and examine the strip with a magnifying glass, the film is seen to spell out the initials of the Royal Bank of Scotland: RBS.

Israeli currency has an opaque magnetic filament that is said to spell out the name of the central bank magnetically, in Morse code.

The Day-Glo colors on many Third World currencies are there for a reason. Bahamian money, for instance, has a "prismatic background"—a delicate pattern of conch shells that grades from turquoise to lilac to pink to orange to gold. A counterfeiter trying to reproduce the pastel tones on a color copier runs into trouble. Fiddle with the color adjustments as he might, at least one of the colors fails to reproduce.

Queen Elizabeth II's hair has been a source of notaphilic

rumors in the Commonwealth nations. The 1954 issue of Canadian dollars contained a remarkably convincing devil's face in the Queen's hair, just to the right of her earring. The portrait was retouched after public discovery of the face. Now the devil's-face dollars are virtually uncirculated (collectors hoard them). The face was claimed to have been the work of an antiroyalist engraver. The current portrait of the Queen on British pound notes has what may be interpreted as a panting Pekinese dog. It is also in the hair, on the right side, directly in line with the Queen's eyes.

7.

Currency Paper

The Treasury Department does not produce the paper used to print money. The paper's manufacture is contracted out to a private company better known for business stationery: Crane and Company of Dalton, Massachusetts. The type of currency paper now used, with the red and blue fibers, was developed by the Treasury Department in conjunction with Crane and Company. It has been in use since 1879.

Officially, the formulation of the paper is a secret. In fact, however, there is very little that isn't known about the paper. Every counterfeiter since 1879 has tried to duplicate it, with varying degrees of success. From time to time, curious paper chemists have broken it down and surmised its salient features. It's known, for instance, that the paper is 75 percent cotton and 25 percent linen. (Originally it was 100 percent linen, then 75 percent, and then 50 percent.) It is permeated with red and blue fibers. U.S. currency has three hidden security features:

1. The paper fluoresces under an ultraviolet lamp.
2. The ink is magnetic—not to a degree you could notice with a pocket magnet, but enough to be detected with special machines.
3. The paper is riddled with tiny, invisible holes. Under a microscope, pinpoints of light shine through. (Many counterfeit papers are solid.)

Money used to be made from used clothing. Crane purchased old cotton shirts, hired ragpickers to remove the buttons, and bleached the fabric white. Now most shirts contain polyester, and the dyes don't bleach out. "New rag cuttings"—small squares of virgin fabric—rather than old shirts are the principal raw material of money today. Crane buys them from textile firms.

The first step in the production of any rag paper is to convert the rag into pulp. The cuttings of cotton and linen (in a three-to-one ratio) are mixed with water—probably just about enough to cover the cloth—and beaten in large machines. Hours later, the mixture is a uniform pulp with no fibers remaining.

The blue and red fibers must be added at this stage. If they were added during the beating, the colored fibers would likewise be reduced to pulp. Examination of the finished currency paper reveals that the fibers are embedded in the paper, not just pasted onto its surface. Therefore they must be mixed into the pulp before the sheets are formed.

The pulp is poured into molds. Paper molds usually consist of a wooden frame with a fine wire mesh bottom. They are somewhat larger than the dry, finished sheets to allow for shrinkage. The pulp must be spread evenly in the mold, and the amount of pulp must be gauged to a final dry-sheet thickness in the range of 0.0042 to 0.0045 inch.

Excess water drips through the wire mesh, leaving a newly formed sheet in the mold. The damp sheets are probably "couched" as most fine paper is—carefully transferred to wool mats or "felts." The sheets and felts are sandwiched together and squeezed in a press to remove further water.

The next step is loft drying, to which currency paper owes much of its durability. The sheets are peeled from the felts and placed on a large screen, the loft, to dry. The faster paper dries, the stronger it becomes; the loft allows it to dry from both sides at once.

Paper to be used for printing must be "sized." Sizing prevents the ink from soaking in and spreading out. If you tried to write on a paper towel (an unsized paper) with a fountain pen, the ink would feather and the writing become illegible. Currency paper, then, obviously is well sized to take the fine engraving. The best sizing material, and the one that paper chemists agree is used for

U.S. currency, is glue. Glue sizing is actually a gelatin made by boiling the hoofs, ears, and other unused parts of slaughtered livestock. It is sold in a dry, flaky form and dissolved in water to yield a thin sizing bath. Dry sheets are immersed in the bath, removed, pressed, and dried.

The exceptional uniformity of currency paper betrays the final step in its manufacture. No matter how carefully the pulp is spread in the molds, even thickness is impossible to ensure without plate finishing. In this step the sheets are sandwiched between polished metal plates. Heavy rollers compress the sandwiched sheets under great pressure. Although mere lagniappe, this finishing is nearly impossible to duplicate with makeshift equipment. High-pressure rollers are expensive machines. (In contrast, all the steps up to plate finishing can be duplicated by amateur papermakers at home.) The thickness of counterfeit paper usually varies outside the Treasury Department tolerances.

The finished sheets are cut to measure 53.5 by 63.0 centimeters—just enough for thirty-two bills, eight down and four across.

8·

Credit Cards

There are at least three types of security devices on credit cards that you aren't supposed to know about. They are the account number, the signature panel, and the magnetic strip.

The Account Number

A Social Security card has nine digits. So do two-part Zip codes. A domestic phone number, including area code, has ten digits. Yet a complete MasterCard number has twenty digits. Why so many?

It is not mathematically necessary for any credit-card account number to have more than eight digits. Each cardholder must, of course, have a unique number. Visa and MasterCard are estimated to have about sixty-five million cardholders each. Thus their numbering systems must have at least sixty-five million available numbers.

There are one hundred million possible combinations of eight digits—00000000, 00000001, 00000002, 00000003, all the way up to 99999999. So eight digits would be enough. To allow for future growth, an issuer the size of Visa or MasterCard could opt for nine digits—enough for a billion different numbers.

In fact, a Visa card has thirteen digits and sometimes more. An American Express card has fifteen digits. Diners Club cards have fourteen. Carte Blanche has ten. Obviously, the card issuers are not projecting that they will have billions and billions of cardholders and need those digits to ensure a different number for each. The extra digits are actually a security device.

Say your Visa number is 4211 503 417 268. Each purchase must be entered into a computer from a sales slip. The account number tags the purchase to your account. The persons who enter account numbers into computers get bored and sometimes make mistakes. They might enter 4211 503 471 268 or 4211 703 417 268 instead.

The advantage of the thirteen-digit numbering system is that it is unlikely any Visa cardholder has 4211 503 471 268 or 4211 703 417 268 for an account number. There are 10 trillion possible thirteen-digit Visa numbers (0000 000 000 000; 0000 000 000 001; . . . 9999 999 999 999). Only about sixty-five million of those numbers are numbers of actual, active accounts. The odds that an incorrectly entered number would correspond to a real number are something like sixty-five million in ten trillion, or about one in one hundred fifty thousand.

Those are slim odds. You could fill up a book the size of this one with random thirteen-digit numbers such as these:

3901	160	943	791
1090	734	231	410
1783	205	995	561
9542	425	195	969
2358	862	307	845
9940	880	814	778
8421	456	150	662
9910	441	036	483
3167	186	869	267
6081	132	670	781
1228	190	300	350
4563	351	105	207

Still you would not duplicate a Visa account number. Whenever an account number is entered incorrectly, it will almost certainly fail to match up with any of the other account numbers in the computer's memory. The computer can then request that the number be entered again.

Other card-numbering systems are even more secure. Of the quadrillion possible fifteen-digit American Express card numbers, only about 11 million are assigned. The chance of a random number happening to correspond to an existing account number is about one in ninety million. Taking into account all twenty digits on a MasterCard, there are one hundred quintillion (100,000,000,000,000,000,000) possible numbers for sixty-five million cardholders. The chance of a random string of digits matching a real MasterCard number is about one in one and a half trillion.

Among other things, this makes possible those television ads inviting holders of credit cards to phone in to order merchandise. The operators who take the calls never see the callers' cards nor their signatures. How can they be sure the callers even have credit cards?

They base their confidence on the security of the credit-card numbering systems. If someone calls in and makes up a credit-card number—even being careful to get the right number of digits—the number surely will not be an existing real credit-card number. The deception can be spotted instantly by plugging into the credit-card company's computers. For all practical purposes, the only way to come up with a genuine credit-card number is to read it off a credit card. The number, not the piece of plastic, is enough.

Neiman-Marcus' Garbage Can

The converse of this is the fact that anyone who knows someone else's card number can charge to that person's account. Police sources say this is a major problem, but card issuers, by and large, do their best to keep these crimes a secret. The fear is that publicizing the crimes may tempt more people to commit them. Worse yet, there is almost nothing the average person can do to prevent being victimized—short of giving up credit cards entirely.

Lots of strangers know your credit-card numbers. Everyone you hand a card to—waiters, sales clerks, ticket agents, hairdressers, gas station attendants, hotel cashiers—sees the account number. Every time a card is put in an imprinter, three copies are made, and two are left with the clerk. If you charge anything by phone or mail order, someone somewhere sees the number.

Crooks don't have to be in a job with normal access to credit-card numbers. Occasional operations have discovered that the garbage cans outside prestige department or specialty stores are sources of high-credit-limit account numbers. The crooks look for the discarded carbon paper from sales slips. The account number is usually legible—as are the expiration date, name, and signature. (A 1981 operation used carbons from Koontz Hardware, a West Hollywood, California, store frequented by many celebrities.)

Converting a number into cash is less risky than using a stolen credit card. The crook need only call an airline, posing as the cardholder, and make a reservation on a heavily traveled flight. He usually requests that tickets be issued in someone else's name for pickup at the airport. The someone else is an accomplice or an identity for which he has bogus ID. Crook or accomplice picks up the tickets at the airport (airlines don't always ask for ID on ticket pickups, but the crook has it if needed) and is set. The tickets can be sold at a discount on the hot-ticket market operating in every major airport.

There are other methods as well. Anyone with a Visa or MasterCard merchant account can fill out invoices for nonexistent sales and submit them to the bank. As long as the account numbers and names are genuine, the bank will pay the merchant immediately.

For an investment of about a thousand dollars, an organized criminal operation can get the pressing machines needed to make counterfeit credit cards. Counterfeiting credit cards is relatively simple. There are no fancy scrolls and filigree work, just blocky logos in primary colors. From the criminal's standpoint, the main advantage of a counterfeit card is that it allows him to get cash advances. For maximum plundering of a line of credit, the crook must know the credit limit as well as the account number. To learn both, he often calls an intended victim, posing as the victim's bank:

> CROOK: This is Bank of America. We're calling to tell you that the credit limit on your Visa card has been raised to twelve hundred dollars.
> VICTIM: But my limit has always been ten thousand dollars.
> CROOK: There must be some problem with the computers. Do you have your card handy? Could you read off the embossed number?

On a smaller scale, many struggling rock groups have discovered the knack of using someone else's telephone company credit card. When a cardholder wants to make a long-distance call from a hotel or pay phone, he or she reads the card number to the operator. The call is then billed to the cardholder's home phone. Musicians on tour sometimes wait by the special credit-card-and-collect-calls-only booths at airports and jot down a few credit-card numbers. In this way unsuspecting businesspeople finance a touring act's calls to friends at home. If the musicians call from public phones, use a given card number only once, and don't stay in one city long, the phone company seems helpless to stop them.

What makes all of these scams so hard to combat is the lead time afforded the criminal. Theft of a credit card—a crime that card issuers will talk about—is generally reported immediately. Within twenty-four hours, a stolen card's number is on the issuer's "hot list" and can no longer be used. But when only a card number is being used illicitly, the crime is not discovered until the cardholder receives his first inflated bill. That's at least two weeks later; it could be as much as six weeks later. As long as the illicit user isn't too greedy, he has at least two weeks to tap into a credit line with little risk.

The Signature Panel

You're not supposed to erase the signature panel, of course. Card issuers fear that crooks might erase the signature on a stolen credit card and replace it with their own. To make alteration more difficult, many card signature panels have a background design that rubs off if anyone tries to erase. There's the "fingerprint" design on the American Express panel, repeated Visa or MasterCard logos on some bank cards, and the "Safesig" design on others. The principle is the same as with the security paper used for checks. If you try to erase a check on security paper, the wavy-line pattern erases, leaving a white area—and it is obvious that the check has been altered.

Rumors hint of a more elaborate gimmick in credit-card panels. It is said that if you erase the panel, a secret word— VOID—appears to prevent use of the card. To test this rumor, fifteen common credit cards were sacrificed.

An ordinary pen eraser will erase credit-card signature panels, if slowly. The panels are more easily removed with a cloth and a dry-cleaning fluid such as Energine. This method dissolves the panels cleanly. Of the fifteen cards tested, six had nothing under the panel (other than a continuation of the card back design, where there was one). Nine cards had the word "VOID" under the panel. In all cases, the VOIDs were printed small and repeated many times under the panel. The breakdown:

VOID Device	*Nothing*
Bloomingdale's	American Express Gold Card
Bonwit Teller	Broadway
Bullock's	MasterCard (Citibank)
Chase Convenience	Neiman-Marcus
Banking Card	Robinson's
First Interstate Bank Card	Saks Fifth Avenue
I. Magnin	
Joseph Magnin	
Montgomery Ward	
Visa (Chase Manhattan)	

When held to a strong light, the VOIDs were visible through the Bloomingdale's card even without removing the panel.

The VOID device isn't foolproof. Any criminal who learns the secret will simply refrain from trying to erase the signature. Most salesclerks don't bother to check signatures anyway.

Moreover, it is possible to paint the signature panel back in, over the VOIDs—at least on those cards that do not have a design on the panel. (Saks' panel is a greenish-tan khaki color that would be difficult to match with paint.) The panel is first removed with dry-cleaning fluid. The back of the card is covered with masking tape, leaving a window where the replacement panel is to go. A thin coat of flat white spray paint simulates the original panel.

The Magnetic Strip

The other security device on the back of the card, the brown magnetic strip, is more difficult to analyze. Some people think there are sundry personal details about the cardholder stored in the strip. But the strip has no more information capacity than a similar snippet of recording tape. For their part, banks are reticent about the strip.

The strip need not contain any information other than the account number or similar indentification. Any further information needed to complete an automatic-teller transaction—such as current account balances—can be called up from bank computers and need not be encoded in the strip.

Evidently, the card expiration date is in the strip. Expired cards are "eaten" by automatic-teller machines even when the expired card has the same account number and name as its valid replacement card. Credit limit, address, phone number, employer, etc., must not be indicated in the strip, for banks do not issue new cards just because this information changes.

It is not clear if the personal identification number is in the strip or called up from the bank computer. Many automatic-teller machines have a secret limit of three attempts for providing the correct personal identification number. After three wrong attempts, the "customer" is assumed to be a crook with a stolen card, going through all the possible permutations—and the card is eaten.

It is possible to scramble the information in the strip by rubbing a pocket magnet over it. Workers in hospitals or research facilities with large electromagnets sometimes find that their cards no longer work in automatic-teller machines. (If you try to use a magnetically doctored card, you usually get a message to the effect, "Your card may be inserted incorrectly. Please remove and insert according to diagram.")

The Bloomingdale's Color Code

Only in a few cases does the color of a credit card mean anything. There are, of course, the American Express, Visa, and Master-Card gold cards for preferred customers. The Air Travel Card comes in red and green, of which green is better. (With red, you can charge tickets for travel within North America only.) The most elaborate color scheme, and a source of some confusion to status-conscious queues, is that of Bloomingdale's credit cards. The five colors of Bloomingdale's cards do not signify credit limits per se, but they do tip off the sales staff as to what type of customer you are. According to Bloomingdale's credit department, here is how it works: Low color in the pecking order is blue, issued to Bloomingdale's employees as a perk in their compensation packages. The basic Bloomie's card is yellow. Like most department store cards, it can be used to spread payments over several months with the payment of a finance charge. The red card gives holders three months' free interest and is issued to customers who regularly make large purchases. The silver card is good for unlimited spending, but as with a travel and entertainment card, all charges must be paid in thirty days. The gold card offers the same payment options as the yellow card but is reserved for the store's biggest spenders.

9.

The VOID Pop-up

What happens if you photocopy something you're not supposed to photocopy? If it is a finely engraved document—money, a traveler's check, a stock certificate—the copy comes out smudged or faded. If it is a simpler document—a money order, a supermarket coupon, a gift certificate—and if you use a good color copier, the copy is often a convincing counterfeit.

The VOID pop-up is a secret gimmick to foil the latter type of counterfeiters. It works simply enough: When a document containing the device is photocopied, the word "VOID" appears on the copy. At best the VOID is faint and fuzzy, like the Shroud of Turin. But users of the pop-up feel it must take a lot more guts to try to pass a counterfeit with the VOID than without it.

The VOID pop-up was invented by the American Bank Note Company but not patented. It has been adopted by other document printers. It is not regarded as effective a security device as currency-quality engraving. The time and expense of engraving make it suitable only for the most important documents, however. The VOID pop-up has been used mostly for medium-security documents, including, according to American Bank Note, Chase Manhattan Bank money orders and Kentucky Fried Chicken gift certificates.

The VOID pop-up uses a screen—a background of dots so fine they appear as an even gray or pastel shade. From a normal viewing distance, the only distinguishing feature of a screen is how dark a gray it is (assuming black dots on a white background; the same argument applies for other ink colors). In turn, the shade of gray depends only on the percentage of the total area that is covered by the dots.

Two different screens can look the same. One screen might have larger dots, a different arrangement of dots, or a different shape from another. But as long as the percentage of black area to white area is the same, and as long as the individual dots are too small to be seen individually, both screens look the same shade of gray.

Two such different but seemingly identical screens can make a VOID pop up. One screen is used to print the letters VOID across the document. The other screen forms a background to the letters. Both screens have exactly the same density, so the original document seems to have an even gray or pastel background.

A Xerox machine sees things differently from the eye. One of the screens is chosen so that the configuration of its dots will bleed together on the copy. This screen comes out darker or of a different quality than the other, and the VOID is visible.

The system isn't foolproof. Copiers vary, so the VOID is conspicuous with some machines, scarcely noticeable with others. Occasionally a ghostly VOID is visible on the original, to the consternation of innocent consumers who aren't intended to know about the pop-up at all. There is a screen attachment for some makes of copiers that defeats the pop-up and allows clean copies.

There are still other ways to prevent illicit photocopying. *Prospects/New Book News,* a New York-based weekly newsletter that summarizes the plots of upcoming novels for motion-picture producers, is printed on red paper. Red shows up nearly black on most black-and-white copiers. (As subscriptions are five hundred dollars a year, producers are sorely tempted to make Xerox copies for associates.) Of course, *Prospects* can be copied on a color copier, and on those black-and-white machines that have red filters.

At the other end of the spectrum, a light, swimming-pool-bottom blue does not reproduce on most copiers. Turquoise felt-tip pens are used to make marginal notes on magazine boards. The notes are invisible in the photographically printed magazines. In 1971 *Computerworld,* a trade publication, postulated the following use of light-blue print:

> The Diners Club, whose accounting system has been attacked by people trying to keep their accounts straight, has

apparently found one way of keeping the complaint level down—particularly those types of complaints that are copied to various federal and state authorities, Better Business Bureaus, Ralph Nader, etc. It won't, of course stop the complaints altogether, but it will certainly reduce their effectiveness in many cases.

What Diners Club did was redesign the forms, printing much of the vital data in non-reproducing blue. As a result, after it has been put into the copying machine, the output simply is almost incomprehensible, and certainly much less persuasive to other people who may want to read it.

According to Diners Club, the color choice was a coincidence—the Diners Club logo is blue.

10·

The Universal Product Code

Supermarkets know better than to trust us anarchists. It is easy enough to take a magic marker and black out a line or two of the Universal Product Code symbol. Lest anyone try to lower prices or sabotage the system, there is a security device built into the code.

The UPC scanner can detect any alteration of a symbol—or, at least, stands a 90 percent chance of detecting it. The secret is a "check digit" encoded in two extra bars at the end of the UPC symbol. The check digit is derived mathematically from the information contained in the other bars of the symbol. Change the symbol, and the check digit probably no longer jibes.

The formula for assigning the check digit was devised by the Uniform Product Code Council, a manufacturers' association based in Dayton, Ohio. It is revealed in *The UPC Guidelines Manual,* a technical bulletin provided to corporate members of the council. Every manufacturer using the Universal Product Code calculates the check digit in the same way.

In its usual form, the code symbol has a number at the left side of the bar pattern and two groups of five digits at the bottom of the bar pattern. A shorter form of the symbol, with only six digits at the bottom, is used on packages too small to take the full symbol. A few products, such as magazines and books, have extra numbers and bars to accommodate large numbers of products from a single manufacturer.

The scanners do not read the numerals. The numerals are there

How to Crack the Universal Product Code

A Two thin "guard bars" don't mean anything; they frame the real message. Repeated in middle and at other end of bar pattern.

B Wide space, bar, narrow space, thin bar encode the 0 at left of symbol. 0 means it's regular groceries. 3 is for drugs.

C Ten spaces and ten bars encode the 12345 at bottom, which identifies the manufacturer. 21000 would be Kraft, etc.

D Encodes the 67890, which identifies the product, including size of package. Price is not encoded.

E A secret "check digit" (here 5) to catch any error or tampering. If someone widens a bar with a felt-tip pen, the check digit helps the scanner detect it.

only for the convenience of the human checkers. If the scanner is down, the checker may enter the numbers by hand. The bars encode the same set of numbers—plus the check digit—in a form that can be read by machine. The check digit is always a whole number from 0 to 9. It is not usually printed in numeral form. (On the few packages where the check digit is printed out, it is smaller than the other digits and appears below the two bars that encode it.)

The other digits of the code are assigned simply enough. The lone digit to the left of the bar pattern is the "number system character." A "0" means the item is an ordinary grocery item; "2" is used for variable-weight items, such as meat and produce; "3" is for drugs and health-related items; "5" is for cents-off coupons.

The first cluster of five digits at the bottom encodes the manufacturer. For instance, 43000 is General Foods; 37000 is Procter & Gamble; 11141 is A&P house brand; 51000 is Campbell Soup. The second cluster of five digits specifies the product and size of package. These five digits are assigned by the manufacturers individually. If 20043 means a ten-ounce can of tomato soup for one manufacturer, it needn't mean tomato soup for another manufacturer.

Once a product is encoded as a number, the next step is to encode the number in a bar pattern. The bar pattern can vary in size; 0.816 inch by 1.175 inches is the minimum; 2.040 inches by 2.938 inches is the maximum. The dark bars may be almost any dark color (not red). The background may be white or pastel.

The first two bars, reading from left to right, signify nothing. They are a sort of punctuation to let the scanner know where to start reading. The same is true for the two bars in the middle, which extend down between the two clusters of visible digits, and for the two bars at the extreme right.

The first two bars to the right of the first set of punctuation bars encode the number system character, the visible digit at left center. If this digit is a zero, there is a space, then a thick bar, then a narrow space, then a narrow bar: the bar code for zero.

Each of the other digits also appears as two bars and two spaces. The portion of the UPC symbol allotted to each digit is composed of seven equal units or "modules," each of which may be either dark or light. The symbol for zero is three light modules (the space), two dark modules (the thick bar), one light module (the narrow space), and one dark module (the narrow bar). This is represented as 0001101, where the 0s are light modules and the 1s are dark modules.

A reversed version of this code is used for the part of the UPC symbol to the right of the two thin bars in the center. A zero appearing on the right becomes 1110010—that is, a thick bar, a space, a narrow bar, a narrow space. Two different codes are used so that the scanner will be able to recognize which side of the symbol it is reading. In this way, packages do not have to be fed to the scanner in one direction only.

The complete code is:

Digit	Left Side of Symbol	Right Side of Symbol
0	0001101	1110010
1	0011001	1100110
2	0010011	1101100
3	0111101	1000010
4	0100011	1011100
5	0110001	1001110
6	0101111	1010000
7	0111011	1000100
8	0110111	1001000
9	0001011	1110100

The check digit, appearing at the far right, is encoded according to the right-side column above. Two narrow bars separated by a triple-wide space signifies a 7, for instance.

Some typical codes, along with their check digits, are as follows:

Ann Page Black Pepper, 2 oz.	0 11141 26230 1
Ronzoni Spinach Fettuccine, 12 oz.	0 71300 00137 0
Campbell's Spanish Style	
Vegetable Soup, 10½ oz.	0 51000 02677 4

The formula? Take the digits of the code (aside from the check digit, of course) and group them according to their sequence in the code. Write the first digit, third digit, fifth digit, etc.—the odd sequence—on one line and the second digit, fourth digit, etc.—the even sequence—below it:

0 11141 26230 ⟶ 0 1 4 2 2 0

⟶ 1 1 1 6 3

Then add each sequence of digits,

$$0 + 1 + 4 + 2 + 2 + 0 = 9$$
$$1 + 1 + 1 + 6 + 3 = 12$$

multiply the sum of the odd sequence by 3,

$$9 \times 3 = 27$$

and add the result to the sum of the even sequence,

$$27 + 12 = 39$$

Subtract this result from the next higher multiple of 10. Here 40 is the next higher multiple of 10:

$$40 - 39 = 1$$

The remainder, 1, is the correct check digit.

Changing any single digit of the code will require a different check digit. In no case could a person with a marking pen expect to change a code to that of a lower-priced item; the best one could do would be to change a code randomly. Perhaps the altered code would be a cheaper item; perhaps it would be more expensive; perhaps it would be an unassigned code. The check digit ensures that any simple alteration will be caught, even if the altered code is an assigned one.

PART THREE

Kids, Don't Try This at Home

Dad's out working, Mom's out networking, and little Elroy and Judy are up to no good. Today's latchkey kids know what puts the "super" in "unsupervised." It's putting Sea Monkeys in the microwave to see if they explode. It's going to the 7-11 and inhaling the nitrous oxide propellant out of Reddi-Wip cans. It's playing William Wegman to the cat's Man Ray. It's drinking mouthwash for the alcohol, it's eating toothpaste to induce vomiting, it's fear and loathing with Procter & Gamble. The kids are *never* all right. And the real consumer education doesn't begin until the role models leave the house. Here are the secret lives of some of our pop consumables.

11·

Perfumes

Nearly all commercial perfume formulations are secret. A typical heavily merchandised fragrance—Chanel No. 5, Bal à Versailles, Joy—is a blend of many scents. Industry conviction is that a perfume that simulates a single, identifiable scent, such as rose or orange blossom, is difficult to market: Consumers assume a complex scent is better. Prospective customers are less likely to reject a scent if they can't explain why they don't like it. Instead of saying, "No, that smells like lily of the valley, and I don't like lily of the valley," they say, "Maybe." Or so the industry postulates.

Blending perfumes is a complex business. Good perfumers command salaries commensurate with those of investment bankers. It often takes years to formulate a fragrance. Some perfumes are reputed to contain as many as three hundred ingredients. Insiders say the large perfume houses routinely analyze each new competing fragrance as it is introduced. The analytic powers of "noses"—skilled perfume blenders—are legendary but have limits. Increasingly, gas chromatography and kindred techniques are used for analysis. Any sufficiently popular new fragrance is soon copied by competing manufacturers and sold under a different name. Thus Estée Lauder's Cinnabar, a cinnamonlike Oriental-type fragrance, seems to have inspired Yves Saint Laurent's Opium.

Is There Bobcat Urine in Perfume?

Most controversial of the hundreds of ingredients used in perfumes are the animal products. All are expensive, all are unsavory in the raw state, and all impart delightful notes when blended properly. Four animal products are used. None is urine (not that what they are is any more appealing).

Ambergris is a wax- or pitchlike substance found floating in tropic seas. It was used for fragrance, flavor, and alleged aphrodisiac properties long before anyone knew what it is. At various times, ambergris was held to be a gum; a bitumen; sea foam mysteriously solidified; the caked excrement of seabirds; a marine fungus; or honeycombs fallen into the sea from cliffside hives. Ambergris is now known to come from the sperm whale. The whale eats squid, and squid have sharp, indigestible "beaks." Ambergris is a secretion produced when the beaks irritate the wall of the whale's intestine. Squid beaks are often found in lumps of ambergris. It is not certain if the ambergris normally passes through the digestive tract or remains in the whale until death (lumps as large as 336 pounds have been reported.) Whaling ships occasionally take ambergris from fresh kills. Then the ambergris is black, tarry, and evil-smelling. Aged ambergris found in the ocean or on beaches may be hard, translucent, and white, gray, yellow, reddish, or striped. At best the odor is sweet, earthy, and lingering—a quality perfumers call "velvetiness."

Civet is a thick, yellowish secretion of anal glands of the civet cat of Asia and Africa. It figures in several confused stories about Chanel No. 5. Civet (or bobcat urine in some variations) is said to be an ingredient of Chanel No. 5. Some cat owners boycott Chanel perfume on the grounds that the animals are tortured. The civet cat is not really in the cat family, but it is a mammal capable of feeling discomfort. The secretion is produced by glands comparable to those that produce the scent in a skunk, and it is collected regularly from living animals. The animals are alleged to produce more civet when closely penned or agitated. As the animals are raised by independent operators unaffiliated with the major perfume houses, the claims of mistreatment are plausible. Civet's odor is objectionably musky at full strength; but pleasant when diluted.

Musk is usually a hardened, granular secretion from the male musk deer of Asia. Musk comes in a pouch, which is cut off and sold. Musk costs about twelve thousand dollars a pound. Frequently the musk is emptied from the pouch, cut with cheaper substances, and replaced. Musk's fragrance is not as lingering as that of ambergris. But musk's odor is so penetrating that it cannot be washed off polished steel. Despite its high price, musk is such a concentrated scent that it is probably never much of a factor in the price of a bottle of perfume. Castoreum, the fourth animal product used in perfumery, is a similar secretion, from the beaver.

How widespread is the use of animal products? One industry observer consulted thought it was decreasing—not so much because of cost as because of animal-protection lobbies. Only free-floating ambergris, of all the animal products, does not involve some form of molestation. Three prominent perfume houses were queried about use of animal products. Estée Lauder responded that it uses castoreum, civet, and musk in its perfume. According to Lauder's spokesperson, ambergris is not used by U.S. firms because of the whale's endangered-species status. Chanel acknowledged the use of civet in Chanel No. 5, noting that "most, if not all, other manufacturers of fine fragrances" do the same. Jean Patou denied use of any animal products in its Joy perfume.

Of course, animal products are only a small part of the picture. Despite trade secrecy, most perfumers have rough ideas of the composition of the major competing perfumes. Fragrance trade journals and books detail representative formulas, including occasional outside analyses of name perfumes. *Big Secrets* canvassed perfumers and fragrance ingredient suppliers for their ideas about several well-known perfumes. What follows are educated guesses. If, as seems likely, some of the actual formulas include dozens of trace ingredients, none of the sources consulted could identify them with any confidence. Nor is it always possible to distinguish a good synthetic component from its natural counterpart. Fragrances are listed in order of increasing retail price as of late 1982.

Eau Sauvage
Christian Dior
$7 per ounce ($13 for a 1.9-ounce bottle)

Bergamot, an obscure citrus fruit, seems to dominate Eau Sauvage. Because most men's colognes imitate the original eau de cologne devised by Johann Maria Farina, it isn't hard to give half a dozen ingredients that are almost certain to be in the Eau Sauvage formula. Basically, colognes blend oils of citrus peels with oils of herbs from the mint family. Oils of bergamot, lemon, neroli, lavender, rosemary, and petitgrain are probably in Eau Sauvage.

The bergamot orange is a misshapen, greenish-rust variety of the bitter orange. The bergamot orange is not eaten, but the oil flavors some candy and prepared foods. Bergamot oil is a universal ingredient in cologne and, along with lemon oil, seems to be responsible for the sharp, refreshing character of Eau Sauvage.

Neroli oil is the distilled essence of bitter orange blossoms; petitgrain is distilled from the leaves and twigs of the same tree. The pine or forest note in Eau Sauvage is probably from rosemary, not pine. Rose oil figures in some cologne formulations. If it is in Eau Sauvage, it is only a bare trace.

Cologne's relative cheapness is due to its dilution. Typically, about 7 grams of essential oils are used per liter of finished product. The rest is alcohol, water, and in some cases orange flower water or rose water. Assuming Eau Sauvage is of typical cologne strength, the 1.9-fluid-ounce bottle contains a scarce 0.39 gram of essential oils. That's about eight drops.

Reputedly, the best colognes are made from potato alcohol. Many modern perfumers dispute the importance of potato alcohol—alcohol should be alcohol, regardless of source. Better colognes are distilled, with the neroli oil and additional alcohol added after distillation. One to six months' aging is often recommended in standard formulas. As one of the most expensive men's colognes, it is likely that Eau Sauvage undergoes aging before being marketed.

Is the greenish-straw color natural? Some cologne essential oil mixtures have an amber color not too different from Eau Sauvage's, but the color is lost upon dilution to final strength. Like the perfumes that follow, Eau Sauvage has had a dye job.

Chanel No. 5
Chanel
$120 per ounce

The big secret here is synthetics. Chanel No. 5 was the first successful perfume to exploit fully a group of chemicals called fatty aldehydes. Despite the unpromising name, fatty aldehydes have revolutionized perfumery. They are usually denoted by the number of carbon atoms they contain—C_{10}, for instance, or C_{12}. Each aldehyde has a distinctive odor that often suggests some natural fragrance. Believed to be in Chanel No. 5 are:

C_9—to chemists, *n*-nonylaldehyde—a liquid with a pleasant rose odor. Chemical formula: $CH_3(CH_2)_7CHO$.

C_{10}, or *n*-decylaldehyde, with a sweet odor unlike that of any natural flower. Chemical formula: $CH_3(CH_2)_8CHO$.

C_{11}, or *n*-undecylaldehyde, with a strong rose odor. Chemical formula: $CH_3(CH_2)_9CHO$.

C_{12}, of which two distinct forms may be used. Lauraldehyde $[CH_3(CH_2)_{10}CHO]$ is a solid with an unpleasant, greasy odor. Diluted, the odor is agreeable. Methyl nonylacetaldehyde $[CH_3(CH_2)_8CH(CH_3)CHO]$ suggests a mixture of orange blossoms and ambergris.

There may be a synthetic vanilla note from vanillin or from coumarin. A likely natural oil is ylang-ylang, produced from the sweet, powerfully scented blossoms of a tree of the same name grown in Madagascar and the West Indies. There seems to be a woody component to Chanel No. 5. This could come from sandalwood, a parasitic tree from the Orient, or vetivert, a grass with aromatic roots. A trace of citrus oil may be present. As mentioned, Chanel's animal note is from civet.

Missoni
Missoni
$150 per ounce

The Missonis know sweaters, not perfume. Not surprisingly, the Missoni fragrance is simply a workmanlike retread of an old standard—the chypre fragrance. Chypre is the generic name for a type of perfume that originated on the island of Cyprus (Chypre to the French) by the twelfth century. Chypre perfumes are heavy, woody/spicy scents. There is less of a flowery character than with most perfumes. Missoni is not the only chypre scent on the market—though it seems to be the most expensive and, one would hope, one of the best made. Aramis and Miss Dior are also chypre scents. Chypre is popular with both sexes.

The three indispensable components of the chypre scent are oakmoss, patchouli, and sandalwood. Vetivert oil is usually present. (Missoni admits to "patchouli, vetivert, and spice" in an ad.) Oakmoss is a lichen—a gray-green encrustation that grows on the

bark of oak and plum trees in the Mediterranean region. It is
collected, made into an extract, and sold to perfumers and soap-
makers wanting a woodsy scent. Patchouli is a shrubby Indonesian mint. Its fragrance suggests both mint and sandalwood. True
sandalwood enters into perfumes as an essential oil produced
largely in India.

Like other modern chypre perfumes, Missoni seems to have a
slight citrus note, perhaps from bergamot. There may be traces of
jasmine and rose (probably natural) and vanilla (probably synthetic). Nearly all chypre formulations contain synthetic musk—
nonanimal substances such as "musk ambrette," "musk ketone,"
and "musk xylene," which simulate the character of musk.

Bal à Versailles
Jean Desprez
$158 per ounce

Once hailed as the world's most expensive perfume, Bal à Versailles now undersells several of its competitors. There seems to be
little argument as to the main components of Bal à Versailles' floral bouquet. They are jasmine, ylang-ylang, patchouli, and vanilla. Ylang-ylang oil is sold in two grades, "Ylang No. 1" and
"Ylang No. 2." Presumably Jean Desprez springs for the better
Ylang No. 1. But there is scarcely any difference between natural
vanilla and synthetic vanillin, so even Bal à Versailles may contain the cheaper synthetic.

Bal à Versailles' scent is relatively easy to simulate. Many perfume houses offer Bal à Versailles knock-offs. This is done with
other perfumes, of course, but Bal à Versailles imitations are often
particularly convincing. Some savvy shoppers are convinced that
one of these reproductions—"Naudet No. 3," sold by Essential
Products Co. of New York—is slightly *better* than the original.
Naudet No. 3 sells for $16 per ounce.

Joy
Jean Patou
**$175 per ounce (regular bottle) or $400 per ounce (Baccarat
crystal bottle)**

For a flavor of the perfume industry doubletalk on pricing, consider: For years, Patou has advertised its Joy perfume as the

"costliest" fragrance in the world. Joy costs $175 per ounce. But Patou also makes 1000 perfume—and 1000 costs $245 an ounce. When challenged, Patou management is said to allow that 1000 is indeed more expensive but insist that Joy is still *costlier*. The distinction, at least in Patou's dictionary, seems to mean that the ingredients of Joy cost more than those of the more expensive 1000. In other words, the markup on 1000 is a lot more. Perhaps to justify its "costlier" ingredients, Patou also offers Joy in a Baccarat crystal bottle for $400.

Joy is nothing more nor less than a very well-made rose perfume. High-quality natural rose oil is undoubtedly the main fragrance ingredient. The other ingredients merely gild the lily— make Joy smell more like a rose ought to smell than a rose does. These ingredients may include bergamot oil, heliotropin (a synthetic suggesting evergreens), and jasmine.

Patou says Joy contains no animal products, so evidently an ambergris substitute is used. One of the most satisfactory is a resin obtained from the Mediterranean labdanum shrub. The sticky, fragrant resin coats the leaves. It is boiled off, extracted with a solvent, or, in the case of a Cyprus variety of the shrub, combed from the wool of sheep or goats that graze among the bushes. It smells like balsam.

The ingredient list on the following page is from a recipe for an imitation of Joy perfume in *A Formulary of Cosmetic Preparations* by Michael Ash and Irene Ash (New York: Chemical Publishing Co., 1977). That recipe suggests ambergris and musk; synthetics have been substituted here to conform with Patou policy.

1000
Jean Patou
$245 per ounce

Patou's ultrastatus scent, 1000, is less sweet-and-conventional. A strong leafy note suggests a mown lawn, growing plants, or the "weedy" nuances of a Cabernet Sauvignon. Floral notes are muted.

There's no grass in 1000. Perfumers create the mown-lawn effect with two substances, coumarin and linalool. Coumarin can be extracted from the tonka bean, the seed of a South American tree. Coumarin is toxic and not permitted as a flavoring in the

Joy Perfume: Ingredients—an Educated Guess

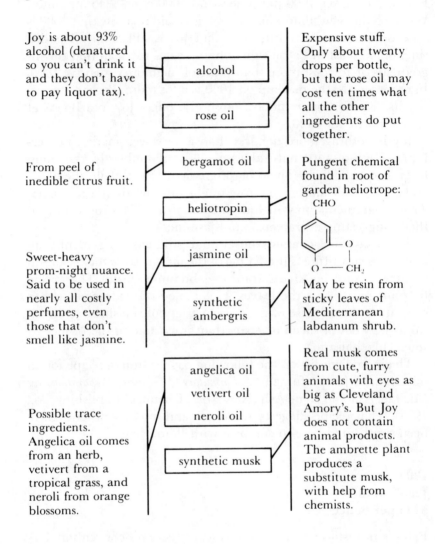

Joy is about 93% alcohol (denatured so you can't drink it and they don't have to pay liquor tax).

alcohol

Expensive stuff. Only about twenty drops per bottle, but the rose oil may cost ten times what all the other ingredients do put together.

rose oil

From peel of inedible citrus fruit.

bergamot oil

heliotropin

Pungent chemical found in root of garden heliotrope:

Sweet-heavy prom-night nuance. Said to be used in nearly all costly perfumes, even those that don't smell like jasmine.

jasmine oil

synthetic ambergris

May be resin from sticky leaves of Mediterranean labdanum shrub.

angelica oil

vetivert oil

neroli oil

Possible trace ingredients. Angelica oil comes from an herb, vetivert from a tropical grass, and neroli from orange blossoms.

synthetic musk

Real musk comes from cute, furry animals with eyes as big as Cleveland Amory's. But Joy does not contain animal products. The ambrette plant produces a substitute musk, with help from chemists.

United States, but it is used in perfumes. Coumarin's chemical formula is:

Linalool is present in bergamot oil. Its formula is:

$$CH_2:CHCOH(CH_3)CH_2CH_2CH:C(CH_3)_2$$

The floral background of 1000 seems to include natural rose and jasmine oils. Violet and tuberose—natural or artificial—may be present.

Are Perfumes Overpriced?

One of the reasons for all the secrecy is the cost. Once the ingredients of a perfume are known, the cost of raw materials can be estimated. In most cases, this cost is a small fraction of the retail sales price—a fact of life in the fragrance industry but one they'd prefer not to publicize.

This is not to say that perfume manufacturers are making a killing. The actual profit to manufacturer is a small part of the gaping difference between ingredient costs and sale price. Manufacturers of fragrances tied to a designer name pay a royalty to the designer (who rarely gives more than a name to the creation). There is often an under-the-table spiff paid to department store salespersons to push a perfume. Bottle and packaging are expensive (if not always to the tune of the $225 you pay for the Baccarat crystal bottle of Joy). Promotion and assorted overhead expenses make up the rest. A 1974 *New York Times* article drew industry ire for estimating these expenses for a then-costly $35 bottle of perfume. The *Times* analysis claimed the following breakdown (here converted from dollar amounts to percentages):

> Fragrance oils, alcohol, and blending 13%
> Bottle (crystal) and packaging 8%
> Royalty for use of couturier or designer name
>   (this arrangement varies considerably with
>   different names) 3%
> Advertising, sales promotion, sampling 11%

Commission paid to salesclerks in stores (usually
    4% to 10% of manufacturing costs) 4%
Administration and overhead 11%
Research, development, and quality control 1%
Taxes 4%
Net profit to manufacturer 4%
Store markup 40%
(Percentages do not total 100% because of rounding.)

Many perfume ingredients are fabulously expensive. The best floral essences can cost $2,000 a pound or more; musk costs about $12,000 a pound. But in most cases a little goes a long way.

Take the *Formulary of Cosmetic Preparations* recipe for imitation Joy. It is hard to say how closely it matches Jean Patou's formula for Joy. However, most perfumes are blended at roughly the same fragrance strength. Joy could hardly contain much more essential oil than specified in the imitation recipe. Moreover, the formulary recipe uses good, expensive ingredients. If the required amounts of ingredients are multiplied by the prices, the results are the ingredient costs—for the imitation Joy, at any rate.

The ingredient prices below are typical. Prices vary according to quality, amount purchased, and market fluctuations. Actual amounts of synthetic ambergris and musk might have to be juggled according to the strength of the substitutes.

Ingredient	Grams per Ounce of Perfume	Price per Pound	Price of Ingredient per Ounce of Perfume
Alcohol	26.3	$.50	$.029
Rose oil	1.06	2,000	4.67
Bergamot oil	0.548	22	.027
Heliotropin	0.274	8.75	.0053
Jasmine oil	0.109	1,500	.36
Synthetic ambergris	0.0547	100 (?)	.012
Angelica oil	0.000155	75	.000026
Vetivert oil	0.000155	50	.000017
Neroli oil	0.0000773	8.50	.000014
Synthetic musk	0.0000773	100 (?)	.000017

Only five ingredients contribute so much as a penny to the final per-ounce cost. The total per-ounce cost: about $5.15, most of it for rose oil.

12·

Playing Cards

1.　　　　2.　　　　3.　　　　4.

1. *Bee:* Nevada casinos use it. Small, busy pattern, no margin. Favored for bottom-dealing.
2. *Aviator:* Does the white margin foil cheaters?
3. *Bicycle:* Popular with the Brach's Bridge Mix crowd but easy to mark—all those little birds, dots, flowers.
4. *United Airlines:* The savvy gambler's choice: more cheatproof than the commercial brands. And you can use the airsick bag to keep score.

It is not easy to design cheatproof playing cards, if possible at all. Most card manufacturers do not even try. Cheaters, however, are aware of the back design as a security device. With certain back designs, it is more difficult to bottom- or second-deal undetected than with other designs. Some backs are easier to mark than others.

For bottom- or second-dealing, the ideal deck would be one

with a solid-color back. With such a deck it would be hard for the other players to tell whether the top card is sliding forward and off the deck (as it should in a legal deal) or staying on top (as in a bottom- or second-deal).

None of the readily available brands of cards has a solid-color back. In practice, bottom-dealers favor brands with small, regular patterns—patterns that are just a blur of color in a brisk deal. Diamond-pattern Bee (back no. 67) and Club Reno are examples.

A white margin ruins a deck for bottom-dealing. As the bottom (or second) card is drawn out, the other players see its white margin, then part of its back pattern, then the top card's white margin, and then the top card's back pattern. This is different from what they see when the top card is drawn off fairly. So decks such as Aviator and Bicycle are relatively cheatproof as far as bottom-dealing is concerned.

Likewise, any conspicuous, localized design works against bottom-dealing. A prominent design acts as a landmark to help players judge whether the top card is removed. It's best if the design is a different color, such as the logos on some airline and promotional decks. Many Las Vegas casinos use custom Bee decks overprinted with the hotel logos.

Gambling lore favors a United Airlines giveaway deck as the most cheatproof. Flight attendants offer the deck (in first class) or supply it if you know enough to ask for it (in coach). Although manufactured by the U.S. Playing Card Company, the deck is in some ways more secure than that company's popular retail decks. The back design is a solid color except for two United Airlines logos. The white logos make it relatively easy to spot bottom-dealing. The simplicity of the back design makes it nearly impossible to mark the deck. Many other airline decks are equally good.

How to Spot Marked Cards

Any complex back design may be marked. One of only two ink colors—navy blue or medium red—will suffice for the well-known U.S. Playing Card brands. The trouble with marking cards at home, however, is that the deck's seal must be broken.

Premarked cards, favored by serious players, come from Louis Tannen, Inc., a New York magic supply house. Tannen's marked decks are genuine U.S. Playing Card decks that have been opened, marked by hand, and resealed with a duplicate U.S. Playing Card stamp, cellophane wrap, and a white tear-band bearing the brand name. Each deck comes with separate instructions for decoding the markings. *Big Secrets* ordered Tannen's Aviator, Bee, and Bicycle decks to see how the markings are concealed.

Aviator

The markings are along the top margin of the back pattern. Ten "sprout" designs run across the top. The two center sprouts encode the rank. Each sprout has six leaves. One of the leaves is disconnected from the sprout—with a dab of ink—to signify ranks 3 through ace. The leaves on the left side of the left center sprout signify ace, king, and queen, from top to bottom. Leaves on the right side of the left sprout are jack, 10, and 9. Similarly, the right center sprout encodes 8, 7, and 6 and 5, 4, and 3. If no leaf is disconnected, the card is a deuce.

Eight of Hearts

			A	J	*8*	5
Diamonds	Clubs	*Hearts*	K	10	7	4
			Q	9	6	3

The three sprouts to the left of the center sprouts give the suit. The "bud" at the top of the sprouts is half blocked out to signify (left to right) diamonds, clubs, and hearts. If all the buds are entire, the card is a spade. All the markings are repeated at the bottom, of course, so the cards may be read from either end.

Bee

On all Bee cards, a column of diamond designs runs just inside the right margin. The top three complete diamonds encode the rank. Look at the uppermost of the three diamonds. A triangular extension of dark ink on the right side of the top point of the diamond means ace. A marking on the top left side means king. Similar markings on the bottom point mean queen (bottom left) and jack (bottom right). The diamond below this one encodes 10, 9, 8, and 7; the diamond below that is for 6, 5, 4, and 3. Deuces are not marked.

Ten of Clubs

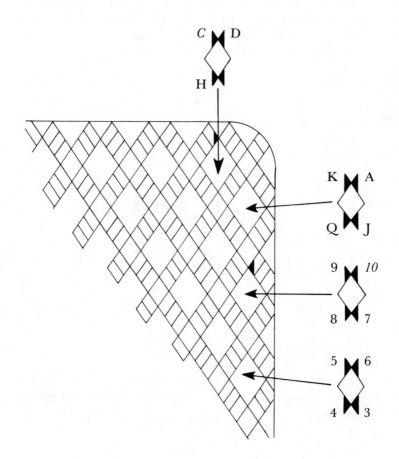

   Above and to the left of the upper diamond is another complete diamond. It is for the suits: Top right is diamonds, top left is clubs, and bottom left is hearts. Spades are not marked.

Bicycle
Find the angel in the upper left corner. His left hand rests on a vine that encircles an eight-petal flower design. The flower gives the rank. When the upper (twelve o'clock) petal is narrowed, the card is an ace. Going clockwise, the position of the narrowed petal signifies king (one-thirty), queen (three o'clock), jack (four-thirty), ten (six o'clock), nine (seven-thirty), eight (nine o'clock), and seven (ten-thirty). For lower ranks, the inner tip of the petal is inked out. A truncated petal at twelve o'clock is six; three o'clock is five; six o'clock is four; nine o'clock is three. All the petals are left entire for a deuce.

Ace of Hearts

Above the angel's arm is a three-part leaf. When the outer, left tip of the leaf is marked out, the card is a heart. The central, upper tip is for clubs; the inner, right tip is for diamonds; no marking signifies spades.

With sharp eyes the Bicycle and Aviator markings can be read passably well at arm's length. The Bee markings are slightly more difficult to read. Persons aware of the markings but not of their precise location may take several minutes to find the marks.

The Hearts and Diamonds Bomb

Chapter 54 of Tom Robbins' 1980 novel, *Still Life with Woodpecker*, describes a fantastic "hearts and diamonds bomb":

> Take a deck of ordinary playing cards, the old-fashioned paper kind, cut out the red spots and soak them overnight like beans. Alcohol is the best soaking solution, but tap water will suffice. Plug one end of a short length of pipe. Pack the soggy hearts and diamonds into the pipe. On pre-plastic playing cards, the red spots were printed with a diazo dye, a chemical that has an unstable, high-energy bond with nitrogen. So you've got nitro, of sorts, now you'll be needing glycerin. Hand lotion will work nicely. Glug a little lotion into the pipe. To activate the quasi-nitroglycerin, you'll require potassium permanganate. That you can find in the snakebite section of any good first-aid chest. Add a dash of the potassium permanganate and plug the other end of the pipe. Heat the pipe. A direct flame is best, but simply laying the pipe atop a hot radiator will turn the trick. Take cover!

In the context, most readers dismiss this as whimsy. But the hearts and diamonds bomb and the other bombs Robbins describes are real. Similar bomb recipes appear in William Powell's *The Anarchist Cookbook*, an underground weapons manual.

What Robbins calls the "jug band bomb" is a working homemade bomb. It is a glass jug containing a few drops of gasoline. The jug is capped and turned around so the gasoline coats the inner surface and evaporates. A few added drops of potassium permanganate solution make the gasoline vapor/air mixture all the more explosive. The bomb is detonated by throwing or forcibly rolling against a wall.

Whether the hearts and diamonds bomb would work is debatable. Robbins makes certain substitutions in the usual recipe: hand lotion rather than pure glycerin, a snakebite nostrum rather than a potassium permanganate solution of known strength.

Assume then that pure glycerin and potasssium permanganate are used. You might get a bomb by mixing diazo compounds with glycerin and potassium permanganate. The question is how much diazo dye could be extracted from red card spots.

The staff historian for the U.S. Playing Card Company admitted hearing of the bomb stories but was not aware of any working bomb having been constructed. In any case, the main problem with the recipe is that there is nothing "ordinary" about old-fashioned paper playing cards. Effectively all cards are now plastic-coated.

13·

Letters, Stamps, and Envelopes

There is little secret coding or gimmickry on U.S. mail. All U.S. postage stamps have an invisible ink coding that fluoresces in ultraviolet light. Partly this is to deter counterfeiting of stamps. Mostly, it is to speed up sorting. Canceling machines shine an ultraviolet beam on letters and check for a glow. Calcium silicate (which glows orange-red) and zinc orthosilicate (which glows yellow-green) are used. They are printed over the entire surface of stamps or in a geometric pattern.

Personal letters to the U.S. President have a secret numerical code. The President often gets 10,000 letters a day. Virtually all must be opened, read, and answered by the White House mail staff. So that letters from friends get to the President and family unopened, all close friends are given a sequence of numbers to write on the outside of the envelope. The code changes with each President. Ronald Reagan's code was described as a number with a special meaning to Reagan and his wife. Jimmy Carter used an old phone number of Rosalynn's.

Wax Seals

Wax seals are not a guarantee against unauthorized opening of a letter. According to the *CIA Flaps and Seals Manual*, edited by John M. Harrison (Boulder, Colo.: Paladin Press, 1975), there is a way to remove and replace seals.

First the opener takes a plaster-of-Paris cast of the seal. This is set aside to harden. The wax is gently heated with an infrared lamp. When soft, it is rolled into a ball and set aside. The flap of the envelope is steamed open, and the letter is taken out and photocopied.

After the envelope's contents are replaced and the flap resealed, the same wax is used to re-create the seal. It is heated till pliable and pressed back into shape with the plaster-of-Paris mold.

One type of seal is secure, even according to the *CIA Flaps and Seals Manual:* one made of two or more colors of wax melted together. The colors inevitably come out different on the second, surreptitious pressing. But a color Polaroid of the seal must be sent under separate cover so that the recipient can compare it with the seal on the message letter.

None of the other common seals are reliable against unauthorized opening, assuming that knowledgeable letter-openers may want to open your mail. Scotch tape across the flap of an envelope comes off cleanly with carbon tetrachloride (applied with a brush or a hypodermic needle). If you suspect that someone is opening your mail, the manual suggests sending yourself a letter containing a sheet of carbon or wax paper. The heat and mechanical treatment of the letter opening will smudge the carbon and melt the wax. Otherwise, you have to examine letters carefully to detect prior opening. A torn flap, smudging of the flap glue, flattened ridges in the flap, or concave (from the back) curling due to steaming are evidence of opening.

A more sophisticated test requires steaming part of the envelope near the flap for fifteen seconds. Then place the envelope under an ultraviolet lamp. If there is a difference in fluorescence between the steamed and unsteamed part of the envelope, then the envelope paper is suitable for the test. If so, examine the unsteamed part of the flap under the ultraviolet lamp. If it shows a different fluorescence than the other unsteamed parts of the envelope, it indicates that the flap may have been previously steamed.

The ultraviolet lamp is also useful in detecting invisible writing. An effective ultraviolet ink need not fluoresce brightly, as the silicate stamp inks do. Any substance that changes the fluorescence of paper in ultraviolet light yet is invisible in ordinary light will work. Prisoners have used human urine as an invisible ink. Salt water, vinegar, milk, fruit juices, saliva, and water solutions of soap or drugs also work, with varying degrees of legibility.

How to Mail Without a Stamp

Postal chiselers used to mail letters unstamped in the knowledge that they would be delivered anyway—postage due to the recipient. It took a niggardly person to mail personal letters this way, but many people did it on bill payments. So the Post Office changed its policy. It stopped delivering letters without stamps. A letter with a stamp—even a one-cent stamp—is delivered (postage due if need be). A letter with no stamp is returned to the sender.

Naturally, this has just opened up a new way of cheating. Letters can now be mailed for free by switching the positions of the delivery address and the return address. If there is no stamp on the envelope, it will be "returned"—that is, delivered to the address in the upper left corner—which is where the sender wanted it to go in the first place. Unlike under the old system, the letter is not postage-due. At most the recipient gets a stamped purple reminder that "The Post Office does not deliver mail without postage."

At least one large company seems to have adapted this principle to its billing. Citibank bases its MasterCard operations in Sioux Falls, South Dakota. The bill payment envelopes have the Citibank Sioux Falls address in both the delivery address and return address positions. (Most bill payment envelopes have three lines for the customer to write in his return address.) Therefore, regardless of whether the customer puts a stamp on the envelope, it is delivered to Citibank. (The return-address gimmick works even when the return address is in a different state from the mailing point.)

Who is cheating whom? If the customer puts correct postage on the envelope, it is delivered to Sioux Falls at customer expense. No one is slighted. If, on the other hand, the customer intentionally omits the stamp, the payment is delivered at Post Office expense. Then the customer has cheated the Post Office. The Post Office also loses out if the customer honestly forgets to put a stamp on the envelope. But then blame ought to be shared with the peculiar design of Citibank's envelope.

Citibank's motive is plain: If payment envelopes are returned to forgetful customers, it delays payment.

14·

Paraphernalia

A Golf Ball That Cheats

Robinhood is the secret brand of golf ball you may have seen advertised in airline magazines. The brand name "is sealed inside the box, a secret between buyer and seller," says the manufacturer, H&L Labs of Norwalk, Connecticut, in an ad. Why the secrecy? The ball's composition and dimple aerodynamics make it fly farther than regular golf balls. Because it sidesteps USGA specs, it cannot be used legally in play. Yet it looks just like a regular ball. If your partners don't know the secret brand name, no one's the wiser. Coyly hints H&L's pitch, "While golf prides itself on being a gentleman's game, it seems that more than 40,000 gentlemen—and ladies—are playing with these innocent-looking buzz bombs. . . . more money is going to change hands with this little white bandit than all the tournament purses put together."

Secret of a Mail-Order Grooming Aid
Klipette nose-hair clipper, another staple of small mail-order ads in the back of magazines, leads a double life. Apparently, a substantial portion of distributor profits has come from rental of a secret mailing list of Klipette customers.

Figure it this way. Anyone can trim nose hair with ordinary cuticle scissors. Those who feel they must have a special clipper can get one at a drugstore. So the folks responding to Klipette ads include people concerned about nose hair but too embarrassed to face a drugstore clerk and ask for a nose-hair clipper. For whatever reason, that mentality is just right for some direct-mail pitches. According to a Consumers Union report, a Washington financial newsletter reported strong response to a mail subscription campaign directed to Klipette buyers—none of whom suspected where the newsletter got their names.

One of the firms that runs magazine ads for the Klipette is the Complex Company of Waipahu, Hawaii. As an experiment for *Big Secrets,* we ordered the Klipette from the Complex Company, using a fictitious name. That way, any subsequent mail arising from the transaction could be identified. Nothing came for about ten months. Then the fake identity resurfaced with a mailing advertising several products, none of them having much to do with nose hair.

There was a free sample of "Potent-8," a sort of alleged aphrodisiac claimed to "arouse and strip any woman of her normal defenses." The sample smelled like ether.

The mailing touted a book, *Seven Steps to Psychic Mind Control,* that helps the reader "turn women into putty" and "will have YOU scoring at work, parties, or on the streets!"

"Pad-A-Panty" is just what it sounds like, a padded bra for the buttocks ("the easy way to a 'wow' figure that men will notice and women will envy").

The mailing also offered an assortment of weight-loss schemes, including a book, an exercise machine, a body wrap, pills (a "mild stimulant"), and a record or cassette containing subliminal messages to discourage overeating.

The Klipette is not the only mail-order gismo used to create mailing lists. What is remarkable about the Klipette list is the profit picture. The Klipette is manufactured by Hollis Co., a New York cutlery firm, but distributed by various mail-order houses nationwide. The distributor profit on the sale of the Klipette cannot be much. If they clear 6 percent of a typical $2.99 retail price, the profit is only $.18. But each purchase can mean another name on the mailing list. Mailing lists sell for anywhere from $.03 to $.75 a name. With luck, a given list may be sold over and over. Are the Klipette retailers in the business of selling nose-hair clippers, or lists of people who buy nose-hair clippers? Apparently both.

According to Consumers Union, other inexpensive items or services that have been used to build mailing lists include the GI Joe Fan Club (it costs money to join, so the membership roster is a list of kids with big allowances and near-zero sales resistance); Hal-bert's, Inc. (an Ohio firm that sells alleged family coats of arms); the Kozak Drywash (a car-buffing cloth; the Republican Party used a list of buyers to solicit contributions); the "ant certificates" purchasers of ant farms must send in (with their name and address) to get their ants; and many mail-refund or free-product offers.

Toothpaste Horror Stories

Crest toothpaste is the object of two secret-ingredient rumors—one about "sand" and another about "rat poison." Actually, Crest has no secret ingredients other than its flavoring. Everything else is spelled out on the ingredients panel. Among those label ingredients is "hydrated silica." Sand is silica. Crest's silica is certainly processed and finely ground. Ultimately, all industrial silica comes from sand, quartz, or the like. So is there sand in Crest? Well, no, not if you mean grains of silica of the size normally called sand. But yes, if you're willing to trace back the chain of raw materials far enough.

The rat-poison story is likewise a matter of interpretation. Crest used to contain something it called Fluoristan. Fluoristan was a trademarked preparation of stannous fluoride, a chemical that prevents cavities. Then Crest's manufacturers discovered that another fluoride preparation, the one now called Fluoristat, is better at preventing cavities. Out went Fluoristan, and in went Fluoristat. The active ingredient of Fluoristat is sodium fluoride. Sodium fluoride, in turn, is a chemical that otherwise finds use as a rat poison. In fact, sodium fluoride has earned something of a bad name among rat poisons because it is toxic to humans as well as to rats. (It was once mistaken for powdered milk at a hospital for the elderly. The patients complained that breakfast tasted soapy, but no one believed them. Some died.) The level of sodium fluoride in Crest is far below the toxic level, of course.

Wholly untrue are the persistent rumors of a secret significance to the Proctor & Gamble logo on Crest and dozens of other familiar products. A story apparently starting in southern Minnesota in 1980 claims that the moon face symbolizes the acquisition of Proctor & Gamble by Reverend Sun Myung Moon and/or his Unification Church. But the Moonies don't own Procter & Gamble, and the logo has been on Procter & Gamble products for over a century.

A variation of the story finds a secret number in the logo's stars. If you take a pencil and connect the stars properly, the result is three not-very-convincing 6s—the biblical number of the beast and, to believers, evidence of Satanism in Cincinnati. The top five stars become a horizontal 6 (with top at right); the middle four stars form a vertical 6; the bottom four become a rotated 6 dipping slightly below the horizontal. Curved lines and considerable imagination must be used. If you count the stars, the total is thirteen—the head count at the Last Supper.

The Drāno Sex Test

Liquid Drāno, meanwhile, enters into a weird ritual for predicting the gender of an unborn child. The Drackett Company, Drāno's manufacturer, tries to discourage the so-called Drāno sex test. Drāno, after all, is dangerous stuff to be playing around with. During the sixth month of pregnancy, a sample of an expectant mother's morning urine is mixed with an equal amount of Liquid Drāno. The concoction will fizz. The color of the resulting liquid is supposed to predict sex: green for a boy, yellow for a girl. It's right about half the time.

Is the Welcome Hostess a Spy?

Welcome Wagon-*type* services are sometimes spies for credit bureaus. Newcomers are a problem for credit reporters. They're the people creditors are most likely to want information on and yet the people most likely to have an empty file. Most welcome services have names patterned after "Welcome Wagon," but not all are affiliated with Welcome Wagon International. Many services are sponsored by the local credit bureau, which hopes you'll tell the smiling Welcome Hostess why you really had to leave town.

Telltale White Lines

Chevrolet, Buick, and Cadillac odometers cannot be rolled back—at least not without it being apparent to any used-car dealer. Since 1969 General Motors cars have had two thin white plastic flags, normally held out of view by a seal, in the odometer case. Tampering with the odometer breaks the seal, and the flags drop into view. They appear as two telltale vertical lines on either side of the thousands' digit—for example, 3|1|820.1.

GM dealers seem to have benefited most from the device. Few customers know what to look for. Absence of the lines is no guarantee of accurate milage. Dealers can buy replacement seals (from independent manufacturers, not GM) to conceal the lines on a doctored car.

Bizarre Hair Treatment

Tia Zolin Placenta, a hair conditioner used in many salons, is said to come from human placentas. It is a straw-colored liquid—with a white sediment—that comes in a single-use sealed vial. The vial is shaken and broken in a towel. The liquid is massaged into the hair. It is not rinsed out—if there really is placenta in Tia Zolin, it is in the hair of anyone who has just used it.

Where do they get human placentas? Tia Zolin Placenta is manufactured by Hask, Inc., of Great Neck, New York. In response to a letter asking about the product, a Hask vice-president confirmed that there is human material in Tia Zolin. But what they call placenta comes from human umbilical cords, not placentas per se. Hask says it gets the umbilical cords from hospitals "in much the same way that human blood and other vital organs are obtained."

Secret Store

Gucci shops have a secret store-within-a-store, the Galeria. Located in the major U.S. Gucci outlets, the Galeria is on a floor of its own above street level. In New York, for instance, it's the fourth floor of the 2 East 54th Street shop. To keep out hoi polloi, the Galeria is accessible only by elevator, and you need a special gold key to get to the right floor. Gucci distributes the gold keys to its best customers. (If you push the floor number of the Galeria without inserting the key, the elevator doesn't move.) Galeria merchandise runs heavily toward jewelry in the high five-figure range.

Secret Bank

Bank of America's Beverly Hills, California, branch at 9461 Wilshire Boulevard has much the same thing—a hush-hush department upstairs for its wealthiest depositors, with no waiting in line for tellers.

Secret Restaurant

Ma Maison, Los Angeles' celebrity eatery at 8368 Melrose Boulevard, keeps out the triptik-and-Bryce-Canyon-decal crowd with an unlisted phone number: (213) 655-1991.

Secret Airline Club

Northwest Orient Airlines' "club" has visibility zero. Like most of the airline clubs, Northwest's "Top Flight Lounges" were started as a free perk for heavy travelers and those in a position to help the airline—corporate travel directors, Civil Aeronautics Board officials, celebrities who might be photographed coming off a plane. In 1966 the CAB decided such invitation-only clubs were unfair. Most airlines started publicizing their clubs, opening them to anyone, and tacking on an annual or lifetime membership fee. But Northwest (and until 1982, Delta) chose not to publicize its club. Officially Northwest's club is not a club at all but a set of free lounges for the enjoyment of all persons holding Northwest tickets. The catch is, Northwest has never made it easy for average passengers to learn where the Top Flight Lounges are— or even that there are such lounges. The lounges are said to be hidden away behind nondescript doors or in airport culs-de-sac. Unless someone with the airline decides that you're Northwest's kind of person, you're on your own.

Suspect Luggage

Samsonite luggage may be prone to extra scrutiny from customs inspectors. The reason is a South American brand of luggage, Saxony, that looks just like Samsonite but features a false bottom that can be used for drugs or other contraband.

Indiscreet Typewriter Ribbon

IBM typewriter ribbon is a boon to industrial spies: The used plastic ribbon contains a razor-sharp impression of everything typed. And only the top-level correspondence is likely to be typed on one-use ribbon. That makes sifting through corporate trash bins all the easier.

Bugs in Books

Tattle-Tape is the name of the bookstore security system requiring electronic detectors at the exits and a rectangular "desensitizer" at the cashier stands. The customer is given to understand that each book must be passed, spine down, over the desensitizer to prevent tripping the alarm. Yet if you've ever searched for an electronic bug in the spine after buying a book, you probably didn't find anything.

The secret of the Tattle-Tape system is that there isn't anything to find in most of the protected inventory. It is a spot-check system. Only a few selected books contain the Tattle-Tape strip. The strip is thin, brownish, and self-adhesive. It is not placed inside the book's spine but rather on one of the pages, as close to the spine as possible. The routine of passing every book over the desensitizer is mainly a deterrent. Desensitized or not, the books not containing a strip can be carted out by the wheelbarrow without setting off the alarm.

The 3M Company, Tattle-Tape's manufacturer, is close-mouthed about the mechanics of the system. The Tattle-Tape seems plainly to be a magnetic strip. If so, it could probably be erased with a pocket magnet. That, perhaps, is what the desensitizer does. Those who purchase a book with a strip may find it objectionable and hard to remove. For this reason, and the labor costs of placing the strips, bookstore managers try to avoid using the strips except where most necessary. Promotional literature of the 3M Company advises using Tattle-Tape strips in "high-theft books," "books near doors," and "volumes over $20.00."

A bookstore using the Tattle-Tape system may return unsold books—with active strips—to their publishers. The publishers, in turn, may ship these books to different stores that don't have the Tattle-Tape system. Books sold at these stores will not be desensitized. If the purchasers take their books into another store or a library, they may trip the alarm system—and be at a loss to explain what has happened.

PART FOUR

Alice, Let's Cheat

L ife is short. One minute you're doing your stretching exercises. The next thing you know, your next of kin are dividing your good silverware. Once it's finally time to roll over and play Parvovirus, you may not care how many Brownie points you racked up for citizenship. In fact, you'll probably wish you stepped on more people as you clawed your way to the top. Here then is a start. There are plenty of annoying tests you have to take after college, and you might as well start cheating on them. Thanks to convenient glitches in test security, some of these post-curricular pop quizzes can be reproduced here with answers—a sort of Cliff's Notes for life. No talking; pencils down; this may go on your permanent record. Please begin.

15·

The Eye Test

Does the optometrist swap answered-the-waffle-iron jokes with the receptionist as soon as you're out of earshot? You never really know because it's not considered good optometric bedside manner to tell the examinee how far down the chart he or she is supposed to be able to read. To qualify for 20/20 vision, you have to be able to read line 8 at the customary examination distance of twenty feet. It's the line just above the red bar: DEFPOTEC. Some slack is built into the definition of normal vision, so many people can read line 9 as well, especially if the light is good.

Helpful hint: only nine letters are used in the standard Snellen eye chart. All occur at least once in easy lines 1 through 5. So if you think you see a G down in the fine print, it's a C or an O.

E	1
F P	2
T O Z	3
L P E D	4
P E C F D	5
E D F C Z P	6
F E L O P Z D	7
D E F P O T E C	8
L E F O D P C T	9
F D P L T C E O	10
P E Z O L C F T D	11

Want to show off? The bottom line is PEZOLCFTD.

117

16·

The Rorschach Test

Most people have heard of the Rorschach test, but few have ever seen a real Rorschach inkblot. The blots are kept secret. When you see an inkblot in a popular article on the test (as in the *Encyclopaedia Britannica* entry on the Rorschach test), it's a fake: *an* inkblot, but not one of *the* inkblots. There are only ten Rorschach inkblots.

Psychologists want the blots to remain a secret from the general public so that reactions to the blots will be spontaneous. Hermann Rorschach hoped these spontaneous reactions would yield valuable clues to the test subject's personality. Whether they do remains controversial. Many psychologists think the Rorschach test is hopelessly unreliable; others see it as one of the cardinal tools of modern psychodiagnosis. Even among those who acknowledge the value of the test, there is disagreement on interpretation of responses.

Just as secret as the blots themselves are the ground rules for administering the test. There are a few things that you, as a subject, are supposed to know and a lot of things you aren't supposed to know. If you ask about something you're not supposed to know, the psychologist will give you a pat answer as prescribed in Rorschach literature. For example, if you ask if it is okay to turn the card upside down, the psychologist will respond that you may do as you like; it's up to you. The psychologist won't say that many of the cards are easier to interpret when turned; that most people do turn the cards; that he or she will make a notation with a little arrowhead every time you do turn a card; and that you lose points in the initiative department if you don't turn the cards.

You'll be handed the cards one by one in the fixed order devised by Rorschach (there are numbers on the backs of the cards for the psychologist's benefit). The first card, for instance, looks like a fox's head or a jack-o'-lantern. The cards are thick, rectangular cardboard, 6⅝ inches by 9½ inches. Half of the blots are black ink on a white background. Two others are black and red ink on white, and the last three blots are multicolored. The psychologist will always put each card in your hands "right" side up.

You aren't supposed to know it, but the psychologist will write down everything you say. This includes any seemingly irrelevant questions you may have. To keep you from getting wise, the psychologist always arranges to sit to your side and a little behind you, so that you can't look at the card and the psychologist at the same time. Most subjects realize the psychologist is taking notes, of course, but they don't realize that the notes are a special shorthand record of *everything* said. Some psychologists use hidden tape recorders.

The psychologist will also time how long it takes you to respond, using a "tickless" watch. The psychologist will not ask you to hurry up or slow down and will not make any reference to time, but response times (in seconds) are one of the things he or she is writing in the notes.

Don't hold the card at an unusual angle. Watch how you phrase things. Say "This looks like . . ." or "This could be . . ." never "This is . . ." After all, you're supposed to realize that it is just a blot of ink on a card. By the same token, don't be too literal and say things as, "This is a blotch of black ink." Don't groan, get emotional, or make irrelevant comments. Don't put your hands on the cards to block out parts. The psychologist will watch for all of the foregoing as signs of brain damage.

If there are no right answers for the test, there are some general guidelines as to what is a normal response. You can probably see images in the inkblots proper and in the white spaces they enclose. Stick to the former. Don't be afraid of being obvious. There are several responses that almost everyone gives; mentioning these shows the psychologist you're a regular guy.

It is okay to be original if you can justify what you see in the shape, shading, or color of the blot. If you see an abalone and can point out why it looks like one, then say so. Justifiable original responses are usually judged to be indicative of creativity or intelligence. You don't want *non sequiturs,* images that don't fit the blot in the judgment of the psychologist. These may be signs of psychosis.

You're expected to see more than one thing on all or most of the cards. Not being able to see anything on a card suggests neurosis. Usually the more things you can see, the better, as long as they fit the form and color of the blot. Of course, you can see things in the whole blot or in parts of it, and images may overlap.

Since time is a factor, it is important to come up with good answers fast. (It looks particularly bad if you take a long time and give a dumb, inappropriate answer.) The most reliable way to come up with good answers is to memorize what the good answers are. Copyright restrictions prevent us from showing you the blots themselves, so we'll use outlines. We'll refer to the blots as psychologists do, as Plates I through X. The psychologist won't mention the numbers to you, but the blots will always be in order.

Plate I

Black ink. A roughly triangular shape, point down, suggesting a broad, fox-like face with prominent ears. Naughty bits: a pair of breasts (rounded projections at top of blot); a vertical female figure, her torso partly visible through a gauzy dress (along center line).

The first blot is easy. How fast you answer is taken as an indication of how well you cope with new situations. The best reaction is to give one of the most common responses immediately. Good answers are bat, butterfly, moth, and (in center of blot) a female figure. Mask, jack-o'-lantern, and animal face are common responses too, but in some interpretation schemes they suggest paranoia. A bad response is any that says something untoward about the central female figure. "She" is often judged to be a projection of your own self-image. Avoid the obvious comment that the figure has two breasts but no head.

If you don't give more than one answer for Plate I, many psychologists will drop a hint—tell you to look closer.

Plate II

Black and red ink. Two dark-gray splotches suggesting dancing figures. Red splotches at top of each figure and at bottom center. Naughty bits: penis (upper center, black ink); vagina (the red area at bottom center).

It is important to see this blot as two human figures—usually females or clowns. If you don't, it's seen as a sign that you have trouble relating to people. You may give other responses as well, such as cave entrance (the triangular white space between the two figures) and butterfly (the red "vagina," bottom center).

Should you mention the penis and vagina? Not necessarily. Every Rorschach plate has at least one obvious representation of sexual anatomy. You're not expected to mention them all. In some interpretation schemes, mentioning more than four sex images in the ten plates is diagnostic of schizophrenia. The trouble is, subjects who took Psychology 101 often assume they should detail every possible sex response, so allowances must be made. Most Rorschach workers believe the sex images should play a part in the interpretation of responses even when not mentioned. You may not say that the lower red area looks like a vagina, but psychologists assume that what you do say will show how you feel about women. Nix on "crab"; stick with "butterfly."

Plate III

Black and red ink. Two obvious figures (black ink) facing each other. But-terfly-shaped red blot between the figures; an elongated red blot behind each figure's head. Naughty bits: penises and breasts (at anatomically appropri-ate positions for each figure).

This is the blot that supposedly can determine sexual prefer-ence. Most people see the two human figures. Both figures have prominent "breasts" and an equally prominent "penis." If you don't volunteer the gender of the figures, you'll be asked to specify it. By the traditional interpretation, seeing the figures as male is a heterosexual response (for test subjects of both sexes). Describing the figures as female or acknowledging the androgynous nature of the blot is supposed to be a homosexual response. Does it work? Not really—many straights describe the figures as women, and not all gays give a gay response. A 1971 study at Mount Sinai Hospital in New York showed the traditionally heterosexual re-sponse (two male figures) to be declining in popularity.

The splotches of red ink are usually perceived separately. Com-mon responses are bow tie or ribbon (inner red area) and a stom-ach and esophagus (outer red areas).

Plate IV

Black ink. A roughly triangular blot, point up, with the two lower corner regions resembling boots or feet. Naughty bits: two penises (on either side of blot, near top of triangle); vagina (on center line near top of blot).

Plate IV is the "father card." At first glance it is a difficult blot to see as a single image. The "boots" are fairly conspicuous; between them is the apparent head of a dog or Chinese dragon. Many subjects see the blot as an animal skin. After a few seconds, though, most can see it as a standing figure seen from below. The boots become the feet, enlarged because of the unusual perspective. The arms and head, at the top, are smaller. Common descriptions are bear, gorilla, or man in a heavy coat. Bad descriptions are monster or *attacking* bear or gorilla—Rorschach theorists equate your description of the figure with your perception of your father or male authority figures.

Plate V

Black ink. A simple, batlike shape. Naughty bits: two penises (the "ears" or "antennae").

Rorschach himself thought this was the easiest blot to interpret. It is a bat or a butterfly, period. You don't want to mention anything else. Seeing the projections on the ends of the bat wings as crocodile heads signifies hostility. Seeing the paired butterfly antennae or feet as scissors or pliers signifies a castration complex. Schizophrenics sometimes see moving people in this blot.

Many psychologists take particular note of the number of responses given to this plate. If you mention more images here than in either Plate IV or VI, it is suggestive of schizophrenia.

Plate VI

Black ink. An irregular shape like that of an animal-skin rug. Naughty bits: penis (center line at top); vagina (below penis).

Plate VI is the most difficult blot. The best-rendered penis of all the blots is at top, but few subjects mention it. The rest of the blot doesn't look like much of anything. Some hold that the value of this blot is to have the subject grope for images and possibly reveal subconscious attitudes about sexuality.

Basically, the secret of this plate is to turn it. A good response is to say it looks like an animal hide (about the only reasonable response when held right side up), then turn it on its side and say it looks like a boat or surfaced submarine with reflection, and then turn it upside down and say it looks like a mushroom cloud, a pair of theater masks, or caricatures of men with long noses and goatees.

Plate VII

Black ink. A U-shaped blot, each side of the U resembling a female figure in a narrow-waisted dress. Naughty bits: a vagina (on center line at bottom of U).

Christina Crawford meets projective psychology: This blot is supposed to reveal how you really feel about your mother. Virtually everyone sees two girls or women. Deprecating descriptions of the figures—"witches," "gossips," "girls fighting," "spinsters"—indicate poor maternal relations. Seeing the blot as thunderclouds instead of female figures suggests anxiety to some psychologists; seeing it as a walnut kernel may mean a vulvar fixation.

There is an entirely different side to this blot, but you're not supposed to see it. The white space between the girls or women can be interpreted as an oil lamp or similar object. It is claimed that only schizophrenics usually see the lamp.

Plate VIII

Pink, blue, gray, and orange ink. An almost circular array of interconnected forms—a gray triangle (point up) at top, a pair of blue rectangles in the center, a pink and orange splotch at bottom, and two pink "animal" shapes forming the right and left sides of the circle. Naughty bits: a vagina (pink-orange area at bottom).

The first full-color card is easy. It is important that you see the four-legged animals—lions, pigs, bears, etc.—on the sides of the blot. They're one of the most common responses on the test, and you're assumed to be a mental defective if you don't see them. Other good responses are tree (gray triangle at top), butterfly (pink and orange area at bottom), and rib cage or anatomy chart (skeletal pattern in center between blue rectangles and gray triangles). The entire configuration can be seen as a heraldic design (good answer) or a Christmas tree with ornaments (reaching). Children tend to like this blot and say a lot about it—the bright colors and animal shapes make it more interesting than your basic penis/vagina number (II, IV, or VI).

Plate IX

Green, orange, and pink ink. A very irregular upright rectangle. Orange at top, protruding green areas at center, pink at bottom. Naughty bits: a vagina (center line at bottom).

There aren't many good answers here. If you're going to throw up your hands (figuratively; see warning about emotional outbursts above) and plead a mental block, this is the place to do it.

The colors clash, apparently by Rorschach's design. Good answers are a fire with smoke, an explosion (but paranoids are claimed more apt to note the pale green mushroom cloud on the center line at top), a map, anatomy, or a flower. If you turn the card ninety degrees, you can make out a man's head in the pink areas at bottom. (The man is identified as Mark Twain, Santa Claus, or Teddy Roosevelt.) A bad response is to describe the orange areas at top as monsters or men fighting—a sign of poor social development. As with Plate V, the psychologist may be counting the number of responses you give to this blot for comparison with the preceding and succeeding blots. You want to give fewer responses to this blot.

Plate X

Pink, blue, gray, green, yellow, and orange ink. A loose assortment of brightly colored shapes, the most chaotic of the plates. Naughty bits: penis and testes (top center, gray ink).

The unspoken purpose of this last blot is to test your organizational ability. Plate X is full of colorful odds and ends easy to identify—blue spiders, gray crabs, paired orange maple seeds, green caterpillars, a light-green rabbit's head, yellow and orange fried eggs—and you're expected to list them. But the psychologist will also be looking for a comprehensive answer, something that shows you grok the whole *Gestalt*. There are two good holistic answers: sea life and a view through a microscope.

Some subjects see two reddish faces at top center, separated by the orange maple key. If you describe them as blowing bubbles or smoking pipes, it may be interpreted as evidence of an oral fixation. Seeing the gray "testes" and "penis" as two animals eating a stick or tree indicates castration anxiety.

17·

The Lie-Detector Test

The polygraph was invented by William Moulton Marston, who was, strangely enough, also the creator of the *Wonder Woman* comic strip (under the name Charles Moulton). The standard polygraph records only three distinct vital signs. A blood-pressure cuff on the upper arm measures changes in blood pressure. Wires attached to the fingers measure changes in electrical resistance of the skin due to sweating. Rubber straps around the torso measure the breathing rate. This information is displayed as four squiggles on a moving strip of graph paper.

Whether or not you believe a polygraph provides useful information (most psychologists have their doubts), there is a good chance you'll be asked to take a polygraph test. The vast majority of lie-detector tests are administered for employee screening— "Have you been using the WATS line for personal calls?" and so forth—not for police work. In *A Tremor in the Blood: Uses and Abuses of the Lie Detector* (New York: McGraw-Hill, 1981), polygraph critic David Thoreson Lykken estimates that as many as one million polygraph examinations are performed on Americans each year. In criminal cases, even the manifestly innocent may be asked to take a polygraph test. All Yakima County, Washington, rape victims are required to take the test; refusal means the case will not be prosecuted.

At best, all the polygraph can indicate is a heightened emotional reaction to a question. It cannot specify what kind of an emotional reaction. Polygraphers try to design question formats so guilt-induced nervousness will be the only emotion invoked and so the subject's reaction to relevant questions can be compared to other, "control" questions.

The Lie-Control Test

This is the question format used in most police investigations. It usually starts with a card trick devised by two pioneer polygraphers, John E. Reid and F. E. Inbau.

The polygrapher hooks the subject to the polygraph and takes out a deck of cards. The polygrapher tells the subject that he must "calibrate" the polygraph with a simple test. He fans the deck and asks the subject to select a card. The subject is told to look at the card but not to show it or mention its name. The polygrapher tells the subject to answer "no" to every question asked about the card. "Is it a black card?" the polygrapher asks. "Is it a high card?" and so on. After each "no" the polygrapher scrutinizes the tracings and fiddles with the dials. If the no answer is incorrect, the polygrapher disagrees. The field is soon narrowed to one card—and it is the correct card.

Needless to say, the polygrapher uses a trick deck. The point is to foster confidence in the machine. After identifying the card, the polygrapher comments that the subject's reactions are particularly easy to read and segues into the interrogation.

Three types of questions are used in a lie-control test. The entire list is read to the subject well in advance of the test. The start of a typical interrogation might run like this:

1. Is your name Sarah Elkins?
2. Is Paris the capital of France?
3. Have you ever failed to report more than fifty dollars of tip, gambling, or gift income on a single year's tax return?
4. Is this apple red?
5. Do you have any idea why the cash receipts for the last quarter are about twenty-two thousand dollars in error?
6. Is there something important that you did not mention on your job application?
7. Have you been embezzling from the company?

The first question is always irrelevant to the matter being investigated. It has to be because many subjects get nervous on the first question no matter what. Other irrelevant questions are asked throughout the interrogation (questions 2 and 4 in the sample list). If the subject gives any thought to these questions, he assumes that they are control questions to provide a yardstick for evaluating responses to the relevant questions. Actually, the irrelevant questions are there to give the subject's vital signs time to return to normal. They aren't the control questions.

Questions 5 and 7 in the list above are relevant questions—the only questions the examiner is really interested in. The relevant questions are asked in several different wordings during the test.

Questions 3 and 6 are control questions. In the pretest discussion of the questions, the polygrapher explains that it is helpful to throw in a few "general honesty" questions. Whoever committed the serious crime, the spiel goes, probably committed less serious crimes in the past. Hence the inclusion of questions about tax cheating, lying on job applications, stealing as a child, etc.

The polygrapher affects the attitude that it would be damaging indeed to admit to any such indiscretions. Frequently this scares the subject into admitting minor crimes. In that case, the polygrapher frowns and agrees to rewrite the question. Should the subject concede failing to report eighty dollars in gambling winnings, question 3 might be changed to "Have you ever failed to report more than a hundred dollars of tip, gambling, or gift income on a single year's tax return?" If necessary, several of the control questions may be reworded before the test—always so that the subject will be able to give the "honest" response.

In reality, the whole point of each control question is to manufacture a lie. It is the secret working premise of polygraphers that everyone commits the minor transgressions that are the subject of the usual control questions. All the subject's denials on the control questions are assumed to be lies. The polygraph tracings during these "lies" establish a base line for interpreting the reaction to the relevant questions.

The reason for rewriting some control questions is so a candid subject will not admit to minor crimes on the test. That would be telling the truth, and the polygrapher wants the subject to lie. The control questions are intentionally broad. Even if a question is reworded to exclude the confessed instance, it is assumed that any denial must be a lie.

The rationale for the lie-control test goes like this: The honest subject will be worried about the control questions. He'll know that he has committed small transgressions or suspect that he must have, even if he can't remember them. So he'll be afraid that the machine will detect his deception on the "general honesty" questions (especially in view of its success with the card trick). That would be embarrassing at least, and it might throw suspicion on him for the larger crime. In contrast, the relevant questions should be less threatening to the honest subject. He knows he didn't commit the crimes they refer to.

The guilty person, on the other hand, should have far more to fear from the relevant questions. If the machine can detect lying on the relevant issue, it matters little that it might also implicate him in petty matters.

By this hypothesis, an innocent person should have greater polygraphic response to the control questions than to the relevant questions. The guilty pattern is just the reverse: greater response to the relevant questions. This, at any rate, is what polygraphers look for when the machine is switched on.

The Relevant-Control Test

The relevant-control test is the type used for most employee screenings. Thus it is the most common type of examination. The interrogation consists only of irrelevant and relevant questions. As with the lie-control test, the first question and a few others are irrelevant. The relevant questions usually test workplace honesty: "Have you ever taken home office supplies for personal use?" "Have you ever clocked in for someone else?"

The premise is that no one will lie about everything. So if a few of the relevant questions produce heightened responses, they are presumed to be the questions on which the subject is lying. Unfortunately, there is no unambiguous way of deciding how much response indicates a lie. Most psychologists agree that the relevant-control test is a poor test of deception.

The Reid/Inbau card trick is eliminated from employee screenings: There is too great of chance of coworkers comparing notes and discovering that everyone picked the ace of spades.

How to Beat the Lie Detector

To the extent that the polygraph works at all, it works because people believe it does. Many criminals confess during polygraph examinations. Many employees are more honest for fear of periodic screenings. But a dummy polygraph that hummed and scribbled preprogrammed tracings would be no less effective in these instances.

David Thoreson Lykken estimates that lie-control polygraph tests are about 70 percent accurate. (Remember, though, that choosing "heads" or "tails" of a flipped coin can be accurate 50 percent of the time.) Accuracy of 70 percent is not impressive, but it is high enough to talk meaningfully of beating a polygraph test.

Just by having read this far, you stand a greater chance of beating a polygraph test. You won't be wowed by the card demonstration. You realize that the polygraph's powers are limited. There are two additional techniques for beating the polygraph. The more obvious is to learn how to repress physiologic responses to stressful questions. Some people are good at this; others are not. Most people can get better by practicing with a polygraph. Of course, this training requires a polygraph, and polygraphs are expensive.

The opposite approach is to pick out the control questions in the pretest discussion and exaggerate reactions to these questions during the test. When the control-question responses are greater than the relevant-question responses, the polygrapher must acquit the subject.

Because breathing is one of the parameters measured, taking a deep breath and holding it will record as an abnormal response. Flexing the arm muscles under the cuff distorts the blood-pressure reading. But a suspicious polygrapher may spot either ruse.

A more subtle method is to hide a tack in one shoe. Stepping on the tack during the control questions produces stress reactions with no outward signs of fidgeting. Biting the tongue forcefully also works.

18·

How to Crash
the Freemasons

Masonry swears its members to secrecy with grisly, anatomically explicit oaths. A Master Freemason must "promise and swear, that I will not write, print, stamp, stain, hew, cut, carve, indent, paint, or engrave" the mysteries of his order "under no less penalty than to have my throat cut across, my tongue torn out by the roots, and my body buried in the rough sands of the sea," according to one version of the oath. Tenth-degree Masons "consent to have my body opened perpendicularly, and to be exposed for eight hours in the open air, that the venomous flies may eat my entrails" if they talk. Even the Shriners, a "fun" order, may incur "the fearful penalty of having my eyeballs pierced to the center with a three-edged blade."

Be that as it may, the secrets of the Masons are preserved in certain arcane tracts, pamphlets, and books. These are sold only by Masonic supply houses—the firms that sell fezzes, banners, plaques, jewels, and other regalia to lodges. The supply houses take the secrecy seriously. Most will not sell booklets containing club secrets to anyone who cannot show a Masonic ID. *Big Secrets* came across a Chicago firm, however, that works by mail order. The Geo. Lauterer Corporation publishes an illustrated catalog of lodge gear. It offers over a hundred Masonic and other fraternal manuscripts. We obtained a sampling of titles.

American Masonry differs in certain particulars from British or Continental Masonry. Rituals may vary from lodge to lodge. Masonic tracts do not always agree. Except where noted, the information below is taken from two of Lauterer's titles, *Richardson's Monitor of Freemasonry* by a pseudonymous Benjamin Henry Day, and *Initiation Stunts* by Lieutenant Beale Cormack.

The Secret Handshake

It's a regular handshake, except that you press your forefinger hard into the other's palm. The thumb presses against the base joints of the second and third fingers. It looks pretty much like any other handshake; only the persons shaking hands can feel the difference.

The Secret Password

"Tubal-Cain" (tōō·bəl·kān′) is the secret password of a Master Mason. But some lodges have their own passwords.

The Secret Word

Not to be confused with the password. The Word (always capitalized) is so secret that initiates are taught it one letter at a time. First they learn A, then O, then M, and finally I. The Word is IAOM.

You never get a straight story as to what it means. As best as anyone can figure, it is the ineffable name of God, or some approximation thereof. The Word (or Name) is a tongue-twister. It takes some practice to get it right. The following pronunciation guide is from *Masonry and Its Symbols in the Light of Thinking and Destiny* by Harold Waldwin Percival:

> The Name is pronounced as follows: It is started by opening the lips with an "ee" sound graduating into a broad "a" as the mouth opens wider with lips forming an oval shape and then graduating the sound to "o" as the lips form a circle, and again modulating to an "m" sound as the lips close to a point. This point resolves itself to a point within the head.
>
> Expressed phonetically the Name is "EE-Ah-Oh-Mmm" and is pronounced with one continuous out-breathing with a slight nasal tone in the manner described above. It can be correctly and properly expressed with its full power only by one who has brought his physical body to a state of perfection . . .

The Secret Code

The Freemasons' cipher is rarely used, but it is mentioned in several sources. You make a diagram like this:

A	B	C
D	E	F
G	H	I

N	O	P
Q	R	S
T	U	V

Each letter is encoded by drawing its cell in the diagram. MASON becomes

The Shriners' Recognition Test

According to a Lauterer manuscript, this is how two Shriners recognize each other:

Q. Then I presume you are a Noble?
A. I am so accepted by all men of noble birth.
Q. Have you traveled any?
A. I have.
Q. From where to what place have you traveled?
A. Traveled east over the hot burning sands of the desert.
Q. Where were you stopped at?
A. At the devil's pass.
Q. What were you requested to do?
A. I was requested to contribute a few drops of urine.
Q. Why were you requested to do this?
A. As a token of my renouncing the wiles and evils of the world and granted permission to worship at the Shrine.
Q. At what Shrine did you worship?
A. At the Shrine of Islam.
Q. Did you ride?
A. Yes, I rode a camel until I paused to dismount.
Q. Then what did you do with your camel?
A. I tied him.
Q. Where did you tie him?

A. I tied him to a date tree, where all True Shriners should do so.

BOTH: Yes, I pulled the Cord, rode the hump, I have traversed the hot arid sands of the desert to find Peace and rest in the quiet shades of the Oasis.

Initiation

There are two sides to Freemason initiations—one a standardized, sedate ritual; the other a highly variable set of hazing stunts.

Prospective Masons must apply of their own free will. Masons may not recruit their friends, at least not in theory. Proposed members are investigated by a committee of lodge members. This is often just a formality but may include, for instance, a credit report. The committee reports on the candidate at a lodge meeting. Members then vote.

The ballot box in the Lauterer catalog uses white balls and black cubes. (Losers are blackcubed, not blackballed.) If there is a single negative vote, the ballot is declared foul. The lodgemaster (who sees how each member voted) may try to convince dissenting members to reconsider. A negative verdict on the second ballot is final.

Successful candidates are invited to the lodge for initiation. There are three basic degrees: Entered Apprentice, Fellow Craft, and Master Mason. Each has its own ritual.

Entered Apprentice candidates begin by taking off their clothes to prove their gender (women may not become Masons). In practice, this means taking off the pants and any jacket. Underwear and shirt are kept on, but the shirt is unbuttoned and pulled down to bare the left arm, shoulder, and breast.

The candidate is hoodwinked (blindfolded). A cabletow (rope) is placed around the neck. (The Lauterer catalog's hoodwink is simply a standard, black satin half-face mask—without eyeholes—secured with an elastic string. The cabletow is a heavy blue rayon cord with tassels at both ends.) Ideally, the cabletow is supposed to have four strands to symbolize the four senses (they don't count touch). The candidate is escorted to a room where three candles are burning. One of the lodge members takes a mason's compass or other sharp instrument and pricks the candidate's bared skin. The candidate is instructed to recite a formula to the effect that what he desires most is light. The other lodge members remove his hookwink and cabletow. Before the candidate are the three candles. He is told that the candles represent the sun, the moon, and the master of the lodge.

The candidate gets a lecture on the symbolism of Masonry. Visual aids are used (Lauterer sells a set of three lecture charts and a set of 118 35-millimeter slides). He is given a "lambskin," a white apron. Lauterer's lambskins are indeed genuine lambskin, lined with cotton. They measure 13 inches by 15 inches or 14 inches by 16 inches. A triangular flap folds down like the flap of an envelope. The lambskin is worn in front, and a tie (tape or cord with tassels) fastens behind the back.

A member of the lodge pretends to be a collector for a needy cause and asks the candidate to donate. Lacking his wallet, the candidate must refuse. The moral: Help the less fortunate. Then the candidate is allowed to put his clothes back on. He is taken before the master of the lodge. The master tells him that he is now a Mason. The candidate is given the working tools of the Apprentice, a twenty-four-inch gauge and a gavel.

The second and third degrees follow a similar pattern. Both repeat the business with the hoodwink and the cabletow. For the Fellow Craft initiation, the right shoulder is bared, and the cabletow is tied around the right biceps. In the Master Mason initiation, the cabletow is wound around the body three times. Each degree has its own lecture on symbolism.

Then there are optional degrees. Their initiation rituals take the form of short plays starring the candidate and other lodge members. The playlets deal with incidents from the mythic history of the Masons, such as the building of King Solomon's Temple and the murder of Temple architect Hiram Abiff. These initiations cost the candidate about $150 a pop, so any thirty-second-degree Mason has dropped over $4,000. Once a Mason has completed the twenty-nine optional degrees of the Scottish rite or the six optional degrees of the York rite, he is eligible to become a Shriner—which means still another initiation.

Depending on the whim of other lodge members, initiations may include a set of burlesque tests to prove a candidate's mettle. These blend sophomoric practical jokes, soft S&M, and an electric carpet (the latter "just the item for initiations," touts the Lauterer catalog, at $4.75 a square foot; jump spark battery extra). Lauterer's *Initiation Stunts* booklet describes over thirty tests judged suitable for fraternal orders, of which the following is a sample. In all cases, candidates are blindfolded. Here's how the Masons keep out the wimps:

"Chewing the Rag"

A lodge member criticizes two candidates for speaking: "They both talk too much and I fear they will someday betray the secrets of our brotherhood." As a lesson, the candidates must "chew the rag." The member says that he has a six-foot length of string with a raisin tied in the middle. Each candidate gets an end of the string. The member instructs the candidates to chew the string from their respective ends: The one who gets the raisin will be excused from "The Test of the Drowning Man." They chew. The "raisin" is really a piece of candy coated with Epsom salts. There is no "Test of the Drowning Man."

"Oriental Dance"

Lodge members strip a candidate and put a skirt on him. As Oriental music is played, he is forced to dance on the electric carpet. This is one of several uses of the carpet, all of which are deemed more effective if the candidate does not know about the carpet. The electric-shock sensation is not immediately identifiable as such, or so the semiwarped reasoning goes. Members may warn the blindfolded candidate to "step high" to avoid burning desert sands, barbed wire, or snakebites.

"A Trip to the Moon"

A member raps his gavel and orders all to be seated. A second member replies that there is no seat for himself and one of the candidates. They are told to sit on the floor. They sit on a spread blanket. As soon as the candidate is seated, the second member steps off the blanket. The candidate is told to sing a song. The lodge members protest his singing and demand that he be punished. All quietly grab the ends of the blanket and toss the candidate in the air.

"The Barber Shop"

A member feels a candidate's chin and calls for a barber. The "barber" lathers the candidate, getting foam in his mouth. He shaves him with what feels like a very, very rough blade. It's a shingle.

"Boxing Match"

Two candidates are selected for a boxing match. Belts are strapped around their waists. A six-foot rope connects the belts so that candidates do not wander blindly off. The boxers are given gloves. Unknown to the candidates, a member also puts on gloves and gives them occasional jabs from unexpected directions.

"Tug-of-War"

Two candidates or groups of candidates play tug-of-war. An unseen member sets the rope afire in the middle. It burns in two, and all fall down—on the electric carpet, if desired.

"The Thirst"

"This neophyte has asked for a drink of water," a member says. Another member replies that there is no water. "Then we must make water," says the first. Several members urinate in a bowl, making sure that the candidate hears. "It is ready," says a member. "Drink, and quench thy thirst." The candidate is handed a bowlful of warm water and forced to drink it.

"Punkin Pie"

This is just a forced pie-eating race, with the candidates' hands bound behind their backs. Other gustatory stunts involve making the blindfolded candidates eat various non- and quasi-edible materials: *Initiation Stunts* suggests ginger ale containing frankfurters and toilet-paper squares.

"The Shampoo"

A candidate is told that he must possess three essentials to be a member: keen vision, a sensitive touch, and an acute sense of smell. An egg is placed in his hand. "What is in your hand?" he is asked. The candidate replies, "An egg." "Correct. Now to test your sense of smell—is it a good egg or a bad egg?" The candidate answers. "We'll see if you are correct," the member says. He crushes an empty eggshell on the candidate's head and pours some water on it. He rubs the "egg" in the candidate's hair. Another member holds a bottle of ammonia or other evil-smelling substance under the candidate's nose.

"The Trained Dog"

A candidate is told that he must meet Fido, the trained dog. An authentic dog is brought in. "Fido snarls at neophytes and sometimes bites them in the calf of the leg," a member warns. Another pinches the candidate's leg. The dog is placed in the candidate's lap. The initiation ceremony proceeds with another candidate so that the first believes that attention has shifted from him. A member sneaks up on the candidate with the dog and trickles some warm water in his lap. He may also hold a smell bottle under the candidate's nose. "Naughty Fido!" all scold.

A variation is the "Bung Hole Test" a standard feature of Shriner initiations. No dog is required. Two blindfolded candidates are directed to opposite ends of a barrel or large metal cylinder lying on its side. They are told to crawl into the barrel or cylinder. The candidates bump heads in the middle. Outside, a lodge member yelps like a dog. Someone sprinkles warm water on the candidate's faces through a hole. A member yells, "Get that dog out of there! It just pissed in his face!"

"The Sacred Stone"

The candidate is told that a "sacred stone" is near his feet. He must make a sign of deference by bending over and placing his forehead as close to the ground as possible. When the candidate bends over, a member paddles him with a paddle containing an exploding cartridge. "The Little Rose" test is the same thing, only the candidate is told to pick a flower.

"The North Pole"

Candidates are forced to climb a greased pole while members paddle them. Afterward, a member hands a candidate a piece of ice: "Here is your share of the North Pole. Hold it as long as you can, and pass it on."

"Molten Lead Test"

A member warns the candidate that the next test may be dangerous if not performed carefully. Proof of a candidate's courage and faith in the order is required, the member explains. "Is the lead good and hot?" he asks another member. "Yes, red hot," he replies. "If you are not a coward, you must plunge your hands into a caldron of red-hot molten lead," the member tells the candidate. A large pot is set before the candidate. It contains any reasonably humane substitute for molten lead. If the candidate refuses to put his hands in the pot, the others force him.

"Good Rich Blood"

An overly "frisky" candidate is selected. "He has too much gall," a member says. "Then we must cut out his gall," another counters. A "doctor" is called for.

The candidate is forced onto a makeshift operating table. The doctor feels for the candidate's pulse. He pronounces the pulse too high. The doctor confers with other members. They decide that drawing a quart of "good rich blood" will make the patient less frisky.

The doctor pricks the candidate with a pencil point and dribbles warm water from a sponge on the wound. If there are other candidates present, a member says, moaning, "Stop! You're killing me!" Doctor and assistants demand "More blood"—"Go in deeper"—"Take some from the heart." The doctor presses a sharp piece of ice against the candidate's chest and draws the ice slowly across the chest. More warm water is dribbled. "He can't take much more of this"—"He's stopped breathing"—"He's dead." The doctor tells his assistants to take the body and throw it on the ash pit.

"The Test of Fire"

Candidates are told a club secret, say a secret number. A member later asks a candidate the secret number. The candidate answers as he has been told. "This infidel knows our secret number," objects the member. "He must not leave here alive. What is to be done with him?" Various tortures or means of execution are proposed: burning at the stake, cutting off the toes, burning out the eyes. The members soon agree on "The Test of Fire."

"You must be branded with the secret number," the blindfolded candidate is told. A fictitious red-hot branding iron is supplied. "Where should we brand him?" a member asks. "The most vital spot," another urges. One member "brands" the candidate's genitals with a warm piece of pipe or a sharp piece of ice while another scorches some raw meat with a candle flame under his nose. If there are other candidates waiting, a member screams. "He fainted," someone says. "Throw the body to the dogs."

"His Majesty, the King"
A candidate is accused of arrogance. "Let's crown him king, then," someone suggests. The candidate is taken to a "throne." This is a folded blanket suspended between two chairs. Lodge members sit on the chairs to hold the blanket in place. The candidate unknowingly sits on the blanket between the two chairs. Underneath the throne is a basinful of water. "Crown him," a member says. A spongeful of molasses is placed on the candidate's head and squeezed. The two members sitting on the blanket get up, dropping the candidate into the water.

"Hazing the Obstreperous"
Initiation Stunts offers the following remedy for unruly initiates: The offender is bound and taken to a special meeting place in the woods. He is securely blindfolded. One member forces him to the ground and holds his mouth open. The other members gather around and make coughing, gagging sounds. They plop a raw oyster into his mouth.

PART FIVE

Pay No Attention to the Man Behind the Curtain

Lose the TV Magic Cards. If you're like most jaded postteens, you don't care about the dinky little card and coin tricks explained in any of the hundreds of magic books for popular consumption. You just want to know how the bitchin' stuff works. How to saw a person in two. How to make a handkerchief dance in a sealed glass bottle. How to make Doug Henning's stage persona actually seem cute. It's fun to be fooled, sure. But it's even more fun to be able to point out the wires and mirrors and ruin it for everyone else.

Magicians get territorial when it comes to the primo material. But even the pros have to learn the secrets somewhere. The somewhere happens to be a handful of professional magic-materials suppliers, including Abbott's Magic Manufacturing Co. (Colon, MI 49040), Flosso Hornmann Magic Co. (304 West 34th Street, New York, NY 10018), U. F. Grant (P.O. Box 44052, Columbus, OH 43204), and Louis Tannen, Inc. (1540 Broadway, New York, NY 10036). All publish large catalogs advertising "workshop plans" for illusions. The plans—short, photocopied manuscripts—detail the secrets of the spectacular stage illusions and sell for a few dollars each. We sent away for some of the real bafflers. Promise you won't be disappointed afterward, and turn the page.

19.

David Copperfield's Dancing Handkerchief in a Bottle

Two of David Copperfield's best-known illusions are levitations of inanimate objects. One uses a large, metal-finish ball, which floats about the stage on command. At one point Copperfield passes the ball through his arms to demonstrate that no wires are used. The other effect, used in a TV commercial for Eastman Kodak, involves a knotted handkerchief. The handkerchief "dances" and jumps from hand to hand. When stuffed in a stoppered glass bottle, the handkerchief thrashes as vigorously as before. It "struggles" to get out and soon pops the stopper and jumps out.

Not only do both tricks seem to rule out all conventional means of support, but also the control of the floating objects is remarkable. Copperfield balances the seemingly heavy ball on a fingertip. It follows a slow, controlled arc to the other hand. The ball retreats from Copperfield, and then it comes back on command. The handkerchief becomes a puppetlike animation.

With cruder forms of levitation, it is a simple matter to decide who is controlling the object: the magician or an unseen flunky offstage. When the magician is in control, the object can strut like a marionette, but—surprise, surprise—it never strays more than an arm's length from the magician. As much of the audience gathers, the object *is* a marionette, just with extra-thin strings. When controlled offstage, the object can vary its distance from the performer and even rise above his head. But movements are slow and awkward. If moved too quickly, the object tends to develop a giveaway sway. Copperfield's method is so much more impressive that some postulate a novel technology—focused air currents or magnetic fields, say.

Copperfield is not the only magician to perform these illusions or variations of them. Mark Wilson first performed the floating-ball trick on national television. Doug Henning levitated an "enchanted silver sphere" in a 1982 TV special and a lighted candle in his Broadway musical, *Merlin*. Larry Wilson performs the dancing-handkerchief trick, with the handkerchief jumping in and out the doorways of a small wooden cabinet. In all cases, the method appears to be the same as Copperfield's.

The Floating Ball

The larger magic catalogs offer two illusions purporting to levitate a metallic ball. The simpler of the two is sold under the trade name Zombie. The Zombie illusion uses a lightweight, metal-finish ball with a secret hole. A cork fits snugly into the hole, and the cork is attached to one of the performer's fingers by a stiff wire. By moving the finger, the performer moves the ball. But the performer must always drape a cloth over or near the ball to hide the wire support. The ball may never vary its distance from the finger supporting it—and this distance is only about a foot.

With practice, the Zombie illusion is not as transparent as it may seem when described. It has the advantage of not requiring an elaborate setup. No amount of skill can conjure away the need for the cloth to conceal the wire support, however. Copperfield does not use a cloth with his floating ball.

The second illusion is described in "The Don Wayne Floating Ball," a manuscript sold by Louis Tannen, Inc. and other magic-materials suppliers. It is a far superior illusion to Zombie, and it is the method Copperfield uses—the manuscript acknowledges that Copperfield and Mark Wilson use it.

The ball is about eight inches across. It is hollow. It may be made of aluminum, acrylic, papier-mâché, or a lightweight plastic. In all cases, it weighs far less than its metal surface suggests.

Size A black silk thread suspends the ball. The average audience little appreciates how invisible a thread may be. For levitations of very small objects, magicians sometimes use a fine nylon that can be invisible at close range in full sunlight to a person of normal vision (they attach bits of adhesive wax to the ends so they will be able to work with it). Size A silk is visible from several yards, but this is remedied by careful choice of lighting and back-drop. If both the silk and the backdrop are black, the silk is very hard to see. The mirrored ball serves a double purpose. It makes the audience think that the ball is quite heavy and thus that any supporting threads would have to be good, thick, and visible. Also, the spotlight play on the ball's mirror surface blinds the audience to the dark threads.

(It doesn't always work that way. On "Doug Henning's Magic on Broadway," an NBC special broadcast November 14, 1982, the thread was visible several times—on home TV screens, yet—as Henning performed the illusion.)

An astute observer might notice that the ball's mobility is limited to a plane. As usually set up, the plane is parallel to the backdrop. It passes through, or just in front of the performer. The diagram shows why.

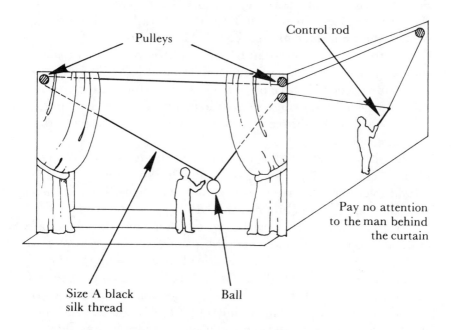

The ball is supported by two threads coming from upper stage right and upper stage left. The two threads and ball actually are part of one continuous loop. At upper stage left, the thread passes over a pulley and then backtracks high over the performer to upper stage right. There it makes a ninety-degree turn over another pulley and passes over an offstage assistant to a pulley far offstage. There it angles down to the assistant, back up to a second pulley at upper stage right, and back to the ball.

Offstage, the thread is tied to an eyelet at the end of a rod held by the assistant. The motions of the eyelet in its plane correspond to the motions of the ball in its plane, with one difference: Vertical motions are reversed. Moving the eyelet up increases the slack in the thread and causes the ball to drop. Moving the eyelet down raises the ball. The ball-bearing pulleys ensure that the ball drops evenly and not from one side only. Horizontal motion of the eyelet moves the ball in the same direction.

The assistant is situated so that he can see the performer at all times. The backdrop may be partially transparent so the assistant can see the spotlighted performer and ball but the audience can't see the assistant in the shadows. Or ordinary curtains may block audience view of the assistant. Because the assistant is watching the performance in real time, he can control the ball almost as well as the performer himself could. Maneuvering the ball with the control rod becomes natural after a little practice. To make the ball jump from the performer's right hand to left hand (move from nine o'clock to three o'clock, clockwise, as seen from the audience), the assistant must swing the control rod eyelet in an arc from nine o'clock to three o'clock counterclockwise, as seen from far stage right.

The beauty of the trick is that no one expects threads to be diagonal. The magician can wave his hands above the ball, below it, and to either side. As far as most of the audience is concerned, this rules out the possibility of threads.

The ball cannot, of course, be passed completely through a fair vertical hoop. The illusion manuscript advises the performer to form his arms into a circle to one side of the ball, with the thread already passing through the arms. The ball can then be directed horizontally through the linked arms. Close observation of Copperfield and other performers shows that this is indeed what they do. If the performer wants to use a metal hoop, it must have a small break for the thread to pass through.

The Dancing Handkerchief

Small objects other than a ball may be levitated as well. Henning's burning candle seems to use the same setup as the floating ball. In principle, a handkerchief (perhaps containing a lead weight for stability) might be levitated in an identical manner. As performed by Copperfield, Larry Wilson, and others, however, the handkerchief trick has some additional features.

Occasionally the handkerchief is borrowed from an audience member. Even if the audience member is a confederate with a prethreaded handkerchief, the threads should be difficult to conceal from those sitting nearby.

Unlike the floating ball, the handkerchief frequently darts in and out of closed containers. It continues to move inside the containers.

The secret is to be found in another illusion manuscript, "Harry Blackstone's 'Spirit Dancing Handkerchief,'" available from Abbott's Magic Manufacturing Co. The illusion, including the routines with the glass bottle and the cabinet, was devised by Harry Blackstone (father of the Harry Blackstone, Jr., now performing). It requires two assistants.

At the beginning of the trick, a size "O" silk thread stretches across the stage at waist height. Each end is held by an offstage assistant.

The magician borrows an unprepared handkerchief from someone in the audience. Going back onstage, he ties a knot in the handkerchief—tying it around the thread. (The magician must turn his back to the audience as he does so, or the assistants must lower the thread briefly so that the magician can step over it and face the audience.)

The handkerchief is subsequently animated by the two assistants working in unison. The manuscript recommends red lights (to make the thread invisible) and a second thread lying on the floor in case the first one breaks.

The only preparation needed for the glass bottle is to shave about one-quarter to three-eighths inch from two opposite sides of the cork. After the handkerchief is placed in the bottle, the stopper must be aligned with the flat sides pointing to the assistants. This allows free space for the thread to slide smoothly over the glass. When inside the bottle, the handkerchief can jump up and down, but it must stay directly under the cork. The cork must, of course, fit very loosely for the handkerchief to pop it off.

The cabinet works the same way. Its edges must be rounded so the thread does not catch. The magician may stuff the handker-

Shaved cork

Fair bottle—no
secret holes,
magnets, or
air jets

Thread to offstage
assistant

chief in one opening and pull it out through another. When the
assistants then both pull on their ends of the thread, the handkerchief enters the cabinet through the latter opening, peeks out the
first opening, and then jumps out.

At the end of the performance, the magician holds the handkerchief in one hand. One assistant lets go of his end of the thread.
The other pulls. The thread slides through the handkerchief knot
and is reeled in by the assistant. Meanwhile, the magician places
his thumb behind the handkerchief knot and reanimates the
handkerchief. It seems to be struggling to free itself. The magician
walks out into the audience (which he couldn't do during the performance) and hands the handkerchief back to its owner.

20·

Harry Blackstone, Jr.'s
Sawing a Woman in Two

Harry Blackstone, Jr., performs the most spectacular of the sawing illusions: He saws through a woman, in plain view, with a buzz saw. The saw looks and sounds real. It cuts through wood. A woman lies down on a platform close to the blade. Unlike other sawing illusions, no cabinet is used. The blade visibly slices through the woman's torso, shredding part of her dress. Even during the sawing, the head and legs move naturally. What makes this illusion so baffling is that there seems to be no room for deception. The audience sees everything, and what it sees is impossible.

Blackstone's buzz saw is, of course, a refinement of the basic sawing-a-woman-in-two illusion. The sawing illusion has been performed in various ways by various magicians ever since 1921. Sexism, not anatomical constraints, dictates that a woman be used. Horace Goldin, who pioneered the trick in the 1920s, originally used a male subject.

The Second-Woman Theory

Goldin's precise method is no matter of conjecture: He patented it in 1923. If you write the U.S. Patent Office and request patent number 1,458,575, they will send a complete description, including diagrams for construction of the cabinet.

A large, rectangular cabinet rests on a table. The cabinet may be lifted off the table and shown at various angles. The top of the cabinet unhinges. A woman gets into the cabinet, possibly assisted by audience volunteers. One end of the cabinet has three openings, for the woman's head and hands. The opposite end has two openings, for her feet. Once the woman's extremities are in place, the top of the cabinet is closed and padlocked. The cabinet may again be lifted to demonstrate that the woman is completely inside. The cabinet is replaced on the table, and the table is spun around to show the apparatus from all angles.

Using a large, genuine saw, the magician and an assistant cut through the cabinet at its center. The cabinet is usually presented to the audience lengthwise so that the woman's head, feet, and hands are visible at all times. If desired, audience volunteers may secure the woman's extremities during the sawing.

The saw is withdrawn. Two metal plates are fitted into preexisting slots just on either side of the cut. The two halves of the cabinet are pulled apart. The metal plates prevent the audience from seeing the (presumably bloody) results of the sawing. The magician points out the head, hands, and feet, which are still moving and obviously not fakes.

Then the two halves are shoved back into contact. The metal plates are removed, the padlocks are unlocked, and the top is opened. The woman steps out of the cabinet, uninjured and in one piece.

Goldin's trick uses two women. The second woman is hidden in the thickish tabletop on which the cabinet rests. Unknown to the audience, the bottom of the foot half of the cabinet has a pair of trapdoors that open upward only. The tabletop has a matching pair of doors. The two pairs of doors must be perfectly aligned. When the cabinet is lifted and replaced on the table, wood ridges on the tabletop help the magician position the cabinet correctly. As the magician spins the table, the feet point away from the audience for a moment. The first woman quickly pulls in her legs, resting her feet on a footrest built into the head half of the cabinet. This places the first woman entirely in the head half. The second woman opens the trapdoors and sticks her feet out the two openings in the end of the cabinet.

The box can then be sawed without harm. The metal plates prevent the audience from glimpsing the illusion's inner workings. Because of the trapdoors, only the head end can be moved.

Rejoining need take only a few seconds. The magician slides

Woman no. 1 rests feet on secret footrest built into box

Saw here

Secret trapdoors in box, table

Innocent-looking tabletop, containing woman no. 2; anorexics preferred

Wooden ridge keeps trapdoors aligned

the head half back into place and removes the metal plates. One plate is casually propped against the cabinet in such a way as to block the audience's view of the feet. The two women switch feet as the magician unlocks the top of the cabinet.

An extra touch, created by Howard Thurston, has the magician snip off part of the woman's sock before the sawing. The magician pretends to hear a heckler protest that the feet are not real. "Spontaneously" he removes the woman's shoes, cuts off part of one sock, and asks an audience volunteer to testify that the foot is real. The second woman, of course, must wear a sock cut in the same manner. Thurston also had volunteers hold the woman's head and feet during the sawing. The person holding the feet was a confederate.

All modern magicians are haunted by the ghost of Goldin's second woman. Word of the second woman leaked out. Sophisticated audiences now expect there to be two women. In consequence, the two-woman method has become operationally extinct. (Abbott's Magic Manufacturing Co. sells a workshop plan for Thurston's method, but none of the well-known contemporary performers dares use it.) The voluminous cabinet and thick tabletop are passé. The modern sawing illusions are designed to banish any suspicion of a second woman.

The "Thin Model" Sawing

The method used by Doug Henning in *Merlin* comes closer to the ideal of a visible sawing. A cabinet is still used, but it is a thin cabinet (about twelve inches thick vs. more than eighteen inches for the old method). Skeptics must concede that even a contortionist cannot draw her knees up under her chin in a foot of crawl space. With the Goldin/Thurston method, the tabletop had to be thick as well. Henning's tabletop is about two inches thick.

The basic scenario is the same, with one innovation: two small doors in the front of the two halves of the cabinet. These may be opened to show the audience the cabinet interior. The cabinet top is opened, and the woman gets in. Stocks secure the head and feet (the arms are inside the cabinet). The two side doors are opened to show that the woman is indeed in the cabinet. The door in the head half shows the woman's arm and torso; the door in the foot half reveals her legs. The woman may stick her arm through the doorway and wave to the audience. The feet move as well. The doors are closed.

The cabinet is sawed through its center. Two metal plates go on either side of the cut. (In Henning's performance, the plate in the head end fails to go down all the way. Henning pulls on the woman's head, and the plate falls into place.) The two halves can then be separated. (The table is in two parts, each with three legs.) The halves may be shown from all angles.

The climax comes when the side doors of the disconnected halves are again opened. The woman's body is seen to be in the same position. Even a spectator thoroughly familiar with the Goldin/Thurston method is likely to conclude that the cabinet affords no room for a second woman and no room for the woman to scrunch up her body in some position other than where it seems to be.

The only thing suspicious about the setup is the triangular arrangement of the table legs. After all, everyone knows about those triangular tables with mirrors between the legs. But this suspicion doesn't pan out. When Henning or an assistant stands behind one of the table halves, their legs are visible underneath it. There are no mirrors.

In due course, the halves are reassembled, and the woman emerges whole. (In *Merlin,* Henning sawed two women in half and interchanged their halves.)

Henning's secret is revealed in a workshop plan titled "Thin Model Sawing A Woman In Half" and available from Louis Tannen, Inc. Henning's use of the "Thin Model" method is mentioned in the plan. Only one woman is used. In brief, the gimmicks are fake feet and a cabinet that is wide enough for the woman to pull up her knees *sideways.*

Invisible thread rotates fake feet

Real arm, side/back visible through this opening

Fake leg visible through this opening

According to the plan, the cabinet is 24½ inches wide. This allows just enough space for a slim woman to draw her legs up to her side. The legs are drawn up on the side away from the side door, of course. The woman's head remains facing upward.

The foot half of the cabinet is equipped with a set of mannequin feet. As soon as the woman gets in the cabinet, she draws herself up into the head half and pushes the fake feet through the opening at the foot end of the cabinet. (This action is in part concealed by the open doors on top of the cabinet.) The woman's real feet are never seen once she gets in the cabinet. The audience sees two feet emerge from the end of the cabinet and assumes them to be the woman's.

The feet must move to be convincing. They have two degrees of freedom. A slide mechanism with a leather grip lets the woman control the in-and-out motion (while the two halves of the cabinet are together). The feet are also on hinges that allow them to rotate inward and outward. This motion is controlled by an invisible monofilament thread operated by the woman or an offstage assistant. A spring attached to the hinges provides a restoring force to counter the string. From a distance, these two motions are sufficient—unless a heckler asks the woman to wiggle her toes.

The open side doors provide but a limited view of the interior. In the head section, you see a genuine arm. Behind it is the woman's costume covering what you take to be her side. Actually, it's the woman's back. The leg in the other side doorway is a built-in fake. It conceals the rotating feet mechanism.

For Henning's *shtick* with the metal plate, the woman evidently blocks the blunt plate with a hand or her feet until the right moment.

The Buzz Saw Illusion

Could fake legs likewise explain Blackstone's buzz saw illusion? The main objection is that there seems to be no opportunity to switch the real legs for the fakes. The woman lies down in full view. The legs are never out of sight. The same is true for the head.

The real secret, as explained in Abbott's "Buzz Saw Illusion" manuscript, is more ingenious yet. Both the head and legs are real. What is fake is the body. In effect, the buzz saw illusion uses a "cabinet" that is shaped like the woman's torso.

The illusion's wood structure incorporates a buzz saw and a mobile table. By means of a crank, the table can be moved under and past the blade of the stationary saw. The table surface hides a large rectangular depression (about 28⅞ inches long by 13½ inches wide by 7¼ inches deep). But the table is just about at audience eye level, so the depression is not noticeable.

As a preliminary demonstration, a strip of wood is secured to the table with a metal holder. The wood and holder bridges the hollowed-out part of the table. Unknown to the audience, the wood has been precut most of the way through. The uncut side is up. The buzz saw is switched on, and the table is drawn under the blade. When the wood is removed, it breaks easily in two.

Under her dress, the woman wears a strip-metal framework conforming to the back of her torso. This is secured with snaps on the abdomen side. The framework includes a strip of flesh-colored cardboard near the intended site of the cut.

As the woman lies down on the table, the billows of her dress—and a conveniently placed assistant—prevent the audience from seeing what is going on. The woman unsnaps the framework. Her midsection sags into the hollow. The framework, held in place by projections, seems to rest on a flat table.

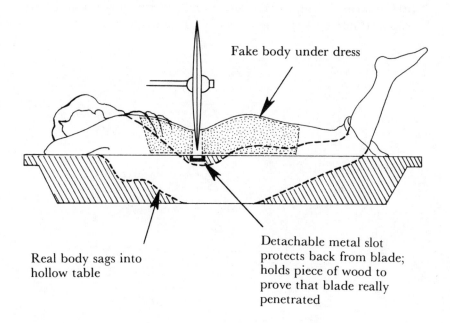

Fake body under dress

Real body sags into
hollow table

Detachable metal slot
protects back from blade;
holds piece of wood to
prove that blade really
penetrated

As a safety measure, the magician and his assistant reinsert the metal holder and a new wood strip "under" the woman's body. Ostensibly this is so the wood will be sawn in two and can be offered as evidence of penetration. Actually, the wood and metal holder go just over the woman's back, through a slot in the torso framework. The wood and metal thus protect the woman's back from the blade.

The swayback position is awkward but safe. Because the fake

body is cloaked in the dress, it does not have to be as well crafted as the fake legs in the "Thin Model" sawing illusion. By and large, audience suspicion is directed to the head and legs, which are genuine. The pink cardboard "back" does not bear close examination, but it is covered up with a cape as soon as the blade is clear. The Abbott's plan recommends dim lighting and a red spotlight on the woman.

If there is any danger to the illusion, it is incidental. The plan warns to take care that the woman's hair does not get caught in the belt driving the blade. The woman must keep her legs vertical, lest they come too close to the blade. The saw is of low power (three-quarter horsepower is suggested). It cuts a dress and pink cardboard but goes through wood with difficulty.

21·

Uri Geller's Blindfold Drive

Uri Geller has, in effect, been blacklisted from national television since talk-show hosts realized his feats were accomplished by trickery. After all, Geller's best-known effects are nontricks—tricks so unspectacular that no avowed magician would bother with them. Seeing a spoon bent or a watch started is exciting only if you believe Geller's claims of some weird supernatural power. Once you know it's a trick, it is easy to figure out.

Geller nonetheless continues to draw crowds of believers to his lectures/demonstrations. And not all of his effects are as easy to explain away as those bent spoons.

His demonstrations include "telepathy." An audience volunteer writes the name of a city or of a color on a blackboard, well out of sight of Geller. Geller correctly identifies the volunteer's choice.

Geller produces ten identical aluminum film cans. A volunteer secretly fills one of the cans with water and reseals it. The ten cans are placed in front of Geller. Without ever touching the cans, he successively eliminates those without water by pointing at them. The last can is found to be the one with the water. (This is one of the tricks that Johnny Carson, a former magician, foiled by keeping a guard on the test materials prior to a Geller *Tonight Show* appearance. Had Geller been a real psychic, Carson's precautions should not have made a difference.)

Geller claims offstage miracles as well. While eating lunch with astronaut Edgar Mitchell, Geller "materialized" a strange piece of metal in a mouthful of vanilla ice cream. Later the same day, another piece of metal materialized out of thin air. When the two pieces were put together, Mitchell recognized them as a tiepin he had lost years earlier.

From the standpoint of conventional magic, the best of Geller's tricks is a blindfold drive sometimes performed as a publicity stunt. Geller is securely blindfolded and then drives a car through city streets. He claims that he sees his way telepathically through the eyes of his passengers.

Geller is not the only performer to do the trick. The Astonishing Neil, another quasipsychic, put on an elaborate, televised version of the stunt for a *Real People* segment. Neil molded a thick layer of clay over his eyes, then blindfolded himself, and then tied a black hood over his head. He was taken to a town he had never been in before and given a map he had never seen before. He drove at moderate speed thus blindfolded, following the directions with the map. He also drove at high speed through a parking lot, managing not to hit volunteers standing at random points in the lot.

In 1975 magician James Randi (The Amazing Randi) wrote an exposé of Geller, *The Magic of Uri Geller* (New York: Ballantine Books), in which Randi insisted that the blindfold drive, as all of Geller's stunts, was done without psychic help. Being a magician himself, however, Randi did not tell how the trick is done.

Everybody Needs Friends

Part of Geller's secret is two friends who hide themselves in the audience during performances. For much of Geller's "telepathy," the entire audience sees the word being transmitted. Geller's accomplices are thought to signal to him.

Shipi Shtrang is a male Israeli several years younger than Geller. Shtrang has dark, wavy hair and looks like he could be Geller's younger brother. Shtrang stays out of the spotlight. He is rarely photographed—though a picture appears in Uri Geller's *My Story* (New York: Praeger, 1975). Geller met Shtrang when Geller was his counselor at a children's camp. The two collaborated on what seems to have been a basic vaudeville mind-reading act ("What is the woman holding up? *Watch* you don't miss it!"), playing small Israeli nightclubs. Leaving Israel, they classed up the act by claiming that Geller has real psychic powers. Shtrang may have helped Geller through his Stanford Research Institute tests by signaling answers.

Geller's other confederate, Solveig Clark, is an attractive, blond, American woman. According to David Marks, a psychologist at the University of Otago in New Zealand who observed Geller during a New Zealand tour, Clark frequently sits in an unoccupied section of the theater, in clear view of Geller. When an audience volunteer writes the name of a color on a chalkboard, Clark relays the name of the color to Geller with hand signals. Geller counts "one, two, three"; the "three" is Clark's cue to signal. Marks identified two of the signals: Waving the hands up and down while the wrists rest on top of the seat in front means "blue." When Clark folds her arms and pats her upper left arm with her right hand, it's "purple."

The Film Cans

There are several ways to do the trick with the ten sealed film cans. Geller eliminates the cans one by one, ending up with the one containing water. The magicians who have exposed the trick seem not to be sure which method Geller uses, but plainly there is little reason to assume clairvoyance. In brief, Geller could (a) breathe on the cans to see which one collects dew; (b) bump the table to see which can moves less; (c) check the adhesive tape around the lids for signs of resealing (before the subject fills one of the cans, Geller could make sure that all cans have a small, precise amount of overlap of the ends of the tape); or (d), the quick and dirty approach, shake the cans during a moment when no one is around.

The Tiepin Miracle

The simplest and most convincing analysis of Geller's offstage miracles credits simple, bold cheating. Geller somehow got hold of a "lost" tiepin of Mitchell's. (Martin Gardner has suggested Geller looked under the seats of Mitchell's car.) Geller broke the pin in two, then popped one piece into his mouth while coughing at lunch. Later he tossed the other piece in the air when no one was looking.

The Blindfold Drive

The blindfold drive is explained in "Sightless Vision," a manuscript that is sold, complete with hood, by Louis Tannen, Inc. The full "Sightless Vision" routine is too slick for Geller's purposes (Geller must take care that his tricks don't look like magic tricks), but the method seems certain to be the same.

The "Sightless Vision" performer produces an assortment of blindfolding gear: a handkerchief, aluminum foil, cotton balls, masking tape, powder puffs, bread dough, cardboard, and a black hood. Audience volunteers are invited to inspect the material. All are indeed found to be opaque. The volunteers assist in blindfolding the performer. A cardboard mask goes over the eyes, then lumps of dough, then silver dollars, and so forth. This material is held in place by wrapping gauze around the head and taping. Then the black hood goes over the head and is tied at the neck.

The performer is able to describe the dress of audience members. He can name objects they hold up. A plank may be placed across two supports, and audience volunteers can place their watches on the plank. The performer can walk the plank without stepping on the watches or falling off. And, of course, the performer can drive a car safely through city streets.

At the end of the demonstration, the sundry layers of the blindfold are ceremoniously removed. All are intact.

There is no way the performer could do all that he does unless he is able to see reasonably well while blindfolded. The trick is to make sure that the gauze or handkerchief is not tied too tightly. Although audience members help in fixing the gauze, they rarely pull it tightly for fear of hurting the performer. As the performer pulls the hood down over his head, he shoves the gauze, dough, cardboard, etc., down just enough to see over them.

Part of the hood is of single-thickness cloth. (When the performer demonstrates the hood to an audience member, he makes sure the opaque part goes over the eyes.) By looking over the gauze/dough assembly and through the thin part of the hood, the performer has serviceable vision. He must hitch up the gauze before removing the hood.

Geller's blindfold is less elaborate, but there can be little doubt that he can see through his blindfold, too. A single thickness of an ordinary silk handkerchief is reasonably transparent when pulled tight close to the eyes. Two thicknesses are nearly opaque. Geller only has to fold a handkerchief so that a crack of single-thickness silk is left to see through.

22.

Doug Henning's Vanishing Horse and Rider

A faked accident draws gasps at the climax of this illusion. As performed in *Merlin,* Doug Henning rides a small horse into a cratelike structure. (On television, Henning has used a motorcycle.) Initially, the front of the wood structure is open so that the audience can see both Henning and the horse. Four heavy chains slowly raise the structure from the floor of the stage. Henning and the horse are still visible, and the crate is isolated from the floor, the sides of the stage, the backdrop, and the ceiling. There seems to be nowhere for Henning and the horse to go. Then the crate—which looked rickety all along—suddenly collapses. A horse's muffled whinny is heard—but Henning and the horse have vanished. Only the edges of the crate remain in place; the bottom and back sides dangle below.

A second or two later, Henning and the horse (or motorcycle) are revealed safe in a distant part of the stage or in a separate, suspended frame. The audience is left wondering not only how the trick was done but also how the horse was trained to perform whatever moves may be required of it.

Vanishing Techniques

There are only three basic ways to make a person vanish. One is to lower the person through a trapdoor in the stage. The second is to conceal the person with a judicious placement of mirrors. The third is to conceal the person behind a panel or curtain that blends into the background. Henning uses all three methods in his repertoire of illusions.

At another point in *Merlin,* for instance, Henning sits in a simple chair, well away from the backdrop and sides of the stage. A blue cloth is draped over Henning and the chair. A few seconds later, the cloth is snatched away. Henning is gone. (The chair is still there.) Henning then reappears from another part of the stage.

This effect appears identical to a very old illusion using a trapdoor under the chair. A wire frame maintains the shape of the body in the chair as the performer drops through the seat of the chair (it's on a hinge) and a trapdoor beneath. The wire frame is drawn away with the cloth.

Use of mirrors was apparent on "Doug Henning's Magic on Broadway" TV special. Henning made a woman and a million dollars appear and disappear from a transparent cubical box. The box rested on what appeared to be a simple four-legged table. For each appearance and disappearance, the box was covered with an opaque screen.

Anyone familiar with magic would have suspected an "Owens table"—a table with vertical mirrors running between the legs. The mirrors reflect the floor or carpet so that it looks as if you are seeing the carpet under and behind the table. Actually, there is a secret space between the mirrors. The woman and the money could have been hidden in this space to effect a disappearance.

The trouble with the Owens table is that the mirrors must be aligned just right for the perspective of the audience (or TV camera). In at least one camera shot of Henning's special, the mirrors were noticeably out of alignment. The reflection of the floor was a little higher than the floor itself. This was particularly evident if you looked at the line where the floor met the backdrop. It zig-zagged as it went "behind" the legs of the table.

The third method is the simplest, but its use is limited. With suitable misdirection, a person may be hidden behind a panel matching the background. This is just the large-scale version of the false bottom in a magician's hat. Usually, the edges of the panel must be concealed. Dark colors, dim lighting, and a distant audience are preferred.

Two Horses, a Henning Look-Alike

If you give the horse-and-rider illusion some thought, you'll realize that there have to be two horses and two riders. The fake Henning has to be the first one, the one who vanishes. Before the illusion, no one expects a substitution. Henning has opportunity to duck offstage and send in his double. The Henning who reappears, however, has to stand up to the scrutiny of a suspicious audience.

The double used in *Merlin* is no dead ringer for Henning. As the crate is being raised, he looks away from the audience and waves, raising his arm so that it blocks his face.

Granting the switch, we are still left with an impressive illusion. The rider, who as it happens is not Henning, and the horse, which is alive, genuine, and heavy, both suddenly disappear far above the stage floor. The illusion is again an old one. It was devised by Clayton L. Jacobsen, who called it the "Vanishing Motorcycle and Rider" and explained it in *The Seven Circles,* a magazine for magicians. The idea of using a horse instead of a motorcycle was likewise Jacobsen's.

The crate must be sturdy. As the crate is being raised, the front is opened. The front is closed just before the disappearance. The bottom of the crate is equipped with a movable shelf that slides out toward the back (away from the audience). In fact, there is no back to the crate, so horse and rider both slide back the instant they are out of the audience's sight. A roller curtain made of the same material as the backdrop is pulled down in front of the horse and rider.

Then the crate "collapses." Actually, the crate edges, the secret shelf, and the curtain remain. The horse and rider are both still up there, behind a curtain that is indistinguishable from the backdrop. (Or, in a variation of the method, the fake backdrop is stretched between two of the supporting chains. Horse and rider are lifted up and out of sight by means of cables and a harness.) The frightened-horse sound is probably a recording. All that either horse must do is stand still and not be frightened by the commotion.

If the audience looked at the crate long enough, they might suspect the false backdrop. But they don't. Before anyone quite realizes what has happened, the real Henning is revealed—and attention shifts to him.

Henning look-alike and
horse hide on secret shelf
behind frame . . .
concealed by a roller
curtain that matches the
backdrop

Audience sees the crate
"fall apart"

Meanwhile, the real
Henning (on identical
horse) is somewhere else
entirely.

23·

The Amazing Kreskin's Social Security Number Divination

The Amazing Kreskin (a.k.a. George Kresge, Jr.) says he has extrasensory perception. Much of what Kreskin does is amazing, but nothing more so than his "telepathic" divination of audience Social Security numbers. Many millions of people have seen the trick on television, and it is one of the most difficult effects to explain. No other well-known magician seems to perform it. Magic catalogs do not sell a manuscript for it. The more gullible among Kreskin's audience readily swallow his claims of supernatural powers. The less gullible are driven to ridiculous extremes in attempting to explain the trickery.

Some think the audience subjects are accomplices. Some think Kreskin lip-reads from subjects who unconsciously mouth the digits while concentrating on their Social Security numbers. It has been suggested seriously that Kreskin plants hidden microphones or cameras in the theaters; that his Coke-bottle-thick glasses are a pair of telescope lenses; that he goes on a pickpocketing spree while mingling with the audience before the show. Or maybe he canvasses the parking lot, takes down license plate numbers, then phones the Department of Motor Vehicles to get the vehicle owners' Social Security numbers.

The intriguing thing about the trick is its apparent simplicity. Kreskin just concentrates on the number and gets it. Sometimes he writes the number on a board; sometimes he announces the digits in slow succession. Kreskin fumbles a lot, but he's rarely if ever wrong. He'll say: "I'm getting a 6, but I'm not sure it's the next digit"; "3-4-0, no, wait, maybe 3-5-0"; and so forth. He solicits minor help from the subject: "Is there a double digit?" "Just tell me, the next digit isn't a 4, is it? I think I'm getting a 4 from somebody else in the audience." But an occasional uh-huh or shake of the head can be of little consequence in selecting the correct nine-digit number out of a billion possibilities.

Sometimes an audience member is chosen before Kreskin starts reading his or her number. At other times, Kreskin starts announcing the digits of a number he is receiving, and then someone recognizes it as his number and stands up.

A few would-be explanations can be dismissed immediately. It is not, it seems, a necessary condition of the trick that the subjects take their Social Security cards out of their wallets. So Kreskin can't depend on spies to read the cards over the subjects' shoulders and signal the digits. Nor are the subjects themselves in cahoots with Kreskin. If you attend consecutive stage performances or videotape talk-show appearances, you'll note that the subjects are indeed different people every time. Unless Kreskin has a veritable army of accomplices, the subjects must be innocent audience members.

A Typical TV Performance

Kreskin's telepathy is not limited to Social Security numbers. In a typical performance, he reads names, dates, places, phone numbers, license plate numbers, and other personal information that he should have no way of knowing.

During an appearance on *The Mike Douglas Entertainment Hour* aired in February 1982, Kreskin scored five hits—and some misses (dialog approximate):

> KRESKIN: I'm getting the names "Chris" and "Elaine."
> (A man stands up.)
> SUBJECT 1: Chris and Elaine are my kids.
> KRESKIN: Do you have another child?
> SUBJECT 1: Yes.
> KRESKIN: Does the initial J mean anything to you?
> SUBJECT 1: Yes.
> KRESKIN: Joan?
> SUBJECT 1: Joan is my third child.
> (Man sits down.)
> KRESKIN: I'm getting something about a right shoulder. Is anyone having problems with a right shoulder? (Pause) I'm also getting the word "Jamaca."
> (Woman stands up.)

SUBJECT 2: That's the street where I live.

KRESKIN: I get something about a wedding ring, too. (Pause) Could you please concentrate on your Social Security number? Three . . . nine . . . three . . . seven . . . zero . . . four . . . seven . . . seven . . . six.

SUBJECT 2: That's correct.

(Woman sits down.)

KRESKIN: Institute of fashion, something about an institute of fashion. I'm getting Chicago, too.

(Woman stands up.)

KRESKIN: Are you from Chicago?

SUBJECT 3: That's right.

KRESKIN: Does institute of fashion mean anything to you?

SUBJECT 3: Not really. I'm going to college . . .

KRESKIN: Does the college have anything to do with fashion?

SUBJECT 3: No.

KRESKIN: But I do get that you're thinking of your favorite actor. Is that correct?

SUBJECT 3: Yes.

KRESKIN: I'm getting . . . Cary Grant.

SUBJECT 3: Right.

(Woman sits down.)

KRESKIN: I'm getting the name "Colleen," or maybe it's "Maureen." (Pause) Someone here had a flat tire last Thursday night.

(Man stands up.)

SUBJECT 4: I did.

KRESKIN: You had a flat tire?

SUBJECT 4: Yes.

KRESKIN: And it was last Thursday night?

SUBJECT 4: Yes.

KRESKIN: Does Colleen or Maureen mean anything to you?

SUBJECT 4: No.

(Man sits down.)

KRESKIN: Golden . . . the word "golden" . . . I'm getting Colorado, it's the town of Golden, Colorado. (Pause) I get skiing . . .

(Man stands up.)

SUBJECT 5: Yes.

KRESKIN: What does Golden, Colorado, mean to you?

SUBJECT 5: I just went skiing there.

KRESKIN: Does the year 1979 mean anything to you?

SUBJECT 5: I was married in 1979.
(Man sits down.)
KRESKIN: Has someone here lost a bracelet? Or found a lost bracelet?
(No one acknowledges it.)

Kreskin's mind reading is far from perfect, but he's right about a lot of things that could not have been lucky guesses.

Does Kreskin Have ESP?

According to Kreskin, it's all perfectly paranormal. He defends his claims of ESP in an autobiography, *The Amazing World of Kreskin* (New York: Random House, 1973):

> ... I do pick up information through a kind of telepathy. By deep concentration, "tuning in," I seek out and then "receive" a single thought, provided the "sender" is concentrating to an almost equal depth. Some debunkers have claimed it is an ability to "muscle read" a subject's face, to decipher clues given unconsciously by the subject. This may well be a factor of ESP, as natural as an eye blink, but I am not aware of it. The reaction on the subject's face may unconsciously increase my perception of the thought, but it does not reveal the thought unless an absolute "yes" or "no" answer is involved. Anyone can usually read a positive or negative simply by studying eye register.
>
> More than all this, if I perceive a Social Security number secreted in a purse at two hundred feet in a darkened theater, muscle reaction is of little help in determining the numbers and their sequence. The only source is the subject's concentration. His or her face, at that distance, is but a small shadowy object. ... I don't have the talents to see through the cloth of a lady's purse or through the leather of a man's wallet, wherein usually lies the small card on which the Social Security number is imprinted. So the only possible method is to read it with and through the mind of the cooperating sitting or standing subject. On receiving his or her signal, I project the numbers, visualizing them almost instantly. "The number is 225-12-6018." ... So while talking to an audience, I'm constantly writing, although I'm not really aware of the pencil movement. The material is usually ahead of what I'm trying to say to the audience or receive from them. ... I do not always look at what the pencil has written on my note pad. *225-12-6018.* I am not always confident it will be cor-

rect. Most of the time, though, the written number will match the verbal projection.

Yet Kreskin admits to using ordinary magician's sleight of hand in other parts of his act. His stage act includes conventional magic (card tricks and the like) and a comic hypnosis routine as well as the mind-reading feats.

How Kreskin Does It

The most comprehensive analysis of Kreskin's mind reading is to be found in *The Psychology of the Psychic* by David Marks and Richard Kammann, two New Zealand psychologists (Buffalo, N.Y.: Prometheus Books, 1980). Marks and Kammann attended a 1974 stage performance by Kreskin in Dunedin, New Zealand. After the show, they advertised in local newspapers for Kreskin's subjects. Interviews with the subjects who responded allowed Marks and Kammann to figure out how Kreskin did what he did.

Of course, the Social Security number trick is performed in the United States only. Marks and Kammann did not see it and thus did not cover it in their explication of Kreskin's techniques.

Big Secrets located one of Kreskin's American subjects. From his description of Kreskin's "mind reading," as well as Marks' and Kammann's analysis and Kreskin's televised performances, it is possible to deduce how Kreskin reads Social Security numbers. The trick is a gem of the magician's art. It uses misdirection, sleight of hand, and an entirely novel means of deception: the television talk show.

To understand how the trick works on television, let's first review Kreskin's stage act. Kreskin warms up his nightclub audience with some routine magic tricks and a few "experiments" to test the audience's vibes. Two examples of the latter:

1. "I am thinking of two simple geometric shapes, one inside the other," says Kreskin. "Concentrate, try to receive my thoughts, and project them on your mental screen."

2. "I'm thinking of a number between 1 and 50. Both digits are odd, but they aren't the same odd digit—15 would be okay, but not 11. Try to project the number on your mental screen."

(Do you have ESP? Draw the two shapes and write the number on a sheet of paper. Then turn to page 179.)

Next comes the mind reading. Kreskin invites the audience to write down any thoughts they want to send. He goes into the audience, dispensing paper, pencils, and envelopes. During the five minutes or so it takes to distribute materials and write messages, Kreskin jokes with audience members or fills up the time with patter about ESP. Then Kreskin instructs the audience to fold their completed messages and place them in envelopes (Marks' and Kammann's subjects) or to throw their messages on the floor (*Big Secrets'* subject). When the envelopes are used, they are given to audience members at the ends of rows for safekeeping. This done, the mind reading begins.

At the performance Marks and Kammann witnessed, Kreskin later went back into the audience, carrying his clipboard (the one he uses to write some of his predictions). He asked some of the people holding the envelopes to take a few folded messages and place them on his clipboard. Kreskin emphasized the fact that he did not so much as touch the slips of paper. Using the clipboard as a tray for the messages, Kreskin returned to the stage, sat down, and placed the clipboard beside him. He explained that he was going to try an experiment in thought transmission. Three volunteers were selected. Each took a message from the clipboard and (per Kreskin's instructions) read it, memorized it, and tore it up. One by one the volunteers concentrated on their messages. Each time, Kreskin divined the messages word for word. The rest of the audience had to take the volunteer's word for the accuracy of Kreskin's mind reading, though.

There is more to Kreskin's stage act, but the foregoing segments are the ones that bear on Kreskin's method for reading Social Security numbers. To the audience, it may seem that Kreskin uses the same technique, whatever it may be, throughout the mind-reading part of his act. In fact, there is reason to believe that Kreskin uses four or more distinct methods.

Let's start with the simplest. Many of Kreskin's readings work by nothing more than well-calculated luck. Take the following hypothetical exchange:

> KRESKIN: Does the date September 11 mean anything special to anyone?
> SUBJECT: Yes.
> KRESKIN: Is it a birthday, an anniversary?
> SUBJECT: It's my daughter's anniversary.

KRESKIN: I see something about your daughter and an automobile.
SUBJECT: She just bought a car.

Now think about it. There are hundreds of people in the audience. Everyone has a birthday. Most people have other special days. No matter what date Kreskin names, it is almost certain to draw a response.

Once someone claims September 11, Kreskin goes for a second match. This time he has to play it safe because he already has his subject. The subject admitted a daughter, so Kreskin sees something about the daughter and an automobile. Again, almost everyone can think of "something about an automobile." Kreskin is vague and lets the subject fill in the details. He knows that much of the audience will soon forget who said what first. Many will go home honestly believing that Kreskin divined the date of a subject's daughter's anniversary and the fact that she had purchased a car.

As it happened, Kreskin's luck was bad on the *Mike Douglas* guest shot mentioned above. Out of five or six attempts at a lucky coincidence, five fell flat. "Right shoulder," "wedding ring," "institute of fashion," "Colleen or Maureen," and "lost bracelet" all seem to have been guesses; "1979" may have been. The trick is to select associations rare enough to astonish those who claim them and yet common enough to make a coincidence likely. Perhaps Kreskin tailors his predictions to the size of the audience, going for more offbeat associations when the house is large. In any case, Kreskin has learned to recognize a dead end and wastes no time moving to another prediction when one fails.

Kreskin's second technique apparently is to steal a few of the messages he has his audience write. *Big Secrets'* informant noted that Kreskin "mind-read" the very same messages his party had written and thrown on the floor. Marks and Kammann say they actually saw Kreskin palm messages and put them in his pocket.

Most of the audience assumes that all the messages are still on the floor or in the envelopes. So they don't necessarily think it suspicious when Kreskin mind-reads the same thoughts they wrote down. Kreskin has told them to write the thoughts they want to transmit. Even if a subject is not concentrating on the same message during the mind reading, his thoughts can hardly help but return to his original message once Kreskin announces a key word of it. The subject *will* be thinking of his written message as Kreskin hems and haws, revealing it bit by bit.

Kreskin scribbles on his note pad a lot, and maybe he uses it as a scratch sheet. It probably isn't always convenient to reveal a palmed message right after looking at it. Kreskin may save himself the trouble of remembering complex messages by writing them on his board.

Speaking of the writing board, Marks and Kammann suspect that it is a "magician's tray"—a standard prop with two bottoms, allowing a quick switch of written messages.

The board looks a little funny. It has two flaps that allow Kreskin to use it as a tray for his "thought transference experiment" messages. But Kreskin does his best to allay suspicion. He uses the board for his notes all along, and he explains that he uses it for the written messages only to demonstrate that he does not touch the messages.

Could Kreskin steal a glance at the messages while they are in the tray? Maybe . . . many people fold their messages only once. If Kreskin is quick enough, he might glimpse a word or two while maintaining his patter and eye contact. But it takes more than that to explain Kreskin's accuracy. Despite his usual false starts, Kreskin reveals the messages verbatim. His accuracy in the thought-transference experiment seems much higher than in his general mind reading.

Marks and Kammann note that Kreskin always sets his tray/writing board down on the stage before proceeding. The flaps fold when the board is set down. When Kreskin picks the board back up, he apparently opens it to a second bottom containing a set of prepared messages. The prepared messages would be written by Kreskin and memorized before the show. Kreskin could get away with this because of the way the thought-transference experiment is set up. The people concentrating on the messages are not the people who wrote them but an arbitrary set of volunteers (often people in the front row). The volunteers have no way of knowing if the messages are fakes. Neither does the rest of the audience.

Kreskin does not ask for the original authors of these messages to reveal themselves. Marks' and Kammann's series of newspaper ads located eight of eleven visible audience participants from the

Kreskin performance they attended. But they failed to locate a single person who had written a message used in the thought-transference experiment. (They located all three of the volunteers who concentrated on the messages.) The most natural conclusion is that no one wrote the messages—no one other than Kreskin himself.

Kreskin may use still a fourth technique. In his biography, Kreskin says that he takes a long walk before every performance to improve his concentration. If so, he could easily manage a detour through the theater or studio parking lot. He could note license plate numbers and makes of cars. (Describing cars often is part of Kreskin's act.) Or better yet, Kreskin may look for bumper stickers and personal articles inside cars. Say Kreskin spots a car with a Missouri license plate, a racquetball sticker, and a child's toy and a Szechuan cookbook in the back seat. It isn't hard to imagine how he could weave this information into a fantastic demonstration of "mind reading."

By mixing these different techniques, Kreskin throws skeptics off the track. An explanation that works for one reading can't work for others. Kreskin mixes techniques even with a single subject. He may read the name of a subject's hometown (from a palmed written message) and then ask if he or she is thinking about a relative (a likely guess). Kreskin probably resorts to occasional ad hoc tricks, too. During a performance, Kreskin once mentioned that he had the feeling someone was wondering what happened to the rest of a twenty-dollar bill. A shocked waitress almost dropped her tray, Kreskin claims. She had just found half of a twenty-dollar bill on the floor, minutes earlier. It isn't hard to guess who lost it.

The Magic of Television

Back to the Social Security number trick. Of the millions who have seen the trick, it is significant that only a slim minority have seen it in person. The rest have seen it only on TV. It's a safe bet that most of those who have seen it live first saw it on TV. The public conception of what the trick is and how Kreskin performs it is derived almost entirely from TV.

That shouldn't make a difference, but it does. Granted, there is a long tradition, going back to the infancy of television, that no camera trickery is used in televised magic, that "you are seeing exactly what the studio audience is seeing." Kreskin, however, has devised the best camera trick of all—that of having the cameras turned off during a part of the Social Security number trick that is essential to understanding how the trick is done. It isn't that Mike, Merv, and Johnny are in on the trick. But Kreskin is aware of the time constraints of a TV talk show and has discovered how to use them to his advantage.

Which of his techniques does Kreskin use for Social Security numbers? A lucky guess is out. So are switched messages—Kreskin reads the numbers of people who stand up for everyone to see. Nothing Kreskin sees in the parking lot is likely to help him, either. That leaves the stolen-message technique.

The only necessary assumption is that some audience members write down their Social Security numbers as a message. Given Kreskin's reputation for reading Social Security numbers, this is an obvious choice. It takes no imagination; it's unique—no one else has the same Social Security number; yet for the shy, it's not too personal. If need be, Kreskin can hint that a Social Security number would be okay as a message.

The farther removed you are from Kreskin's "mind reading," the better it looks. Kreskin's subjects know they wrote the messages Kreskin reads. If they are of a skeptical turn of mind, they must suspect trickery. Nonsubject audience members know the entire audience wrote messages beforehand—but they probably attach little importance to it. Kreskin's TV audience is even more at a loss.

Obviously, Kreskin can't do his whole act on TV. What you usually see is this: The host introduces Kreskin, they chat briefly, and Kreskin goes right into his mind reading. He reads Social Security numbers, names, addresses, license plates, and other personal information, much of which couldn't be a lucky guess.

What you *don't* see is Kreskin passing out slips of paper for written messages, just as in the stage act. He may do this before the taping begins, in a commercial break, or within the sequence of the show if the tape will be edited for broadcast.

Kreskin explains the messages as a means of preparing the audience for telepathy and improving his rapport. Kreskin makes sure it takes several minutes to distribute paper, write messages, and collect them—dull, boring minutes in which nothing is happening; bad television. A tightly scheduled talk show cannot possibly allow five or ten minutes of what amounts to dead air. (An entire guest segment may be less than ten minutes.) So the host and producer see nothing wrong with handling Kreskin's preliminaries off-camera.

The omission is crucial. To the studio audience, Kreskin's Social Security number trick is pretty good. But to the home TV audience, which never suspects the written messages, it is incredible and seamless—a trick so inexplicable that many are prepared to believe it is no mere trick at all.

Finding the Paycheck

Kreskin does another trick that seems beyond the realm of ordinary prestidigitation. Near the end of each stage show, he locates his hidden paycheck "telepathically."

While Kreskin is offstage, a team of about four persons hides the paycheck. They are permitted to hide the check anywhere in the theater. It need not be in plain sight. After Kreskin returns, he warns the audience not to do or say anything to give the hiding place away. Kreskin wanders the theater with the team of hiders, looking for the check. Usually Kreskin holds one end of a handkerchief, and a hider holds the other end as Kreskin searches.

Kreskin is remarkably accurate. He forefeits his check (it goes to a charity of his choosing, actually) if he fails to find it. This has happened three times. Kreskin almost always finds the check before people start to get bored. He is expected actually to produce the check: If, say, it is hidden in a woman's purse, he must not only find the right woman but also ask her to open her purse and find the check inside.

Kreskin has a standing offer of twenty thousand dollars to anyone who can prove that he uses confederates in this trick. Moreover, the hiders are typically people known to many members of the audience—local celebrities, such as mayors, police chiefs, casino executives—so that complicity will not be suspected.

If Kreskin seems paranoid on this point, it's because the trick would be very easy to perform with a confederate. Everyone in the audience sees where the check is hidden, so a plant could direct Kreskin with a few discreet signals.

Most likely, the trick is legitimate. Kreskin probably does it by skillfully observing the reactions of the hiders and his audience. As in some of his mind-reading tricks, there's safety in numbers. Kreskin can count on there being a few people in every large audience who will give things away. They may keep glancing back to the hiding place or muttering to their neighbors when he makes a crucial turn. As to Kreskin's hiders, his admonitions not to show any reaction make it all the harder for them not to do so.

Other magicians can do cruder versions of this stunt; Kreskin is simply very good at it from years of practice. As he explains in his biography, he started as a child, playing the game of Hot and Cold:

> A player leaves the room and the rest of the class hides a bean bag. The player returns and begins to look for the bag, with the class shouting "Getting hotter" or "Getting colder." . . . Wouldn't it be great, I told my parents, if the object could be found without all the directions, just by having the "hiders" think about where it was? With the blessing of childhood, I didn't know the rules—what could be done, what couldn't. I tried it with my parents and had no success, naturally. They lost interest.
>
> But then I persuaded [my brother] Joe to try it. I literally forced him to practice with me for about four months. By the end of that time I could find almost any object in our small, cluttered room without him saying "hot" or "cold." I had no idea what I was doing, nor how much I was reading his facial expressions (a lot, probably) as I neared the object, but now I realize I was blindly beginning to train myself in sensitivity and ESP.

ESP? If Kreskin had it, he wouldn't need to palm messages for the mind reading. Kreskin's skill in finding his paycheck is remarkable, but there's no reason to assume it is anything supernatural.

Answers to ESP Test

Look at the opposite page. No ESP here. These tricks work because most people's minds work much the same way. No. 1? Figure that there are only three simple shapes (circle, square, triangle) that people are likely to think of. The most popular pair is the circle and triangle—no one knows why, but that's how it works out—and the civil defense symbol configuration is slightly

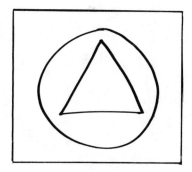

1. "A triangle in a circle—or the other way around."

2. "Thirty-seven. Actually, I was thinking of 35 first, but I changed my mind."

favored. As usual, Kreskin plays both sides of the street. No. 2? It sounds as if there are almost twenty-five numbers to choose from. Really there are only eight: 13, 15, 17, 19, 31, 35, 37, and 39. And hardly anyone picks 15 because Kreskin mentioned it. About a third of the population picks 37, and another quarter pick 35. Those that pick 35 are scarcely less impressed to hear that Kreskin rejected it.

The catch is, these tricks can't be done for the same audience twice. Kreskin doesn't repeat them when he has more than one show in a town. He can't ever do them on national television.

PART SIX

Always the Last to Know

You should have suspected that something important was being bumped when they started running Wishing Well and Jumble on the front page. But aren't all newspapers playing up features to compete with TV? A few weeks later, you can't remember either of your state's senators. You're living in a soft-news fantasy world—a world where nothing that happens in Washington or Beijing is ever more important than local high school basketball. A world called Knight-Ridder, Gannett, or Newhouse. Everyone said it couldn't happen in your town—until the day the capitalists took over the newspapers.

Soon there's a new managing editor—and a new slant to the lead photo captions ("The weatherman says fall doesn't arrive till 2:09 P.M. Friday, but try telling that to these little pixies . . . the Molenar quads of 2491 Euclid Avenue.") There's an increased emphasis on TV listings, Erma Bombeck, and 4-H news (each in a separate four-color pullout). Then one day you wake up and realize you're reading the kind of newspaper that gets excerpted at the bottom of columns in *The New Yorker*. Rest assured—obscene though your paper's return on investment may be, it is never too late to find out what is really going on. With today's media, you have to read between the lines.

24·

Did Neil Armstrong
Blow His Lines?

Yep. What Neil Armstrong meant to say was, "That's one small step for a man, one giant leap for mankind." But that isn't quite what he said.

The radio transmissions from the *Apollo 11* lunar module were of somewhat poor quality. If you listen to a tape of the transmissions, however, there can be little doubt as to what Armstrong did say. After setting foot on the moon, Armstrong pauses a second or two and says,

> *That's one small step for man,*
> *one giant leap for mankind.*

The omitted "a" is a small mistake but a particularly unfortunate one. "Man" without a preceding article means not one man but man in general, mankind. So Armstrong said, in effect, that's one small step for mankind and one giant leap for mankind. He managed to create a logical contradiction in the first eleven words spoken while standing on another planet.

The slip of the tongue is understandable. What's harder to understand is the way the blunder has been ignored. Despite the massive buildup given the first words on the moon's surface, no major news source seems to have mentioned the mistake, even in passing. Most newspapers and magazines at the time reported the quote accurately but without comment. *The New York Times* for July 21, 1969, noted,

> ... Mr. Armstrong opened the landing craft's hatch, stepped slowly down the ladder and declared as he planted the first human footprint on the lunar crust:

"That's one small step for man, one giant leap for mankind."

Life magazine didn't print Armstrong's historic words, an unusual omission even in a picture magazine.

Other sources have become more charitable yet (see table). Quite a few respectable sources now give a corrected version of the line. The 1980 edition of the *Encyclopaedia Britannica* says,

> At 10:56 PM EDT, July 20, 1969, Armstrong stepped from the "Eagle" onto the Moon's dusty surface with the words, "That's one small step for a man, one giant leap for mankind."

Accurate Quote but No Mention of Mistake	"Corrected" Quote	No Quote
The New York Times	Encyclopaedia Britannica	Life
The Washington Post	Encyclopedia Americana	
The Los Angeles Times	Collier's Encyclopedia	
Time	World Book Encyclope-	
Newsweek	dia (entry co-written	
Famous First Facts	by Wernher von	
	Braun)	
	People's Almanac	
	Reader's Digest	
	National Geographic	
	(article by Arm-	
	strong, Aldrin, and	
	Collins)	

Big Secrets' search of reference sources found only one complete account of Armstrong's words. This was in the relatively obscure *Academic American Encyclopedia,* 1980 edition (Princeton, N.J.: Aretê Publishing Company). David Dooling's entry on Neil Armstrong gives the real story:

> ... he planted his left foot on the lunar surface and proclaimed: "That's one small step for [a] man, one giant leap for mankind." He later said that he intended to say "a," but static on the tapes leaves this detail uncertain.

25·

Secret Radio Frequencies

Sandwiched into the gap between the AM and FM dials are hundreds of secret communications frequencies—some so secret that no one owns up to them. The usual consumer gear—AM/FM radios, TVs, CB radios—brings in only a small portion of the electromagnetic spectrum. To pick up the secret signals, you need a shortwave receiver—and you need to know the unlisted frequencies.

Allocation of radio frequencies is quirky. When you flip the TV dial from channel 6 to channel 7, you unknowingly jump over the entire FM radio band as well as such exotica as Secret Service communications and a special frequency designated for emergency use during prison riots. The U.S. government will provide information on unclassified allocations (those for the Coast Guard, Forestry Service, weather reports, etc.). But it is quiet about secret government frequencies and those of mysterious illegal broadcasters here and abroad.

Many shortwave-radio hobbyists keep track of the secret frequencies, however. Their findings appear in such publications as the *Confidential Frequency List* by Oliver P. Ferrell (Park Ridge, N.J.: Gilfer Associates, 1982 [periodically updated]), *How to Tune the Secret Shortwave Spectrum* by Harry L. Helms (Blue Ridge Summit, Pa.: TAB Books, 1981), and *The "Top Secret" Registry of U.S. Government Radio Frequencies* by Tom Kneitel (Commack, N.Y.: CRB Research, 1981 [periodically updated]). These and similar publications should be consulted for the most up-to-date listings. The selection below includes only the most noteworthy or inexplicable broadcasts.

Air Force One

Many of the in-flight phone calls from *Air Force One* are not scrambled and can be picked up by anyone with a shortwave radio. You just have to watch the newspapers for information on the President's travels and listen to the right frequencies shortly before landing or after takeoff at Andrews Air Force Base (when calls are less likely to be scrambled electronically). A presidential phone call is usually prefaced by a request for "Crown," the White House communications center.

Air Force One uses several frequencies, including those assigned to Andrews Air Force Base. Transmissions are on single, usually upper, sideband. The frequencies are nominally secret, but the frequency numbers have long since leaked out or have been discovered independently. It is suspected that wire services and TV news operations monitor them for leads. The reported frequencies (in kilohertz) are:

6,731	13,201
6,756	13,215
8,967	13,247
9,018	15,048
11,180	18,027

In addition, 162.685 MHz and 171.235 MHz are Secret Service frequencies used for *Air Force One* communications. The White House staff uses 162.850 MHz and 167.825 MHz. Secret Service channel "Oscar," 164.885 MHz, is used for the President's limousine. *Air Force Two* uses the same frequencies as *Air Force One*.

Although everyone concerned must know that outsiders may be eavesdropping, conversations are often surprisingly candid. (Shortwave-radio listeners heard the White House staff urging *Air Force Two* back to Washington after the 1981 attempt on President Reagan's life, complete with reports that then-Secretary of State Alexander Haig was "confusing everybody" with his claim of being "in control.") No law seems to forbid such eavesdropping. Ironically, it is illegal (Section 605 of the Communications Act of 1934) to reveal intercepted conversations to anyone else—that being regarded as the wireless equivalent of wiretapping. Even so, *The New York Times* has run snippets of *Air Force One* conversations.

Central Intelligence Agency

The CIA and other government agencies with clandestine operations are believed to have dozens of authorized frequencies, which may be rotated as needed to throw eavesdroppers off the track. Call letters are rarely used, and several government agencies may share the same frequencies. A further, rather thin veneer of security comes from the use of code words. Government surveillance operations use a common code: "Our friend" or "our boy" is the person being followed. "O" is his office; "R" is his residence. A "boat" is a car. Once apprehended, a suspect is a "package" and may be taken to the "kennel," the agents' headquarters. Does this fool anyone? Probably not.

Not all U.S. government broadcasts can be identified as to agency. Conversations are cryptic; letters to the Federal Communications Commission and Commerce Department bring form replies. These frequencies (in megahertz) have been identified with the CIA:

163.81
165.01
165.11
165.385
408.60

Drug Enforcement Administration

Reported frequencies are:

11,076 KHz	418.625
14,686	418.675
18,666	418.70
163.185MHz	418.725
163.535	418.75
165.235	418.775
165.285	418.80
165.29	418.825
172.00	418.875
172.05	418.90
172.20	418.925
415.60	418.95
416.05	418.975
416.20	419.00

Federal Bureau of Investigation

Reported frequencies are:

7,905 KHz	167.395
9,240	167.40
10,500	167.41
120.425 MHz (?)	167.425
149.375	167.435
163.31	167.45
163.485	167.46
163.81	167.475
163.825	167.485
163.835	167.50
163.875	167.51
163.885	167.525
163.91	167.55
163.925	167.56
163.935	167.575
163.95	167.585
163.96	167.60
163.975	167.61
163.985	167.625
164.26	167.635
164.275	167.65
164.41	167.66
164.46	167.675
165.525	167.685
166.50	167.70
167.15	167.71
167.21	167.725
167.22	167.735
167.235	167.75
167.25	167.76
167.26	167.775
167.275	167.785
167.285	167.805
167.30	167.875
167.31	167.925
167.325	167.985
167.335	168.885
167.36	406.20
167.375	406.25
167.385	406.275

406.30	414.30
406.325	414.35
406.35	414.375
406.375	414.40
406.40	414.425
406.45	414.45
408.85	414.475
408.875	414.50
408.90	414.525
408.925	414.55
408.95	414.575
408.975	415.75
409.00	417.075
409.025	417.15
409.05	417.40
409.10	417.45
409.15	417.50
409.175	417.55
409.20	419.20
409.25	419.225
411.025	419.25
411.075	419.275
412.425	419.30
412.45	419.325
412.475	419.35
412.50	419.375
412.55	419.40
412.575	419.425
413.425	419.45
413.55	419.475
413.975	419.50
414.00	419.525
414.025	419.55
414.05	419.575
414.075	467.95
414.10	
414.125	
414.15	
414.175	
414.20	
414.225	
414.25	
414.275	

Secret Service

Reported frequencies (in megahertz) are:

162.375	165.76
162.685	165.785
163.36	165.90
163.40	166.21
163.81	166.405
164.75	166.51
164.885	166.615
165.025	166.70
165.085	168.40
165.21	168.45
165.235	169.625
165.375	169.925
165.675	171.235
165.685	

Bugs

Room bugs are miniature radio stations. As such, anyone can tune them in. This rarely happens, though, because the range is limited and the frequency is known only to the person who placed the bug.

In practice, most bugs transmit by frequency modulation, on or near the standard FM broadcast band (88 to 108 MHz). There is a toy called Mr. Microphone that is, in effect, a bug shaped like a large hand-held microphone. The user speaks into the microphone, and others may hear his voice on their FM radios. Clandestine bugs work similarly but are more likely to transmit just off either end of the FM band—from 86 to 88 MHz (which infringes on a band allocated to television channels 5 and 6) or 108 to 110 MHz. In that way, the chance of accidental interception or of someone complaining to the Federal Communications Commission is less. The Watergate bug was to have transmitted at 110 MHz.

You can check for bugs using an FM radio. Turn the tuner to the extreme left side of the dial, as far as it will go, and turn the volume up. Although 88 MHz is the lowest frequency marked, most receivers have enough "overcoverage" to pick up 87 or 86

MHz. No FM stations are assigned below 88 MHz, so anything you may hear there is suspicious. Slowly move the dial to the right until you come to the first commercial FM station. Sweep over the FM band proper, and then check the overcoverage region above 108 MHz. Any bug you hear will be in your immediate neighborhood: Typical transmitters use a few milliwatts of power and have a range of a few hundred yards. If you suspect the bug is in a nearby room, have someone talk or play music while you scan.

A few bugs can be picked up only with special shortwave receivers. The frequencies from 48 to 50 MHz and 72 to 75 MHz are sometimes used. Several shortwave operators have reported conversations that seem to be from room bugs at 167.485 MHz— an FBI frequency.

Morse Code Letter Beacons

Dozens of low-power stations transmit only a letter of Morse code endlessly. No one, including government agencies and the International Telecommunications Union, admits to knowing where the signals are coming from, who is sending them, or why.

"K" (dash-dot-dash) is the most common letter. Letters are repeated every two to seven seconds, depending on the station. The stations never identify themselves. The frequency used for the broadcast shifts slowly with time, so this list is only an approximate guide:

Frequency (KHz)	Letter
4,005	K
4,466	U
5,306	D and W
5,307	F
5,795	K
5,890	K
5,920	K
6,203	P
6,770	A and N
6,800	F and K
6,806	Q
7,590	W
7,656	W

Frequency (KHz)	Letter
7,954	K
8,137	U
8,144	K
8,647	F
8,703	E
8,752	K
9,043	K
9,058	U
10,211	U
10,446	E
10,570	K
10,614	F
10,638	K
10,644	D
10,645	F
10,646	R and K
11,156	K
12,151	K
12,185	U
12,329	U
13,328	U
13,637	F
14,478	K
14,587	K
14,967	K
15,656	U
15,700	U
15,705	U
17,015	D
17,016	C
17,017	F
17,018	UE and TA
18,343	K
20,456	E
20,992	O and C

These stations broadcast mostly during the night hours of North America. They are most often picked up in North America, Australia, and the Orient. But because of the easy propagation of shortwave signals, no one is sure where they are coming from.

An analysis in the *Confidential Frequency List* holds that the signals are coming from 25- to 100-watt unattended transmitters somewhere in the South Pacific. An alternate theory places the Morse code "beacons" in Cuba. It is known that there used to be a "W" station operating at 3,584 KHz, a frequency supposedly reserved for amateur use. When American amateurs protested to the Federal Communications Commission about the interference, the FCC complained to the Cuban government. The station disappeared shortly thereafter.

Actually, all of the beacons must be presumed illegal. Short-wave stations are supposed to be registered with the International Telecommunications Union; none of those listed above are. The purpose of the stations is as unclear as their location. A single letter conveys no information. There are legitimate navigational beacon stations, which broadcast their call letters. But such stations are registered and operate on fixed frequencies from known locations. Keeping location and frequency information secret would defeat their purpose.

Maybe, then, the letter beacons are navigational stations operated for the benefit of a select few. Some think they are operated by the Soviet Union, in Cuba, for some military purpose. Still, the globe is crosshatched with legitimate navigational beacons. It is hard to see what further navigational aid the Soviets could expect to derive from their own secret network of beacons.

It has also been suggested that the beacon stations are really teletype or other data-transmission stations and that the Morse code letters are just a way of keeping the channel clear between data transmissions. A few of the stations started transmitting some sort of data—audible as a characteristic high-speed typewriterlike sound—in 1980. There are other ways of keeping a data channel open, though. Most radioteletype stations transmit the signal for a "space" (as between words) or a similar device between transmissions. (The radioteletype code is different from Morse code.)

Finally, still others think the letter transmissions are themselves some sort of coded message. Granted, the letter can't mean anything, but some wonder if the precise length of the interval between the letters means something. Or the frequency shifts may hold the message.

The number of Morse code letter stations seems to be increasing.

Numbers Stations

Well over a hundred "numbers" or "spy" stations have been reported, all rather closely following a pattern. On the typical numbers station, the announcer is—or seems to be—a woman. No one knows who the woman is or where she is broadcasting from. She speaks in Spanish, German, or Korean. Save for a few words at the beginning and end of the transmission, the message consists of random numbers, announced in groups of five, four, or, rarely, three digits. As with the Morse code stations, the numbers stations are all on unauthorized frequencies. No government or organization owns up to the broadcasts; officially, at least, the FCC claims no knowledge of them.

Many of those who have listened to the broadcasts carefully are convinced that the woman is in fact a robot. The voice has a mechanical ring, sometimes with a click between each digit. It seems to be the same sort of device used by the telephone company to give the time or forwarding phone numbers.

The exact format of the messages varies with the language and number of digits per group. With Spanish, five-digit groups, for instance, a typical message might be:

> *Atención* 290 22 . . . *Atención* 290 22 . . . *Atención*
> 290 22 . . . 39876 . . . 11203 . . . 58888 . . .
> 30957 . . . 11219 . . . 95804 . . . 38502 . . .
> 21230 . . . 49801 . . . 98205 . . . 48290 . . .
> 81101 . . . 86038 . . . 28194 . . . 69301 . . .
> 72067 . . . 19473 . . . 18637 . . . 02731 . . .
> 33082 . . . 89063 . . . 99120 . . . *Final, final.*

Broadcasts are during the night hours of North America and seem to start shortly after the hour. After the *"final, final,"* the transmission stops. It is claimed that a given transmission is repeated a few minutes later on a slightly different frequency.

There seems to be no escaping the conclusion that the messages are a numerical code. The second number after the *"Atención"*—22 in the example—is the number of digit groups in the message. There doesn't seem to be any demonstrable significance to the first number. Some suspect it is an identifying number for the sender or, more likely, the receiver.

The four-digit transmissions in Spanish are different. A three-digit number (perhaps that of the sender or receiver) is repeated several times, followed by the digits 1 through 0 (*"uno, dos, tres, cuatro, cinco, seis, siete, ocho, nueve, cero"*) and a string of Morse-code dashes. The word *grupo* is followed by the number of four-digit groups to come and repeated once—for example, *"Grupo 22, grupo 22."* The message—groups of four Spanish-language numbers—follows. At the end the voice says, *"Repito grupo 22,"* and the message repeats. The station goes off the air after the repeat.

Any attempt to explain these stations is complicated by numbers broadcasts in other languages. There are also broadcasts in German (they start with *"Achtung"* and terminate with *"Ende"*), Korean, and English. Occasional transmissions in Russian, French, Portuguese, and even Serbo-Croatian are reported. Sometimes a male (mechanical?) voice reads the numbers. The female robot voice doing English-language broadcasts is often described as having an Oriental or German accent. Typical of the uncertainty surrounding numbers stations are the reported English-language messages prefaced with a female voice saying "Groups disinformation" and ending with "End of disinformation." At least, it sounds like "disinformation." Perhaps the voice machine has a bad rendering of "this information."

Still other stations transmit messages consisting of letters from the phonetic alphabet (Alpha, Bravo, Charlie, etc.). Some spice their programs with music, which ranges from ethnic tunes to weird tones that may or may not conceal a message.

Reported frequencies for numbers and phonetic-alphabet stations include:

Frequency (KHz)	Description
3,060	Female reading numbers in Spanish
3,090	Female reading numbers in Spanish
3,365	Male reading numbers in Serbo-Croatian
4,640	Male reading numbers in Spanish
4,642	Female reading numbers in French
4,670	Female reading numbers and phonetic-alphabet letters in Spanish and English
4,740	Male reading numbers in Spanish and Portuguese; musical interlude from *Aïda*
4,770	Female reading numbers in German
4,792	Female reading numbers in Spanish

Frequency (KHz)	Description
5,020	Female reading numbers in Spanish
5,075	Female reading numbers in Spanish
5,110	Male reading numbers in Czech; Slavic musical interludes
5,812	Female reading numbers in Spanish
6,770	Female reading numbers in Spanish
6,790	Female reading numbers in Spanish
8,875	Female reading numbers in Spanish
9,040	Female reading numbers in English and Spanish
9,345	Female reading numbers in Spanish
9,450	Female reading numbers in English; musical tones
9,463	Female reading numbers in Spanish
9,950	Female reading numbers in Spanish
10,450	Female reading numbers in Korean
10,500	Female reading numbers in German
11,532	Female reading numbers in Spanish
11,545	Female reading numbers in German
11,618	Female reading numbers in German
11,635	Female reading numbers in Spanish
13,320	Male reading numbers in Russian
14,947	Female reading numbers in German
14,970	Female reading numbers in English; beep tones
23,120	Female reading numbers in German
30,050	English numbers
30,250	English numbers
30,420	English numbers
30,470	English numbers

Whatever is going on, it's a big operation. Harry L. Helms' *How to Tune the Secret Shortwave Spectrum* has a list of sixty-two stations that includes only those with a female voice reading five-digit numbers in Spanish. Much time and effort are going into the broadcasts. Some numbers stations transmit on upper sideband rather than amplitude modulation (upper sideband requires more elaborate and expensive equipment). Signals are usually strong. Because of ionospheric reflection, they can be picked up over most of the globe. This makes direction-finding difficult.

Two explanations are offered for the numbers stations. It is rumored that some of the stations are communications links in the drug traffic between the United States and Latin America. If so,

Spanish is a logical language. The numerically coded messages could tell couriers where drops will be made, how much to expect, and other minutiae that would change from day to day. Weak support for this explanation comes from some amateur direction-finding, which seems to place many of the Spanish-language stations somewhere south of the United States.

But even those who subscribe to this explanation agree that other numbers stations, probably most of them worldwide, are engaged in espionage—governmental or organizational communication with agents in the field.

Which government? The Spanish-language stations are usually heard between 7:00 P.M. and 6:00 A.M. Eastern Standard Time. The night hours are best for clandestine broadcasting, as weak signals propagate farther. So the Spanish-language broadcasts are probably coming from a time zone not far removed from Eastern Standard Time. (The EST zone includes the central Caribbean, Colombia, Ecuador, and Peru.)

On the basis of broadcast times and signal strengths, it can similarly be postulated that the German-language stations are coming from Europe or maybe Africa, and the Korean-language stations are coming from the Orient—reasonably enough.

As far as the Spanish-language stations are concerned, suspicion points to Cuba. In 1975 U.S. listeners reported muffled Radio Havana broadcasts in the background of some of the Spanish-language stations. A station at 9,920 KHz is said to have used the same theme music as Radio Havana.

But then there are American ham radio operators who swear that the Spanish-language stations must be in the United States. *How to Tune the Secret Shortwave Spectrum* tells of listeners in Ohio who reported four-digit-numbers stations coming in stronger than anything else on the dial except a 50-kilowatt broadcast-band station a few miles distant. Similar reports come from the Washington, D.C., area.

Probably the simplest of all the many possible explanations is that the Spanish-language stations are operated by Cuba for the benefit of Cuban agents in the United States. The Radio Havana broadcasts in the background would have been a mistake. The engineer was listening to Radio Havana and forgot the mike was on, or maybe Radio Havana and some of the numbers stations share facilities and the signals got mixed. The local-quality broadcasts heard in the United States could be Cuban agents reporting back to Havana. Each agent would have to have his own mechanical-voice setup.

The actual explanation may not be the simplest, though. According to Helms, some shortwave listeners believe that the four- and five-digit Spanish-language broadcasts are entirely different operations. The four-digit transmissions, at least some of which seem to originate in the United States, may be the work of the U.S. government. Only the five-digit transmissions may come from Latin America—and may be associated with local governments or U.S. foreign agents. Harry L. Helms speculates that the United States may have faked the Radio Havana background just to divert suspicion from an American espionage operation.

Any glib explanation of the numbers stations is further challenged by another incident Helms cites. An unnamed listener was receiving a five-digit-numbers broadcast in a female voice in Spanish. At the end of the transmission, the station (accidentally?) stayed on the air, and faint female voices were heard reading numbers in English and German. If the report is accurate, then the numbers stations could be the work of one worldwide operation. Choice of languages could be arbitrary. Whatever his or her native tongue, an agent need only learn ten words of, say, Korean in order to receive a numerical code in Korean.

No one willing to talk about it has broken the code or codes used for the transmissions. If the operation or operations are sophisticated enough, it may be pointless even to try. A random four- or five-digit number added to each number group before transmission will scramble the code. The numbers must be agreed upon by sender and receiver beforehand. If a different number is used for each number block and if they are not repeated, it is mathematically impossible for outsiders to crack the code.

Beeps, Screeches, and the Russian Woodpecker

There are still other inexplicable radio transmissions.

At 3,820 KHz there is a four-note electronic tune. The station never identifies itself; no one knows where the signal is coming from or why.

At 12,700 KHz there is a plaintive, twenty-one-note, flutelike melody.

At 15,507 KHz there are beeps.

The "Russian woodpecker" is a mysterious noise heard on frequencies ranging from 3,261 to 17,540 KHz. It is variously described as like a woodpecker or buzz saw. It was first heard in late 1976 or early 1977, seems to be coming from the Soviet Union, and is so powerful that it drowns out all other signals on its band. The usual hypothesis is that it is an experimental Soviet over-the-horizon radar system. Similarly, some think that 388.0 MHz—a frequency between VHF and UHF television carrier frequencies—is a resonant frequency of the human body being used in secret "death ray" experiments.

The most secret of transmissions are not even recognizable as transmissions. *Without Cloak or Dagger*, a 1974 book by former CIA agent Miles Copeland, tells of "screech" transmissions. These are tape-recorded messages speeded up or scrambled in such a way that they sound like radio interference. Only the intended recipient, with a variable-speed tape recorder or descrambler, can recover the messages.

More subtle yet is a device called the SC/16, manufactured by Transcript/International of Lincoln, Nebraska. The SC/16 is a "frequency-hopping" transmitter and receiver. Two synchronized units broadcast and receive at a frequency that changes every twelfth second. As many as twenty-four different frequencies are used, all between 145 and 166 MHz.

Any outsider tuning into this range would hear, at most, one-twelfth-second bursts of speech. The bursts are too fleeting to be recognized as speech; they sound like static.

26·

Secret Messages on Records

Two mentalities are at work here: 1960s rock fans and 1980s fundamentalist Christians. The idea of phonographically concealed messages dates from the Paul McCartney death scare of 1969. For hard-core types, the secret-message rumors never really died. Avid rock fans have auditioned every album release since the late 1960s for hidden nuances. Backward messages, barely audible messages, and messages on one stereo track only have been alleged. At the other end of the sociosensual spectrum, fundamentalist Christians have gotten into the act. TV programs such as *Praise the Lord* and *The 700 Club* have propagated rumors of a satanic plot in the recording industry, no less, in which various albums conceal "backward-masked" demonic murmurings. If *that* sounds too spacey to be taken seriously, consider that it was the fundamentalist groups who were behind House Resolution 6363, a bill introduced in the U.S. House of Representatives by Robert K. Dornan (R., Calif.) in 1982 to label all suspect records: "WARNING: THIS RECORD CONTAINS BACKWARD MASKING THAT MAKES A VERBAL STATEMENT WHICH IS AUDIBLE WHEN THIS RECORD IS PLAYED BACKWARD AND WHICH MAY BE PERCEPTIBLE AT A SUBLIMINAL LEVEL WHEN THIS RECORD IS PLAYED FORWARD." In February 1983, the Arkansas State Senate passed a similar record-labeling bill by a vote of 86 to 0.

Contributing to the quasi-occult status of these rumors is the difficulty of checking them out on home audio equipment. You pretty much have to take someone else's word for it, or dismiss the rumors out of hand.

From a technical standpoint, there are four simple ways to conceal a verbal message on a recording. The most obvious is to record the message at a very low volume. The message may then be recovered by turning the volume up while playing the record or tape. If the message is faint enough, though, noise levels of home equipment may garble it. If the accompanying music or lyrics are loud enough, or if the message itself is indistinct or electronically modified, it may be hard to hear on any equipment.

A second gimmick is to record a message on one stereo track only. Records and tapes have two independent recordings, of course, normally played simultaneously for stereo effect. On a record, each stereo track occupies one side of the V-shaped groove for the needle. On a tape, the tracks are recorded in parallel lanes of the magnetic material. The two tracks are called "right" and "left" after the stereo speakers they will play on. Otherwise, the tracks are interchangeable—the sound mixer can put anything he or she wants on each track. (High notes do not have to go on one track and low notes on the other.) A message on one track can be masked by simultaneous loud music or lyrics on the opposite track. With normal stereo balance (or mono equipment) the loud track drowns out the message track. At home, single-track messages can be recovered by adjusting the stereo balance so that only the desired track plays. Sometimes this trick also makes indistinct words clearer. Even if the words are not exclusively on one track, they may happen to be more audible on one track.

A message could be recorded at a speed different from the rest of the record. Then the record would have to be played faster or slower than usual to recover the message. Unless the message was at one of the standard speeds (say, 45 rpm on a 33⅓ rpm record), it could not be played normally on home equipment.

The fourth and most commonly alleged trick is to record a verbal message backward. Reversed speech has several unexpected features. One is that syllables are not a constant in the reversal process. A one-syllable word can have two or three syllables when played backward. Thus "number nine" in the Beatles' *Revolution 9* reverses to "Turn me on, dead man" (or something like it), a jump from three to five syllables.

There is no simple way to predict what a word or phrase will sound like reversed. Obviously, you can't just reverse the letters. The slightly less naïve approach of reversing phonetic spellings—

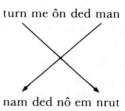

Reversed messages are difficult to recover at home. Record turntables are not built to go backward. Some have a neutral setting, in which the pickup and amplifier remain active and you can turn the record backward by hand. But hardly anyone has a steady enough hand to produce satisfactory results.

With patience, it is possible to reverse a cassette recording. Transfer the music from the original record or tape onto a blank tape cassette. Place the cassette flat on a table. Draw out the part of the tape with the suspected message and snip it off at both ends. Hold the tape segment horizontally. Rotate it 180 degrees, keeping it horizontal at all times. This turns the tape end for end. Splice the reversed tape segment back onto the two loose ends of the cassette with strong adhesive tape. Reel the tape back inside the cassette. The spliced segment will play backward on an ordinary cassette player.

Big Secrets rented a recording studio to test the secret-message rumors. New copies of the records in question were transcribed on quarter-inch master tape. Where rumor alleged that a single stereo track contained a message, right and left stereo tracks were transcribed separately. Records with alleged inaudible messages were treated similarly. To test claims of reversed messages, recordings on the master tape were edited out and spliced in backward. Twenty cuts or portions of cuts from sixteen albums were tested.

"Another One Bites the Dust"
Queen, *The Game*

Rumor: When played backward, the lyrics say, "It's fun to smoke marijuana."

Findings: There is something that sounds like "It's fun to smoke marijuana" in the reversed music. It is repeated over and over. It might be rendered no less faithfully, however, as "sfun to scout mare wanna." This "message" is the reversal of the song title, which is repeated as a line in the song.

Let's make a distinction between engineered and phonetic reversals. When an artist records a verbal statement, reverses it by turning the tape end for end, mixes the reversed statement onto a master tape, and has records and tapes produced from the master, that is an engineered reversal. When the phonetic properties of song lyrics are such that they can be reversed to sound like something else, that is a phonetic reversal.

"It's fun to smoke marijuana" is clearly a phonetic reversal. The lyrics are perfectly plain played forward ("Another one bites the dust"), not so plain played backward ("sfun to scout mare wanna"). With an engineered reversal, the opposite should hold true: gibberish forward, clear as a bell backward. Some are prepared to believe that phonetic reversals are just as intentional as engineered reversals—that the songwriter painstakingly planned the phonetic *double-entendre*. In the absence of confirming evidence, that just doesn't wash. It's too easy to find coincidences. If, for instance, the letters of the alphabet are recited in conventional fashion (Ay, Bee, Cee, etc.) and reversed, at least five sound like English language words. D reverses to "eden," F becomes "pray," S becomes "say," V becomes "even," and Z becomes "easy." "It's fun to smoke marijuana" is likewise a coincidence.

"A Child Is Coming"
Jefferson Starship, *Blows Against the Empire*

Rumor: When played backward, "son of Satan."
Findings: Another phonetic coincidence. The repeated "It's getting better" reverses to an iffy "son of Satan," the "of" drawn out and the "Satan" strongly accented on the first syllable.

"Eldorado"
Electric Light Orchestra, *Eldorado*

Rumor: When played backward, "He is the nasty one/Christ, you're infernal/It is said we're dead men/Everyone who has the mark will live."
Findings: Coincidence. The supposed message lurks around the line "On a voyage of no return to see." Reversed, this passage be-

comes the expected syllable salad—no one hearing it cold would describe it as anything but reversed music. Only if you listen while reading along with what you're supposed to hear will you get anything. The rumored version of the message is somewhat fudged. The passage sounds more like "He's to nasty one/Christ you are, Christ, you're fernal/There wiss suh, we're dead men . . ." There is no "in" in what is taken to be "infernal." The line that is supposed to be "Everyone who has the mark will live" isn't even close, though the syllable count is about right.

"Shoo Be Doo"
The Cars, *Candy-O*

Rumor: When played backward, the word "Satan" repeated approximately eleven times.
Findings: Coincidence. The rumor refers to the reversal of the "Shoo be doo, shoo be doo, shoo be doo . . ." near the end of the song. Given the mysterious logic of reversed phonemes, these three-syllable units can be heard as a repeated two-syllable word. The word sounds a little like "Satan."

"Snowblind"
Styx, *Paradise Theater*

Rumor: According to a mimeographed list of suspect records distributed by Congressman Dornan, the words "Satan move through our voices" when played backward.
Findings: Negative. Despite repeated listenings, it was not even possible to identify the part of the reversed track that Dornan et al. are talking about.

"Stairway to Heaven"
Led Zeppelin, untitled, a.k.a. *Stairway to Heaven*

Rumor: In reverse, "I live for Satan . . . The Lord turns me off . . . There's no escaping it . . . Here's to my sweet Satan . . . There's power in Satan . . . He will give you 666."
Findings: Coincidence. If you listen very carefully to the "And it makes me wonder" lines in reverse, you'll hear something approaching "There's no escaping it." A better description is

"There's no escape do." Knock off the last syllable, and you have "There's no escape," a complete, intelligible sentence in reverse. It's there, all right, but it's not an unlikely enough coincidence to—well, make you wonder.

The "Satan" in "I live for Satan" is good and clear. The "I live for" part isn't. The other alleged lines are unremarkable. All are phonetic reversals of the entirely lucid forward lyrics and obviously just accidents.

"When Electricity Came to Arkansas"
Black Oak Arkansas, *Black Oak Arkansas* and *Ronch and Roll*

Rumor: In reverse, "Satan, Satan, Satan, Satan, Satan. He is God. He is God."
Findings: The *Black Oak Arkansas* cut was reversed. Again, pairs of reversed syllables are being freely interpreted as "Satan." "He is God" was not identifiable.

"Rain"
The Beatles, *Hey Jude*

Rumor: The unintelligible lyrics at the end are reversed.
Findings: A true engineered reversal and not really a secret. "Rain" seems to have been the first popular recording to incorporate an obviously reversed lyric. The story is that John Lennon accidentally spliced the last part of the song in backward and liked the effect. When reversed, the strange-sounding vocals at the end become intelligible as a reprise starting with the drawn-out word "sunshine."

The reversal is less apparent to the casual listener than it might be because the accompanying music is not reversed. The ending fits in smoothly with the rest of the song, the vocals suggesting a foreign language.

"Fire on High"
Electric Light Orchestra, *Face the Music*

Rumor: When played backward, "The music is reversible, but time—turn back!"
Findings: "Fire on High" is instrumental. About twenty-six sec-

onds into the music, scrambled speech is heard. It is mostly louder than the accompanying music and begins with a two-syllable unit repeated several times. The seeming speech lasts for about fourteen seconds.

Reversing the music confirms that that there is a true, engineered message. In reverse, a voice (Jeff Lynne's?) says, "The music is reversible, but time—turn back! Turn back! Turn back! Turn back!" All the words are clear and unambiguous. Anyone comparing this to the alleged reversal on ELO's "Eldorado" will have no trouble telling which is genuine.

"Goodbye Blue Sky"
Pink Floyd, *The Wall*

Rumor: In reverse, "You have just discovered the secret message."
Findings: The "secret message" is at the very end of the instrumental passage following the "Goodbye Blue Sky" vocals. It comes just before the words "What shall we do" at the start of the song that is identified as "Empty Spaces" on the record label and as "What shall we do now?" on the record sleeve. Played forward, the message is less apparent than the "Face the Music" reversal: A reasonably attentive listener might play *The Wall* through and not catch it. It suggests speech not quite close enough to be overheard. In context this is not unusual because the "Goodbye Blue Sky" instrumental passage includes "airport noises" and other sound effects. A loud climax in the music further masks the unintelligible voice.

When played backward, the voice (Roger Waters'?) plainly intones, "Congratulations, you have just discovered the secret message. Please send your answer to old Pink, care of the funny farm . . ." As the voice fades out, there may be another word—perhaps "Chalfonte" or "Chelsea"—after "funny farm."

"Heavy Metal Poisoning"
Styx, *Kilroy Was Here*

Rumor: A red sticker on the *Kilroy Was Here* album cover warns, "By order of the Majority for Musical Morality, this album contains secret backward messages . . ."
Findings: This is a case of second-generation backward-masking. Styx' *Paradise Theater* did not contain a backward message, though

a lot of people said it did. So Styx has included a sure enough backward message on *Kilroy Was Here*. It is at the very beginning of "Heavy Metal Poisoning." The reversed speech lasts about three seconds. There is no musical background. The words reverse to *"Annuit cœptis. Novus ordo seclorum."* This is the Latin motto encircling the pyramid on the back of a dollar bill. The usual translation: "God has favored our undertakings. A new order of the ages."

The cover sticker's "Majority for Musical Morality" is a fictitious Falwellesque group in the *Kilroy Was Here* video. Although the sticker suggests a plurality of "messages," only one was found.

Space between "I'm so tired" and "Blackbird"
The Beatles, untitled, a.k.a. *The White Album*

Rumor: A reversed message. At the time of the Paul-is-dead stories, the segue from "I'm so tired" to "Blackbird" was offered as evidence. It was held to contain John Lennon's voice, reversed, saying, "Paul is dead, miss him, miss him, miss him." That interpretation seems unlikely now, but there is a mysterious low muttering between the songs.
Findings: The mumbling is actually just to the "I'm so tired" side of the shiny "space" between cuts on the record. Each of the stereo tracks was recorded separately, twice, and a copy of each track was reversed. This produced four versions of the two-second passage: right forward, left forward, right reversed, and left reversed. All were equally unintelligible. It was not even apparent whether the voice is forward or reversed. Nor could John Lennon be identified as the speaker. There are nine or ten syllables. The first six (when played forward) are a two-syllable unit repeated three times. There is little or no difference between the stereo tracks. Any claimed interpretation of the sounds seems doubtful.

"Strawberry Fields Forever"
The Beatles, *Magical Mystery Tour*

Rumor: It was, of course, claimed that John Lennon says "I buried Paul" at the end. (It's forward, at the very end after the music fades to complete silence, returns, and starts to fade out again.) But Lennon told *Rolling Stone* that the words are "cranberry sauce."
Findings: They are "cranberry sauce." The "sauce"/"Paul" part

is indistinct, but the first syllable sounds a lot more like "cran" than "I."

"Baby You're a Rich Man"
The Beatles, *Magical Mystery Tour*

Rumor: On one of the tracks the line "Baby you're a rich man too" is sung as "Baby you're a rich fag Jew," a dig at Brian Epstein. Or some think it's "rich fat Jew" and claim it as evidence of Beatle anti-Semitism.
Findings: Negative. The two stereo tracks are nearly identical. It's always possible to hear words as similar-sounding words, but basically, the lyrics jibe with the published version.

"Lord Have Mercy on My Soul"
Black Oak Arkansas, *Black Oak Arkansas*

Rumor: Simulated sex in the background behind Jim Dandy Mangrum's spoken prologue. Also, different voices saying different things on the two stereo tracks.
Findings: The rumors refer not to the song itself but to the prologue and the whispering behind it. The whispering starts after Mangrum's words, "God and the Devil, however you want it." Played in stereo, the whispering seems to be someone saying, "I want it, I need it, I want it, I need it . . ."

When the stereo tracks are split, it is apparent that there are two voices. The right track contains some low breathing or moaning before the whispering starts, and then a male voice repeating "I want it." The "I need it" 's begin a moment later, in a female voice on the left track. Another left-track voice repeats "Good" between the "I need it" 's in a more or less sexual 1½-second rhythm. The running-water sound at the end of the prologue is on both stereo tracks.

"Wild and Loose"
The Time, *What Time Is It?*

Rumor: Different voices on the two tracks, in the party conversation in the middle of the song.
Findings: The same assignment of genders to stereo tracks as

above: male voices on the right track and female voices on the left. The main female voice switches over to the right stereo track when she talks to lead singer Morris Day.

"I Am the Walrus"
The Beatles, *Magical Mystery Tour*

Rumor: The fadeout contains several lines from *King Lear*. According to *The Beatles A to Z* by Goldie Friede, Robin Titone, and Sue Weiner (New York: Methuen, 1980), Lennon taped the lines from a BBC radio production and did not even know what play it was until years later.

Findings: Right and left stereo tracks of the ending were compared, but there was little difference. There seem to be four vocal components to the ending of "I Am the Walrus":

1. A chanted "Goo goo goo joob"—which is in the published lyrics and is taken from *Finnegans Wake*.
2. Another chant that seems to be "Oom pah, oom pah."
3. A third chant that has been identified as "Everybody's got one," beginning approximately when the "Goo goo goo joob" chant dies away.
4. The lines from *King Lear*.

Chant no. 3 makes it nearly impossible to understand the *Lear* dialog. But it fades away just before the last line from the play. For a moment at the very, very end of the record, there is only the *King Lear* recitation. If you turn the volume way up, you can hear (on both tracks) "Sit you down, Father; rest you." This is a line from Act IV, Scene iv. Once you turn to the right place in the play, it isn't too hard to hear the other lines spoken as you read along. "I Am the Walrus" contains eleven lines from *Lear*, the three characters speaking in distinct—not the Beatles'—voices:

OSWALD   Slave, thou hast slain me. Villain,
                take my purse:
          If ever thou wilt thrive, bury my body,
          And give the letters which thou find'st
                about me
          To Edmund, Earl of Gloucester; seek him
                out

	Upon the English party. Oh, untimely death! Death!
EDGAR	I know thee well. A serviceable villain, As duteous to the vices of thy mistress As badness would desire.
GLOUCESTER	What, is he dead?
EDGAR	Sit you down, Father; rest you.

"Sheep"
Pink Floyd, *Animals*

Rumor: A Moog-modified voice recites a parody of the Twenty-third Psalm.

Findings: The part in question begins six minutes, thirty-five seconds into the cut, in an otherwise instrumental passage. In stereo you can barely hear a muffled, electronically modified voice begin, "The Lord is my shepherd/I shall not want . . ." The voice continues but is drowned out by the music and the bleating of sheep.

The two stereo tracks were split. The voice is relatively clear on the left track, all but absent from the right. Only the first two lines are directly from the Twenty-third Psalm. The rest (thirteen lines) is a passably clever parody of man/God and man/sheep relationships: "He converteth me to lamb cutlets." Pink Floyd's music publisher refused permission to print the lyrics here.

"Revolution 9"
The Beatles, untitled, a.k.a. *The White Album*

Rumor: Various reversed and/or one-track speech. The reversal of "Number nine" to "Turn me on, dead man" has pretty much been discounted as coincidence (though it is mentioned on Congressman Dornan's list).

Findings: Distinction between lyrics and any hidden message blurs on "Revolution 9." The eight-minute cut is a montage of sounds collected by John Lennon and Yoko Ono (and not by credited cowriter Paul McCartney, per *White Album* usage). It includes discordant music, radio broadcasts, sirens, applause, gunfights, sports cheers, the crackling of a fire, screams, a baby gurgling, a choir singing, and much that cannot be identified. For this investigation, "Revolution 9" was transcribed four times, twice on each stereo channel. One copy of each of the tracks was reversed. The four resulting versions were compared against each other and against the original two-channel version.

"Revolution 9" contains a lot of talking. Played in stereo, forward, the longest stretch of understandable speech is probably an announcer saying, ". . . every one of them knew that as time went by they'd get a little bit older and a little bit slower . . ."

One believable instance of reversed speech occurs: someone saying "Let me out! Let me out!" (once held to represent McCartney in his totaled Aston-Martin). Two iffy reversals occur on the backward recording of the right stereo track: "She used to be assistant" and "There were two men . . ." Neither is clear enough or long enough to be convincing. Some of the music, including the recurring theme, sounds more natural in reverse.

"Turn me on, dead man" is a typical phonetic reversal. The forward "number nine" (repeated throughout the cut) is clear; the reversal is slurred—something like "turn me on dedmun." It has been claimed that "number nine" must be pronounced with a British accent or with some careful inflection in order to reverse to "Turn me on, dead man." This seems not to be so. As an experiment, three American-accent renderings of "number nine" were reversed. All sounded about as much like "Turn me on, dead man" as the record did. Like the other phonetic reversals, "Turn me on, dead man" must be considered a coincidence.

Much of "Revolution 9" is on one stereo track only. Near the end a voice says "A fine natural imbalance . . . the Watusi . . . the twist . . . Eldorado . . . Eldorado." "A fine natural imbalance" is on the right track only, though the words that follow are in stereo. One of the longer bits of speech—"Who could tell what he was saying? His voice was low and his [unintelligible] was high and his eyes were low"—is clear on the left track, a bare whisper on the right.

There is a stereophonically concealed "secret message" on "Revolution 9." The words are on the right track. They begin about four minutes, fifty-eight seconds into the cut and run for about twenty-two seconds. They are not likely to be noticed in stereo because of the much louder left track. The sound of applause begins on the left track at about five minutes, one second into the cut. Deafening noises—the clapping, sirens, music—continue on the left track until five minutes, forty seconds. It may or may not have been Lennon's and Ono's intention to conceal the spoken passage. Given the haphazard quality of "Revolution 9," the concealment may have been accidental. To recover the passage, the left track must be switched off. The right track can then be heard to contain a sound like a stopwatch ticking, behind these words:

> So the wife called, and we better go to see a surgeon. . . . [a *scream muffles a line that sounds like* Well, what with the prices, the prices have snowballed, no wonder it's closed.] . . . So any and all, we went to see the dentist instead, who gave him a pair of teeth, which wasn't any good at all. So instead of that he joined the bloody navy and went to sea.

"A Day in the Life"
The Beatles, *Sgt. Pepper's Lonely Hearts Club Band*

Rumor: The seemingly blank grooves at the end of the record contain a note so high that only dogs can hear it, intended for Paul McCartney's dog, Martha.

Findings: Anyone who examines the record carefully will notice fifteen widely spaced grooves at the end of "A Day in the Life." They seem to contain no music. The record label lists the length of "A Day in the Life" as five minutes, three seconds. Yet, if you time it, the music seems to be over in about four and a half minutes. Certainly the "full" five minutes, three seconds are not played on the radio.

"A Day in the Life" was recorded with a forty-two-piece orchestra from the London Philharmonic. The loud climaxes were created by playing in different keys simultaneously. A synthesizer was also used.

Could a record contain a note too high-pitched for humans to hear? The sound engineer *Big Secrets* consulted didn't think so. Recording hardware is tuned to the human range of hearing and has a very poor response outside that range. The same is true for the equipment that plays back the sound. Even if the Beatles had somehow managed to record such a note, no commercial tweeter would respond to it—not if it was much more than twenty thousand cycles per second, anyway. So much for the idea of Fru-Fru being hypnotized by "A Day in the Life."

Those fifteen grooves aren't really empty, though. The end of "A Day in the Life"—starting with the final loud "daaa" and going all the way into the center of the record—was transferred to master tape and the stereo levels monitored. Initially, the final note is split evenly between stereo tracks. As it tails off, most of the note is on the right channel. The level never hits zero until the end of the record. By turning the volume up repeatedly, the final note can be heard all the way to the end.

Dogs can hear fainter sounds as well as higher sounds than humans. So at a given volume setting, a dog should be able to hear the final note longer than a human. Whether the dog hears the entire recorded note depends on the volume level and the dog.

27·

Subliminal Shots in Movies

Bona fide subliminal shots—significant action that flashes on the movie screen too quickly to be perceived consciously—are rare. The few recent examples use a different technology from the "Drink Coca-Cola" experiments in the 1950s.

The 1950s experiments used a tachistoscope, a sort of slide projector capable of flashing a still image on a screen for a split second. The movies themselves were projected separately. At a Fort Lee, New Jersey, movie theater, marketing researcher James Vicary pointed his tachistoscope at the screen and flashed two written messages during movies: "Hungry? Eat popcorn" and "Drink Coca-Cola." After trying the device for six weeks (on a total audience of about forty-five thousand people), Vicary concluded the messages were getting through. His report on the experiment claimed that sales of popcorn rose 57.8 percent and those of Coca-Cola increased 18 percent.

Vicary's experiments sparked a public outcry against subliminal advertising. What isn't so well known is that Vicary's experiments have been discredited scientifically as well as ethically. His tachistoscopic messages were on the screen for a fleeting one-three-thousandth second. Previous experiments in psychology laboratories had shown that information could be conveyed at a sub- or semiconscious level by the tachistoscope. But the shutter speeds in the laboratory experiments were usually around one-hundredth second—about thirty times slower than Vicary's device.

No scientist himself, Vicary did not design the experiment very well. Popcorn sales may have surged, but there was no control. Psychologists have since countered that the increase may have been a random fluctuation, a seasonal change of taste, or the result of expectant vendors pushing their product harder. No one else has since shown that one-three-thousandth-second messages can dictate behavior. Vicary's experiments raised an offbeat, perhaps important ethical issue, but if they caused even one person to buy popcorn or Coke, he did not demonstrate it in a way that most psychologists will accept.

So effectively did Vicary's tachistoscope blacken the name of subliminal advertising that only one instance of a high-speed ad has turned up in all the years since. This was in a Christmas-season-1973 TV commercial for a child's game, "Hūsker Dū?" Four times during the commercial, the words "Get it!" flashed for a split second. By then, the National Association of Broadcasters had long since banned subliminal material on member stations; the stations running the spot apparently were not aware of the high-speed inserts. A Federal Communications Commission warning resulted in the spots being pulled from the air in the United States.

A subliminal message need not have a commercial purpose. A very short message or shot edited into the final print of a movie will appear every time the movie is shown; no special equipment is needed.

Such tinkering is quantized. The briefest image possible is one that occupies a single frame of the film. A message or shot can last for one frame, two frames, three frames, but never less than a whole frame. Movies are projected at a rate of twenty-four frames a second. So each frame is on the screen for one-twenty-fourth second—actually, a hair less than that because the screen flickers to black for an instant while the next frame shifts into place.

A blink of an eye lasts about one-tenth second—long enough to blot out a one- or two-frame insert for a given viewer. But even a single-frame shot lasts several times longer than typical (one-hundredth-second) tachistoscopic stimuli of psych labs. How noticeable a shot is depends on the surrounding cinematography. Projected in a darkened theater, a single all-white frame surrounded by an opaque leader is visible as a flash on the screen. Of course, in a normal movie, the illusion of motion demands that single frames not be consciously perceptible.

Expectations influence perception. Movie projectionists have no trouble spotting the reel-change indicators (rough circles scratched into the upper right corner of a dozen or so consecutive frames). Yet the average viewer may sit through a two-hour movie without consciously perceiving the markings. Depending on the filmmaker's intentions and ingenuity, a shot may linger on the screen for some time and still be missed by those who don't know exactly what to look for. The subliminal grades into the merely inconspicuous.

Some avant-garde filmmakers have toyed with single-frame shots. Robert Breer's *Images by Images I* (1954) consists entirely of single-frame images. In a sense, the whole film is "subliminal" material. The eye adjusts to the visual anarchy enough to pick out many individual images, though.

Tony Conrad's *The Flicker* (1966) alternates all-black and all-white frames for an effect aptly described by the title. (The film is claimed to be dangerous for epileptics.)

Narrative films with significant hidden content are few and far between. The short list below does not include one sometime candidate, *The Texas Chainsaw Massacre* (New Line Cinema, 1974). Director/cowriter Tobe Hooper raised eyebrows in a 1977 *New Times* interview by acknowledging subliminal techniques in the film. Hooper denied any one-frame shots, however. If there is hidden content in *Chainsaw*, no one seems to have identified it.

My World Dies Screaming, retitled *Terror in the Haunted House* Precon Process and Equipment Corporation, c. 1958

Psychologist Robert Corrigan and engineer Hal C. Becker founded the Precon Process and Equipment Corporation in New Orleans to exploit a tachistoscopic device of their invention, the "Precon." In the late 1950s, they produced two ultralow budget horror films "in Psychorama." The first, *My World Dies Screaming,* was shown in the United States and (as *Terror in the Haunted House*) Great Britain. Apparently it is no longer in release. According to descriptions, there are four embedded images. A tachistoscopic skull is supposed to evoke death; a pair of beating hearts suggests love; a snake projects hate; the word "BLOOD" reinforces fear. There is no indication that the film was any more emotionally riveting because of these devices.

A Date with Death
Precon Process and Equipment Corporation, c. 1959

Corrigan and Becker's other film.

The Exorcist
Warner Brothers, 1973

The Exorcist is apparently the only major-studio release to use sub-liminal inserts. The plot follows a young girl, Regan, who is pos-sessed by the devil. A priest, Father Karras, is called in to exorcise the demon. Of the many special effects used by director William Friedkin, one is very brief shots of a ghoulish face. In a dream, Karras sees his mother coming out of a subway—and the face flashes on the screen. Later, Karras tries to kill Regan, and the face shot is repeated.

If you examine a print of the film, you find that the shots last two frames. The face is on the screen for one-twelfth second—rather on the longish side of subliminal. No one who knows about the face should have much trouble getting a glimpse of it. But nearly everyone who did not know about the face when they saw the movie does not remember seeing it.

The spliced-in frames show a ghostly white face looking some-thing like Father Karras (perhaps it is Karras with different makeup). The mouth and eyes are outlined in red. The face wears a white shroud. Later in the film, when Karras becomes possessed, his face turns pale, much like the subliminal face.

It has also been claimed that the word "PIG" appears sublim-inally. The word appears as a graffito near the stairs behind the house. It is never on the screen for more than a moment.

It is a moot point whether the subliminal material makes the film any scarier. Neither the two-frame face nor the graffito "PIG" is particularly gruesome compared to the rest of the film. If they have any effect at all, it can only be to create a sense of ap-prehension. They may not even do that.

Dark Star
Jack H. Harris, 1974

Dark Star, John Carpenter's first film, has a cult following on late-night television. It is a science-fiction comedy shot for sixty thousand dollars with a group of Carpenter's fellow University of Southern California students. The script is bright, the special effects cheesy: One "space suit" was reportedly made from a cookie tin, a vacuum-cleaner hose, and styrofoam packing material from a typewriter case. The *Dark Star* is a spaceship that locates "unstable" worlds and destroys them. The lately psychotic crew is captained by a dead but still conscious commander in the ship's deep freeze. One of the ship's cache of introspective bombs must be talked out of premature explosion. The film's brief hidden message is flashed momentarily on a computer panel: "FUCK YOU HARRIS."

Who is Harris? He is Jack H. Harris, the film's producer and distributor. Best known for *The Blob* and *The Eyes of Laura Mars,* Harris backed *Dark Star* after Carpenter and friends' self-funding (some six thousand dollars) ran out. In its first celluloid incarnation, *Dark Star* ran for forty-five minutes on sixteen-millimeter stock. Harris' money bankrolled another thirty-eight minutes' worth of footage and the transfer to thirty-five-millimeter stock necessary for commercial release. Be that as it may, a rift developed between Carpenter and Harris. Carpenter and cowriter Dan O'Bannon were perfectionists; Harris was a corner-cutter. At one point Carpenter and O'Bannon allegedly sabotaged the sound track so that Harris would have to move the work from a discount film dubber to Metro-Goldwyn-Mayer.

Dark Star had limited distribution in its 1974 release. It was rereleased after *Star Wars* and has been popular in revival since. Local TV stations presumably are not aware of the fleeting obscenity, but the film is often heavily edited for television.

28·

Is Walt Disney Frozen?

Lots of people think that Walt Disney is frozen. Some say his icy remains are in a special chamber beneath the Pirates of the Caribbean exhibit at Disneyland. Some think his body is in a Salt Lake City deep freeze. It is known that there is a secret apartment in one of the spires of the Cinderella Castle at the Orlando Disney World, built for Disney and family but (they say) never occupied. Is the late animator awaiting reanimation? The story gets a lot of play at Holmby Hills cocktail parties and elsewhere. The Disney family never has said what it did with Walt's body. And as Disney's studio told the press after his death, "The entire corporation is carrying on exactly as if Walt were here."

The rumor of Disney's "cryonic suspension" has been floating around the Disney organization, cryonics groups, and much of the nation since the cartoonist's 1966 death. No one seems to know where or how the story started. Anthony Haden-Guest mentioned it in a 1973 book, *The Paradise Program* (New York: William Morrow). It has turned up in the pages of *Playboy*. Cryonics popularizer Robert C. W. Ettinger has acknowledged the rumor but discounts it. One version of the tale, it should be noted, contends that Disney was frozen but his family had second thoughts and thawed him out again. Poor Walt—first everyone said he was a pothead and now this.

The premise of cryonics is that bodies may be preserved at or before death by freezing and kept in a changeless frozen state indefinitely. It is postulated that the supertechnology of a future age will be able to revive the frozen bodies and cure them of disease or injury now untreatable. The cryonics movement generated popular interest after the publication of *The Prospect of Immortality* by Robert C. W. Ettinger, a Michigan college instructor, in 1964 (Garden City, N.Y.: Doubleday). Since then at least thirty-two people have been frozen.

No celebrities have been frozen. There are stories that Omar Bradley and Dwight Eisenhower considered it, but they most certainly were not frozen. Among living notables, sixties guru Timothy Leary and Columbia University physicist Gerald Feinberg are said to have expressed interest. TV comedy writer Dick Clair (half of the team that includes wife Jenna McMahon) plans to be suspended. But nearly all the people frozen so far are middle-class Americans—housewives, a few kids, salesmen, teachers. That's it, unless there is something to the Disney rumors.

Disney had opportunity to hear about cryonics. Ettinger's theories received widespread attention in the two years before Disney's death. (Ettinger made a tour of talk shows, getting into a televised argument with Buddy Hackett when Hackett made jokes about cryonics. Ettinger didn't see what was so funny.) If Disney was frozen, he would have been the first, barring any other clandestine freezings. Disney died just a month before Dr. James Bedford, a Glendale, California, psychology professor who received publicity as "the first frozen man."

An Old Polo Injury

There was no news coverage of Disney's funeral. Likewise, even as Disney's health failed in late 1966, he kept tight rein on media coverage of his condition.

On November 2, 1966, Disney was admitted to St. Joseph's Hospital, just across the street from his Burbank studios. Studio officials, who handled all of Disney's personal publicity, said he was to be treated for an old neck injury received while playing polo.

While in the hospital, surgeons removed part of Disney's left lung on November 21. A tumor had been found, according to a press release, but the studio refused to say whether it had been malignant. Disney was released. He was readmitted on December 5. This time he was said to be undergoing a routine postoperative checkup. Disney remained in the hospital until his death.

Hospital sources said that Disney died at nine thirty-five on the morning of December 15. Cause of death was not announced: A press release said only that Disney had suffered "acute circulatory collapse." In other words, his heart suddenly stopped beating—which, presumably, is how they decided he was dead in the first place.

On the evening of December 16, the studio unexpectedly announced that funeral services had already been held. "The services were a closely guarded family secret," observed the *Los Angeles Times*, "and were announced only after they had been concluded." The ceremony was conducted at the Little Church of the Flowers in Forest Lawn Memorial Park, Glendale. The *Los Angeles Times* reported that studio and Forest Lawn officials refused to reveal any further details of the service, including the disposition of the body. "Mr. Disney's wishes were very specific and had been spelled out in great detail," the *Times* quoted a Forest Lawn spokesman.

If you want to believe the cryonics rumor, there is further circumstantial evidence. Disney had a long preoccupation with death.

In *The Paradise Program*, Anthony Haden-Guest notes Disney's "sombre sense of death" and "occasional touch of the horrors," telling of a gruesome seven-minute Mickey Mouse cartoon made in 1933, two years after Disney's nervous collapse. In it, a mad scientist tries to cut off Pluto's head and put it on a chicken. The film was withdrawn from the Rank film library in 1970.

In *The Story of Walt Disney*, a 1957 biography, daughter Diane Disney Miller and Pete Martin write:

> It may have been while he was undergoing the nervous wear and tear which led to his crack-up that he became concerned with the inevitability of death. Mother [Mrs. Lillian Disney] says that she first noticed his brooding about that after a party twenty years ago when a fortuneteller told him that he would die when he was thirty-five.
>
> But my mother's sister, Aunt Hazel, says he still worried about that prophecy even after he passed his thirty-fifth year. Whenever father gets depressed, he discusses his impending demise. He never goes to a funeral if he can help it. If he has to go to one it plunges him into a reverie which lasts for hours after he's home. At such times he says, "When I'm dead I don't want a funeral. I want people to remember me alive."

Cryonics is expensive. Ettinger estimated the cost of a cryonics suspension in the mid-1960s as eighty-five hundred dollars minimum. Currently Trans Time, a Berkeley, California, cryonics organization, sets sixty thousand dollars as rock bottom for undertaking and for setting up a fund to pay for the costs of suspension in perpetuity. Disney's estate was said to be worth many millions of dollars. He did set up three trust funds and a foundation, the details of which were not released. (One of the trust funds endows the California Institute of the Arts, a Valencia, California, creative arts college since nicknamed Walt's Tomb or the Magic Mausoleum.)

Add to that the fact that Disney was the ultimate technology freak. Tomorrowland, monorails, Space Mountain, EPCOT ... it isn't hard to believe that he might have been intrigued with cryonics.

A Search for Disney's Grave

What, then, happened to the body?

Regardless of the family's wishes, a death certificate must be filed, and certain information must be provided on it. Disney's death certificate is available—to anyone—from the Los Angeles County registrar-recorder's office.

It contains information that did not appear in any newspaper account of the death. The attending physician, Dr. Bert H. Cotton, listed the cause of death as "cardiac arrest" due to "bronchogenic ca lt lung." The latter is shorthand for bronchogenic *carcinoma, left* lung—that is, a cancer arising in the air passages of the left lung. Three months is given as the approximate interval between onset and death. Disney probably knew about the cancer well before the "polo injury" trip to the hospital.

The cause-of-death information on the certificate is said to have been determined from an operation November 7. This was prior to the operation disclosed to the press, which took place on November 21. The November 21 operation seems to have been his last.

The certificate says that Disney's body was cremated at Forest Lawn, Glendale, on December 17, 1966. No autopsy was performed, but there is an embalmer's signature—"Dean Fluss"—indicating that the body was embalmed.

The embalmer's name and license number check out. Fluss was indeed a real embalmer working at Forest Lawn and not a fake identity cooked up to cover a cryonics trail. When contacted, Fluss's wife said she had never heard of the cryonics rumor.

The death certificate does not say what was done with the remains. Generally speaking, though, the Forest Lawn mortuary is for those who will be interred at Forest Lawn.

The Forest Lawn management is circumspect with a vengeance. Excavated earth from fresh graves is covered with Astro-turf, lest anyone be reminded that the deceased are buried in ordinary dirt. No photographs taken at Forest Lawn, including several taken for this chapter, are ever allowed to be published. The information office usually refuses to say where famous people are buried. But if you ask for the location of the marker for Walter Elias Disney, the attendant first looks in the records and then says that they are not allowed to give out that information—thus confirming that Disney *is* at Forest Lawn after all.

Big Secrets located Disney's gravesite. Much like Disneyland, Forest Lawn is divided into thematic sections: Slumberland, Vale of Memory, Babyland, etc. Disney's gravesite is in an area known as the Court of Freedom. This is on the eastern extremity of the park, about as far from the entrance as possible.

At the eastern end of the Court of Freedom is a majestic marble building, the Freedom Mausoleum. It contains the remains of several celebrities (Gracie Allen, Francis X. Bushman, Gummo Mark, Larry of the Three Stooges). Disney's site is not inside the mausoleum but in a small private garden snug against the front wall and far to the left of the mausoleum's main entrance. It is in the corner formed where the front of the mausoleum abuts a gray brick wall. The garden is enclosed with a low wall and gate (not locked). Inside is a marble bench, azalea and holly plantings, and a green-patinaed statue of a small girl. A metal plaque on the brick wall contains spaces for eight names. Disney's name is in the top space. Robert B. Brown, a son-in-law, is listed third.

The only thing even slightly unusual about the site is the wall on which the plaque rests or, more exactly, what's behind it. The wall continues far beyond the Disney family's small garden. The wall has only a few doors, normally kept locked. Behind the wall is an enclosed area not accessible from any side.

A secret cryonics vault? No. A workman left one of the wall

doors open on the day of this investigation. The hidden space is a storage area, with tools and nursery stock. The only thing on the part of the wall opposite from the Disney marker is a paper-towel dispenser for workers. Walt Disney was cremated, if in secrecy, and has a perfectly ordinary gravesite.

It is easy to guess how the cryonics rumor may have gotten started. Disney had a neurotic fear of death. He wanted people to remember him alive. So he arranged beforehand for there to be no press coverage of his funeral. He specified that the public never be told the location of his grave. The utter secrecy was unusual; it stuck in people's minds. A few weeks later and purely by coincidence, the first cryonics suspension took place. Somebody made the connection and wondered if Disney had been frozen too.

Index

Biggest
Secrets

OTHER BOOKS BY WILLIAM POUNDSTONE

Big Secrets
The Recursive Universe
Bigger Secrets
Labyrinths of Reason
The Ultimate
Prisoner's Dilemma

BIGGEST SECRETS

More Uncensored Truth About All Sorts of Stuff You Are Never Supposed to Know

William Poundstone

It is the policy of William Morrow and Company, Inc., and its imprints and affiliates, recognizing the importance of preserving what has been written, to print the books we publish on acid-free paper, and we exert our best efforts to that end.

Library of Congress Cataloging-in-Publication Data

Poundstone, William.
    Biggest secrets: more uncensored truth about all sorts of stuff you are never supposed to know /William Poundstone.
        p.   cm.
    Includes bibliographical references and index.
    ISBN 0-688-13792-X
    1.United States—Social life and customs—20th Century—Miscellanea. 2. United States—Popular culture—History—20th Century—miscellanea. 3. Secrecy—Miscellanea.
    4. Handbooks, vademecums, etc. I. Title.
E169.1.P73 1993
973.92—dc20   92-33948
                                                           CIP

Printed in the United States of America

First Quill Edition

     5 6 7 8 9 10

BOOK DESIGN BY BERNARD SCHLEIFER

To Kathy Poundstone

Acknowledgments

Revealing secrets is a tricky business. Many individuals in many walks of life have offered their inside information, assistance, ideas, and advice. Thanks go, first of all, to those requesting anonymity. Among the others, particularly helpful were Mike Backes, Muff Rollins Bobo, Kris G. Bonner, Michael L. Camarano, Janet Coglianese, Professor Irwin Corey, Mikolas Crews, Michael Cronin, Elizabeth L. Diefendorf and the staff of the Research Libraries of the New York Public Library, Alison Ewington, Paul V. Ferris, Sharon L. Focht, Allan B. Goodrich, William Handwerker, Merton P. Haynes, Eva Hedger, William Hilliard, Jr., Larry Hussar, Amy Kakacek, Gerry Kroll, Stuart C. Lerner and the staff of Associated Analytical Laboratories, John M. Meyers, James G. Moser, Scott Parker, Janet Pawlowski, Marilyn A. Phipps, Jen Blair Polin, Réunion des Musées Nationaux (Photographic Service), William Robbins, Thomas L. Ruble, Kate Seago, Colleen T. Sherman, Harvey Shore, Steve Stoliar, Mark Turcotte, and Sean Wade. Finally, thanks to all the readers of *Big Secrets* and *Bigger Secrets* who wrote to offer their knowledge and/or suspicions.

Contents

I: People

1·

People's Real Ages

Lots of people try to keep their age a secret. They forget that everyone born in the civilized world has a birth certificate. Moldering away in some cobwebbed hall of records, these documents are matters of public record. In many cases, that means that *anyone* can obtain a copy for a nominal fee. The trick to learning the ages of celebrities is to find the person's real name and place of birth and to apply to the relevant hall of records for a certified copy of the person's birth certificate. That's just what we did.

Some people lie about their age; others simply keep it a secret. Then there are people who say one thing on a résumé but refuse to be quoted; refuse to comment on the accuracy of published ages, and so on. As a rule, TV networks don't give ages of stars in their press kits. This is more honest than the old movie-studio practice of disseminating blatantly false ages and birth dates.

Here's an eye-opener. Go to the library and peruse old copies of *The World Almanac*. Since 1922, it has printed a section on the places and years of birth of living entertainers. To the average browser, this data is rock-solid, incontestable truth, no more open to question than census figures or World Series scores. Actually, a lot of the dates are wrong. Successive editions of *The World Almanac* frequently give different dates for the same person's birth.

Almanacs don't have the resources to check each and every year of birth. They get their dates from scanning recent articles on entertainers. The writers of these same articles rarely trouble to confirm years of birth, either. They usually accept the celebrity's word; ages on résumés and PR releases; previous articles on the celebrity; or, um, *The World Almanac*. Other sources are even less fastidious. *Who's Who* and like references almost always print whatever birth date the person puts on the questionnaire.

As the first step into our exploration of creative chronology, we consulted back and current editions of *The World Almanac; Who's Who;* a special horoscope issue of the *National Enquirer* that listed celebrity birthdays; and selected biographies and magazine and newspaper articles. When a person refused to give an age, or when the given dates of birth conflicted by two years or more, we tried to find the real date of birth from public records.

How to Find Out Anyone's Age

Halls of records aren't set up to satisfy idle curiosity. Bureaucracy almost uniformly dictates that you give the exact day of a person's birth, his or her original name, and the names of both parents, including the mother's maiden name, on the application for a copy of a birth certificate. In practice this information is what keeps birth certificates relatively inaccessible to curious nonrelatives.

Don't let this faze you. *Who's Who* may be a pushover for press-release ages, but it makes a point of giving mothers' maiden names. It usually has the rest of the information you'll need, too, including an authentic date of birth. Fortunately for our purposes, people hardly ever lie about their birthday. They lie about the year, not the month and day. That makes it fun, easy, and profitable to do a fishing expedition in the birth records.

It works like this. First you find out where the person was born. Big cities usually have bureaus of vital statistics. The state keeps certificates for small-town births, normally at a vital-records bureau in the state capital. You send a check to the appropriate hall of records, asking for a copy of so-and-so's birth certificate and giving the required information—including your best guess on the person's year of birth.

If you're lucky, they send you a certified copy of the birth certificate—sometimes a mere photocopy, more often a handsomely engraved document on prismatic paper with an impressive embossed seal. Should you ever need to prove that celebrity's age in court, you can submit it as evidence!

If your guess about the year is wrong, you may be out a few dollars. Big-city bureaus usually refuse to issue a certificate if any information supplied (such as the year) is wrong—they keep the fee, too. More forgiving bureaus may check other years for free. In any case, record searches are cheap (three to fifteen dollars). You can usually hit on the correct year in a few tries. The upshot is that almost anyone's real age may be had for a few sawbucks and a little persistence.

It isn't always that easy. Some municipalities issue certificates only to the person named on it. Others require nit-picking information difficult to find. The New York City Department of Health is a real stickler. They want not only the borough in which the person was born but the name of the hospital or building as well. Sometimes no birth certificate can be found under the relevant name, for whatever reason; records for adopted children can be tricky to locate; whole years of records get lost in fires or floods. Where birth certificates are missing or unavailable, early marriage certificates can be nearly as informative. A person applying for such a certificate has to give his or her age and sometimes the full date of birth. Although people of a certain age *do* shave years off their age on marriage certificates, those barely of legal age presumably don't (they may lie about being older than they really are, however). The particulars of marriages are available from newspapers or *Who's Who*.

As a last resort, there are school records or yearbooks. Most people enter college at the age of 17 or 18 and graduate from a four-year program at 21 or 22. This pins down their age (to a high degree of probability, anyway) to within a year or two.

A pattern emerged in our research. Many of the ages or dates of birth given by the press are wrong. Some ages and dates are off by just a year, a discrepancy that may be innocently explained. Someone may have computed the year of birth from an article in which the person's age was stated. But when a date of birth was wrong by at least two years, it was virtually always wrong in the same direction, namely, *later* so that the person appears to be *younger*.

The reported month and day almost always agree with the birth certificate. This supports the cynical position that it is indeed the celebrity, or his or her minions, who is consciously lying.

Contrary to expectations, the *National Enquirer* tends to accept dates of birth provided in press releases. Stars often turn up a year or two younger in the *Enquirer's* pages than they do in almanacs or ordinary newspapers. You have to assume that the people at the *Enquirer* are well aware that different and earlier birth dates appear elsewhere. This suggests an uneasy predator-prey relationship between the stars and the *Enquirer,* which deals in puff pieces, funny photos, and Phyllis Diller quips as much as scandal. There are some puzzling exceptions. Occasionally the *Enquirer* says a person is *older* than ages given in other references. They couldn't have gotten the earlier year of birth from a press release or an almanac. And it often turns out that the anomalous *Enquirer* year is *wrong.* The birth certificate proved the person to be younger. Sloppy journalism? Or a tabloid vendetta against targeted celebrities (for example Tyne Daly and Diana Ross)?

For the record, many famous people we checked *weren't* misrepresenting their ages—not by a single day. Let's look at some who were.

Singers

E. J. Kahn's Frank Sinatra biography, *The Voice* (1947), says Sinatra was then twenty-nine years old, implying he was born c. 1918. This birth date was accepted and commonly used for years. More recent sources push Sinatra's birth date back to 1915. Some would push it back even further. In a 1990 interview in the *Palm Beach Post,* rival crooner Perry Como revealed his age and added, "I'll tell you a secret. Frank Sinatra and I were both born in 1912. But he's celebrating his 75th birthday, and I'm celebrating my 78th. Our wives were pregnant at the same time, but his daughter is 36 and my son is 51."

The Hoboken, New Jersey, Board of Health says Francis Albert Sinatra was born on December 12, 1915. The birth certificate they send out is a signed and notarized typewritten document containing information copied from the original records, and not the more common photocopy of those records. Granting the possibility that someone with Sinatra's pull might manage to "correct" civic records, it's easier to believe Hoboken city hall than Como (who couldn't remember being born at the same time as Sinatra anyway). Most references say Nancy Sinatra was born in Jersey City on June 8, 1940.

The World Almanac has long given Diana Ross's year of birth as 1944. The *National Enquirer* claims it's 1941. Biographical sources say Ross was begging Berry Gordy for a job at Motown even before she graduated from high school. Motown was founded in January 1959, so the 1941 date (implying high school graduation circa 1959) can't be ruled out. It looks like the *Almanac* date is the right one, though. The Michigan Department of Health says Ross was born in Detroit on March 26, 1944.

Eydie Gorme—or her publicists—has perpetuated the myth that she is the same age as husband Steve Lawrence (no date at all appears in her *Who's Who* entry). Born Edith Gormezano in the Bronx on August 16, 1932, she's three years older than him. According to *Who's Who*, Dinah Shore was born in 1921. More objective sources says Frances Rose Shore was born in Winchester, Tennessee, on March 1, 1917. *Who's Who*, old editions of *The World Almanac*, and many newspapers give 1923 as Cyd Charisse's year of birth. Recent *World Almanacs* have turned the clock back two years to 1921 (born Tula Finklea in Amarillo, Texas, March 8). Eartha Kitt has been reticent about her age, but mid-1950s press coverage of her career gave it correctly (born in North, South Carolina, January 26, 1928).

James Brown's alleged years of birth have spanned 1928 through 1934 (born Pulaski, Tennessee, June 17, 1928). Ray Charles's year of birth is given as 1932, but it's actually a couple of years earlier (born Ray Charles Robinson, Albany, Georgia, September 23, 1930). Tina Turner was born not in 1941, but a couple of years earlier (as Annie Mae Bullock, in Nutbush, Tennessee, on November 26).

The singing cowboy or cowgirl is not immune from big-city pretense. Of chronically misreported age are Gene Autry (1908 and 1911 reported; actually born Orvon Gene Autry, Tioga, Texas, September 29, 1907) and Dale Evans (reported 1918; born Frances Octavia Smith, in Uvalde, Texas, October 31, 1912). Loretta Lynn has that rare distinction, a dash for the year of birth in *The World Almanac* (1935 in *Who's Who*). She was born Loretta Webb in Butcher Hollow, Kentucky. We didn't get her birth certificate, but some sources say she was born on April 14, 1932.

People don't have to be all that old to be shy on the topic of age. Evasive Cyndi Lauper (quoted as being "around 30" in 1986) was born in New York City, on June 20, 1953. Notice how "around 30" can mean 33 but never 27. Despite a propensity for autobiography, Prince is closemouthed about age and other specifics of his early life. Even his real name was not known until several years after he became famous. Though most sources give his original name as Prince Rogers Nelson, the middle name of his birth certificate is *Roger*, not *Rogers* (which may be a clerical error), and he was born in Minneapolis on June 7, 1958.

Actors and Actresses

In her autobiography, Joan Collins said she was born in London on "May 23, sometime between the end of the Great Depression and the beginning of the war." Okay, the end of the Depression is a pretty vague concept. The designated historical window is compatible with Collins's string of tellingly ancient movies and TV shows. She appeared in a 1952 film, *Lady Godiva Rides Again*, in which she played a grown-up. Joan Collins is her real name, and her actual birth date is May 23, 1933. You'd have a hard time finding a historian who would say the Depression was over in Britain by the spring of 1933.

Quite a few television actresses refuse to discuss their age. Bea Arthur won't, and her reported ages have varied by several years (1926 in *Who's Who*; born Bernice Frankel in New York City, May 13, 1923). Ditto for Barbara Eden (born Barbara Huffman in Tucson, August 23, 1934). "I will not embarrass myself by pretending to be thirty when I'm fifty," Angie Dickinson once said. True to her word, at the half-century mark she was claiming to be only forty-five (reported year of birth, 1936; actually born Angeline Brown in Kulm, North Dakota, September 30, 1931).

As a rule of thumb, actresses who have played Hot Lips Houlihan are at least half a decade older than has been reported in the press. Sally Kellerman's claimed ages imply a birth date of 1942. Her birth certificate says she was born five years earlier in Long Beach, California (June 2, 1937). Loretta Swit's reported ages point to a year of birth in 1944 or 1946. In fact Swit was born in Passaic, New Jersey, on November 4, 1937. That's a *nine-year* discrepancy.

Many references say Diane Keaton was born in Santa Ana, California, in 1949. Orange County had no record of her birth; the missing certificate was in Los Angeles County records. Keaton was born Diane Hall in Los Angeles, and her date of birth is January 5, 1946.

Like many with a list of vintage credits as long as your arm, Ann

Miller claims to have had an early start in show business. An age of fourteen was reported for Miller's bit part as a grown-up woman in the Marx Brothers' *Room Service* (1938). That would make her year of birth around 1924. No day or year of birth appears in Miller's *Who's Who* entry. *The World Almanac* says Miller was born on April 12, 1919. That may be right, but neither Houston nor the state of Texas had a record of a Lucille Collier (Miller's original name) being born on that date.

The years of birth for sisters Jayne and Audrey Meadows present another conundrum. Were they born in 1926 and 1929, respectively, or in 1926 and 1924, or was it 1920 and 1924? Each pair of dates has made it into reference books. It's not even certain who's the older sister. We gave up on trying to obtain their birth certificates. The Meadows sisters were born as Jane and Audrey Cotter, daughters of a missionary, in Wu Chang, China. An old (1958) *Current Biography* says Jayne is two years older than Audrey. If we accept the two-year age difference and go with the earliest year reported for Jayne, that would give birth dates of September 27, 1920, for Jayne and February 8, 1922, for Audrey.

Why a woman with the unshakable self-assurance to pitch diapers for the incontinent would be squeamish about a few years is a mystery, but June Allyson's reported birth date is seven years late. The official studio-released date was long October 7, 1924. Allyson was born Jan Allyson in New York City in 1917.

These folks have good company. A small sampling of other wobbly years of birth includes those of Don Ameche (as late as 1908 has been claimed; born in Kenosha, Wisconsin, May 31, 1904), Dana Andrews (supposedly 1915; born Carver Dana Andrews in Collins, Mississippi, January 1, 1909), Martin Balsam (1923 claimed; born in New York City, November 4, 1919), Robert Blake (as late as 1938 reported; born Michael Gubitosi in Nutley, New Jersey, September 18, 1933), Alistair Cooke (1912 claimed; born Alfred Alistair Cooke in Manchester, England, on November 20, 1908), Tyne Daly (1947 in *World Almanac* vs. 1944 in *National Enquirer;* but really born Ellen Tyne Daly in Dane County, Wisconsin, on February 21, 1946), Douglas Fairbanks, Jr. (1909 in authorized biography; born in New York City on December 9, 1907), Mary Beth Hurt (no year in *Who's Who*, 1948 in the *National Enquirer*, 1949 elsewhere; born Mary Supinger, Marshalltown, Iowa, September 26, 1946), Glenda Jackson (1938 reported, but gave correct age of fifty-five during her 1992 political campaign; born Liverpool, England, May 9, 1936), Louis Jourdan (1922; born Louis Gendre in Marseilles, France, June 19, 1919), Angela Lansbury (allegedly 1927; born in London, October 16, 1925), Ida Lupino (said to be 1915 or 1918; born in London, February 4, 1914), Walter Matthau (1922 reported; born in New York City, October 1, 1920), Yvette Mimieux (claimed 1942; born in Los Angeles, January 8, 1939), Tony Musante (1941 given; born Bridgeport, Connecticut, June 30, 1936), Barry Nelson (officially 1925; born in San Francisco, April 16, 1920), Hugh O'Brian (claimed 1930; born Hugh Krampke—good name change—in Rochester, New York, April 19, 1925), George Peppard (1933 cited; born in Detroit, October 1, 1926), Sidney Poitier (February 20, 1927, in *Who's Who* and *World Almanac* vs. 1925 in *National Enquirer;* we are unable to confirm because Miami refuses to release birth information to anyone other than the person concerned), Telly Savalas (1927 given; born in Garden City, New York, January 21, 1924), Roy Scheider (1935 in *Who's Who;* born in Orange, New Jersey, November 10, 1932), and Shelley Winters (ostensibly 1925; born Shirley Schrift in St. Louis, August 18, 1922). None of the current crop of prevaricators can touch the achievement of the late Rosalind Russell, whose year of birth is given as early as 1892 and as late as 1912, an incredible two-decade difference. Russell died in 1976—they're pretty sure of that.

It is not hard to believe that the aging sex kitten or long-in-the-tooth heartthrob would lie about age, especially if their talent-to-sex-appeal ratio is low. The surprising thing is that they generally don't lie that much, at least no more than other performers. For Raquel Welch, we've got a reported year of birth of 1942 (born Raquel Tejada in Chicago, September 5, 1940); 1938 for Ursula Andress (born in Berne, Switzerland, March 19, 1936); 1929 for Melina Mercouri (born in Athens, October 18, 1925). We are unable to obtain definitive proof of Sophia Loren's date of birth in Rome (original name, Sophia Scicoloni), but years of 1932 and 1934 are quoted, and a press release gives her birthday as September 20. Hedy Lamarr listed 1914 as year of birth when she petitioned to change her name. In her 1966 autobiography, the date becomes 1915. Lamarr was born Hedwig Eva Maria Kiesler in Vienna, and most sources now agree on November 9, 1913, as her date of birth. These discrepancies are trifling, as these things go.

The passing years inspire some people to tell the truth. In *Me*, Katharine Hepburn admitted to having been born in 1907, "despite everything I might have said to the contrary." Recent *World Almanacs* concurred with Charles Higham's 1975 biography in placing her year of birth in 1909. Hepburn was born in Hartford, Connecticut, on November 8. A frank Mickey Rooney (born in Brooklyn, New York, September 23, 1920, or possibly 1922) gives 1920 the nod in his 1965 *I.E.: An Autobiography*.

On Reflection, Helen Hayes's 1968 autobiography, says its subject was born at the turn of the century. Kinder sources have said 1901. Yet when the century was still young, for years *The World Almanac* said Helen Hayes was born in 1895. District of Columbia records confirm Hayes's own story. She was born Helen Brown in Washington in 1900. Hayes celebrates October 10 as her birthday, and all published sources we've seen concur, but the birth certificate says October 11.

Comics

Fudged ages are well and fine for romantic leads. The likes of (say) an Arte Johnson can be honest about his age. Right?

Some of the biggest liars are comedians. Way back in 1965, a *National Observer* interviewer asked Joan Rivers her age. "I don't think it's anybody's business," she told him. She has stonewalled ever since. If press reports can be believed, Rivers has *forbidden* Barnard College, her alma mater, to say when she attended. A lot of people didn't even know you could do that. Older editions of *Who's Who* had Rivers born in 1937 and graduating in 1958. The current edition moves the year of birth back to 1933, but still has her getting her B.A. in 1958. Rivers's autobiography doesn't say when she was born yet volunteers the information that she was thirty-one when she first appeared on *The Tonight Show*. You can't go by her looks. Rivers wasn't joking when she told *TV Guide*, "Plastic surgery is like a tool in a career tool chest." For all this reticence, Rivers got a lot of mileage out of a turning-fifty routine in the late 1980s.

Rivers appears in the 1954 Barnard yearbook. Her *Tonight Show* debut was on February 17, 1965. If she was thirty-one then, she would have been born in 1933, as her birthday is in June. Rivers was born Joan Sandra Molinsky in Brooklyn, June 8, 1933.

Don Rickles is missing a mere two years (1928 reported; born in New York City on May 8, 1926); ditto for Morey Amsterdam (1914 reported; born in Chicago, December 14, 1912). *Who's Who* says Tom Poston was born in 1927, but it also has him entering Bethany College (as an eleven-year-old prodigy?) in 1938. Poston was born in Columbus, Ohio, on October 17, 1921. In 1980 Red Skelton fessed up to *People* magazine that he was "in my 70s," despite a theoretical age of sixty-six computed from the almanacs (born July 18, 1913, or thereabouts, in Vincennes, Indiana).

One of the most incredible cases is that of Imogene Coca. Older sources, such as the 1970 *World Almanac*, give her year of birth as 1920. More recent accounts push this back a whole *decade* (Coca was eighty-two in 1992, according to the *San Francisco Chronicle*). In interviews Coca refuses to discuss her age.

It's unclear who was responsible for the 1920 date. Coca is fourteen years older than *Show of Shows* costar Sid Caesar, and frequently played his wife. Maybe relationships between older women and younger men were taboo on 1950s TV, and they wanted to play down the age difference. In any case, the 1920 date is way, way off. It would have meant Coca was five when she made her Broadway debut as a chorus girl in *When You Smile* (October 5, 1925)—this after *years* of working in vaudeville, according to biographies. The date on her birth certificate (born Emogeani Coca in Philadelphia, November 18, 1908) is a full twelve years earlier than the commonly used date.

The alumni of *Laugh-In* are staving off late middle age with massive injections of denial. Arte Johnson has shed five years (1934 year of birth reported; born in Benton Harbor, Michigan, January 20, 1929). Dick Martin's reported age has varied by six years (1922 through 1928; born January 30, 1922). This is nothing next to Tiny Tim. At the time of his 1969 marriage on *The Tonight Show*, Tim claimed a 1932 birth. 1933 has also been reported. He was actually born Herbert Buckingham Khaury in New York City on April 12, 1923. Tim was forty-six, claiming to be thirty-seven, in 1969. Not many people can lop off 20 percent of their age and keep a straight face.

Emcees

Everyone wants to believe that Dick Clark is really about ninety. Nope. When Clark was sworn in as a character witness in a 1991 investment-fraud trial in Dallas, the prosecutor took advantage of the situation to ask his age. Clark answered that he was sixty-one. That agrees with records showing that he was born in Mount Vernon, New York, on November 30, 1929, and attended Syracuse University from 1947 to 1951.

Who's Who gives Bob Barker's birthday (December 12), charitably omitting the year. Barker's birth certificate is more informative (born Robert William Barker, Darrington, Washington, in 1923). Monty Hall's 1973 autobiography has nary a mention of a date of birth. He was supposedly born with the surname Halparin in Winnipeg, Manitoba. Manitoba's vital-statistics bureau was unable to find a record of the birth, though. Birth dates of August 25, 1923, and 1925, have been given in the press.

Cosmetics Tycoons

If you ever make it big in the cosmetics business, you will be expected to become an ageless icon yourself. That is the message of the incredible secrecy surrounding the ages of Estée Lauder and Mary Kay Ash (of Mary Kay Cosmetics), each a hostage to the promise of eternal youth on which their fortunes are based.

Ash gives out her birthday (May 12) but won't say how many of them she's celebrated. The photo that appears over and over in the company brochures (wearing a black outfit with a gold bee broach) is a haunting image that makes her look like she's in her mid-thirties. Her eye shadow, not to mention her eyebrows, appears to have been airbrushed onto an utterly unlined face. About the only date ever mentioned in company literature is 1963. That's when Ash founded the company. She wasn't a kid then (she had "retired from a long and prosperous career in direct sales"). So the official photo is either *very* old or *very* flattering.

Ash was born May Kay Wagner in Hot Wells, Texas. She was a student at the University of Texas from 1942 to 1943. If she attended right after high school, that would put her birth around 1924, and she'd be old enough to collect social security.

Estée Lauder has been known to say that age is an "irrelevancy." According to *Who's Who*, Lauder has been chairman of the board of her eponymous company since 1946. Her first marriage was in 1930. Lauder, too, has a Dorian Gray photo that makes her remarkably young-looking in view of how old you know she *has* to be. Lauder's birth certificate is filed in the archives division of New York City's records, which is home to documentation of births registered before 1910. She was born Josephine Esther Mentzer in Corona (Queens), New York, on July 1, 1908.

Nancy Reagan

It's darned near impossible to survive eight years of the fishbowl world of a president's wife with any secrets intact. Nancy Reagan sure tried. Press kits distributed in her husband's presidential campaigns and throughout his presidency gave Nancy's birthday as July 6, 1923. The press soon discovered that Nancy Davis had attended Smith College from 1939 to 1943. Now it's conceivable that Nancy was such a brain that she skipped two grades and entered college early. But Miss Davis was also a Chicago debutante in 1939. As far as we can tell, there's no such thing as a deb qualifying for an "advanced-placement" coming out. It has been ascertained that Nancy was born Anne Frances Robbins in Manhattan, on July 6, 1921. In her autobiography Nancy says she forgets the name of the hospital where she was born—a convenient lapse of memory, considering New York City's insistence on that datum when applying for a copy of a birth certificate. She was born in Sloane Hospital.

Two years is no big deal for a former actress. But there are some old-fashioned enough to think that a First Lady shouldn't lie about anything that can be checked. Magazines ran snippy items like "Nancy Reagan, 62, celebrated her 60th birthday." *Current Biography* lists her birth date as "July 6, 1921(?)" and then goes on to make it clear that this is a lie and everyone knows it. Kitty Kelley's biography reproduced the birth certificate. Nancy was confronted repeatedly on the matter, and some of her comebacks were pretty good. Asked when she was born, she replied, "I haven't decided yet."

The Gabor Sisters

Where age is concerned, one of the few things the chronologically challenged Gabor sisters agree upon is that Eva is the youngest of the trio. Otherwise, details are either missing or relatively inaccessible in a Hungarian record bureau. Absurd, presumably, is the urban legend about the Gabor sisters being unrelated ex-whores who immigrated to the U.S. with their madam, the woman who pretends to be their mother. Modern DNA fingerprinting could put the lie to this story, should the Gabors care to submit tissue samples.

The September 6, 1952, issue of *Collier's* ran a photo-feature on the Gabor clan. "Though their exact ages are classified top secret," the article said, "Mama Jolie is certainly the oldest, Magda is late thirtyish; Zsa Zsa early thirtyish. Eva admits to being past twenty-five and below thirty-one." The article quotes Zsa Zsa as calling Eva "my younger—but not much younger—sister." This implies ballpark years of birth of 1915 for Magda, 1924 for Zsa Zsa, and later but also circa 1924 for Eva. *Collier's* reported that the Gabors were "somewhat witty." "We are a very simple, average family," Magda told the magazine.

Orchids and Salami, Eva Gabor's 1954 autobiography, insists petulantly that "to this very day I am not thirty-three. . . ." Eva was taking umbrage at a 1950 magazine article that claimed her to be thirty-three then. Eva said the writer was settling a personal score. If that article was true, she would have been born about 1917. Taking Eva at her word, she would have been born no earlier than 1921.

The *Celebrity Register* gives a kinder birth date of "February 11 circa 1924." *Current Biography* (1968) gives 1926 with a question mark, and the yet more generous 1970 *World Almanac* made it 1929. Eva was "reportedly 67" in the *Los Angeles Times* (June 7, 1988), which jibes with recent editions of *The World Almanac* (born 1921). The *National Enquirer* buys 1923. The range of reported dates of Eva Gabor's birth thus runs from circa 1917 to 1929.

The 1929 date is just short of physically impossible. Eva married Dr. Eric Drimmer and moved to Hollywood in 1939 (at age ten?). She was the leading lady in the extremely bad movie, *Forced Landing* in 1941 (age twelve?). Her acting was so deficient in the worthless 1942 film *Pacific Blackout* that Paramount dropped her contract (a has-been and divorcée at thirteen?).

The 1929 date means Gabor would have been only thirty-six for the first season of TV's *Green Acres*, a fact hard to square with the heroic means used to keep her looking youthful for the show. Reportedly, makeup artist Gene Hibbs rigged up a sort of mechanical face-lift. Flesh-colored adhesive-tape patches were affixed to Gabor's forehead. Elastic bands running around her head kept tension on the tape patches, lifting folds of sagging skin. This somewhat grotesque setup was concealed by Lisa Douglas's stylish hairdos.

Eva was born in Hungary, of course, and her first marriage took place in Europe. Her paper trail starts on this side of the Atlantic with her marriage to real estate millionaire Charles Isaacs in September 1943. On that certificate, she listed her age as *twenty-two*. It is hard to believe that the May half of a May-December marriage would subtract years from her age when applying for the marriage license. A quick computation gives us a year of birth of 1921. Evidently Eva was being truthful in her biography. She was lying, or permitting lies to be told, during the late-1960s run of *Green Acres*. The maximum downward revision was eight years (approximately 16 percent of her age in 1970).

This pales next to the riddle wrapped in an enigma that is sister Zsa Zsa's age. The tactful *World Almanac* gives only an agnostic dash in lieu of Zsa Zsa's birth date, equating it with such unknowables as the fate of the lost dauphin. Who else but Zsa Zsa would hand out alleged copies of her Hungarian birth certificate at a press conference? These bore the date February 6, 1928.

A date of 1919 was long the one generally used by the wire services in calculating Zsa Zsa's age for parenthetical mention in items on her zany doings. A January 1989 Associated Press story found "Gabor, 69," being kicked off a plane for releasing her Shih Tzus from their travel kennels and letting them frolic in the cabin. "If I live to be 100 I'll never understand why five policemen would have to come and take me off the plane," Gabor complained, insinuating that she was still shy of the century mark.

The 1919 date is cited in the *Television and Video Almanac* (1987 edition), *The World Almanac* (1980 edition), and, with question mark appended, *Current Biography* (1988). *Celebrity Register* (1986 update) gives February 6 in either 1921 or 1923. Older sources often use 1923 (*World Almanac*, 1970 edition). A 1986 piece in the *Los Angeles Times* found Zsa Zsa claiming 1928, while "experts" favored 1919.

When Zsa Zsa went on trial for roughing up a Beverly Hills police officer in 1989, she claimed *in court* to be sixty-six. Lying about age while under oath is perjury, but enforcement is lax. Officer Paul Kramer testified that the birth date on Gabor's expired license had been altered. The prosecution produced a blown-up facsimile of Gabor's driver's license, issued in 1986. It was a remarkable document. One *entire line* of data (sex, hair, eyes, height, weight, *and* date of birth!) had been altered, the new information entered in pen over the typewritten original. The changes recall the ingenuity of a third grader with a bad report card. Rather than alter just the crucial items, trace over the other information too. Out of court, Zsa Zsa said the license had been stolen by Mexicans and returned with the alterations.

The license birth date was changed from 06-06-23 to 02-06-28, and the weight from 130 to 110. It's tough to change a 3 to a 1, and a lesser woman might have settled for a 2. Zsa Zsa ingeniously bent the bottom of the 1 left into a serif to cover the down stroke of the 3.

Also in 1989 Zsa Zsa proved her ability to live with contradiction when she swore—literally *swore* in a legal document—to being born in 1930. The document in question was an application for a license to marry her eighth husband, Frederick von Anhalt. Von Anhalt's former girlfriend, Silla Molnar, had recently committed suicide after he refused to marry her. Molnar was seventeen years old.

The 1930 date seems to be the most recent that Zsa Zsa has (yet) dared claim. It would make her a six-year-old Miss Hungary contestant in 1936 and a jail-bait bride at seven. (Of that unsuccessful 1937 marriage to Burhan Belge, press director of the Foreign Ministry of Turkey, Zsa Zsa has said that she wasn't ready for marriage.) It would also mean that Zsa Zsa had divorced Belge, married Conrad Hilton, divorced him, and married third husband George Sanders all before the usual age of consent.

Not too surprisingly, no date of birth figures in the first authorized biography, *Zsa Zsa Gabor: My Story,* "written for me by Gerald Frank" and published in 1960. Emboldened by advancing age, Zsa Zsa teased readers of her 1991 autobiography with the promise of *partial* disclosure of her age: "They will be able to figure it out," she claimed. The new bio was titled, with what might be disarming frankness, *One Lifetime Is Not Enough*. It used such devices as a passage set "somewhere in time" in which Zsa Zsa regresses in memory to when she was twelve years old and the world was a lot younger.

There's no need to bother with arcane hints. In the wake of the publicity attending Gabor's cop-slugging trial, Elizabeth Nussbaum of Seattle, a former classmate of Zsa Zsa's at the exclusive Madame Subilia's School for Young Ladies in Lausanne, Switzerland, produced an incriminating school photo. It gave Zsa Zsa's birth date as February 6, 1917.

This appears to make sense in view of other clues dropped over the years. Biographies say that Zsa Zsa attended Madame Subilia's from age thirteen to fifteen and that during her second summer vacation, she was first runner-up in the Miss Hungary contest. In *Women Confidential* (1960), columnist Lee Mortimer said there was "a picture of her winning some beauty contest in Budapest in 1933," a statement that would be hard to accept *if* the picture is identified with Zsa Zsa's 1936 victory. Were Mortimer talking about a picture of Zsa Zsa "winning" first runner-up at age fifteen or so, it would be consistent with the 1917 date.

Nussbaum was not the first classmate to dispute Zsa Zsa's chronology. There's a Budapest grade-school classmate who goes around claiming Zsa Zsa was born in 1914. Mere recollections can be clouded by time and spite. It's the documentation that makes Nussbaum's claim believable.

That makes Zsa Zsa four years older than Eva. Never, ever, or so it seems, has she publicly admitted to her real age as an adult. Zsa Zsa's claimed year of birth has actually been advancing faster than the passage of time itself. It leaped *seven* years forward in the *three*-year interval between applying for her 1986 driver's license and the 1989 marriage certificate. If this trend continues unchecked, Zsa Zsa will be claiming to be twenty-one years old by the year 2018.

Charo

The Tennessee legislature may have once mulled over a bill making pi equal to three, but a Nevada court *legally* changed the age of Charo. Other stars may lie until they're blue in the face. Charo alone has a legal document asserting the birthday of her choice.

Charo was born Charro Baeza in Murcia, Spain. For eons, town records said this event took place on March 13, 1941. To her credit, Charo has consistently maintained that that date is wrong. She has wavered only in how many years it's wrong. When Charo came to attention in the mid 1960s, she said she was born in 1947. A few years later, she started counting from 1949. In 1966 Charo married sixty-six-year-old band leader Xavier Cugat. She was then just barely of legal age (she said) or twenty-five (really). As the years went by, Charo was determined to stay twenty-something, even though when she stopped jiggling, she looked older.

By 1977 Charo was so fed up with the skeptics that she went to court. Wisely choosing the venue (Las Vegas), Charo told a U.S. judge that the birth date on her naturalization papers and passport was wrong. Clerical error had got a digit wrong; instead of 1941, it was 1951. This would have made her fifteen when she married Cugat. As evidence, Charo supplied affidavits from her parents. The judge officially moved the perpetual calendar ahead to 1951. Crazy? Just crazy enough to work. *The World Almanac, National Enquirer*, and many other fine publications accept the 1951 date.

2.

Secret Identities

Secret identities are common in comic books. They're not that common in real life. We mean an actual Superman/Clark Kent deal, where the person is famous in one context, yet manages to keep secret a "real" name, appearance, biography, and/or whereabouts. This narrows the field considerably. A mere stage name doesn't count. Nor do people who do American Express commercials. We mean people who are serious about keeping a secret identity secret—preferably to an obsessive degree.

Many performers are reluctant to mention their "real" names. Few who ascend to the *People* magazine-cover level of celebrity succeed in keeping that name a secret. The most famous person in America today who keeps her legal name secret is probably Whoopi Goldberg. In 1984 she told *The Washington Post*, "I can go home and live as this other person and even though I look like Whoopi Goldberg on the street, I can whip out my driver's license and say, 'Hey, but I'm not.' " Goldberg's cover has been blown. Her real name is Caryn Johnson (born in New York City, November 13, 1949).

Trevanian

In 1979 Trevanian, best-selling author of spy thrillers, reluctantly agreed to an interview with a writer for *The New York Times Book Review*. Trevanian is a pen name, and the author "is adamant about avoiding publicity—just as he is adamant about hiding his real identity," claimed the *Times*. To that end, the paper ran a head shot of the author sitting in the dark, his face turned away from the camera.

"He talked fast, sounding self-confident and at times arrogant, and always referring to his pseudonymous self in the third person," wrote the *Times* interviewer. The article also reported that Trevanian looked a little like Clint Eastwood. Eastwood starred in the film version of *The Eiger Sanction*.

Who is Trevanian, really? In interviews he stonewalls not only on his name but also on his date and place of birth. The few facts he has divulged sound like something out of his novels. Like the hero of *Shibumi*, Trevanian says he was in Japan during the aftermath of Hiroshima, lives in a small Basque village, and doesn't like the United States much.

It's not such a bad publicity angle for a writer of spy novels to have a secret identity. Trevanian's real-life cloak-and-dagger mystery has inspired at least two rumors that haven't hurt sales of his books. One is that Trevanian is a former CIA agent. The other is that Trevanian is really Robert Ludlum.

The case for the Ludlum theory is that (a) Ludlum has used pseudonyms—Jonathan Ryder and Michael Shepherd—that we know about; (b) Ludlum's first book was published the year before the first Trevanian book appeared; (c) Ludlum's 1973 novel *The Matlock Paper* is about a tweedy English professor who's really a secret agent, while Trevanian's 1972 *The Eiger Sanction* and 1973 *The Loo Sanction* are about a tweedy art professor who's a spy; (d) all those three-word titles sound alike; and (e) one of Ludlum's pseudonymous books was titled *Trevayne*, which sounds like Trevanian.

Trevanian blasted the Ludlum idea in his 1979 *New York Times* interview: "I don't even know who he is. I read Proust, but not much else written in the 20th century." *Oh.*

The key to Trevanian's real identity is the fact that he was once a college professor. Nat Wartels, who published Trevanian at Crown, told *The New York Times* that Trevanian was teaching film at the University of Texas when he submitted *The Eiger Sanction*.

Numerous references to academia occur in Trevanian's works (among them his professor/superspy Jonathan Hemlock). A character in *The Main* jokes that someone was "so dumb he'd have difficulty making the faculty of a polytechnic in Britain, or getting his Ph.D. in journalism in the States. . . . That line would get a laugh in an academic crowd."

Academic personnel are well documented in college catalogs and faculty directories. There weren't that many lecturers on film at the University of Texas circa 1971. We quickly determined that Trevanian's true identity is Rodney Whitaker, Ph.D. (1925–   ). A university-supplied photo shows that, yes, Whitaker looks a little like Clint Eastwood. He doesn't look like Robert Ludlum. Whitaker later taught at Emerson College in Boston.

In 1970 Whitaker published a scholarly tome, *The Language of Film*. A typical line from the first page: "We shall seek to trace the linguistic and mechanical development of the medium; to describe the content implications of image and sound; to suggest the contributions of editing and montage; to examine the cohesive envelopes of plot, theme, narrative organization, and histrionics; to deal with the role of meaning in the modern film; and finally to take an overview of the nonlinguistic modes of the avant-garde and the underground."

Whitaker's name appears in the credits for the film version of *The Eiger Sanction*. A check of library catalogs and periodical indexes flushed out other Whitaker/Trevanian pseudonyms: Nicholas Seare and Beñat LeCagot. Oddly, *The Language of Film* is credited to Nicholas Seare in some catalogs, even though the name Rod Whitaker appears on the title page. This Nicholas Seare is identified as R. Whitaker in catalogs and has written medieval tales: *1339 . . . or So: Being an Apology for a Pedlar* (1975) and *Rude Tales and Glorious: Being the Only True Account of Diverse Feats of Brawn and Bawd Performed by King Arthur and His Knights of the Table Round* (1983). Beñat LeCagot, on the other hand, has published a story in *Harper's*. LeCagot is supposedly the pen name of Arnaud Etcheberria (1902–1971), author of Basque verse, which is said to be untranslatable. LeCagot also happens to be a fictional character in Trevanian's *Shibumi*. As *Harper's* gives Trevanian a translation credit for the story, we think LeCagot/Etcheberria equals Whitaker/Trevanian/Seare.

The clincher is that Trevanian alludes to his real identity in *The Loo Sanction*. The versatile Jonathan Hemlock rattles on in an impromptu lecture on film, commenting that "the intensity of the visual beat is a function of what Whitaker, in his lean description of film linguistics, has called 'cutting volume.' "

Ghostwriters

There are, of course, many writers who remain anonymous to some degree. For years the Stratemeyer Syndicate, the organization behind the Nancy Drew and Hardy Boys books, thought it necessary to perpetuate the myth that the bylined Carolyn Keene and Franklin W. Dixon were real authors. Syndicate contracts required that the people who wrote the books never reveal their identities. Each series has been written from syndicate-supplied plot outlines by many ghostwriters over the years.

The first Carolyn Keene was Harriet S. Adams (circa 1893–1982). She had the good fortune to be the daughter of syndicate founder Edward Stratemeyer and thereby shared in her books' financial success. Not so lucky was the original Franklin W. Dixon, Canadian author and filmmaker Leslie McFarlane (1902–1977). McFarlane got a flat fee of $125 per book. As he once noted, McFarlane never learned what the *W.* in Franklin W. Dixon stood for, but it wasn't *Wealthy.* In the early years McFarlane was so cowed by the secrecy clause in his contract that he barely worked up the courage to tell his mother about the Hardy Boys books—and he lived with her at the time. After penning his last Hardy Boys book, McFarlane made several documentaries, one of which, *Herring Hunt* (RKO, 1953), was nominated for an Academy Award. To confuse things further, Adams also wrote some of the Hardy Boys books under the Dixon pen name, and McFarlane wrote some Dana Girls books under the Keene name.

Though not credited, it's well known that *New Republic* columnist T.R.B. was Richard Strout (1940s–1983), succeeded by Michael Kinsley (1983–). Incidentally, T.R.B. is a registered trademark.

We hate to blow a fellow vade mecum author's cover, but *Straight Dope* columnist Cecil Adams (variously described as "one of the world's legendary recluses" and "reputedly the world's smartest human being," and never photographed) is a guy named Ed Zotti. Zotti is credited as Adams's "editor and confidant."

Thomas Pynchon

Surely the most secretive literary figure of the late twentieth century is Thomas Pynchon. There are more, and clearer, photos of Bigfoot than of Thomas Pynchon. The only photo generally available is from his 1953 high school yearbook. Remember, the guy is in his *fifties* now. Pynchon had turned camera shy by his freshman year at Cornell, when he refused to submit a photo for the freshman register. The publication of *V* resulted in *Life* photographers stalking Pynchon through Mexico. They didn't find him. The jacket of Pynchon's *The Crying of Lot 49* had a black rectangle where the author's photo would normally be.

No reclusive writer's fame is complete without the rumor that he is really someone else entirely. Pynchon has been rumored to be J. D. Salinger (who has himself been in relative seclusion since the 1950s). In support of this: (a) Salinger's last book, *Raise High the Roofbeam, Carpenters and Seymour: An Introduction*, appeared in 1963. Pynchon's first book, *V*, appeared in 1963. (b) Salinger's publisher is Little, Brown. Pynchon's publisher is also Little, Brown. (c) The cover of the current paperback edition of *Catcher in the Rye* has a set of diagonal colored stripes in the upper left corner—a "rainbow" not unlike a similar device on the right side of the paperback cover of *Gravity's Rainbow*. (d) No one has ever seen Salinger and Pynchon together.

The ultimate source of the Pynchon-equals-Salinger rumor is novelist John Calvin Batchelor (*The Birth of the People's Republic of Antarctica*). In 1976 and 1977 Batchelor aired his suspicion in a series of articles in the *Soho Weekly News*. In the mid-1960s, noted Batchelor, Salinger said he was writing about his experiences in World War II. Salinger had been a counterintelligence agent whose job it was to interrogate SS and Gestapo agents. Well, *Gravity's Rainbow* is about the war, and it describes the interrogation of a German officer. Salinger was known to admire Emily Dickinson and Rainer Maria Rilke. Both are quoted in *Gravity's Rainbow*. "A nom de plume now afforded Salinger the anonymity he had sought but failed to find as Caulfield's creator," wrote Batchelor. "It was the perfect cover."

But in 1977 Batchelor got a letter from Pynchon—or from someone claiming to be Pynchon. It was on Metro-Goldwyn-Mayer stationery (as far as anyone knows, Pynchon never worked there) and contained the enigmatic advice, "Some of it is true, but none of the interesting parts. Keep trying."

Batchelor compared the signature to existing specimens of Pynchon's handwriting. He decided it was legitimate. By then the story had a life of its own.

We were able, with little trouble, to confirm Pynchon's existence from a couple of sources that seem unlikely to be in collusion: Professor Irwin Corey, the comic Pynchon hired to accept his National Book Award for him, and the employment department of Boeing Aircraft, where Pynchon once wrote for the *Minuteman Service News*, a house organ for missile workers. Boeing couldn't release any writing samples because the *Service News* was produced for the air force and is still considered a secret document. They could say that Pynchon was hired on February 22, 1960, and resigned on September 13, 1962.

Pynchon's whereabouts have been a secret ever since. Common accounts place him (at some point) somewhere in Mexico; in the bohemian enclave of Arcata, California, about two hundred miles north of San Francisco; somewhere in Oregon. According to a *Biggest Secrets* informant, Pynchon has settled down and now resides quietly in the upper west side of a large East Coast city. Pynchon is slim, a little over six feet tall, with gray hair and a mustache. If you want an idea of what he looked like in high school, go to a library and look at page 450 of the 1987 *Current Biography Yearbook*.

Gael Greene

Gael Greene's lavishly photographed restaurant pieces in *New York* magazine show assorted beautiful diners, but never Greene herself. Greene takes her mystery-reviewer persona seriously enough to hide her features with a large floppy hat for TV interviews. Were her face generally known, she would get special treatment, and her reviews would be invalid. That's the theory, anyway, and it's not so paranoid as it sounds.

It is a near-universal practice for major restaurant reviewers to make reservations under someone else's name. That way, the restaurant can't prepare something special for the critic. More corruptible reviewers are content to leave it at that, and are only too glad to accept any special treatment they might get once recognized. Others consider it their duty to pay with a credit card issued in another name; to don glasses, wigs, or other disguises; and, most important of all, to keep their likenesses out of the media.

Restaurants have been known to post photos of food critics and offer a reward to the first waiter to spot them. Greene herself told of an incident where a companion raved about his lamb. Greene, who had ordered the same dish, found it only so-so. As she happened to know the chef, she told him about it, and he said, "But *he* must have gotten the plate I sent out for *you*."

As one of the most respected, powerful, and anonymous of American restaurant reviewers, Greene is prime meat for New York's paparazzi. Enough candid shots exist to assemble a photo mosaic of the rarely seen face under the hat. Greene is a female Caucasian in her late fifties, with shoulder-length graying hair, given to funky outfits with a hat and lots of costume jewelry. A suspected Greene sighting may be confirmed by the presence of a ring on the little finger of the right hand—noticeable on the looming, flash-overexposed hand of paparazzi photos.

Guerrilla Girls

Life imitates Mexican wrestler movies. There are grown-up people in America today who appear in public *only in masks*. The curiously fetishistic outfit of gorilla mask, miniskirt, and fishnet stockings is the trademark of the Guerrilla Girls, a band of feminist artists who periodically paper Manhattan with their broadsides. Articles insist that no one ("even close friends and significant others") knows who they are or how many of them there are. They appear masked for TV guest shots and lecture dates (before they hit on the obvious pun, they used stockings or ski masks to conceal their faces).

At the absolute minimum, there are five Guerrilla Girls (group photos show that many). In 1990 *The New York Times* guessed that there were "three dozen to four dozen" members, basing its estimate on phone interviews with "about six." The Guerrilla Girls themselves talk of a diverse group with a wide range of ages, ethnicities, and professions. That sounds like a fair number.

Any would-be unmasker must address a 1989 poster in which the Guerrilla Girls unmasked themselves—or did they? Under the headline "GUERRILLA GIRLS' IDENTITIES EXPOSED!" the poster listed five hundred names and claimed there were many others.

Like most of the organization's efforts, the posters lasted only a few days in New York City's mean streets (some people were peeling them off as collectibles). Among the prominent artists named were Jennifer Bartlett, Audrey Flack, April Gornik, Nancy

Graves, Jenny Holzer, Holly Hughes, Mary Miss, Elizabeth Murray, Judy Pfaff, Adrian Piper, Erika Rothenberg, Alison Saar, and Cindy Sherman.

Are these women Guerrillas? *Vanity Fair*'s Anthony Hayden-Guest thought not. He ingeniously postulated that the *real* Guerrilla Girls would never reveal their names; ergo, the women on the list can be *definitely ruled out* as suspects. It seems more likely that the women listed agreed with the organization's aims and said it was okay to use their names. That at least ought to make them honorary members. Most of them probably never donned a plastic gorilla head, though. A plausible candidate for the inner circle of guerrilladom: Martha Wilson, director of the Franklin Furnace arts facility in SoHo. The Guerrilla Girls operate out of the Franklin Furnace building, and Wilson's name is included on the "Exposed" poster.

The Residents

Never, in concert or in their videos, does the band calling itself the Residents let you see their faces. "Despite 13 albums in 11 years, the four members of the sexually indeterminate band—anonymous Bay Area cult heroes—give no interviews and no clues to their identity, and never appear in public unmasked," noted *People* magazine in 1984. A 1986 *Rolling Stone* write-up observed that the group "stripped down to black-hooded body stockings (revealing rather feminine figures—are the Residents half-female?)" and wondered facetiously "if Alice Cooper, Laurie Anderson, Rod Serling, and Igor Stravinsky weren't hiding behind those big bloodshot orbs." In recent years the speculation has centered on the now-defunct Talking Heads. By one theory, the Residents *are* the Talking Heads, or an offshoot à la the Tom-Tom Club. A related theory is that there's really just one Resident, and he is David Byrne.

Considerable ingenuity has been expended in attempts to find out who the Residents are. On a European tour photographers learned the hotel where the group was staying and began knocking on doors and photographing everyone who answered. Complained spokesman Hardy Fox in 1990, "It's the kind of stuff they might do with Jacqueline Onassis or something. It's all rather stupid. The Residents don't really care. It doesn't matter. Why it matters to someone is totally beyond them."

The trouble with being so anonymous is that it's tough to do the interviews more or less demanded of a touring rock group. The Residents have resorted to "spokesmen" Fox (identified as a studio engineer and officer of the Residents' aptly named production company, the Cryptic Corporation) and Homer Flynn (claimed to be a San Francisco artist) for interviews. Stephen Ronon of *Mondo 2000* magazine plied both Fox and Flynn with drink yet failed to come up with band members' identities.

According to Fox and Flynn, the future band members went to school together in Shreveport, Louisiana, and moved to the Bay Area during 1967's "Summer of Love." There they lived over an auto body shop in San Mateo. Both Fox and Flynn have distinct southern accents. Could, uh, they actually *be* Residents? You rarely ever see an article on the Residents where the writer doesn't mention rumors to that effect, quickly followed by Fox or Flynn's unequivocal denial. Both are scrupulous about referring to the Residents in the third person.

Four Residents appear on stage and in videos. The trademark disguise consists of bloodshot eyeballs in tuxes and top hats, with a black skull for the fourth Resident. It does not necessarily follow that there are four Residents in the recording studio. Flynn hinted as much when he told *Mondo 2000*, "There's lots of pictures and always four in each one. I make those pictures, and I've always been extremely careful."

Biggest Secrets sneaked a tape recorder into a lecture Homer Flynn gave on music video to get a sample of his speaking voice. Flynn's voice, it turns out, sounds extremely similar to that of someone on the Residents' albums. Vocals on "Toddler Lullaby" (*The Big Bubble* album), "Loss of Innocence" (*Commercial Album*), and "Nobody Laughs When They Leave" (*Freak Show*) sound like Flynn.

To confirm our suspicions, we compared voiceprints of Flynn, the Resident who sounds like Flynn, and David Byrne. Voiceprinting, which has been accepted as evidence of identity in court, uses taped samples of known and unknown persons saying the same word or phrase. Normally, a known person is asked to recite the text of a taped sample of an unknown person's voice. We had to settle for coincidental occurrences of the same phrase in the Flynn speech, Residents albums, and Byrne/Talking Heads albums.

Much of the vocals on Residents albums are electronically modified. We found a long monologue by the Flynn sound-alike at the end of "Toddler Lullaby." This is spoken rather than sung, sounds undoctored or relatively so, and is plainly audible above the music. The monologue had many words in common with the tape of Flynn's speech. In establishing identity on the basis of voice samples, phrases are preferred to isolated words, as syllables are intoned differently according to context. We found four pairs of words occurring in "Toddler Lullaby" and in the tape of Flynn's speech. They were "I guess," "I think," "and they," and "of the." The first two phrases were clear; the latter two, less so. We were also able to find a sample of David Byrne singing "I think" in "Girls on My Mind" on his solo album *Uh-oh*. These phrases were digitized and fed into software that produces spectrograms (time vs. frequency vs. power graphs). Normally these spectrograms ("voiceprints") are characteristic of each speaker.

The "I think" spectrogram for David Byrne was distinctly different from the same spectrogram of the Resident who sounds like Flynn—not surprising, since Byrne sounds nothing at all like the southern-accented Resident in "Toddler Lullaby." We could not find any vocals on several Residents albums that sounded much like they could be Byrne.

The spectrograms for Flynn and the "Toddler Lullaby" voice appeared to match well, *except* that the latter is higher in pitch. The characteristic formants (peaks in strength) are shifted about 15 percent higher up the frequency spectrum. For instance, the beginning of the word *think* contains a striking V-shaped pattern in both Flynn's and the Resident's voiceprints (but not in Byrne's or that of another speaker we tested). The top of the V is about 2,800 hertz in Flynn's spectrogram; about 3,200 in the voice of the singer in "Toddler Lullaby." The pronoun *I* has three strong formants in Flynn's spectrogram (at about 600, 1,400, and 2,800 hertz). The Resident's spectrogram has formants at about 600, 1,600, and 3,200 hertz.

The "I guess" spectrograms for Flynn and the mystery Resident were also similar, aside from an identical frequency shift. In both, the word *guess* has a prominent parenthesis-shaped formant. The center of the parenthesis is at about 2,000 hertz for Flynn; 2,400 hertz for the Resident.

This essential similarity suggests that the voice on "Toddler Lullaby" is Flynn's voice, raised slightly in pitch in the recording

studio. One of the advantages of voiceprints is that the characteristic patterns are not changed by such manipulation. While two-
word samples are shorter than voiceprint experts like to use in a
courtroom setting, the similarities in the spectrograms second the
convincing subjective impression that the voices are identical.

One Residents video, "Moisture," includes frenetic shots of a
gyrating and grimacing but barely disguised guitar player who looks
a lot like Flynn. The glasses that the guitar player is wearing look
like the glasses Flynn wore at the lecture.

The most obvious reason why Homer Flynn would be appearing in all those Residents albums and videos is that he is not just a
friend of the Residents but *is* a Resident himself. You have to
wonder if "spokesman" Hardy Fox isn't a Resident, too. It is even
possible that the creative core of the Residents is the duo of Flynn
and Fox.

II: Merchandise

3·

Mrs. Fields Cookies

For someone who dots her *i*'s with little hearts, Debbi Fields is a shrewd businesswoman. She has built a worldwide empire of cookie stores on the strength of the top-secret recipe she invented —a secret that earns her company a 6 percent royalty on every cookie sold at investor-owned stores. In her 1987 biography, *One Smart Cookie*, Fields writes that "the cookie recipes were in my head and nowhere else. I'd never even written them down. This used to scare some people—I mean, somebody runs a red light and that's the end of Mrs. Fields Cookies."

Formerly a foul-line girl for the Oakland A's, a Christmas elf for Mervyn's department store, and a water skier in Marine World's human pyramid, Debbi thought she had left the exciting and glamorous service economy behind when she married at nineteen. Fields credits her business success to the rude remark of an overbearing associate of her husband's. The businessman asked Debbi what she intended to do with her life. Debbi said she was trying to get "orientated." The man walked over to a bookcase, pulled out a dictionary, and tossed it in Debbi's lap. "The word is *oriented*," he said. "There is no such word as *orientated*. Learn to use the English language."

Fields was so upset that she cried on the way home from dinner, resolving to get a life. She had experimented with cookies since childhood and had devised a formula for a buttery chocolate-chip cookie that was popular with friends. So Fields opened a cookie boutique at a Palo Alto, California, supermarket in 1977. Not a single customer had come in by noon of her first day in business. In desperation, Fields filled a tray with cookies and tried to give them away to customers in the shopping center. People didn't want to take them for free. But those who tried the cookies liked them. Mrs. Fields cookies were bigger, softer, and richer than the chocolate-chip cookies people were used to.

A 1985 *Consumer Reports* article on chocolate-chip cookies rated Mrs. Fields the best store-bought fresh cookie. The magazine's tasters found Mrs. Fields cookies better than David's or Famous Amos; better than any of the several dozen chocolate-chip cookies tested *except*, oddly, those made at home with Duncan Hines mix. A 1990 survey of seven thousand households reported in the trade journal *Restaurants and Institutions* gave Mrs. Fields the "highest food-quality rating" of any fast-food chain of any description. There is something unique about Mrs. Fields cookies, and not many people know what it is.

The secrecy has had peculiar consequences. One is a spate of knockoff Mrs. Fields cookies recipes appearing in women's magazines and even in chain letters. Particularly worrisome was a counterfeit recipe for Mrs. Fields cookies that was widely circulated as a chain letter beginning in 1986. "In the beginning, we just shrugged it off as a sick joke," Marketing Director Candy Johnson told *The Wall Street Journal*. Debbi Fields found it necessary to post signs branding the alleged recipe a fake and insisting that the real recipe remained safe in Park City, Utah, a "tasty trade secret." The company then claimed, incredibly, that only three people in the entire world knew the real recipe. None had squealed.

Three people? How do all the cookies in all the malls of the world get made if only three people are in on the secret? Someone at each of the six hundred Mrs. Fields outlets must know a bit more than they're letting on. Asked about the Mrs. Fields recipe, Don Sawyer, president of the archrival Famous Amos Chocolate Chip Cookie Company, sniped, "Any home economics teacher worth her salt could figure it out."

The classic chocolate-chip cookie recipe was devised circa 1931 by Ruth Wakefield at her Toll House Inn in Massachusetts. There were no chocolate chips back then. Wakefield chopped up a Nestlé chocolate bar. The Nestlé company knew a good thing when they saw it. When they came out with chocolate chips, they put the Toll House recipe on the package. Rarely does any cookbook or magazine recipe differ greatly from Wakefield's public-domain recipe.

They all contain flour, butter or margarine, white and brown sugar, eggs, vanilla extract; sometimes baking powder or baking soda, and salt; and, of course, loads of chocolate chips. Variations in published chocolate-chip-cookie recipes are limited mostly to the nut question, specifics of oven temperature and baking time, and novel ingredients like M&M's or coconut.

Given the basic recipe, it ought to be a cinch to determine what sets Mrs. Fields cookies apart. There have been several attempts to do so. One is that chain letter. The Mrs. Fields cookies chain letter is (at least in our specimen) an incredibly grainy, zillionth-generation photocopy. The main body of text appears to be type-written. A few lines of awkwardly expanded text at top and bottom look like an old dot-matrix printer's output. The recipe looks like it was originally on monarch-sized stationery and was copied, many Xerox generations ago, onto a larger but odd-sized (eight-and-a-half- by twelve-inch) sheet of paper.

The story behind the letter may be relevant, so here's the complete text (grammar and spellings are *sic*). Once again, this is *not* the correct Mrs. Fields recipe.

No one knows who the people named are. The anecdote is an old story, though, older than the Mrs. Fields company. Chain letters and flyers bearing virtually the same sad tale have been connected to other commercial recipes (most notably a fictitious "red-velvet cake" said to be a specialty of the Waldorf-Astoria Hotel). In each case someone asked for a famous recipe, ended up paying more than they bargained for, and sought revenge by distributing copies. It always turns out that the distributed recipe *isn't* what it claims to be, too.

Lose those touchy-feely notions about the cookie business. "Some of our competitors are not the nicest people in the world and they would do anything they could to besmirch our reputation," Debbi's husband, Randy, told the press after the chain letter appeared. He suspected that unnamed parties (David's Cookies? Häagen-Dazs? one of those frozen-yogurt outfits?) had distributed the recipe to undermine public confidence in his wife's cookies. The Mrs. Fields company took great pains to track down the source of the disinformation campaign. Reportedly, they found the original woman somewhere in Texas and offered her a thousand dollars to show proof of purchase. She refused.

The company was, of course, vehement in asserting that the

RECIPE OF THE MONTH
MRS. FIELDS COOKIES

I was given this recipe by Pauline Seligman. I am going to reprint it as I received it.

EILEEN BIANCHI

A woman who works with Jean's mother at the American Bar Association called Mrs. Field Cookies and asked for the following recipe. She was told there was a two fifty charge for the recipe. She assumed it was $2.50 and she charged it to her VISA. It was not $2.50, but $250.00. In order to get her monies worth, she is passing the recipe out to everyone.

MRS. FIELDS COOKIES

Cream Together:
  2 Cups butter
  2 Cups sugar
  2 Cups brown sugar
Add:
  4 eggs
  2 teaspoons vanilla
Mix together:
  4 Cups flour
  5 Cups oatmeal (put small amounts in blender--after measuring--until it turns to powder)
  1 teaspoon salt
  2 teaspoons baking powder
  2 teaspoons baking soda
  Mix together all ingredients and 24 ounces of chocolate chips, and 8 ounce Hershey bar (grated) and 3 cups of chopped nuts (any kind). Bake on an ungreased cookie sheet. Make golf ball sized cookies, 2 inches apart. Bake at 375 degrees F for 6 minutes*.
*Slightly longer if necessary--cookies should be soft.
THIS IS AS A $250.00 RECIPE--GIVE IT TO EVERYONE!!!!

circulating recipe is wrong. "That recipe isn't even close," said Randy Fields. "We made it, and it's not a good cookie."

Well, yes and no. We tried the chain-letter recipe in the *Biggest Secrets* test kitchens. The recipe is sabotaged. Six minutes isn't nearly enough cooking time. Even in an oven scrupulously preheated to 375 degrees Fahrenheit, the cookies were oozing globs that dripped through a spatula's slots at the end of the prescribed time.

Anyone who had gone to the trouble of preparing the recipe would have sense enough to let it cook longer. At the end of about fifteen minutes, the counterfeit dough baked up into a batch of perfectly good cookies.

Perfectly good, but not Mrs. Fields. Our panel of tasters felt that the resulting cookies were both delicious and (within the wide gamut of store-bought and homemade chocolate-chip cookies) comparable to the authentic Mrs. Fields product. They were distinguishable from the real thing in side-by-side comparison, though. The counterfeits were thicker than Mrs. Fields cookies, a shade heavier in texture, and lighter in color.

The dubious recipe's product doesn't correspond exactly to any of the several varieties of cookies sold by Mrs. Fields. The only cookies obviously containing oatmeal are the so-called Debbi's Favorites, which contain raisins, walnuts, and oatmeal. In these, the oatmeal is visible. But the cookies made with the chain-letter recipe, in which the oatmeal was reduced to an unrecognizable powder in a food processor, gave no hint of oatmeal as an ingredient.

The real Mrs. Fields cookies had the edge in taste. A sweet, rich nuance—redolent of fudge or butterscotch—in the Mrs. Fields cookies was lacking in the fakes. The chain-letter cookies were hard a day later. The Mrs. Fields cookies remained soft and chewy.

Chain letters never die. They mutate. A recent text we came across, said to have been given out by a Mrs. Fields baker, omits the story. It's just a photocopied recipe. It adds some new ingredients (2 tablespoons of cream or milk, an optional ½ teaspoon almond extract, and an also optional 1 teaspoon of rum extract). The shredded Hershey bar is omitted in favor of a "pkg. of milk chocolate chips and/or 1½ Cups crushed Walnuts and 1½ Cups crushed Pecans," and cooking time is adjusted to a more reasonable 15 minutes at 375 degrees Fahrenheit. But the wording and layout on the page bear suspicious similarities to the Bianchi version.

We tried the mutant recipe, too. The end product had a flavor somewhat closer to real Mrs. Fields cookies, but the texture was still wrong.

Meanwhile, essentially the same oatmeal chocolate-chip-cookie recipe and tale of woe have lately turned up as the putative formula for a cookie sold in Neiman-Marcus department stores. This is more reason not to believe a chain letter.

The March 3, 1988, issue of *Woman's Day* offered its own Mrs. Fields wannabes. "Now you can make your own versions of the cookies you drive miles to buy—and save up to $5.83 a pound," reads the article. "Ours are every crumb as delectable as the famous ones that inspired them."

The *Woman's Day* recipes purported to simulate eight varieties of Mrs. Fields and David's cookies (without drawing any distinction between the two brands). They are conventional oatmeal-free chocolate-chip-cookie recipes, though modestly atypical in omitting baking soda, baking powder, and salt. The magazine advised an electric mixer and baking at 325 degrees Fahrenheit for about 17 minutes.

We tried two of the *Woman's Day* recipes. They produced tasty cookies that looked like the poor sisters of the ones in the magazine's color spreads. Once again, they weren't Mrs. Fields cookies. The rich, buttery fillip was still missing.

Are there any secret ingredients in the Mrs. Fields recipe? The general impression is that Mrs. Fields cookies are fat-laden but natural products, and that it is the *absence* of arcane additives that distinguishes them from Chips Ahoy! The company's consumer-line voice-mail recording states there are no artificial colors, flavorings, or preservatives in the product. If Mrs. Fields cookies are merely exceptionally rich confections of sugar, butter, flour, eggs, chocolate, nuts, and such, would not any Mrs. Fields employee know the recipe?

Well, Randy Fields claimed that "virtually every one of our ingredients is specially formulated to our specifications. Even if you tried to buy them from our suppliers you couldn't and we wouldn't even reveal their names."

We hope those suppliers aren't charging the Fieldses too much extra for specially formulated sugar, butter, eggs, and salt.

Employees Talk

The aggregate Mrs. Fields work force consists of about five thousand people. Most earn the minimum wage, or close to it, and regard working in a cookie store as a dead-end job. *Biggest Secrets* advertised on college campuses for employees or ex-employees of Mrs. Fields willing to talk about the recipe. We found *lots* of Mrs. Fields workers willing to spill the beans.

A worldwide operation can take steps to preserve the secrecy of its recipe even from the people who bake the product. If need be, just one person can buy, prepare, or measure the ingredients, seal them in packages, and send them to rank-and-file employees across the country. In the early days, that's exactly what Debbi Fields did, measuring the ingredients into Tupperware containers. Regular employees did the mundane work of mixing and baking according to not-so-secret directions.

Our informants reported three sources of dough and dough ingredients in their own work experiences. One ex-employee had worked in a Mrs. Fields outlet in London. She said that the dough was shipped frozen to the British store. The people at the London outlet simply thawed and baked the dough and didn't know the recipe.

All but one of those who worked at American stores concurred that the cookie dough was made fresh on the premises. In most stores the dough was made partly from packages of premeasured ingredients that came from the corporate headquarters in Utah and partly from locally purchased dairy products. No one was mystified as to what the packaged ingredients were: flour, sugar, brown sugar, etc.

Finally, one informant reported that the cookies at his store had been made entirely from locally purchased ingredients. Flour, sugar, *everything*, were measured out and mixed up by the store's employees. Unfortunately, this informant was no longer employed at the store, and did not have a copy of the recipe used. His recollection of the ingredients confirmed that of the other employees, however.

We enlisted the aid of employees in reconstructing the Mrs. Fields recipe as accurately as possible. First of all, forget the oatmeal theory. Oatmeal was added to oatmeal cookies, of course, but not to the regular chocolate-chip cookies. Still, we wondered if there might be finely ground oatmeal in the supplied flour mix. Rank-and-file employees might not know that. To double-check, we contacted the Mrs. Fields company on their toll-free information line. Our caller feigned a virulent allergy to oatmeal and asked point blank if Mrs. Fields chocolate-chip cookies contained oatmeal (a handy technique in checking any company's suspected secret ingredient). We figured that they wouldn't lie where someone's health was at stake, and also that they wouldn't turn away a customer needlessly. The spokeswoman said that *only* the oatmeal raisin cookies contained oatmeal (she warned, however, that bowls are not washed between batches, and a crumb of oatmeal might find its way into the regular cookies).

There *is* a secret ingredient in Mrs. Fields cookies. It is added at each outlet, and may have something to do with the fudgelike taste of real Mrs. Fields cookies. The secret ingredient is *milk.*

There's hardly ever milk in cookies. A survey of standard cookbooks failed to turn up any published recipe for chocolate-chip cookies that called for milk. It is possible that whoever was responsible for the second photocopied recipe had heard that milk was used (but the recipe is wrong in other respects). Milk is an ingredient of fudge and praline. Fudge is made by cooking milk with sugar, butter, and (usually) chocolate or nuts. Praline contains milk but no butter and, like chocolate-chip cookies, is made with brown and white sugar. It's possible the use of milk, along with the generous amounts of butter and sugar, results in a cookie that's· less breadlike and more fudge- or pralinelike in flavor. It's watered-down milk. Employees said they used equal parts of water and milk. No one knew why; that was just the way it was done.

According to our sources, the list of ingredients ran as follows: flour, brown sugar, white sugar, butter, margarine, eggs, milk, water, vanilla extract, salt, baking soda, chocolate chips, and walnuts. For the record, cinnamon, toffee, peanut butter, cream, and oatmeal were used in some Mrs. Fields cookies, but not in the regular chocolate-chip variety we sought to emulate. Cream was added to brownies and the peanut butter toffee cookies, though not, as a rule, to the regular chocolate-chip cookies. But one employee said, "If we had extra cream, we'd use it" in the chocolate chip cookies.

The Mrs. Fields organization makes much of their specially formulated ingredients, so let's give some brand names. Not everyone knew the brand names, except for the dairy products (which were local and varied with region). But several informants said they saw, heard, or were given to understand that a certain brand was used, and they often concurred. These sources mentioned C&H sugar, Diamond walnuts, and Hershey chocolate chips (a single person mentioned Ghirardelli). Company lore says that the first chocolate company Fields called out of the phone book sneered that her company was too small to bother with. The second company she called was nice, and out of gratitude, Fields has stuck with them ever since, even as her firm has become one of the country's biggest buyers of chocolate. A guess is that the chocolate company with attitude was Nestlé (Fields has mentioned using Nestlé chocolate chips in her childhood baking), and the nice second company was Hershey. In any case, the chips are the usual "kiss"-shaped chips, not the chocolate chunks you find in David's Cookies. Surprisingly, no one recalled using the Mrs. Fields brand of chocolate chips, sold primarily in midwestern supermarkets. (The packages have cookie recipes on the back, but the company emphasizes that these are "recipes Debbi has developed for use at home" and *not* the secret recipes used in Mrs. Fields stores.)

The reported use of margarine (a half-and-half blend of margarine and butter, our informants said) was surprising, for Fields has long insisted on butter, not margarine, in her cookies. In her autobiography she tells of a salesman who tried to sell her on a fifty-fifty butter-margarine blend. Fields stonily replied, "I can't believe you're even calling me." She finally agreed to try the stuff, and pronounced the resulting batch of cookies "dreadful. The difference is night and day." Fields adds, "Sadly, there are any number of businesses pretty much based on the theory that the American consumer is too dumb to know good from bad. . . . When I hear about some scheme based on that idea, it actually seems *evil* to me. . . ." Barring the possibility that all our informants had worked at maverick outlets that were cutting corners, the Mrs. Fields organization may have relented on the margarine issue since 1987.

Crucial and easily overlooked is the *slow* baking at relatively *low* temperature. Doughy-soft when taken from the oven, the cookies remain pleasantly chewy when cool. Our experiments suggest that this, as much as any other single factor, is responsible for the seductively gooey texture and all-around Mrs. Fields gestalt.

There are differences between making cookies on an industrial scale and making them at home. The ingredients are mixed in large mixers—"very powerful and dangerous," one informant said. No one thought the official Mrs. Fields mixers (made by Proctor-Silex, according to one employee) did anything your home mixer wouldn't do, except make bigger batches faster. Convection ovens ensure uniform baking. Best use of limited manpower dictates that the dough is sometimes made in advance and chilled. Cooking time must be adjusted upward for chilled dough. The extra moisture may counteract the drying effect of storage. In our experiments, the surface texture of the finished cookies varied with length of refrigeration of the dough. It best matched the appearance of store-bought Mrs. Fields cookies—with their network of little cracks—when the dough had been refrigerated about a day before baking.

Mrs. Fields cookies are a nice even tan color, not much darker on the bottom. We had some difficulty reproducing that color in a home oven. Our cookies tended to come out too dark on the bottom. The answer lies in the use of a lightweight baking sheet. We had good results using heavy-duty aluminum foil.

Not everyone would care to match the Mrs. Fields obsession with quality at home. Cookies may be rejected for poor chip placement and other cosmetic defects. Many an article on the company claims that only cookies no more than two hours old may be sold. Fields talks of the "Mr. Thumb" test. Employees are supposed to press their thumb into the underside of a cookie just before slipping it into a bag. If it's not soft, the cookie goes in the reject bin. These "cookie orphans," as they're known in Mrs. Fields corporate culture, are donated to food banks and "worthwhile groups," according to a company press release.

Few of the Mrs. Fields employees we spoke to had even heard of the two-hour rule. Asked how long cookies could be kept before being withdrawn from sale, answers ranged from a minimum of six hours to an incredible two days. Some employees did recall giving old cookies to community groups, but others spoke of giving out old cookies as "free samples"; of selling "day-old" cookies at a steep discount; of taking home stale cookies themselves; and in one case, of an autocratic store manager who insisted there shouldn't *be* any unsold cookies.

MRS. FIELDS COOKIES: INGREDIENTS

Butter **Margarine**	Debbi favors butter, but employees say they used a blend to get butter flavor at margarine prices. Quantities for our home-version recipe: (*½ cup butter, ½ cup margarine*).
Flour **Sugar** **Brown sugar** **Eggs** **Vanilla extract** **Chocolate chips** **Walnuts**	All standard chocolate-chip cookie ingredients. For authenticity, use C&H sugar, Hershey's chocolate chips, and Diamond walnuts. Chips may be semisweet or milk chocolate (Mrs. Fields sells both varieties). Extract is the real kind, made from vanilla beans, per the Mrs. Fields ban on artificial flavorings. (*2¼ cups flour, 1 cup brown sugar, ½ cup granulated sugar, two medium eggs, beaten, 2 teaspoons vanilla extract, 12 ounces chocolate chips, 1 cup chopped walnuts*).
Milk **Water**	The only "secret" ingredient, milk, adds moisture, cooks into a fudge with butter and sugar. (*½ teaspoon milk, ½ teaspoon water*).
Baking soda **Salt**	Soda creates an airy, cake-like texture (*1 teaspoon baking soda, ½ teaspoon salt*).

Directions: Mix sugars, butter, and margarine in an electric mixer. Add other wet ingredients, mixing well; then mix in flour, baking soda, and salt; then chocolate and nuts. Wear a plastic glove when forming golf ball–sized lumps of dough (a spoon is useful). Chill in refrigerator about a day. Set dough on ungreased lightweight baking sheet and flatten with gloved hand. Cook at 325 degrees Fahrenheit for about 15½ minutes (time may vary with oven and temperature of dough). Cookies will be very soft when taken from oven. Carefully lift with spatula and place on rack to cool. Target thickness of finished cookie: one-half inch. Day-old cookies may be donated to the homeless.

4·

Kellogg's Frosted Flakes

"Made with Tony's Secret Formula," reads a banner on each box of Kellogg's Frosted Flakes. You might be forgiven for thinking that this is anything more than kid stuff. Tony is not the company's CEO or director of research. He is a cartoon character for *babies*. In commercials, Tony battles bad guys who want to steal the secret recipe for frosted corn flakes. How secret can corn flakes be?

The answer is that it's secret enough for Kellogg's to alienate the citizenry of Battle Creek, Michigan, and sue people. In April 1986 the Kellogg Company stopped giving tours of its Battle Creek factory. It charged that industrial spies had been taking the tour to ferret out its cereal secrets. A Kellogg's vice president, Joseph M. Stewart, griped that engineers from a foreign firm took the free tour twenty times, then set up their own cereal factory. Stewart said, "We are about to put $500 million into this plant, and we want to be the only ones who know what's inside."

Termination of the tours was a big deal to the citizens of Battle Creek. With its giant statue of Tony the Tiger, the Kellogg factory dominates the skyline of Battle Creek. Watching cereal being made may not sound like much of a thrill, but it drew an estimated six and a half million of the curious and patient over an eighty-year period. Many of those out-of-towners had money and an itch to spend it on Kellogg-themed T-shirts, commemorative plates, and junk. Mayor John J. H. Schwarz feared that without the factory tours, tourists would begin to bypass Battle Creek. That proved to be a well-founded fear. Talk of a slick new cereal museum remains just that—talk.

On the last day of the tour, *The New York Times* interviewed Paul Siebert, a Plymouth, Michigan, resident who was one of the last outsiders to enter Kellogg's forbidden cereal kingdom. "I didn't see anything in there that was secret," he said. For Siebert, the tour had a bittersweet edge. "Until now this has been a friendly place. Now it will be part of some mysterious corporate structure. The cereal will be the same, I guess, but the feeling won't be the same when I sit down to eat breakfast."

A few months later, Kellogg's get-tough stance led to a restraining order against an executive who had taken a job with a competitor. Roger D. Billingsley, who had been director of cereal product development for Kellogg, took what the company charged was a similar position at Nabisco. The restraining order barred Billingsley from formulation, development, testing, or marketing of ready-to-eat cereals, and from using "confidential proprietary and trade secret" information of Kellogg. Nabisco denied that it had any intention of using the priceless secrets in its new executive's brain.

The Brothers Kellogg

Secret cereal recipes have brought tragedy and fabulous wealth to the Kellogg family. The corn-flake recipe was the invention of two jealous, resentful brothers who spent a big part of their lives suing each other over it.

The chain of events leading to today's bowl of corn flakes can be traced back to 1844. An anonymous farmer stopped in his field for a smoke. As he drew on his tobacco, he reflected that were Christ to return that instant, he would not want Him to find him smoking the devil's weed. The farmer threw the pipe under his plow and ground it into the earth. At the next meeting of the prim Adventist sect, the farmer spoke so enthusiastically about his decision to quit smoking that other Adventists followed suit. Within a few years, church members were swearing off not only tobacco but liquor, spicy foods, and meat. Dietary restrictions became part of Adventist doctrine.

The Adventists established a health resort in Michigan. Head of the Battle Creek Sanitarium was Dr. John Harvey Kellogg, a sincere, charismatic man who would handily qualify as a quack by current FDA standards. Wealthy folk traveled from all over the world to take the cure, which consisted of a bland vegetarian diet.

The term *health food* was in use even then. The cereals served at the sanitarium were considered quintessential examples. Dr. Kellogg saw his invention of flaked cereal as part of a vast program to reform the American diet. He saw cereal as an all-around meat substitute—something people could eat at any meal. Many Adventists further believed that a vegetarian diet would make people lose interest in sex (which they held to be a good thing). Dr. Kellogg's pride and joy was Duke, a husky Saint Bernard said to subsist entirely on vegetables. The buzz in Battle Creek was that a local butcher was secretly feeding the dog bones and scraps.

But it is not John Harvey's freely adapted signature you see on today's cereal boxes. That Kellogg was the doctor's brother, Will Keith Kellogg. For years, Will was an underpaid lackey in the shadow of his brother, the big, famous doctor. Will was a quiet sort who did everything from bookkeeping to capturing escaped mental cases. For this he drew a modest salary at an institution not noted for generosity to its help. (Dr. Kellogg once announced that he was cutting everyone's salaries because "all of us are doing the Lord's work.")

Dr. Kellogg was interested in finding a digestible substitute for bread. (Bread is now considered a digestible food.) The doctor and his brother performed gloppy experiments with boiled grain in the sanitarium's kitchens. Testimony in later lawsuits is sometimes contradictory about who did what, but by 1894 the brothers had invented a flaked-wheat cereal.

The brothers were trying unsuccessfully to make appetizing cereal from boiled wheat. On one occasion they left a vat of boiled wheat standing at the end of a workday. They forgot about it, and a day or two later, the mush was moldy. The brothers tried flaking it anyway. When the stuff was run through the rollers, they were able to peel away nice thin flakes. The vital point was that the grain mush had to set a couple of hours before flaking.

The doctor was uneasy about the flakes. He thought they should break up the flakes into crumbs, and serve people the crumbs. Will thought the flakes were fine as they were. He prevailed, and the sanitarium started serving the flakes under the name Granose.

Given the wheat-flake recipe, it wouldn't take an Einstein to conceive of corn flakes. But neither brother got around to trying corn until three or four years later. When Will finally did mix up a batch of corn, he found it wasn't as easy to work with as wheat. The first corn flakes produced were thick and bland.

Will continued to experiment. Unlike the doctor, Will was not so set on making a health food. He wanted something that would sell because of its taste. Will made several changes to create a better-tasting flake—most of them nutritionally detrimental by today's standards.

Will found that corn grits made a better flake than whole corn. So grits he used, and today's corn flakes remain a refined food, shorn of the fibrous bran and the nutrient-laden germ.

The flakes still didn't have much flavor. Will found remedies in malt, sugar, and salt. Malt is sprouted barley, a flavorful component of beer. Added to the corn flakes, it produced a nutty taste.

Sugar was a controversial matter. The doctor strictly forbade white sugar in sanitarium products. While Dr. Kellogg was wintering in Europe, Will said the hell with it. He started making the flakes with sugar; salt, too. This produced the first Kellogg's Corn Flakes as we know them today (*not* Frosted Flakes, of course, but the regular corn flakes, which contain a good deal of sugar themselves).

When the doctor returned from the Continent, he hit the roof. Shortly thereafter, Will set out on his own. He formed the Battle Creek Toasted Corn Flake Company in 1906.

Every success of his brother's company was a jab at the heart of Dr. Kellogg. An early flaked-cereal patent the doctor took out had been overturned, so Will had every right to make corn flakes—all the more so, since he had been co-inventor. Just to make everything aboveboard, Will struck a deal with the doctor to buy the right to use the recipe. A few days after agreeing to sell worldwide rights to the corn-flake recipe, the doctor reneged and decided he meant only the U.S. rights. As Will's company grew, the doctor did a brisk business selling corn flakes of his own. Not only was the doctor's cereal also called Kellogg's Corn Flakes but it was packed in a similar box, and salesmen for the doctor's company did nothing to clear up the natural confusion. Another time, the doctor decided that since he had sold only a corn-flake recipe, he had every right to sell a very similar rice-flake recipe to another company.

Will could be just as spiteful. There was the time the doctor began producing a cereal called Pep. Will found out that Pep was already a registered trademark, and bought the rights to it. He forced his brother to destroy thousands of already-printed cereal cartons.

From the beginning, the Kelloggs were plagued by security

leaks. A number of start-up firms in Battle Creek were making money selling the foods that the Kelloggs had invented. The Kelloggs invented peanut butter but didn't patent it, and it was others who made fortunes off of it. The cruelest blow was that a certain C. W. Post had been a patient at the sanitarium. After taking the cure, Post launched a new career making something called Grape Nuts. Many felt Grape Nuts bore a suspicious resemblance to Granola, a cereal the sanitarium had been serving for years. At one point, there were over forty breakfast-cereal companies in Battle Creek, which then had a population of only about thirty thousand. Other companies often hired Kellogg employees to learn the formulas of Kellogg products.

By 1909 the two Kellogg brothers weren't on speaking terms. Both spent much of the following decade suing each other. These complex legal actions resulted in the ruling that only Will's company could market cereal under the Kellogg name, and in lifelong mutual enmity for the two brothers.

"Only the most discerning of acquaintances would have labeled W. K. Kellogg a 'very human man,'" observed Horace B. Powell's tactful 1956 biography of Will. By all accounts, Will was a hardworking, decent, not especially lovable man who neglected his family. The Adventists eventually ousted Will for his worldliness. Kellogg was interested in little besides the cereal business, a company baseball team, and the number seven. He told people, "I was my father's seventh son, born on the seventh day of the week and the seventh day of the month. My father was a seventh child, and the name 'Kellogg' has seven letters." When he traveled, he booked rooms on the seventh floor; his Michigan license plates had to end in a seven.

Will's prescient recognition of the value of advertising guided the company on its path to worldwide success. After the 1929 stock-market crash, Will told his board of directors, "Double our advertising budget!" Kellogg's managed to grow during the Depression because a bowl of corn flakes was cheaper than eggs and ham.

Will groomed his grandson, John L. Kellogg, Jr., to take over the company reins. Working on company time in the company research lab, the grandson perfected a method of puffing corn grits. It was to be to corn what the already successful Rice Krispies were to rice. The grandson magnanimously offered to *sell* the process to the company. Will replied that anything invented on company time already *was* the company's. The disagreement ended in the grandson's resignation. In 1937 the young man started his own company to make the new cereal under the name Nu-Korn, and Kellogg lawyers sued with a fury. Depressed over the suit, John Kellogg, Jr., committed suicide in his Chicago factory. As an unidentified source told biographer Powell, "The Kelloggs were the suing-est people."

Tony's Secret Formula

Now, about this secret formula business: Go to any supermarket, and you'll see other brands of corn flakes that appear to be very similar to the Kellogg's product. The basic corn-flake formula appears in the technical literature of food processing. A prime reference for that is an invalid patent that Dr. Kellogg took out. On May 31, 1894, Dr. Kellogg filed an application to patent "flaked cereals and process of preparing same." This gave the full recipe as it then existed (which was then used for wheat flakes, though the patent mentions barley, oats, and corn). The patent was later ruled invalid in a 1903 suit brought by a competitor, the Voight Cereal Company of Grand Rapids, Michigan. What distinguishes Kellogg's Corn Flakes are the added vitamins and the frosting. Nowadays, most competing corn flakes are fortified, and many are frosted, too.

The ingredients of Kellogg's Corn Flakes are no secret. They're listed on the label, as required by law: "corn, sugar, salt, malt flavoring, corn syrup," plus a list of added vitamins and iron. The label has a disclaimer: "No artificial colors or flavors."

Ingredients must be listed in descending order of their quantities on the label. So corn is the main ingredient, sugar is second, salt is third, and so on. The box of Kellogg's Corn Flakes gives the same ingredient list as Frosted Flakes. Sugar is the number-two ingredient, even in the plain flakes.

At Kellogg's, the manufacture of corn flakes takes place in a high-tech wonderland of custom-built industrial grinders, pressure cookers, flakers, and dryers. However, the entire process can be (and once was) done on a stove-top scale.

Take hybrid yellow corn and mill to remove bran, crown starch, and germ. (One of the neat facts they *used* to tell you on the tour was that the crushing machine could exert forty tons of force on a bit of corn.) The resulting grits should be small enough to pass through a 4-mesh sieve and big enough to be stopped by a 5-mesh. This means that the typical kernel is stripped of its fibrous outer coat and split into two pieces—each a frosted flake in the making. The bits retain their identity throughout the cooking process. Kellogg's could not make the flakes much larger or smaller than they are. That's why competing corn flakes (or your own!) look nearly identical to the Kellogg's version.

For each two thousand pounds of corn, Kellogg adds about forty-two gallons of a malted syrup for flavor. The syrup is composed of sugar dissolved in water with malt and salt for flavoring. Cook in a pressure cooker at eighteen pounds per square inch for an hour or two. In industrial practice, the pressure cooker rotates slowly like a cement mixer. Because cooking time varies with the lot of corn, the cooker is supplied with a valve that lets an inspector blow out a sample of corn to see how it's doing. It's done when all the split kernels are translucent. The mix absorbs considerable moisture from the steam of the pressure cooker, becoming approximately one-third water.

Release the pressure and pour the cooked corn out onto a conveyer belt. Break up the clumps formed during cooking (normally, this is done with a special machine). After that, the corn goes to dryers (usually large silolike buildings). The corn enters at the top and dribbles down walls where it is dried by hot (150 degrees Fahrenheit) dry air forced upward.

By the time the moisture level is reduced to about 20 percent, the product is an unpleasant, dark brown granular mass. Because it is unevenly dried, it must be stored in bins (for up to a day) to redistribute the moisture throughout. The lumps are then broken into individual flakes (another custom-machine job).

Further drying and toasting take place in a heated (550–575 degrees) rotating drum (50 seconds to 3 minutes depending on temperature and moisture content). This creates the characteristic surface texture. The finished flakes have a moisture content of no more than 3 percent.

As the flakes cool on an air-conditioned conveyer belt, they are sprayed with a solution of water-soluble vitamins. This operation is performed at the last minute because vitamins are easily destroyed by heat. The vitamins are not an integral part of the corn flake recipe, just a guilt-induced afterthought to make up for all the sugar. We know *which* vitamins from the label, but what are the proportions? They could be added in any amount.

The label breaks down the nutritional content of the cereal under the headings "Nutrition information" and "Percentage of U.S. recommended daily allowances (U.S. RDA)." Figures are not only provided for calories, protein, carbohydrate, and fat but also for vitamins and minerals, including all of the added vitamins and iron, per one-ounce serving of cereal.

Some of the vitamins come from the corn. Fresh yellow corn is rich in vitamin A and has substantial amounts of iron and several B vitamins. Cooking nukes the vitamin A, leaving just traces of the B vitamins. The vitamin content of generic, unfortified corn flakes is known. By subtracting the unfortified flakes' vitamins from the Kellogg's label amounts, we can deduce the amount of vitamins that must be added to get the advertised vitamin content—to a nice degree of precision.

According to our reverse engineering, only the iron content of Kellogg's Corn Flakes derives primarily from the corn itself (some extra iron is added). A fraction of the thiamin, riboflavin, and niacin is natural. The other vitamins on the label are present entirely or almost entirely as additives.

Per ton of dry flakes, the folks at Kellogg spritz on 4.8 million international units of vitamin A palmitate preserved with BHT, 8.3 grams of thiamin hydrochloride (vitamin B_1), 12.7 grams of riboflavin (vitamin B_2), 132 grams of niacinamide, 16 grams of vitamin B_6, 1.6 grams of folic acid, 480 grams of vitamin C in the form of sodium ascorbate and ascorbic acid, 32 milligrams of vitamin D, and 12 grams of digestible iron salts. Even with industrial sprayers, vitamin coating is spotty, so the flakes must be mixed thoroughly to distribute the vitamins.

The manufacture of regular corn flakes ends there. The final piece of Tony's Secret Formula is the frosting. Kellogg's frosting is neither a granular dusting of sugar nor a wet, doughnutty glaze. It is a nonstick transparent coating impervious to humidity. British Patent No. 754,771 details the flake frosting process. The frosting agent is a syrup made with ordinary table sugar (sucrose) and a small amount of a simpler sugar (evidently corn syrup in the Kellogg's version) that is applied to the flakes and allowed to dry thoroughly. Ultimate sugar content for frosted flakes: a taste bud–hammering 39 percent (versus 7 percent for regular corn flakes).

5·

Grey Poupon Mustard

It's the most natural thing in the world to think that the Grey Poupon on your supermarket shelves came straight from Dijon. The label's half in French and fancied up with heraldic crests. The proud French tricolor runs around the lid. Sure, the fine print says something about Nabisco Brands of East Hanover, New Jersey. They *wouldn't* make Grey Poupon in New Jersey! They make it in Oxnard, California.

What makes Grey Poupon Grey Poupon is a secret formula. The year prominently featured on the label (1777) is *not* when the recipe was invented, though. Basically, it's how far back the company that makes Grey Poupon can trace its roots. In 1777 a man named Nicolas Foret opened a mustard and vinegar shop in Dijon. At his retirement, he was succeeded by another mustard maker doing business at the same place, and so on and so on, several times. In 1823 an Englishman named Grey bought the firm.

Dijon was by then the mustard capital of the world. As the city was formerly on a Roman spice route, its citizens got used to highly spiced foods. When trade patterns shifted, the Dijonnais craved something to jazz up their food. They hit on the mustard growing as a weed in the area. They mixed the dried seeds with verjuice (juice of unripe grapes, sometimes fermented). Differences in processing methods and additional ingredients produced different products. Most of the firms, including Grey's, kept their recipes secret from competitors.

Grey had big ideas for the mustard business. In 1850 he invented the first machine for crushing the mustard seed—previously, a smelly manual operation that literally brought the workers to tears. The machines gave Grey a leg up on the competition. Napoleon III named Grey his official mustard maker. Needing money to expand further, Grey took on the wealthy Frenchman Auguste Poupon as his partner. Meanwhile, Grey invented a recipe for a strong mustard made with local white wine. Dijon is the gateway to the Burgundy wine region, home of true Chablis.

The Grey Poupon brand is said to date from 1866, when the firm requested permission from the mayor to put up a sign that read, "GREY F^R DE MOUTARDE, A. POUPON SUC^{SEUR}." Besides acknowledging the new partner, the name change helped distinguish the new mustard from a horde of competitors, some of whom were using the name Grey without authorization. Americans are wrong, of course, to think that Grey refers to the *color*. We're so used to the fluorescent yellow mustard sold at the ballparks that Grey Poupon looks neutral-toned in comparison.

Literature put out by the French Grey Poupon operation boasts, "From the very first days of its existence the firm won great renown for a product which today is still made from exactly the same unaltered recipe: a natural verjuice mustard prepared solely from very young white wine and the finest of mustard seeds. It may be added that, in spite of innumerable attempts by competitors to discover the secret of this recipe, not one has yet succeeded in doing so." At least a generation older than the Coca-Cola formula, the Grey Poupon recipe is one of the oldest secret recipes of commercial importance.

The Poupon family still manages the business in France. There can't be many enterprises more narrowly defined than the Grey Poupon Boutique in Dijon (32, rue de la Liberté). There's a bit more variety than you'd think. Through a series of mergers from 1952 on, Grey Poupon has gobbled up a number of competitors, so the shop stocks brands of mustard other than Grey Poupon. You can get mustard in exotic flavors (honey, tarragon, shallot, green peppercorn, etc.). If you really don't like mustard that much, you can buy vinegar, cornichons, or piccalilli. The shop is partly a museum of antique mustard pots. Modern reproductions, filled with mustard, of course, can run over a hundred dollars a jar.

Mysteries of Oxnard

In 1946 the French operation sold the secret recipe and rights to the Grey Poupon name to Connecticut-based food and liquor processor Heublein Inc. The agreement forbids export of the U.S. product. The bilingual labeling on the American mustard is strictly for show.

In fact, Dijon mustard is now an *appellation contrôlée* in France. It is against the law to sell "Dijon" mustard from the U.S. in France. Though Heublein came by the name and recipe honestly, the U.S. product draws a mixture of amusement and contempt from Francophiles. A brochure put out by Food and Wines from France, an import trade group, mentions "a delicate, indeed an embarrassing situation. There are mustards on the market whose labels and advertisements mention 'Dijon' to convey a certain image. But note the caveat, the escape clause: they write, they say: in the style of, based on a recipe from, and so on. . . . These mustards, it should be understood, are not made in Dijon or in any part of France. So much for authenticity."

Heublein admits that "Dijon-style mustards aren't always made in Dijon, but wherever they're made, there's a culinary kinship which unites them all." The flip side of the Heublein agreement is that you can't find French-made Grey Poupon in the U.S., even though it is sold in Canada and other nations.

In any case, Heublein's Grey Poupon was a stunning success. Through ads playing on American awe of French cuisine, the U.S. manufacture has exceeded that of France. James Beard praised Grey Poupon—*Heublein's* Grey Poupon—as the best American-made mustard in a 1975 article in *Esquire*. Of twenty-eight domestic and imported mustards sampled by Beard, Grey Poupon came in third, behind the imports Maille Dijon and Maître Jacques Grained. (Beard's *worst* mustard: French's.)

Heublein made Grey Poupon first in Connecticut, then moved production to the West Coast in 1975. The American label reads, "Based on the original Dijon, France recipe." As the "based on" wording implies, the current American recipe is *not* identical to the original. A press release from the French company says that their Grey Poupon is "made exclusively from white Burgundy wine. . . . Containing neither acid, vinegar nor spices, it can in no way irritate even the most delicate stomach."

Acid, vinegar, and spices figure prominently in the American product. The American label's ingredient list runs as follows: "water, mustard seed, distilled vinegar, salt, white wine, citric acid, tartaric acid and spices."

It's unlikely that *les messieurs* decided, right off the top of their *têtes*, to use citric and tartaric acid. They are the principal acids in citrus fruits and grapes, respectively. Maybe the real original recipe used lemon and grape juice?

The wheeling, dealing eighties saw Heublein merging with the diversification-happy tobacco colossus R. J. Reynolds in 1982, and the latter gobbling up Nabisco in 1985. This triggered a corporate realignment in which Grey Poupon was transferred to Nabisco.

The Grey Poupon recipe is presently kept under guard in New Jersey. Corporate spokesperson Mark Gutsche was quoted in 1989 as saying, "The formula is locked in a safe at Nabisco's research and development headquarters in New Jersey. Only four people back there know the formula. The secret is the spices, which are blended in New Jersey and shipped to Oxnard." Indeed, the people in Oxnard turn out thirty million jars of mustard each year without knowing the formula.

Analysis

We sent a jar of the American Grey Poupon to Associated Analytical Laboratories, a prominent food-chemistry firm, to have it analyzed. We used the standard Heublein Grey Poupon, not the Johnny-come-lately Country Dijon and Parisian mustards. This is what they came up with.

The main solid ingredient is, of course, mustard seed. The lab found a protein content of 6.5 percent (essentially all of that would come from the mustard seed) and reported the level of allylisocyanate, a compound responsible for mustard's tang, at 0.07 percent.

A few facts about the mustard seed have appeared in the press. The mustard seed for the American Grey Poupon comes from Canada. There's nothing wrong with that; the Dijon area no longer grows much mustard seed. Even the French version uses Canadian seed. Many say the Canadian seed is superior.

France regulates its mustards more strictly than America does. A French Dijon mustard must be made from black or brown mus-

GREY POUPON MUSTARD: INGREDIENTS

Water Mustard seed	The mustard seed is from Canada. As far as we can tell, nothing in the American-made Grey Poupon comes from France.
Vinegar Salt	Grey Poupon contains 1.5 percent acetic acid, implying plenty of vinegar (about 30 percent). It's pretty salty (over 6 percent).
White wine	Kosher white wine from New York, the kind that would come with a screw top. The lab found an alcohol content of 0.04 percent.
Citric acid Tartaric acid	Much of the tartness is due to citric acid [HOC $(CH_2CO_2H)_2CO_2H$], also an ingredient of Tang and Kool-Aid. Tartaric acid [$HO_2CCH(OH)CH(OH)CO_2H$] content is much less (0.03 percent, much of that from the wine).
Black pepper Allspice Nutmeg Cinnamon	Secret spices differentiate Grey Poupon from the competition, lend a subliminal pumpkin-pie note.

tard seed (*Brassica nigra* or *B. juncea*, which are stronger than other varieties). Turmeric, a common ingredient of American hot-dog mustards, is forbidden. Technically a spice, turmeric dyes mustard a brighter color. American Grey Poupon is evidently made with the same mustard species. No turmeric was found in the lab analysis.

One innovation is grinding the (initially whole) mustard seed *after* mixing it in with the liquid ingredients. This produces a fresher, sharper product. A strainer removes the tasteless husks, and another machine removes air bubbles quickly (reportedly in an hour or so, versus several days by traditional hand-stirring).

The mustard contained 1.5 percent acetic acid. All of that would come from vinegar. Raw vinegar is usually about 7 percent acetic acid, but it is frequently diluted to a standard 5 percent. The vinegar content of the mustard would therefore be around 30 percent (down to about 21 percent if stronger vinegar was used). The lab reported a salt content (ordinary sodium chloride) of 6.23 percent.

The least that Heublein could do, as a concession to authenticity, would be to import the wine from France, right? No such luck.

The company has admitted that it uses a kosher white wine from upstate New York. For all the big deal the company makes about the wine, it's a fairly minor ingredient. The lab detected an alcohol level of a modest 0.04 percent. Wine is about 12 percent alcohol. Even allowing for loss of alcohol in processing, the initial wine content can hardly be more than a percent or so.

Grey Poupon has as much in common with Kool-Aid as with Chablis. The reason is a dollop of citric acid, the powdery white chemical used to mock up fruit-juice flavors on the cheap. There was much less tartaric acid, some of that from the wine.

As Nabisco asserts, the principal secret is the spices. Ordinary black pepper was most prominent, recognizable by the presence of piperine in the mustard. Traces of allspice, nutmeg, and cinnamon—pumpkin-pie seasonings—add an unexpected sweetness to an otherwise sharp tang.

6·

Mystery Meat

For every pair of hams brought to market, there's a whole pig, snout to chitlins. Of course, all that nasty stuff is ground up into cat food and fertilizer. *Or is it?* The fact is that pig hearts and salivary glands don't always end up in a butcher's trash bin. America's meat processors package these and other strange morsels into luncheon meats.

Who knows what's *really* in Spam, Underwood Deviled Ham, or Oscar Mayer Head Cheese? The place to look is in the technical literature of meat processing. The dirty little secrets of butchery might be passed privately from generation to generation. Not so the secrets of pickle loaf. Modern meat is a science. Formulation of today's hyperprocessed luncheon meats is the subject of sophisticated research reported (with appalling photos) in trade journals that the average consumer mercifully never sees. The pages of *Meat Science, Advances in Meat Research,* and the *Journal of Dairy Science* find high-powered specialists discoursing frankly on such matters as the pros and cons of gut casings for wieners, the aesthetics of ground cardiac muscle, and the age-old problem of upgrading abattoir waste. For our investigation, we chose several popular brand-name processed meats and went to the experts. What's in this stuff, anyway?

A sometimes adversarial relationship exists between the public and the cold-cut cartel. Much of the potentially edible weight of a pig or cow carcass is in organ meats or other nonmuscle tissue. Protein is protein; parts are parts. Processed into a formed and spiced cold cut or sandwich spread, offal is arguably palatable, certainly unrecognizable. Meat processors have every incentive to use leftover cuts—and also to be quiet about it. Not everyone likes the idea of lunching on pig lips.

As they say, the public shouldn't see how laws or sausages are made. What's on a processed-meat label depends on how successful the meat lobby has been in structuring the label laws. Current U.S. labels give, at the very least, the species of animals used, barring only bona fide accidental contaminants (insects and rats, mostly, which are kept to an absolute minimum by federal inspection). Labels also give a near-complete breakdown of additives, a few hidden under umbrella terms like *flavorings*.

Labels reveal, for instance, that it is almost impossible to find a luncheon meat that doesn't have a sugar fix. It *is* impossible to find a luncheon meat that doesn't contain sodium nitrite or nitrate. Federal law requires these purportedly carcinogenic compounds in cured meat. The risk of sudden death from botulism without nitrites is thought to outweigh the slight risk of cancer with nitrites.

Spam

In 1937 the George A. Hormel company discovered the secret of eternal shelf life. The result was Spam—real meat that lasts practically forever. At first Hormel didn't know what to call the stuff. They ran a contest to name it. The winning name was a contraction of "spiced ham." That's odd, because there is less ham in it than you might think, and it contains no spices at all. You can stick cloves in it if you want, but you're on your own.

Spam is a joke food. Generations of American doughboys scarfed Spam in trenches or jungles. Few GIs liked it, and those who did stopped after they'd sampled it a few times. Even Hormel has belatedly caught on to the fact that most people think Spam is funny or disgusting or both. Austin, Minnesota, where Spam was invented and is still made, went all out with silly promotions for Spam's jubilee (1987). They had people dressed like cans of Spam and cook-offs that backfired when the press noted that nobody wanted to eat the stuff. Hormel now markets a campy Spam gift pack via gourmet catalogs. ("More 'In' Now Than Ever/SPAM is the perfect tongue-in-cheek gift.") Somehow these efforts don't quite work. You can't make Spam *and* make fun of it.

Somebody out there is eating Spam. Over a hundred million

cans of Spam roll out of the factory each year. Had you uncannily sensitive hearing, you would detect the faint staccato rhythm of three Spam vacuum seals being broken, somewhere in the globe, each *second*. Sales of Spam increase each year.

The basic concept behind Spam is simple: hermetically sealed, heat-sterilized meat. If there are no living bacteria or mold spores inside the can, the meat can't go bad. That is, it can't get any worse than it already is. It *is* Spam.

The can's short ingredient list reads, "Chopped pork shoulder meat with ham meat added and salt, water, sugar, sodium nitrite." Spam is thus mainly made from pigs' shoulders, with an admixture of costlier ham. That's it; lunchroom scare stories aside, there are no tongues or organ meats.

Meat used for canning contains adjacent fat and connective tissues that need not be spelled out on the label, though. "The presence of tendons in canned meat is considered . . . permissible if the amount is not in excess of 10 per cent," state Andrew L. Winton and Kate Barber Winton in *The Structure and Composition of Foods* (1937), who add reassuringly, "In the presence of other protein, finely ground tendons are believed to be digestible."

There is a lot of fat in Spam. As so-called reformed meat, Spam requires more fat to taste as juicy as fresh meat. In 1987 *People* magazine stated Spam's fat content was "more than 70 percent." That *has* to be wrong. If it was that high, you could grease skillets with it. Even sausages top out at 50 percent fat, uncooked. Spam is somewhat leaner than that, based on the relatively modest amount of grease rendered during cooking.

You can find the basic recipe for Spam, or at least for an incredible simulation thereof, in food-processing literature. The *Food Products Formulary* (1974) put out by AVI Publishing of Westport, Connecticut, gives a formula for "Chopped Ham in 12-Oz Oblong Cans" that is "commercially sterile" and needs no refrigeration. For every hundred pounds of meat (pork shoulders and ham), you'll need about three and a half pounds of salt, a pound of sugar, and about an ounce of sodium nitrite. Nitrite is the chemical you have to thank for Spam's almost eerie pinkness. Without it, Spam would fade to a drab meat-loaf gray.

Spam's texture is unlike the flesh of any animal that ever walked the earth. Too rubbery to be a meat loaf, each Spam module is a sturdy, man-made cutlet constructed on the principle of concrete.

Coarse chunks of meat are held together by a pâté of finely ground meat. To get the proper consistency, grind about three-quarters of the meat coarsely (through the three-eighths-inch plate of the grinder), the remaining quarter finely (one-eighth-inch plate). Grinding, mixing, and curing must be done in a chilled factory (34 to 36 degrees Fahrenheit) to minimize bacterial growth. Mix the two grades of meat with the salt, sugar, and sodium nitrite in a vacuum mixer set to a twenty-seven-inch vacuum, for five minutes. Release vacuum and let the mixture cure overnight, maintaining refrigeration. The next day, mix in the vacuum mixer for about ten minutes at a twenty-seven-inch vacuum. The chilled meat is then ready for canning.

Though the canning plant does not have to be refrigerated, the meat must not warm more than a few degrees (to no more than 40 degrees Fahrenheit) in transit. Spray the inner surfaces of the cans with oil for easy removal, then pack with meat mixture and seal under a twenty-seven-inch vacuum.

Spam is still raw when canned. Cooking and sterilization take place in the sealed can. The time required to sterilize depends on the size and shape of the can. The classic $3\frac{7}{8}'' \times 3\frac{1}{4}'' \times 2\frac{1}{8}''$ oblong can takes about 70 minutes in an oven set to 230 degrees Fahrenheit. The can's sturdy design and the internal vacuum prevent explosion.

The last step: Open and enjoy. You don't even have to heat it. The sterilization kills any trichinosis organisms. Spam is the pork to have when you're having it tepid.

It's tough to figure out how old a can of Spam is. Unlike wine, Spam does not display its vintage date proudly. Hormel's dating code is a five-digit number on the bottom of the can. For Spam, it's something like F04173, where *F* encodes the processing plant. The first two digits refer to the month (04 means April), the next two, to the day (17 stands for April 17), and the last, to the year (3 means 1993 unless it's a really old can).

There is a record of canned meat (not Spam, obviously) remaining edible for 114 years. However, a Hormel brochure suggests using all canned foods within two years. Says Hormel, "It is important to keep in mind that all foods are substances which are derived from living matter. All living things have life spans that are characteristic of the species." Even Spam.

Oscar Mayer Wieners

The central fact about hot dogs is that most of the "meat" is just plain fat. So basic is fat to hot dogs that manufacturers aren't required to list it on the label. Oscar Mayer's standard mid-American hot-dog label says it is made with pork and turkey. It doesn't say pork and turkey fat; that is supposed to be obvious. Nutritional analyses have shown that typical hot dogs are about 26 percent fat, and only 13 percent protein. Nearly all the rest is water.

Hot dogs are allowed to contain up to 3.5 percent of nonmeat extenders. This can include cereal, starch, and vegetable protein. Hebrew National claims its all-beef hot dogs contain "no fillers." The fine print on the label admits to hydrolyzed vegetable protein "for flavoring." Hydrolyzed vegetable protein is an ingredient of Hamburger Helper. You don't get much more filleresque than that.

Another 2 to 3 percent of the typical hot dog is salt. There is no government limit on sugar content. According to a company brochure, Oscar Mayer meats contain approximately 2 percent sugar. They're boasting about how *low* that is. Assuming that figure applies to hot dogs, the standard one-pound ten pack of Oscar Mayer Wieners contains about 9 grams of sugar (in the form of corn syrup and dextrose). That's more than three teaspoons. Wieners are low in sugar only if your normal impulse is to add *more* than three teaspoons of sugar to a pound of meat. Hot dogs are seasoned, typically with black pepper, nutmeg, mace, cinnamon, mustard, and garlic.

All things considered, what goes into hot dogs is not necessarily as repellent as you might think. The U.S. Department of Agriculture draws a distinction between *skeletal meat* and *meat by-products*. The former is any muscle that was once attached to the skeleton (plus adjacent fat), and is therefore a reasonable approximation of the average person's concept of meat. By-products are low-menu-appeal scraps like lips, tongues, stomachs, and hearts.

Hot dogs used to contain meat by-products routinely. They still can. Then they have to be sold as "wieners with variety meats"—or language to that effect—and the by-products must be spelled out on the label, with little left to the imagination. A hot dog made with pork snouts has to have the words *pork snouts* on the label. In practice, the major brands of hot dogs forgo the use of by-products to avoid label shock.

Another misconception is that hot-dog casings are made from intestines. Hot-dog and sausage casings *can* be made from gut, of course, and sometimes still are in the case of "dry" sausages like salami. Small intestine, large intestine, rectum, and sometimes the esophagus are used. The trouble is that gut casings vary too much in thickness and diameter to be used in today's high-tech hot-dog factories. The big factories use machine-made casings of collagen (a protein usually made by boiling cowhides), cellulose (made by boiling cotton linters, a textile-factory waste), cloth, or plastic. At that, most supermarket hot dogs have no casing at all when you buy them. Typical is Oscar Mayer's procedure. They form and cook wieners in cellulose casings, then strip off the casings before they're packaged in plastic.

Farmer John Liverwurst

The liver at the butcher counter hails from inside a cow. It's the humble, neglected pig liver that figures in wursts and other popularly priced luncheon meats. There is one ironclad rule of processed liver: The bitter gallbladder is always snipped off.

Just because pig livers are cheap doesn't mean there aren't other porcine oddments in a liverwurst. Farmer John Liverwurst contains pig snouts, as well as some fancy skeletal meat, including bacon. Those preferring their pig livers snout-free should try braunschweiger. Technically a liverwurst made from smoked livers, braunschweiger is (in contemporary luncheon-counter practice) a bit upscale in comparison to liverwurst. It's less likely to contain snouts, fillers, or quite so much leftover fat.

Spices have a lot to do with a liverwurst's flavor. Using the feigned allergy technique, we got a Farmer John spokesperson to divulge their liverwurst's secret spices: salt, pepper, marjoram, onion powder, basil, tarragon, thyme, and allspice. There's also a dollop of corn syrup for sweetening.

Underwood Deviled Ham

Time was when deviled ham was a catchall for slaughterhouse leftovers and uncredited fillers. Lunch-box staple Underwood Deviled Ham has not entirely shed the shady reputation of its ilk. Food writer Roy Andries de Groot once accused Underwood Deviled Ham of covertly containing finely ground peanuts to simulate ham from peanut-fed porkers (*Esquire* magazine, June 1975). That's not likely. Peanuts would have to be listed on the label, and they're not. The main novelty is that the smoky taste is artificial. Underwood Deviled Ham is made with unsmoked hams plus artificial smoke. While most processed meat contains a great deal of fat, Underwood actually uses trimmed fat as an ingredient. It's made from ham (probably not so lean itself) *plus* fat trimmings from ham. Underwood Liverwurst Spread contains cooked pork fat, defatted wheat germ, and yeast.

Oscar Mayer Olive Loaf

Vague and inoffensive, *loaf* is a loaded word. That's *loaf* as in honey loaf, luncheon loaf, luxury loaf, old-fashioned loaf, olive loaf, peppered loaf, pickle and pimento loaf, and picnic loaf (all of which are currently marketed by Oscar Mayer alone). Provided the word *meat* does not appear in the designation, a loaf is exempt from the 3.5 percent limit on extenders that applies to sausage-type meats. A strong pickle-loaf lobby convinced the Feds that binders are necessary to keep America's cold cuts in one piece. The most commonly used binder, good for gluing flecks of pimento into cold cuts, is dried nonfat milk.

Oscar Mayer Head Cheese

And then there's head cheese. Swift thought the man brave who first ate an oyster. What fired some unsung pioneer to fricassee a pig's face in gelatin and eat it for lunch? Like *loaf, cheese* is one of those magic regulatory words that tells you no holds are barred. Oscar Mayer's Head Cheese consists of pig snouts, tongues, and hearts arrayed in a dishwater-colored gelatin made with flavored sugar water and vinegar. The gelatin proper is a denatured collagen protein made by boiling skins and other nitrogen-rich refuse.

Libby's Potted Meat Food Product

Upton Sinclair's *The Jungle* tells of a fictional "potted chicken" made from "tripe, and the fat of pork, and beef suet, and hearts of beef, and finally the waste ends of veal, when they had any." That was the bad old days of the packing industry. Today no one would dream of such deceptive labeling. That doesn't mean you're out of luck if you've got a hankering for tinned tripe, suet, and cow hearts. You can still buy it; it just goes by another name, the bizarrely noncommittal "potted meat food product."

Unlike Sinclair's horrible example, Libby's Potted Meat Food Product actually has some chicken in it. It doesn't have veal, and it has pork stomachs but no pork fat per se. The gourmand who lifts the flip top lid of Libby's Potted Meat is rewarded with the sight of a puttylike appetizer suffused with a delicate flush of rose. Could those mashed hearts be responsible for the color? "Heart and cheek meats are good sources of [the pigment] myoglobin and may be used to advantage in products that tend to be pale in color," writes G. R. Schmidt in *Muscle as Food* (1986; edited by Peter J. Bechtel).

Tripe is the rubbery stomach lining of a cow, trimmed of fat. Whether it's a pig or cow stomach, there's no need for morbid reflection about biting into some poor creature's last supper. The *contents* of the stomach are discarded at the packing house. Then the whole organ is thoroughly washed and scrubbed to remove mucous membrane. No matter what the organs used, the assumption definitely is zero consumer tolerance for mucus.

The Libby's label also speaks of something called "partially defatted beef fatty tissue." Much trimmed fat contains a bit of lean meat clinging to it. Someone discovered that low temperature rendering (at about 120 degrees Fahrenheit, low enough to avoid cooking the lean part) upgrades this waste into, well, not *meat*, exactly, but something that has more protein and less fat than it did. The result isn't pretty to look at. Mixed in an emulsified product, no one's the wiser. "This ingredient is a good source of protein," a company spokesperson assured us.

You have to admire Libby's chutzpah. Whoever wrote the potted-meat label is intent upon sipping champagne from the very gutter of charcuterie: "We take pride in providing you with only products of the finest quality." The label has a picture of a meat cleaver inscribed with the proud motto, "A cut above." A cut above what? Tumors?

Carmelita Pork Chorizo

Enough already? There are parts of the pig still unaccounted for. Where do the least appetizing parts of the pig go? In a word: *chorizo.*

Chorizo is the spicy Latin American sausage made with cuts some people don't like to think about. Try pig salivary glands and lymph nodes. That's not a biopsy, it's dinner.

You do get warning. The Carmelita Pork Chorizo label admits, in five-point, orange-on-yellow print, that it contains "pork salivary glands, lymph nodes and fat (cheeks and tongues)" as well as otherwise unspecified "pork." Note that salivary glands and lymph nodes head the list. Once again, labeling laws require that ingredients be listed in descending order of quantity. We're not talking about a *soupçon* of salivary gland, a dash of lymph node. They're the main ingredients. The company logo is a grinning, baseball-capped pig, blissfully unaware of the Carmelita folks' designs on its immune system.

According to industry sources, cheeks are pretty much what they sound like (synonymous with the folksy *jowls*). Tongues have salivary glands connected to them. A "long-cut" tongue has the glands still attached; a "short-cut" tongue has had the glands removed and is considered a choicer cut. With Carmelita Chorizo, you're getting the whole shebang. Tongues are *always* scalded to remove saliva and mucous membrane.

Carmelita Chorizo appears to be free of fillers. Not so with some brands. Reynaldo's Cured Pork Chorizo resorts to soy flour to stretch its offal.

Trying to cut down on pork snouts? Here's a handy chart to demystify meat.

Just for the record, there *are* parts of the pig and cow so intensely appetite-deadening that they aren't used in luncheon meats. As far as can be gathered, no one even thinks of turning pork eyeballs into food. Other tidbits that some people eat and enjoy (brain, thymus, small intestines) have not found a place in the cold-cut aisle. R. A. Lawrie's *Meat Science* (a 1985 book, not to be confused with the journal) bids the industry reader to "reassess the potential for making edible and attractive foods from the substantial amounts of slaughterhouse protein which are currently wasted." The biggest

Mystery Meat

	Hormel Spam	Oscar Mayer Wieners	Oscar Mayer Olive Loaf	Oscar Mayer Head Cheese	Farmer John Liverwurst	Underwood Deviled Ham	Libby's Potted Meat Food Product	Carmelita Pork Chorizo
Pork:								
Snouts				✔	✔			
Cheeks								✔
Tongues				✔				✔
Salivary glands								✔
Lymph nodes								✔
Hearts				✔				
Stomachs							✔	
Livers					✔			
Skeletal meat	✔	✔	✔	✔	✔	✔		✔
Trimmed fat						✔		✔
Beef:								
Hearts							✔	
Tripe (stomach linings)							✔	
Milk			✔					
Partially defatted fatty tissue							✔	
Chicken:								
Skeletal meat							✔	
Turkey:								
Skeletal meat		✔	✔					
Sugar*	✔	✔	✔	✔	✔	✔	✔	

* In some cases, in the form of corn syrup, dextrose, or brown sugar.

wastes: lungs (richer in protein than hot dogs), stomachs (remember, cows have four), and blood (blood sausages are a drop in the bucket next to mighty rivers of discarded plasma and corpuscles).

Not that these are wasted, exactly. Meat by-products and even diseased meat (nothing *too* virulent, mind you) are used in pet foods. Heat sterilization prevents livestock diseases from being passed to pets. The stuff that can't even make it as pet food (by now we're down to dried blood, crushed bone, and wisps of protein left after the fat is rendered) is mixed with such fillers as citrus peels, boiled feathers, cardboard boxes, newsprint, and municipal waste to become feed for the next generation of cows and pigs.

7.

Secret Ingredients

Is There Saltpeter in Army Coffee?

Many soldiers and sailors sincerely believe there is saltpeter in army or navy coffee. In *Western Folklore* (1973) George W. Rich and David F. Jacobs surveyed 140 people and reported that an amazing 38 percent of males believed that they *personally* had been given saltpeter as a sexual depressant, a chemical that reduces or eliminates sex drive. Rumor claims that saltpeter has also been sneaked into food at summer camps, boarding schools, religious colleges, and prisons.

Saltpeter, also known as niter or potassium nitrate (KNO_3), is a crystalline powder readily soluble in water. It is colorless: Water containing saltpeter looks the same as pure water. It is not especially toxic and has been used to preserve meats, but sodium nitrate or nitrite is used much more commonly. Rich and Jacobs asked their group what foods they thought contained saltpeter. Besides coffee, popular answers were milk, soup, stew, mashed potatoes, scrambled eggs; "mushy foods" generally. In Vietnam, the story was that penicillin pills issued freely to soldiers in the field were really saltpeter. Rich and Jacobs wrote, "The conviction that selected foods are riddled with saltpeter is so strong among some military personnel that dosage schedules are even imagined. Some sea-going sailors, for example, imagine that the ship's coffee and soup take on the peculiar taste of saltpeter the day before going into port."

The saltpeter rumor is dead wrong. First of all, we asked a former marine cook about the story. Never had he knowingly added saltpeter to food or beverage, nor had he added any mysterious ingredient under orders from higher-ups. The ingredients for coffee were coffee beans and water, period.

Secondly, saltpeter has an extremely bitter taste. The taste could not easily be disguised in coffee or milk.

The best refutation of the rumor is that saltpeter *doesn't* have any medically recognized effect on libido. Just as all those alleged aphrodisiacs don't do anything, neither does saltpeter. The main physiological effect of small doses of saltpeter is to increase urination.

Similar beliefs have been and are held by armies of many nations, not always with saltpeter as the culprit. The English in World War II thought they were being dosed with copper sulfate; the Germans suspected iodine (in coffee) or sodium bicarbonate (in meat); the French thought their wine contained bromides; women in the English military thought their tea had bromides. All believed that these disparate, mostly toxic substances reduced interest in sex, and thus minimized frustration, venereal disease, rape, pregnancy, and other problems the high command didn't want to be bothered with for the duration.

Equally false is the rumor that Church's Fried Chicken is owned by the Ku Klux Klan and that it contains a "secret spice" that makes black men impotent. The *Biggest Secrets* grapevine of fast-food employees located a Church's employee. She (a black woman) denied that the chicken had any such effect. She warned rather of the marinade: "If we used too much, you'd have diarrhea the next day." Like most franchise chains, Church's does not let employees know the seasoning formula. Our informant was of the opinion that the main ingredient in the marinade was garlic (which has no known effect on libido).

Seaweed in Eskimo Pies

Seaweed is a staple in Japan. To many Americans, the word still connotes an unpleasant green slime hanging to pilings. In fact, seaweed is one of the great American secret ingredients. There's a good chance you've eaten some in the past twenty-four hours, only it's never, ever called seaweed on the label. The FDA allows the term *carrageenin* instead, and food-processing companies opt to puzzle rather than put off potential customers.

The seaweed in question is called carrageen or Irish moss. It's a common red, green, brown, or purple weed of rocky shores. It is harvested with rakes in the U.S. European custom is to gather it from the line of decaying wrack on beaches. Either way, it's washed to get rid of grit. Strictly speaking, carrageen is the seaweed and carrageenin is a colloid made by boiling or alcohol extraction from carrageen. Some Philippine processors began selling the crushed seaweed itself as carrageenin. When competitors complained, the FDA decided, what the heck, as long as it's the right kind of seaweed, it's okay to call it carrageenin. The distinction between carrageen and carrageenin is no longer enforced.

There's nothing wrong with seaweed as food. Far from it; carrageenin must rank among the more nutritious components of the junk foods in which it is often used. Carrageenin is a stabilizer that prevents complex emulsions from separating. When a food aspires to be something it's not—especially to be a dairy product it's not—that food is a candidate for carrageenin. It plays a featured role in Carnation Coffee-mate (the liquid), Fleischman's Egg Beaters, and Kraft Free Singles (the "lite" version of the double plastic-wrapped product you possibly call American cheese—Kraft *can't* call it that). A small sample of major brand-name products using carrageenin/seaweed: Eskimo Pies, Dove Bars, Ovaltine Chocolate, Mocha Mix Lite, McDonald's McLean Deluxe burger, Royal Vanilla Pudding, Jell-O Tapioca Pudding, Reddi Wip, Ultra Slim Fast and Seago diet products, Aqua-Fresh Fluoride Toothpaste, and Gerber Baby Formula. Carrageenin is also used in some shoe polishes.

Labels That Lie

Every now and then an irate diner makes a fuss over a restaurant's "Maine lobster" being from somewhere other than Maine. Several localities have passed menu laws forbidding inaccurate geographical designations. Not so well known is the fact the federal government permits certain types of blatantly false labeling on supermarket foods. Take Norwegian salmon. The naive would think that this is salmon from Norway, or perhaps that there is a species known as Norwegian salmon. Nope. In the U.S., any salmon, of any species, from anywhere, can be sold as Norwegian salmon. In 1991 Maine salmon producers complained that Norway was dumping (selling at below cost) salmon in the U.S. The result was a prohibitive tariff that pretty well drove the Norwegian product from the U.S. marketplace. Now the "Norwegian salmon" in American markets is almost certain to be from the U.S., Canada, or Chile—anywhere but Norway.

It is perfectly legal to label maple syrup from Canada as "Vermont" syrup. Vermont conjures up postcard-perfect scenes of snow-clad hills and church steeples, but it's a small state, and three quarters of the world supply of maple syrup comes from Canada.

Chocolate-Covered Cherries

There are people who would gladly drink bath water rather than have anything to do with the pinkish goo inside a chocolate-covered cherry. Nevertheless, the chocolate-covered cherry is an integral part of a Whitman Sampler (there regally enrobed in gold foil). Hard-core chocophiles favor the no-nonsense Brach's box—*all* chocolate-covered cherries, no foil to peel off, and a great oozing cutaway diagram on the label. A somewhat déclassé reputation has hindered the chocolate-covered cherry's jump to the finer confectionery lines. Godiva resorts to the discreetly bilingual "Cherry Cordials/Cerises à la liqueur."

When you think of it, the chocolate-covered cherry is a peculiar confection. A maraschino cherry swims in a viscous liquid, hermetically sealed inside a chocolate shell. "The secret of how the fruit got inside the liquid-filled, chocolate-covered cherries is almost as much a mystery as how the ship got inside the bottle," declared an Associated Press story. For many, the first explanation that comes to mind is a two-part chocolate shell. Cherry and goo are poured into a concave shell, then a flat "lid" (which becomes the bottom of the candy) is attached. But the chocolate coating looks much like that on regular dipped candies, not like something made in a mold. Close inspection fails to reveal any sign of a seam. The ingenious ice-cube theory (cherry frozen into a block of goo, dipped in chocolate) is closer to the truth.

The real explanation involves an ingredient not on most pantry shelves: enzymes. Cherries are coated with a paste of sugar and the enzyme invertase. This is allowed to harden, creating a sugar-coated cherry, which is then dipped in chocolate.

Over the next couple of weeks, the enzymes go to work. No harsh industrial chemical, invertase is a completely natural enzyme found in your own digestive juices. (The chocolate companies get it from yeast.) The enzyme breaks down ordinary sugar into its components, glucose and fructose. It's almost as if the candy makers were thoughtful enough to spit in the candy to give you a head start on digestion. The simple sugars are more soluble than sucrose is. They dissolve in the moisture content of the sugar, forming a syrup around the cherry.

8·

Fakes

It's easy to fool some people. That's what sells cubic zirconias and swap-meet Guccis. It's hard to fool *everybody*. That doesn't stop people from trying. There exist among us major, Potemkin village–style public shams, intended to fool everyone in the world. Welcome to the land of the totally bogus.

Trump Tower's Missing Floors

Building management wants you to think that mid-Manhattan's glamorous Trump Tower is sixty-eight stories high. Most reference sources list the building as having sixty-eight stories. There *is* a button for the sixty-eighth floor on the elevator. Pushing that button takes you to a real floor whose apartment numbers start with sixty-eight. Yet Trump Tower doesn't have sixty-eight stories. A sharp-eyed observer on the ground can verify by patient counting that Trump Tower has only fifty-eight stories.

Donald Trump was well aware that prices of condos rise in proportion to height. Building management fudged by having the top floors designated sixty-six through sixty-eight on the elevator. As a result, many a Manhattan building taller than Trump Tower has fewer stories than Trump Tower supposedly does. The General Motors Building a few blocks up Fifth Avenue is 705 feet high (vs. 664 for Trump Tower), but it has only fifty stories.

Of course, you can't blame Trump for the fact that his casinos are missing a floor. All casinos (and many other buildings) omit a thirteenth floor for fear that people would refuse to stay on the "unlucky" floor.

Parade Crowds

In November 1990, President Bush addressed cheering crowds in Prague. The Czechs estimated the size of the crowd at about 100,000 people. The Bush staff insisted it was 800,000. That would have meant that two thirds of the population of Prague—men, women, children, babes in arms, and invalids—were in attendance. When newspapers used the more realistic 100,000 figure, a Bush staffer complained that the lowball figure had "insulted the Czech people and the President."

Few factoids in the respectable news media are as dependably undependable as estimates of the size of crowds. The *Columbia Journalism Review* once called crowd figures the "last area of fantasy" in journalism.

No one has ever counted the people who show up in Times Square each New Year's Eve. Even an earnest mathematical estimate requires a lot of eyeballing. The maximum shoulder-to-shoulder density is about 0.5 people per square foot. When it comes to determining whether this maximum density exists, or how it falls off toward the fringes, you're back to guesswork. Should people on side streets be counted? People watching from buildings? For all these reasons, people rarely bother with the math. The usual Times Square estimate ("about two hundred thousand revelers") is pulled out of the chilly night air.

Crowd estimates of political demonstrations are not trivia. The attention a cause gets depends partly on how many people it draws. Rallies for an "anti-establishment" cause often claim crowds two to eight times larger than police estimates. TV and newspapers select guesstimates to match their political slants.

With parade-crowd estimates, there's only the "official" figure. PR types have discovered they can get away with murder. However speculative the Times Square crowd estimates, no one has a vested interest in distorting the numbers. Not so with those flotillas of corporate-sponsored commercials, America's big holiday parades. Asking if parade sponsors would exaggerate crowd figures is like asking if TV networks would inflate their Nielsen ratings if given the opportunity, with no chance of being caught. Journalists don't have time to challenge numbers in a soft-news story—on a holiday yet.

Each year press agents for the Rose Bowl Parade drag out the tall tale that "over a million people" lined the parade route. That is, for starters, five times the size of the crowd claimed on the previous night in Times Square. It's almost ten times the population of Pasadena. How did these million out-of-towners get to Pasadena, a city with poor public transportation? Where are their 250,000 cars parked?

The alleged million are crowded onto a 5.5-mile route. That would require that the throngs be packed, *at physical maximum density,* 34 feet deep on *both* sides of the street. Hmmm. . . . We measured the sidewalk near the reviewing stand at Colorado Boulevard. It was 14′6″ wide. But that was atypical; across the street, the sidewalk is only 6′11″ wide.

In fact, the attendance varies from year to year. In 1992 newspapers commented on the sparse crowds: "It was possible to walk down the sidewalk along the parade route . . . compared to the shoulder-to-shoulder crowds of previous years," reported the *Los Angeles Times.* The official crowd tally was, once again, "over a million." Soberer minds have put the typical attendance at no more than 400,000.

The most extreme case of PR hype may be the Hollywood Christmas Parade. Its organizers have claimed 750,000 spectators in recent years. This would entail packing people shoulder-to-shoulder 44 feet deep on each side of the street all along the 3.2-mile route. Even allowing for a large proportion of children and their lesser space-and-oxygen requirements, it may safely be predicted that the year 750,000 people show up for the Hollywood Christmas Parade is the year that the bodies will be stacked like cordwood, with no way of carrying out the suffocated dead.

The White House Christmas Tree Lighting Ceremony

The next thing you'll say is that the president doesn't light up the national Christmas tree. Historians now agree that President Reagan resorted to a fake button for the annual tree-lighting ceremony. The tree's outside in the Ellipse, and it gets *cold.* Reagan stood out on a White House balcony for the ceremony and pushed an ostensible remote-control button to light the tree. It was pretty obvious that there wasn't an extension cord running all the way from the White House to the tree (it would have had to cross E Street). The press corps doubted that anyone would bother to rig up a radio or microwave link for a once-a-year deal. To this day, Reagan's aides have never admitted that the president used a fake button. Bush braved the weather and used a real button, physically connected to the tree and a live power source.

Fake Speed Traps

People slow down when they see a cop parked by the side of the road. The trouble is that cops expect salary, health plans, and pensions. More cost-effective are mannequins dressed in police outfits and posed realistically in a police car. Among the police departments reported as using fake cops are the Minnesota State Police.

Fake Towns on Maps

Map publishers allegedly put fake features on their maps to protect their copyrights. Wouldn't that be a fine kettle of fish if you packed up the car and spent your vacation driving to a town that doesn't exist? "Are we there yet?" "Sorry kids, it was just one of those, you know, copyright-enforcement towns."

Okay, they wouldn't use major towns. Still, the idea that anything on a map is fake is kind of scary. We wondered if we could verify this story with any specific examples.

No one "owns" the configuration of land and sea, of towns and political boundaries. No publisher wants to put in years of work making a map and then have someone else copy it, either. The idea is that if someone publishes a map with the town of Gotcha, Illinois, on it, and someone else copies the map illegally, the pirated map will also include Gotcha. The publisher could then sue the pirates and make a good impression on the judge or jury by revealing that the fictitious Gotcha is on the copied map.

Map publishers we talked to insisted there are many ways of telling if a map has been cribbed *without* resorting to fake towns. No atlas map shows every tributary of every river all the way to their sources. If it did, any reasonably humid nation would be a spiderweb of blue ink. The decision of which portions of which rivers to show is at least somewhat arbitrary. If one detailed map's drainage pattern *consistently* matched another map's, that would be ample proof of copying. The same thing goes for thematic maps such as road atlases. The choice of towns or roads is always somewhat arbitrary and provides proof of copying on any detailed map.

Biggest Secrets canvassed several major map publishers to see if they used fake features. The National Geographic Society and Times Books of London (publisher of *The Times Atlas*) said definitely not; there is no false information on their maps if they can help it. The Times Books cartographer said she'd never come across such a practice in ten years in the business.

Rand McNally and Hammond said no, too. According to a Hammond spokesman, "Not now, nor has it ever been our policy to include fictional towns. . . ."

Two other map publishers, ADC and Thomas Brothers, did admit to using fake features. Both firms specialize in city and regional atlases. A street atlas is supposed to show every street, period. There is no editorial choice involved, and that makes it difficult to prove copying—unless they slip in a few fake streets.

ADC's spokesman was at first reluctant to reply to our inquiries. As far as they're concerned, even the fact that copyright traps exist is supposed to be a secret. The spokesman wouldn't give a specific example but said they have a set of guidelines for the copyright traps. The fake features range from nonexistent streets and area names to mere misspellings and index doctoring. A nonexistent street may be in the index but not on the map; or it may be on the map but not listed in the index. The fake streets are chosen so as to pose no confusion to travelers. They're not through roads, just itty-bitty cul-de-sacs. ADC keeps careful records of the traps in its files and changes them with each edition of their maps. Their spokesman could not recall any case of a person getting lost because of a copyright trap. "Occasionally customers will notify us of them as an error," he said.

We had more luck coaxing a specific example from Thomas Brothers. A fictitious "Eamon Court" appears in the town of Rocklin, California, on their Sacramento atlas. Directions to nowhere: Take Interstate 80 north from Sacramento, get off at the Pacific Street exit, and continue north to Sunset Boulevard. Turn left on Sunset, right on Whitney Boulevard, and right on Midas Avenue. Eamon Court would be the first street on your right.

USA, Japan

A recurring story claims that a Japanese city changed its name to "Usa" so that goods could be exported to the U.S. with the label "MADE IN USA." This turned up in a 1991 letter to Dear Abby. Another Abby correspondent said the story had been published in *Reader's Digest* "back in the 1960s."

There *is* a town called Usa in Japan. It's on the island of Kyushu, about eighty miles northeast of Nagasaki. But the name seems innocent enough. Usa isn't far from towns called Ozu, Udo, and Usuki. Made in Usa or not, goods could not be imported into the U.S. with a "MADE IN USA" label. Imports must be labeled by nation of origin, not city. The Usa, Japan, story appears to be a case of someone's tall tale that someone else took seriously.

Bogus Batters

Pranksters have attempted to achieve a slice of immortality by getting their names into official baseball statistics. The most successful (that we know of) is Lou Proctor, long listed as a member of the 1912 St. Louis Browns. The real Lou Proctor was but a mild-mannered telegraph operator in the St. Louis press box. Just once, he slipped his own name and some phony stats into the box score. Just once! No one much noticed or cared. At season's end, Proctor's one-game career was duly tabulated in the 1912 statistics. Proctor made the first six editions of *The Baseball Encyclopedia* (editors got wise when preparing the seventh) and keeps turning up in baseball references eighty years later.

This is but one example of the false information that finds its way in trusted references. Some of the people listed in *Who's Who in America* don't exist. The fakes are there so that the *Who's Who* people can monitor the junk mail being sent to people listed. The fake entries have the addresses and last names of *Who's Who* employees. Thus most of the ringers have addresses in the Chicago area, where the book is published. One example from past editions: Edward Petchenik, supposedly a Highland Park, Illinois, surgeon and esteemed member of the Elks, Knights of Columbus, and Democratic party. *Kenneth* Petchenik was actually the president of the *Who's Who* company.

Fake Autographs

Most people know that the U.S. president is too busy to sign letters to average citizens. How can you tell if a famous person's signature is for real? You won't get much help from the International Autopen Co., the Sterling, Virginia, firm that makes the machines presidents and other busy people use to forge their own signatures. International Autopen rarely divulges who its customers are. When you get right down to it, the whole point of the machine is to make people think that someone signed something when that someone didn't. "You're getting into the cloudy business of who you're fooling," company owner Robert DeShazo told *The Washington Post* in 1989. A company brochure lists a few corporate or organizational purchasers who said it was okay to name them: American Telephone and Telegraph, United Airlines, the Democratic National Committee, the Brookings Institution, and the Brotherhood of Electrical Workers. No word on who uses the machines at these organizations, but it's not going to be middle management. The company claims—ominously for autograph collectors—that a certain customer's signature has been reproduced over 100,000 times on the machine.

The cheaper of the two models of the machine costs about three thousand dollars. That buys a table with a rig holding a pen. It's 34 inches high, semi-portable (100 pounds), and plugs into a standard 110-volt outlet. The owner submits two good typical signatures, and the company cuts a special "matrix" to reproduce the motions used to sign. The machine isn't completely automatic. An underling has to feed in letters and operate the machine. DeShazo estimated that three thousand to four thousand were in use, many inside the Beltway, where they are often perceived as status symbols.

Kennedy was the first president to use the machine. Autograph dealer Charles Hamilton noticed that an awful lot of Kennedy autographs matched *exactly*. He could superimpose one signature over another, hold them up to the light, and detect no difference. Informed of Hamilton's suspicions, Press Secretary Pierre Salinger countered, "Absolutely untrue, there is no such machine." He was lying. Gerald Ford was the first president to admit to using the machine. Autograph dealers now contend that nearly all senators and Supreme Court justices, and many congressmen and astronauts, use the machines. Courts have ruled that robot signatures are legal and binding. A bill signed by a machine in a legislator's absence is valid. Lyndon Johnson's oath of office as vice president was signed with an Autopen—the Kennedy administration was nuts about the machines.

The Autopen works with pencils and felt-tip, ballpoint, and fountain pens. The machine can be adjusted to sign unusually shaped and/or fragile objects. It does not follow that the autograph in a copy of Nixon's autobiography is legitimate, or even that a Ronald Reagan–signed White House Easter egg is.

The company suggests that the signatures used for cutting the matrix be somewhat simplified: "Do not use periods, dashes or extra marks unless necessary. Connect letters and name as much as possible." It's not that the machine can't dot *i*'s and cough out jittery doodads; it just slows it down. As a rule, real signatures are a bit gnarlier and less calligraphic than the machine signatures.

The only *sure* way to identify an Autopen signature is by comparing it to known Autopen signatures. Unlike humans, an Autopen matrix turns out identical signatures. Or nearly so. The paper can slip a bit, offsetting part of the signature. The pressure varies, depending on how well the pen contacts the document. Beyond that the basic form of the signature is the same.

Signature matrices are cheap (they cost about one hundred dollars) and interchangeable. Bigwigs often order several matrices to churn out several different versions of the signature. Kennedy had seven machine signatures (mostly "John Kennedy" but also "Jack Kennedy"); Nixon had nine full signatures and three versions of his initials; Reagan had about twelve machine patterns, including versions of "Ronald Reagan," "Ron," "Ronnie," and, for those who knew him way back when, "Dutch."

Jimmy Carter had an Autopen but is more notorious among autograph hounds for letting presidential secretary Susan Clough churn out his signature. Clough's Carter signatures look great and are considered almost worthless. Reportedly, Clough once signed Carter's name to a photograph that had been signed—*personally* —by Menachem Begin and Anwar Sadat.

Our research suggests that the place to get a genuine presidential autograph is at the gift shops of the presidential libraries. We examined quite a few copies of signed autobiographies in the Richard Nixon and Ronald Reagan presidential libraries. No two signatures (on bookplatelike paper inserts) were alike. As the Autopen machine is perfectly capable of signing books, there would be little reason to use the inserts except for convenience of the former presidents. Reagan's jaggy penmanship could be the clever dissimulation of a proxy signer, but the price of the autographed books (about twenty-five dollars more than the cover price) suggests that the former president would be able to recoup his billing rate. Nixon's autographed books sell for cover price. People at both gift shops insisted that the signatures were genuine. Nixon even autographs books and other memorabilia that people *send* to him, according to a Nixon Library gift-shop spokesperson.

That kind of dedication is sadly lacking in the world of sports. Unless it's one of those deals where you shell out money to have a former star sign a ball in your presence, they're apt to have a secretary sign. Autopens are rarely used by ballplayers, but rubber-stamp signatures are widely used.

In 1990 the Charlotte Hornets admitted that many of their autographed basketballs were not all they might be. Asked Hornets vice president Tony Renaud, "When you have somebody who has a sick kid in the hospital, and you're going to send them a ball, and the players aren't here, what do you do?" The answer was that they send a ball forged with players' autographs by authentic Charlotte Hornets office personnel.

Sports Collectors Digest columnist Dave Miedema reported the case of a binocular-equipped fan who observed a Yankee coach signing baseballs in the bullpen. There's nothing wrong with that, except that the coach signed balls two and three times. He signed for Willie Randolph and Lou Piniella. Both have rare and valuable signatures, given their known reluctance to sign!

According to sports-memorabilia dealers, the list of baseball greats known to have used proxy signers includes Hank Aaron, Johnny Bench, Yogi Berra, Roy Campanella, Lou Gehrig, Mickey Mantle, Roger Maris, Willie Mays, Babe Ruth, Ted Williams, and Carl Yastrzemski. Some players (like Joe DiMaggio) are so fed up with the commercialization of baseball autographs that they rarely sign anything for anyone. Consequently, there are forged DiMaggio signatures on the market. *All* "Shoeless" Joe Jackson signatures (there are many) are problematic. It remains a point of debate whether the illiterate Jackson ever learned to write.

Less is often more with sports autographs. A star player's signature, alone, on a ball or bat is usually worth more than the same ball or bat signed by the whole team. Collectors prefer the former, and they're often rare. Multiple-signature balls are usually the result of a determined kid of long ago having gotten players on two opposing teams to sign, creating an odd mixture of nobodies and a recognized star or two. Currently, Rod Carew is said to have a policy of not signing bats unless other players have signed. Shrewd fans have been known to obtain near worthless signatures on a bat before presenting it to Carew. After Carew signs, they erase the other signatures.

9.

The Formula for Play-Doh

Make no mistake about it, Play-Doh is not modeling clay. Clay comes out of the earth. Play-Doh comes out of a big fun factory somewhere. Feature articles on the stuff talk of a "top secret" formula. About all you'll learn from the manufacturer is that Play-Doh is "clean, non-toxic, not a clay." Because Play-Doh isn't food, the manufacturer doesn't have to divulge ingredients. That is, it's not a food to *adults*. The "non-toxic" part has always been a big selling point because, uh, children eat so much of it. Play-Doh's crumby, chocolate-truffle-cake texture and addictive aroma are the stuff of schoolyard picas.

Kids sometimes mix up a homemade "clay" from baking soda, cornstarch, and water. This has a cold mashed-potato consistency distinctly inferior to Play-Doh's. The smell isn't even close. Play-Doh was invented in Cincinnati in 1956 by Noah W. McVicker and Joseph S. McVicker. The McVickers worked for a company called Rainbow Crafts, which made soap. Kenner acquired Play-Doh and made a game effort to run the rival Super Dough out of the business with a lawsuit that—while dead serious—is kind of silly when you try to explain it. Kenner claimed that Super Dough maker Tyco Toys had stolen all sorts of confidential trade secrets, among them the "extruding buds" used in Tyco's Flower Makin' Basket, which Kenner claimed were similar to its unrealized plans for a toy that, in turn, was a logical extension of the concept embodied in its Fuzzy Pumper Barber Shop, a device that squeezes Play-Doh "hair" through a plastic human head. A federal judge rejected the latter claim.

Hasbro bought out Kenner's parent company and, with inscrutable corporate logic, transferred Play-Doh to its Playskool division, an outfit that has quietly amassed the rights to a staggering variety of classic toys (Mr. Potato Head, Tinkertoys, Raggedy Ann, Lincoln Logs).

There is a patent for Play-Doh—not under that name, of course—and anyone can get it. Just send three dollars to the Commissioner of Patents and Trademarks, Washington, DC 20321 and ask for U.S. Patent No. 3,167,440. Filed by the McVickers in 1960, this document describes a "plastic modeling composition of a soft, pliable working consistency" that can only be you-know-what. The patent was granted in 1965.

Play-Doh is real dough, first of all. All the several sample formulations in the patent agree in using a dough of ordinary wheat flour and tap water. That Proustian aroma? It's deodorized petroleum distillates, a.k.a. kerosene. The odor, of course, is a serendipitous by-product. The kerosene is in there to keep the dough soft and nicely moldable. To this, various chemicals are added to kill bacteria (otherwise Play-Doh would turn into sourdough pretty fast), and facilitate drying (so you can make permanent mugs or ashtrays by letting it dry).

You wouldn't want to drink kerosene straight up, or sample some of the other chemicals mentioned in the patent. These are minor ingredients by weight, and evidently there's little chance of a child eating so much as to cause harm. The McVickers write that the compound is "not recommended for eating but no harm is done should a child accidentally swallow a piece of it."

Think Play-Doh is just kid stuff? The patent confesses, "We are unable to state definitely the theory upon which this process operates, because the reactions taking place in the mass are complicated." Science has harnessed Play-Doh, but it may never understand it.

Play-Doh: Ingredients

Water **Flour** **Salt**	Play-Doh is about 97–98 percent real dough. Use equal amounts of tap water and flour, adjusting if necessary to obtain desired consistency. The McVicker patent suggests "hard winter wheat flour, first clears" for best results. Add several percent of ordinary table salt.
Kerosene	A 1 percent admixture of kerosene keeps the dough velvety, prevents sticking to hands, hair, and clothing. Deodorized kerosene is *de rigueur* for the Play-Doh aroma. For your own sake, use a kerosene with a boiling point of about 150 degrees Celsius (there's less risk of explosion!).
Alum	Use $Al_2(SO_4)_3 \cdot 18H_2O$, about 0.8 percent by weight of final product, to bind the mixture. Iron-containing alums are out—they stain fabrics.
Borax	$Na_2B_4O_7 \cdot 4H_2O$ prevents mold, allows dough to last indefinitely in its can. Use about 0.5 percent.
Artificial color and fragrance	Approved red, yellow, and blue food dyes give a complete color set (white dough is natural). Trace of perfume enlivens kerosene buzz.

10·

How They Get a Ship in a Bottle

a b c

d e f g

Had enough of smug old geezers who build ships in bottles and won't tell how it was done? The next time you're craft fair–bound, use this identification template. Faced with a taciturn folk artist, find the problem curio above and read the explanation. *Bargaining tactic:* Try reading the explanation aloud.

(a) *A penny in a tiny bottle just large enough to hold it.* The mouth of the bottle is way too small (about one quarter inch diameter) and stopped with an elfin cork. The maker put the penny in an open-mouthed glass cup, then heated the top and formed it into a narrow mouth. The bottle gets hot, hence use of a coin rather than a wooden object.

(b) *The classic ship in a bottle.* Builders want you to think they assembled the ship, piece by piece, inside the bottle. All the carving, painting, and niggling work is actually done outside the bottle. The guy built a fully rigged model ship with hinged masts that collapse like an umbrella.

The solid hull of the ship is just narrow enough to fit inside the bottleneck. Sails and masts (often ordinary toothpicks hinged to the hull with pieces of bent pins) make the ship look bigger than it is. Long threads are attached to the masts to form the rigging. These are then run through strategically placed holes (usually on the bowsprint, extending from the front of the ship) to allow the collapsed masts to be raised by remote control. The ship is collapsed and inserted into the bottle, with the long control threads still hanging out the bottleneck.

Builders of ships in bottles need various long, narrow tools. Tweezers, needle-nose pliers, and scalpels may suffice for small bottles. Most workers improvise their own tools. Useful are a long thin tong that fits in the bottleneck and dowels or bamboo skewers for gluing and untangling. First the builder glues the base of the ship to the bottle. Long cotton swabs (the sort used for cleaning audio equipment) are useful for swabbing excess or spilled glue. Once the glue is dry, the maker pulls the control threads to expand the masts and sails. He tapes the threads temporarily to the outside of the bottle, keeping them taut, and applies drops of glue to the holes where the control threads exit from the ship. The glue solidifies, leaving the rigging, masts, and sails in the expanded state. When the glue is completely dry, the builder snips the control threads off with a tool consisting of part of a razor blade on the end of a dowel. An ocean is simulated by packing in blue clay, piece by piece, and patting it down with a spoonlike instrument.

Ships in bottles "still filled" with liquid are frauds. They put the ship in a empty bottle, then fill it with water for "gin" or tea for "whiskey" and cap tightly. Note: People who make curios from liquor bottles often don't have to go far for their raw material, if you catch our drift.

(c) *A glass ship in a bottle.* The ship is one of those glasswork tchotchkes with frilly threads of glass for the rigging. It's a cute variation, but insofar as the guy who made it was an expert glass-worker, the bottle is suspect. The glass ship is made normally. Once cool, it's inserted in an open-ended bottle, then fixed in place with a blowtorch. Finally the open end is carefully sealed. With practice the close is nicely inconspicuous. There will always be some telltale unevenness where the glass has been melted.

(d) *A Crucifixion scene in a bottle.* A cross of two pieces of wood secured with a single nail is collapsible. The maker applies glue to the juncture of crosspiece and upright. Immediately (while glue is wet) he rotates the crosspiece so that it is parallel to the upright. Thus collapsed, the cross fits easily through the bottleneck. Once inside, the cross is opened with dowels or tongs and allowed to dry. The corpus Christi is just narrow enough to fit in the neck of the bottle. Arms are hinged or flexible. The builder applies glue to the back, then inserts and carefully positions the figure on the cross. Elaborate models include crucified thieves.

(e) *A bottle with an impossibly placed screw or peg.* A long cork extends down some distance into the body of the bottle. A large screw penetrates the cork perpendicularly. The screw is longer than the width of the bottleneck, and it is impossible to remove the cork from the bottle. To make this, the artisan drills two holes in the cork (which is actually made of a more solid wood). One is the hole the screw will go in, and the other is a secret hole down the center of the cork. The latter hole ends at, and intersects with, the screw hole.

There are two ways of getting the screw in the hole. In one, you put the screw in the bottle, insert the cork, and jiggle the bottle, for hours or days on end if necessary, until a miracle happens and the screw lands partly inside the perpendicular hole. When that happens, you carefully angle the cork, pressing the screw head against the inside of the bottle. This forces the screw further into the hole. The screw fits loosely in the hole; otherwise it *would* be impossible.

Next, you immobilize the screw by ramming a fitted dowel down the secret hole. The final step is to glue a decorative cap onto the top of the cork to hide the secret hole.

Second method: Take the screw and wind a thin strong wire around the center portion of its threads. One end of the wire then goes into the cork's screw hole, up through the secret hole, and out the top of the cork. Put the screw and the cork in the bottle. Pull carefully on the wire at the top of the cork. With luck, the screw will thread itself into the hole as the wire unwinds.

(f) *A Coca-Cola bottle penetrated by a wooden arrow.* It's a legitimate bottle with a hole drilled through it. The shaft of the arrow enters the bottle through the holes. Arrowhead and tail are much too large to fit through either hole, yet the arrow is all one piece of wood. The secret is that the arrow is made of basswood (*Tilia* spp.), a light, compressible wood that expands when exposed to steam. The arrowhead is compressed and pushed through predrilled holes. Steam expands the arrowhead to its original dimensions.

(g) *A pear inside a bottle of brandy.* The empty bottle is placed over a branch pruned of all but a single pollinated bloom. The fruit grows inside the bottle. When ripe, the fruit is snipped off with a tool, the bottle cleaned and filled with brandy.

11·

Secret Places

Wyoming's Jackson Hole ski resort has a secret run that's on the official trail map. Upstate New York has a Secret Caverns that advertises itself with billboards. Tour guides point out the Secret Garden at Miami's Vizcaya estate. Secret beaches are too common to enumerate, and add to that years of travel-section hyperbole ("Finland is Scandinavia's best-kept secret"). For some reason, the travel industry thinks that secrecy sells. The trouble is that none of these promotion-savvy places is much of a secret.

Still, there *are* genuinely secret places—places someone is trying ever so hard to keep you from knowing about—places you can visit on your next vacation. Here are directions.

The Capitol's Secret Conference Room

America's roster of secret places starts at the Capitol in Washington, D.C. Pay no attention to the tour guides' cornball story about the "whispering gallery" having been kept secret by Washington insiders in order to allow eavesdropping on rivals. There's a much better, fully authenticated secret beneath the Capitol dome. Since the mid-1970s, Congress has maintained a special room for secret conferences. Directly under the dome, it's a soundproof cone of silence, invulnerable (they hope) to electronic eavesdropping.

The dome you see is steel, painted to look like marble. This provides some electronic shielding itself. The walls of the conference room are lead-lined. A little information on the room came to light in 1986, when Senator Bob Dole complained that the room's shielding was easy pickings with new eavesdropping techniques. The shielding has, one gathers, been beefed up since then. A principal user of the room is the House Intelligence Committee.

The Greenbrier Relocation Center

Many hotels have a special room set aside for an unexpected V.I.P. guest. The posh Greenbrier Hotel (on U.S. 60, White Sulphur Springs, West Virginia) has 800 such rooms. In the late 1950s the government built a cavernous fallout shelter beneath the resort. It includes separate subterranean meeting chambers for the Senate and House of Representatives. *The Washington Post* blew the Greenbrier site's cover in 1992, and what with easing nuclear fears, the government isn't sure it wants to maintain the facility. The Greenbrier facility is merely the toniest of a whole string of federal fallout shelters in the mountains west of Washington. Unusual for a bomb shelter, the Greenbrier facility is leased. The reported rent ($50,000 to $60,000 a year) isn't so bad considering that you'd need about $35 million to rent all 700 of the Greenbrier's above-ground units for a year.

Tourist Trap

The Thing? is a living tribute to the laxity of Arizona's consumer-protection statutes. Claimed to be the first of several remarkably similar attractions scattered over the country, it is the great American tourist trap. For years, The Thing? has existed solely to hook customers on the strength of an overblown "secret" that is revealed only to those who pay the price of admission. Repeat business is minimal.

Over a dozen billboards in each direction on Interstate 10 advertise The Thing? without telling you what it is. "THE INEVITABLE AWAITS YOU," says one sign. "SEE FANTASIA WOOD," urges another. Then there's "MUSEUM OF GHOSTS." Just to keep you guessing, the billboards also let you know that cactus candy and liquor miniatures are to be had at The Thing? Located on a boring stretch of open road between Tucson and El Paso, the self-proclaimed Mystery of the Desert snares all but the most monomaniacal of drivers.

So you take Exit 322, near Dragoon, Arizona, and find that the exit ramp leads to a mundane gas station/gift shop. Inside the gift shop is a weird grotto surrounded by colored lights. This portal leads to The Thing? You pay the cashier and enter. On the other side of the impressive door is a revolving door like those in subway exits. You can't get out the way you came in. All of a sudden you are outside again, in a squalid back lot of sheds and trailers. Never mind that; on the sidewalk in front of you are painted gigantic footprints leading to a carportlike structure.

Inside is a pointless assortment of unrelated junk. A sign above an old car says, "1932 BUICK—THIS ANTIQUE CAR WAS REALLY *THE THING*." Oh-oh! Is it too late to get a refund? Unfortunately, you're now on the wrong side of that revolving door.

There's a car that belonged to Hitler—"*THE THING* IS, WE CAN'T PROVE IT." Next to the cars is a gruesome, life-size diorama of medieval tortures. Hanging from the ceiling and scattered along the walkway are pieces of driftwood carved into hideous monsters. The more sensitive tykes are already crying their eyes out. But this is only the first of three non-air-conditioned exhibits.

The third and final shack of this dime-museum hell contains The Thing? itself. "THE THING—WHAT IS IT?" asks a sign. It's a tomblike structure of whitewashed cinder blocks, covered on top with a sheet of glass. Inside is a fake mummy clutching a fake mummified child. That's all it is. Now you know.

The Marine Mammals Program

You've probably heard stories about how the U.S. Navy is training cute, lovable dolphins and seals to plant bombs and outsmart bad guys. The navy really does have a Marine Mammal System. They concede that the program exists, though almost everything else about it is secret—including where it is located and what the mammals are being trained to do.

The secret boot camp for navy seals, the real kind, is near San Diego. You won't find it on maps. Even the massive breakwaters and piers are curiously missing from civilian maps that show comparable structures elsewhere in the harbor. San Diego street maps show the Fort Rosecrans Naval Reservation. The marine-mammal facility is a small part of that. The training site is on the San Diego Bay side of the peninsula, in the water, of course, just north of Ballast Point.

The coast guard tips its hand by enforcing a "restricted zone" north of Ballast Point. No civilian craft are allowed within 700 yards of the shore between Buoy 15 and the Naval Supply Systems fueling pier. There are also signs posted in the vicinity barring swimming, surfing, and fishing.

The marine mammal program reportedly has about 140 animals, 100 of them Atlantic bottle-nose dolphins (*Tursiops truncatus*). That's what Flipper was. The program also uses a couple of dozen California sea lions (*Zalophus californianus*), the circus seal that balances balls and plays horns. There are other species of dolphins, three beluga whales, and a false killer whale. After training at the San Diego base, some mammals go to smaller bases in Florida and Hawaii. It is generally conjectured that the mammals would be used to locate mines or enemy divers and, conceivably, to place bombs near enemy ships.

Of late the navy has seemed more worried about animal-rights activists than spies. It considered evacuating the facility for the 1992 Americas Cup race, fearing not only that foreign agents would use the opportunity to spy on the operation but also that media attention brought to the area might lead to unwanted publicity.

The curious can get a panoramic view of the base by hiking through a naval cemetery. Highway 209 (Cabrillo Memorial Drive) runs down the center of the Point Loma peninsula to the Cabrillo National Monument. On either side of the road are signs forbidding entry of unauthorized personnel into the fort. Turn left into the Fort Rosecrans National Cemetery (which is open to the public). Find Section M and walk to the chain-link fence. Directly below, at the bottom of the cliff, is the marine-mammal base. You can see piers and a series of holding pens. You're close enough to watch training going on, particularly with binoculars. Forgot your binoculars? Two of the coin-operated telescopes behind the gift shop at nearby Cabrillo National Monument can be trained on the base.

The Secret Face-Lift Hotel

Le Petit Hermitage Hotel is a *Mondo Cane*–quality aberration in Beverly Hills catering to the celebrity who wants to keep a face-lift a secret. Tabloids would pay big bucks for photos of famous people with telltale black eyes. Reportedly, Le Petit Hermitage's high-profile guests check in discreetly and take a limo with jet black glass to and from their elective surgery. The limo heads off the yellow press by ducking into a secret tunnel leading to a private elevator. Inside, the once and future beautiful person dines on gourmet meals—soft, mushy gourmet meals—and never need leave the elegant prison his or her own fame has created.

Officially, Le Petit Hermitage doesn't exist. It's not in the phone book or the *AAA TourBook.* It's under the management of the exclusive but not secret L'Ermitage Hotel. By having a confederate pose as a potential customer, we learned the specifics.

Le Petit Hermitage is located at 9293 Burton Way. It's on the north side of the street, east of Foothill Road, a two-story building immediately to the west of L'Ermitage Hotel. The unlisted phone number is actually the same as that of L'Ermitage, except for an extension: (310) 278-3344, ext. 222. The fax number is (310) 271-4490. Though inconspicuous from the street, Le Petit Hermitage has a sign (concealed by plantings) and a posted street number. The front entrance, which most customers shun, opens after a screened caller has pressed a doorbell. Security cameras scan the perimeter. Fourteen rooms go from a rock-bottom $350 to $500 a day at this writing. That includes meals. Nurses and a physician are on call, and a pharmaceutical service, a chauffeur, a makeup artist, and a personal shopper are available. All major credit cards are accepted.

Given the expense of excavation, the secret tunnel has to be nearby. There's nothing you could call a tunnel in the alley behind the hotel; it is unlikely that the older apartment building to the west would be admitting Le Petit Hermitage clients via its parking garage; there are only private houses south of the wide greenbelt of Burton Way. That leaves L'Ermitage Hotel's parking entrance. Given that the two hotels even share a phone number, it seems likely that the underground entrance beneath L'Ermitage is what they're talking about. It is on the east (far) side of L'Ermitage, and has two mirrors that provide visibility for drivers entering traffic. The L'Ermitage parking structure does indeed extend west under the hotel (and Le Petit Hermitage?) and has elevators. However, fanny-lift and liposuction cases requiring wheelchair access will have to use the ramp—in plain sight—leading from the alley in back.

Unlisted Restaurant

A recent entry to the small rank of restaurants with unlisted phone numbers is Olive (119 South Fairfax Avenue, Los Angeles). Olive raises commerical camouflage to new heights. It's practically in the parking lot of the Farmer's Daughter Motel, which caters to ordinary folks in town to see game-show tapings. Olive has no window, the door's unmarked, and there's no sign, unless you count the mosaic of hexagonal bathroom tiles that serves as welcome mat. Unlisted number notwithstanding, references are required just to get a dinner reservation. Say you're a friend of Julia Roberts. That ultrasecret number: (213) 939-2001.

Century House

Long reputed to be the most secretive of intelligence agencies, Britain's Secret Intelligence Service (SIS or MI6) has eased up a bit in recent years. Yet MI6 remains cloistered in an unmarked and unlisted London building, Century House.

Any intelligence operation deals in secrets. But the very existence of Britain's two intelligence agencies was technically a secret for most of the twentieth century. MI6 (MI refers to "military intelligence") is Britain's spy agency. MI5 is the internal security agency, charged with capturing foreign spies and terrorists in Britain. Because the British government denied that either agency existed, the location of their headquarters, the identity of their heads, and many other basic data were necessarily classified.

James Bond's boss was "M." To those in the know, this was a jab at the real head of MI6, "C." The designation "C" dates from the days of the first chief, Mansfield Cumming. A former navy man retired for chronic seasickness, Cumming headed the agency from 1909 until his death in 1923. Cumming was a monocled eccentric who liked disguises and gadgets more than was strictly necessary. Visitors to his office in Whitehall Court had to enter by a secret panel leading to a hidden staircase. Cumming had a wooden leg—he hacked the real one off with a pen knife to extricate himself from an overturned car—and was fond of navigating the halls of the SIS with his prosthesis propped on a toy scooter.

Cumming signed documents with the initial C, always in green ink. Like J. Edgar Hoover, Cumming became synonymous with his agency—so much so that it was considered impolitic to let on that he had passed on. His successor, Sir Hugh Sinclair, continued to sign documents with a C, as have Sinclair's successors.

A "D-notice" long forbade British papers from publishing information on C. Each new appointment led to a round of C outing in the European press, starting with riddlelike hints and inevitably leading to the publication of the new C's name and picture. Based on these well-confirmed leaks, the list of covert C's runs as follows: Sir Hugh Sinclair (took over in 1923), Sir Stewart Menzies (1939), Sir John Sinclair (1953), Sir Dick White (1956), Sir John Rennie (1968), Sir Maurice Oldfield (1973), Sir Arthur Franks (1979), Sir Colin Figures (1982), and Sir Christopher Curwen (1985).

This degree of secrecy no longer prevails. Britain now admits that its intelligence agencies exist, and in 1991 it took the unprecedented step of naming (though not releasing a picture of) Stella Rimington, the newly chosen head of MI5.

Both agencies are hidden behind unmarked doors in London. The headquarters of MI5 is Leconfield House, at 22 Curzon Street in the fashionable Mayfair district, about a block from the London Hilton. The entrance to the glass lobby says LECONFIELD HOUSE in gold letters. There's no indication that this is the headquarters of a big government agency.

Tacky in comparison is MI6's headquarters in South London. Century House is the oddly anonymous and ugly free-standing twenty-story building at the corner of Westminster Bridge Road and Pearman Street, near the Lambeth North station of the underground. Despite the generous setback from the street, the property is bare of plants or ornament other than a wall of cheap-looking gray bricks. Gates restrict auto access. The only tip-offs that this isn't just another office block are the video cameras trained on the entrance and an occasional security guard with a walkie-talkie. The ostensible name of the building is the Government Communications Bureau. No sign says that, but there is a modest sign on the Westminster Bridge Road side saying, "CENTURY HOUSE." The only conspicuous sign at the entrance says, "USE CENTRE DOOR." The London phone book has no entry for MI6, Secret Intelligence Service, Government Communications Bureau, or Century House.

III: Codes

12.

Lottery Tickets

Ever wonder what all those stray numbers on a lottery ticket mean? The answer is simple, though state lottery boards don't like to talk about it. The numbers are there to prevent counterfeiting, now a huge problem. Lottery tickets are easy to duplicate. They don't use fancy engraving or watermarks. Their commerical-grade card stock, foil, and inks are all too readily matched by a good print shop. But hardly anyone gets away with lottery fraud. Thanks to secret devices and codes, forged or stolen tickets are easy to identify. States have even arranged sting operations in which lottery cheats are invited to a "big spin"—then arrested. Here's how it works.

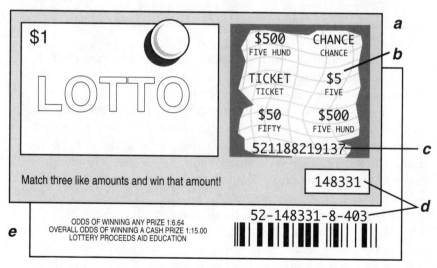

(a) The foil is not just for show. The 0.002-inch thick aluminum laminate (coated with a resin to accept printing) is dense enough to set off sensitive metal detectors at the exits of the plants where lottery tickets are printed. That keeps winning tickets from walking out with sticky-fingered employees. The foil also makes it impossible to read numbers by holding tickets to a strong light.

(b) Yes, people sometimes try to change a $5 amount to a $500. Prize amounts are printed in such a way that illicitly added digits are apparent. Attempts to erase printing rub off the decorative background, making alteration obvious.

(c) A secret verification code defeats counterfeiters. It's an extra number somewhere on the ticket, often hidden underneath a scratch-off patch, sometimes under a special patch you're instructed *not* to remove. The verification code is a computer-generated string of numbers or letters produced from the ticket's number or configuration of instant-winner items. Only someone knowing the encoding algorithm can generate a proper verification code. Let's say that the winning number in a jackpot drawing is 926577, and that the verification code (kept secret) is 502284010. Ticket 926577 has gone unclaimed long enough that it's unlikely a winner will ever turn up. A counterfeiter might then be tempted to print up a card with the winning number 926577. The counterfeiter won't know the correct verification code, though. Should he make up a code or copy one from a losing ticket, it wouldn't be the right one for ticket 926577, and the ticket could be quickly identified as fake.

(d) The inventory control number helps detect ticket theft. It's a visible serial number, usually on the back of the ticket, often accompanied by a bar code. (The regular UPC, encoding the price only, also appears on some lottery tickets.) Part of the inventory control number may also appear on the front of the ticket so that it's readily visible. The control number, too, must agree with the assigned ticket number/verification code, as recorded in computer tapes at the ticket factory. The lottery board keeps track of where each package of tickets was sent. All the tickets on a hijacked delivery truck will be consecutively numbered, making it easy to identify stolen tickets. One winner in the California lottery flashed a $10,000 ticket while celebrating in a San Pedro bar. Another patron failed to partake of the festive spirit of camaraderie and grabbed the ticket and ran out the door. When the thief tried to cash in the ticket, lottery officials asked him where he bought it. His story didn't jibe with the serial number. Ticket and prize were restored to the doubly lucky legitimate winner.

(e) Like it or not, winning numbers *are* random, whether chosen by computer in the printing plant or by Ping-Pong balls in a TV drawing. That means all lottery systems are worthless except to those who make money selling them. Lotteries dangle the carrot of a big win. Actually, the return is poor. Most state lotteries are inefficient enterprises that are required to donate a share of their take to good works, and much of what's left is budgeted for measly $5 and $10 prizes.

Only about 50 cents of a ticket buyer's $1 is returned as winnings. Many casino games pay over 90 cents on the dollar; race tracks pay about 80 cents; a slot machine paying back 75 cents is considered a bad deal. About half of the state-lottery prize budget typically goes to the cheapest prizes. A 1 in 15 shot at a $5 prize eats up 33 cents of the prize budget per ticket.

The remote chance of a big win, rarely disclosed, is camouflaged by compartmentalizing the winning process into successive drawings and big spins. Many "winning" tickets (of a chance at a drawing, or of other lottery tickets) ultimately return naught. The real chance at a ten-million-dollar jackpot can hardly be better than 1 in 40 million, given a 50 percent return and assuming that half the return funds small prizes. The chance of winning that kind of jackpot, *ever*, even if you buy a ticket every day of your life, is well under a tenth of 1 percent.

13.

The Beale Cipher

Legends of buried treasure are a dime a dozen. There's the $3 million in Confederate treasury gold supposedly buried near the James River to spite invading Union forces, the Lost Dutchman Mine of Arizona, the hellish Money Pit of Nova Scotia, and half a dozen other conjectured sites of Captain Kidd's loot. The biggest secret of the lot is that of the Beale Cipher.

Between 1819 and 1822, frontiersman Thomas J. Beale is said to have buried 2,921 pounds of gold—not ounces, *pounds*—5,100 pounds of silver, and a king's ransom of jewels in an underground vault four miles from the town now called Montvale, Virginia. The location is described in a numerical cipher that has puzzled romantics, cryptographers, and the plain greedy for a century. Today the Beale hoard would be worth something like $17 million.

Very likely, more time and effort have been spent on finding the Beale fortune than any other, mainly because treasure hunters can work indoors. Directions to the treasure exist. They just have to be deciphered. Even as you read this, determined souls are trying to solve the cipher.

The Story

Let's start with the conventional Beale narrative—with the warning that some of this story may be a fabrication. Thomas Beale is a mysterious figure from Virginia. He is said to have ventured west with about thirty others to hunt buffalo and grizzly bear. In March 1818, somewhere 250 miles north of Santa Fe (in what's now Colorado) they struck gold. The party took it back to Virginia. Beale made two trips between the gold mine and Virginia.

While in Virginia, Beale stayed at the Washington Hotel in Lynchburg. There he became friends with innkeeper Robert Morriss. Morriss is the first person in this story who indisputably existed. Records unrelated to the cipher legend establish that he lived in Lynchburg and ran the hotel. When Beale again headed west in 1822, he left an iron strongbox with Morriss for safekeeping. Morriss was never to see Beale again.

Two months later Morriss received a letter from Beale postmarked St. Louis. Beale explained that the strongbox contained three coded letters "unintelligible without the aid of a key. . . . Such a key I have left in the hands of a friend in this place, sealed, addressed to yourself and endorsed not to be delivered until June 1832." Beale told Morriss to open the box if he had not shown up by then.

The decade passed with no word from Beale and no key letter. Not until 1845, thirteen years after the appointed date, did Morriss finally break into the box. Inside he found two letters addressed to himself, some "receipts," and three ciphers, each consisting of a long sequence of numbers. None of these original documents survives, only copies.

According to the letters, the three ciphers give directions to the treasure, describe it, and give the names and addresses of the next of kin to those in Beale's party. The letters instructed Morriss to recover the treasure and divide it into thirty-one equal parts. One part was for Morriss himself, and the others were to be distributed to the thirty members of the syndicate or their survivors.

Morriss had a go at solving the ciphers without the key. He never solved them; never came close. Seventeen years after opening the box, he gave the ciphers and letters to a friend—the anonymous author of an 1885 pamphlet called *The Beale Papers*. This author may or may not be one James B. Ward, a Virginian who registered the pamphlet with the copyright office.

The pamphlet's author says he devoted himself full-time to working on the ciphers. It was a decision he regretted. He spent two decades "wasting" his life and frittering away his fortune. The ciphers betrayed but one of their secrets—not, however, the one he would have chosen. The pamphleteer managed to crack the second cipher.

The pamphlet author took the text of the Declaration of Independence and numbered all the words: "When(1) in(2) the(3) Course(4) of(5) human(6) Events(7) . . ." He then matched the numbers of the cipher to the first letters of the corresponding numbered words in the Declaration of Independence.

For instance, the number 7, which appears several times in the cipher, refers to the word *Events* and therefore stands for the letter *E*.

The cipher is consequently much more secure than a simple number/letter substitution. A given letter may be enciphered by many different numbers. The Declaration of Independence contains many words beginning with *E*, and any of their numbers is an equally valid encipherment of *E*. Just in the opening lines, the numbers 7, 37, 49, and 79 all stand for *E*. Beale appears to have chosen valid numbers at random.

The pamphlet author obtained this deciphered message:

I HAVE DEPOSITED IN THE COUNTY OF BEDFORD ABOUT FOUR MILES FROM BUFORD'S IN AN EXCAVATION OR VAULT SIX FEET BELOW THE SURFACE OF THE GROUND THE FOLLOWING ARTICLES BELONGING JOINTLY TO THE PARTIES WHOSE NAMES ARE GIVEN IN NUMBER THREE HEREWITH. THE FIRST DEPOSIT CONSISTED OF TEN HUNDRED AND FOURTEEN POUNDS OF GOLD AND THIRTY EIGHT HUNDRED AND TWELVE POUNDS OF SILVER DEPOSITED NOV. EIGHTEEN NINETEEN. THE SECOND WAS MADE DEC. EIGHTEEN TWENTY ONE AND CONSISTED OF NINETEEN HUNDRED AND SEVEN POUNDS OF GOLD AND TWELVE HUNDRED AND EIGHTY EIGHT OF SILVER, ALSO JEWELS OBTAINED IN ST. LOUIS IN EXCHANGE TO SAVE TRANSPORTATION AND VALUED AT THIRTEEN THOUSAND DOLLARS. THE ABOVE IS SECURELY PACKED IN IRON POTS WITH IRON COVERS. THE VAULT IS ROUGHLY LINED WITH STONE AND THE VESSELS REST ON SOLID STONE AND ARE COVERED WITH OTHERS. PAPER NUMBER ONE DESCRIBES THE EXACT LOCALITY OF THE VAULT SO THAT NO DIFFICULTY WILL BE HAD IN FINDING IT.

Or this is *nearly* the message he obtained. If you go back and apply the method to the cipher given in *The Beale Papers*, it's not quite that pat. There are no spaces between the words in the message, and there are lots of misspellings that the pamphlet author never mentions. The actual deciphered message starts: IHAIEDEPOSOTEDINTHE . . . Eyestrain notwithstanding, the pamphlet's cleaned-up version of the message seems accurate and genuine.

Naturally, this made the mysterious author of *The Beale Papers* all the more eager to solve Cipher No. 1. The Declaration of Independence was of no help this time around, nor could the strategy be applied to the third cipher. The solution never came. Faced with "pecuniary embarrassments of a pressing character," he threw in the towel. He published the ciphers to remove the temptation to keep working on them. The author explained that he was "compelled, however unwillingly, to relinquish to others the elucidation of the Beale Papers, not doubting that of the many who will give the subject attention, some one, through fortune or accident, will speedily solve their mystery and secure the prize that has eluded him."

The Beale Papers was printed by the Virginian Book and Job Print of Lynchburg. It appears that some parties didn't think the ciphers should be made public. A fire broke out in the printer's office and conveniently destroyed nearly all the copies of the pamphlet in existence—or so it's said, anyway.

The Ciphers

For some time afterward, the ciphers were again a virtual secret. Owners of the pamphlet refused to share it with others; bootleg handwritten copies of the ciphers were in circulation, some error-laden.

Let's pause here to give the ciphers. A few numbers vary depending on whose copy you use. This is the version that appears in the original edition of *The Beale Papers*.

Cipher No. 1 (Location of the Treasure)

71	194	38	1701	89	76	11	83	1629	48
94	63	132	16	111	95	84	341	975	14
40	64	27	81	139	213	63	90	1120	8

15	3	126	2018	40	74	758	485	604	230
436	664	582	150	251	284	308	231	124	211
486	225	401	370	11	101	305	139	189	17
33	88	208	193	145	1	94	73	416	918
263	28	500	538	356	117	136	219	27	176
130	10	460	25	485	18	436	65	84	200
283	118	320	138	36	416	280	15	71	224
961	44	16	401	39	88	61	304	12	21
24	283	134	92	63	246	486	682	7	219
184	360	780	18	64	463	474	131	160	79
73	440	95	18	64	581	34	69	128	367
460	17	81	12	103	880	62	116	97	103
862	70	60	1317	471	540	208	121	890	346
36	150	59	568	614	13	120	63	219	812
2160	1780	99	35	18	21	136	872	15	28
170	88	4	30	44	112	18	147	436	195
320	37	122	113	6	140	8	120	305	42
58	461	44	106	301	13	408	680	93	86
116	530	82	568	9	102	38	416	89	71
216	728	965	818	2	38	121	195	14	326
148	234	18	55	131	234	361	824	5	81
623	48	961	19	26	33	10	1101	365	92
88	181	275	346	201	206	86	36	219	324
829	840	64	326	19	48	122	85	216	284
919	861	326	985	233	64	68	232	431	960
50	29	81	216	321	603	14	612	81	360
36	51	62	194	78	60	200	314	676	112
4	28	18	61	136	247	819	921	1060	464
895	10	6	66	119	38	41	49	602	423
962	302	294	875	78	14	23	111	109	62
31	501	823	216	280	34	24	150	1000	162
286	19	21	17	340	19	242	31	86	234
140	607	115	33	191	67	104	86	52	88
16	80	121	67	95	122	216	548	96	11
201	77	364	218	65	667	890	236	154	211
10	98	34	119	56	216	119	71	218	1164
1496	1817	51	39	210	36	3	19	540	232
22	141	617	84	290	80	46	207	411	150
29	38	46	172	85	194	39	261	543	897
624	18	212	416	127	931	19	4	63	96

12	101	418	16	140	230	460	538	19	27
88	612	1431	90	716	275	74	83	11	426
89	72	84	1300	1706	814	221	132	40	102
34	868	975	1101	84	16	79	23	16	81
122	324	403	912	227	936	447	55	86	34
43	212	107	96	314	264	1065	323	428	601
203	124	95	216	814	2906	654	820	2	301
112	176	213	71	87	96	202	35	10	2
41	17	84	221	736	820	214	11	60	760

Cipher No. 2 *(Description of the Treasure)*

115	73	24	807	37	52	49	17	31	62
647	22	7	15	140	47	29	107	79	84
56	239	10	26	811	5	196	308	85	52
160	136	59	211	36	9	46	316	554	122
106	96	53	58	2	42	7	35	122	53
31	82	77	250	196	56	96	118	71	140
287	28	353	37	1005	65	147	807	24	3
8	12	47	43	59	807	45	316	101	41
78	154	1005	122	138	191	16	77	49	102
57	72	34	73	85	35	371	59	196	81
92	191	106	273	60	394	620	270	220	106
388	287	63	3	6	191	122	43	234	400
106	290	314	47	48	81	96	26	115	92
158	191	110	77	85	197	46	10	113	140
353	48	120	106	2	607	61	420	811	29
125	14	20	37	105	28	248	16	159	7
35	19	301	125	110	486	287	98	117	511
62	51	220	37	113	140	807	138	540	8
44	287	388	117	18	79	344	34	20	59
511	548	107	603	220	7	66	154	41	20
50	6	575	122	154	248	110	61	52	33
30	5	38	8	14	84	57	540	217	115
71	29	85	63	43	131	29	138	47	73
239	540	52	53	79	118	51	44	63	196
12	239	112	3	49	79	353	105	56	371
557	211	505	125	360	133	143	101	15	284
540	252	14	205	140	344	26	811	138	115

48	73	34	205	316	607	63	220	7	52
150	44	52	16	40	37	158	807	37	121
12	96	10	15	35	12	131	62	115	102
807	49	53	135	138	30	31	62	67	41
85	63	10	106	807	138	8	113	20	32
33	37	353	287	140	47	85	50	37	49
47	64	6	7	71	33	4	43	47	63
1	27	600	208	230	15	191	246	85	94
511	2	270	20	39	7	33	44	22	40
7	10	3	811	106	44	486	230	353	211
200	31	10	38	140	297	61	603	320	302
666	287	2	44	33	32	511	548	10	6
250	557	246	53	37	52	83	47	320	38
33	807	7	44	30	31	250	10	15	35
106	160	113	31	102	406	230	540	320	29
66	33	101	807	138	301	316	353	320	220
37	52	28	540	320	33	8	48	107	50
811	7	2	113	73	16	125	11	110	67
102	807	33	59	81	158	38	43	581	138
19	85	400	38	43	77	14	27	8	47
138	63	140	44	35	22	177	106	250	314
217	2	10	7	1005	4	20	25	44	48
7	26	46	110	230	807	191	34	112	147
44	110	121	125	96	41	51	50	140	56
47	152	540	63	807	28	42	250	138	582
98	643	32	107	140	112	26	85	138	540
53	20	125	371	38	36	10	52	118	136
102	420	150	112	71	14	20	7	24	18
12	807	37	67	110	62	33	21	96	220
511	102	811	30	83	84	305	620	15	2
10	8	220	106	353	105	106	60	275	72
8	50	205	185	112	125	540	65	106	807
188	96	110	16	73	33	807	150	409	400
50	154	285	96	106	316	270	205	101	811
400	8	44	37	52	40	241	34	205	38
16	46	47	85	24	44	15	64	73	138
807	85	78	110	33	420	505	53	37	38
22	31	10	110	106	101	140	15	38	3
5	44	7	98	287	135	150	96	33	84
125	807	191	96	511	118	440	370	643	466

106	41	107	603	220	275	30	150	105	49
53	287	250	208	134	7	53	12	47	85
63	138	110	21	112	140	485	486	505	14
73	84	575	1005	150	200	16	42	5	4
25	42	8	16	811	125	160	32	205	603
807	81	96	405	41	600	136	14	20	28
26	353	302	246	8	131	160	140	84	440
42	16	811	40	67	101	102	194	138	205
51	63	241	540	122	8	10	63	140	47
48	140	288							

Cipher No. 3 (Addresses of Next of Kin)

317	8	92	73	112	89	67	318	28	96
107	41	631	78	146	397	118	98	114	246
348	116	74	88	12	65	32	14	81	19
76	121	216	85	33	66	15	108	68	77
43	24	122	96	117	36	211	301	15	44
11	46	89	18	136	68	317	28	90	82
304	71	43	221	198	176	310	319	81	99
264	380	56	37	319	2	44	53	28	44
75	98	102	37	85	107	117	64	88	136
48	154	99	175	89	315	326	78	96	214
218	311	43	89	51	90	75	128	96	33
28	103	84	65	26	41	246	84	270	98
116	32	59	74	66	69	240	15	8	121
20	77	89	31	11	106	81	191	224	328
18	75	52	82	117	201	39	23	217	27
21	83	35	54	109	128	49	77	88	1
81	217	64	55	83	116	251	269	311	96
54	32	120	18	132	102	219	211	84	150
219	275	312	64	10	106	87	75	47	21
29	37	81	44	18	126	115	132	160	181
203	76	81	299	314	337	351	96	11	28
97	318	238	106	24	93	3	19	17	26
60	73	88	14	126	138	234	286	297	321
365	264	19	22	84	56	107	98	123	111
214	136	7	33	45	40	13	28	46	42
107	196	227	344	198	203	247	116	19	8

212	230	31	6	328	65	48	52	59	41
122	33	117	11	18	25	71	36	45	83
76	89	92	31	65	70	83	96	27	33
44	50	61	24	112	136	149	176	180	194
143	171	205	296	87	12	44	51	89	98
34	41	208	173	66	9	35	16	95	8
113	175	90	56	203	19	177	183	206	157
200	218	260	291	305	618	951	320	18	124
78	65	19	32	124	48	53	57	84	96
207	244	66	82	119	71	11	86	77	213
54	82	316	245	303	86	97	106	212	18
37	15	81	89	16	7	81	39	96	14
43	216	118	29	55	109	136	172	213	64
8	227	304	611	221	364	819	375	128	296
1	18	53	76	10	15	23	19	71	84
120	134	66	73	89	96	230	48	77	26
101	127	936	218	439	178	171	61	226	313
215	102	18	167	262	114	218	66	59	48
27	19	13	82	48	162	119	34	127	139
34	128	129	74	63	120	11	54	61	73
92	180	66	75	101	124	265	89	96	126
274	896	917	434	461	235	890	312	413	328
381	96	105	217	66	118	22	77	64	42
12	7	55	24	83	67	97	109	121	135
181	203	219	228	256	21	34	77	319	374
382	675	684	717	864	203	4	18	92	16
63	82	22	46	55	69	74	112	134	186
175	119	213	416	312	343	264	119	186	218
343	417	845	951	124	209	49	617	856	924
936	72	19	28	11	35	42	40	66	85
94	112	65	82	115	119	236	244	186	172
112	85	6	56	38	44	85	72	32	47
63	96	124	217	314	319	221	644	817	821
934	922	416	975	10	22	18	46	137	181
101	39	86	103	116	138	164	212	218	296
815	380	412	460	495	675	820	952		

Finders, Keepers

It sounds so simple. Solve the cipher, get the treasure. Central to the contemporary Beale legend is the belief that Virginia law says the treasure would belong to whoever finds it, even if they found it on someone else's property, unless the direct descendants of the original owners could be located. Accurate or not, this statement has appeared in article after article. You can bet there'd be some fancy legal challenges *were* the treasure found, not to mention heirs coming out of the woodwork. There is legal incentive *not* to decipher the third cipher, the one with the next of kin's names.

By now, residents of Bedford and Botetourt counties don't much cotton to treasure hunters. People are always trespassing on their lands with shovels, metal detectors, and dynamite. Cattle have fallen into excavations. Some of the property owners have taken to expressing their lack of interest with potshots at trespassers. More enlightened landowners have drawn up contracts splitting any treasure found.

With its seminars and publications, the Beale Cypher Association (P.O. Box 975, Beaver Falls, PA 15010) attempts to bring order to this roiling chaos. The association's "confidential" newsletter is easily worth the subscription price for its glimpse into the twisted mental landscape of crackpot America. Editorials gripe about people who attend association seminars under a false name, sit in back, don't say anything, and take copious notes. Many of the newsletter contributors are people who say they've solved the ciphers personally or know someone who has. Not that they're necessarily going to reveal their solutions. They just want *you* to know that *they* know.

The March 1992 issue has news of no less than three solutions of the Beale mystery. A solution to Cipher 1 starts out this way: "USE DOUAY NOTLE START O SV SET HINDU/AU TINE IN L NYE POG BASE N LIT TIENE AU E E E E RULO PASS . . ." A rival solution in the same issue ignores the ciphers entirely and "decodes" one of Beale's letters as "This prophecy, eye shall see, bare record word of the seven churches, things which are him to shew. . . ." *This* Beale rambles on about vague church matters and has nothing to say about buried treasure.

"Solvers" must come to terms with the delicate issue of why they aren't rich. Popular excuses: Beale or the pamphlet author omitted or scrambled some of the numbers (so that solvers would have to deal with him for the *complete* cipher); someone else got there first and kept quiet about it to duck taxes or heirs; the treasure is on patrolled private or federal property; a massive structure is built right on the spot; the spot is now under water.

It's not only cranks who are drawn to the Beale cipher. Spurred by Montvale's proximity to Washington, cryptographers at the National Security Agency have taken up the Beale Cipher as a pastime. Why haven't the NSA folks or other competent parties solved it?

A logical assumption is that the two unsolved ciphers work the same way as the solved one, using a different text as a key. In that case the simplest approach is to find the missing key document. Treasure seekers have tried familiar and obscure governmental, religious, and literary works—to no avail. They've used passages from the Bible and Shakespeare; the Magna Charta, the Mayflower Compact, the charter of Virginia, the 1733 Molasses Act, and "The Star-Spangled Banner." All failed.

It is possible for experts to crack a cipher of this type even without the key. To do so, the solver requires large amounts of enciphered text so that subtle patterns are evident. Large streams of enciphered text often do exist for military and diplomatic ciphers. The Beale ciphers are so short that it would be almost impossible to solve them without the key or other information (such as part of the deciphered message). And there the matter rests.

Is It a Hoax?

Other people suspect the ciphers are a hoax. The most colorful theory is that they were a prank perpetrated by Edgar Allan Poe. His story "The Gold Bug" demonstrates an interest in cryptography, and he was in the area when he attended the University of Virginia in the 1820s. It is easier to believe that the pamphleteer was an unknown con artist who concocted the ciphers just to make money. The pamphlet sold for 50 cents, a steep price at the time. The author wrote that he anticipated "a large circulation." It has also been speculated that the treasure story was fabricated to launder proceeds from a bank robbery or gold hijacking.

People have advanced all sorts of arguments, pro and con, on the ciphers' legitimacy. Let's list the main points.

Pro: The author's description of his experience with the papers is in many ways convincing, well supplied with telling detail. There's the right tone of sour grapes. He hints, ever so subtly, that whoever finds the treasure ought to give him a share. ("Having now lost all hope of benefit from this source to himself, he is not unwilling that others may receive it, and only hopes that the prize may fall to some poor, but honest man, who will use his discovery not solely for the promotion of his own enjoyment, but for the welfare of others," he writes.)

One of the strongest and most repeated arguments for the ciphers' authenticity is a study by Dr. Carl Hammer of Sperry Univac. Hammer determined that the unsolved ciphers show the patterns to be expected of an enciphered text and were not just a bunch of random numbers. He concluded, "They contain intelligent messages of some sort. The method used for encoding Ciphers One and Three is similar to that used for Number Two."

Hoaxes tend to get exposed, eventually. No one, on his deathbed or otherwise, confessed to faking the ciphers or admitted knowledge of a hoax, as far as is known.

Con: The main arguments against the legitimacy of the ciphers are circumstantial. We have only Beale's word *via an anonymous author* that the treasure exists. We have only the anonymous author's word that Beale existed. By the time the pamphleteer went public, Morriss, the one documented figure, was dead. More than casual research has failed to turn up any third-party evidence that the Beale we're talking about existed, that the gold was found, that it was transported across the country, or that it was buried in Virginia.

Why there are three ciphers is hard to fathom. It's not like pirates splitting a treasure map in several pieces, each essential to recovering the treasure. The complete "treasure map" is in cipher 1. Beale would have wanted to make certain that anyone who deciphered the directions would have the next-of-kin information also. So why have the next of kin in a separate cipher with a different key?

The cracked cipher 2 touts cipher 1—almost as if it were intended all along that just cipher 2 would be broken, creating the tantalizing mystery we have. Beale intended to send a key that would allow Morriss to decipher all three messages in short order. Why the cross-references?

Cipher 3 appears too short to give the names and addresses of the next of kin of thirty members of the treasure syndicate. If each number is a letter, the 618 numbers of cipher 3 would yield about 100 words, or about 3 words per syndicate member. (Even if the ciphers are numbered incorrectly, the other uncracked cipher is shorter yet.)

A curious discrepancy: Old records say Morriss took over the

Washington Hotel in 1823 or 1824. His testimony in *The Beale Papers* has him running the Washington Hotel in 1820.

The Hammer study cannot guarantee that the unsolved ciphers lead to a treasure. The message could be something like "Ha! Ha! Fooled you! . . ."

One argument against the cipher's legitimacy is subjective. Because the pamphlet quotes extensively from letters, it really has several principal authors. Yet anyone who takes the trouble to read *The Beale Papers* is apt to come away with the impression that all the collected texts share a single voice.

The anonymous pamphleteer is long-winded. He writes sentences like, "Regardless of the entreaties of his family and the persistent advice of his friends, who were formerly as sanguine as himself, he stubbornly continued his investigation, until absolute want stared him in the face and forced him to yield to their persuasions."

This takes 42 words to say the writer's friends thought he was crazy for working on the cipher until he ran out of money. Just so you get the idea, he says nearly the same thing elsewhere: "I have been reduced from comparative affluence to absolute penury, entailing suffering upon those it was my duty to protect, and this, too, in spite of their remonstrances." The author's style is often unintentionally amusing. The odd thing is that it doesn't get *less* amusing when the author quotes someone else.

In his quoted letters, rough-and-tumble Beale also speaks like a Victorian novelist: "All the pleasures and temptations which had lured them to the plains were now forgotten, and visions of boundless wealth and future grandeur were the only ideas entertained."

Morriss, too, is unaccountably wordy. His description of Beale goes, "His form was symmetrical, and gave evidence of unusual strength and activity; but his distinguishing feature was a dark and swarthy complexion, as if much exposure to the sun and weather had thoroughly tanned and discolored him; this, however, did not detract from his appearance, and I thought him the handsomest man I had ever seen. Altogether, he was a model of manly beauty, favored by the ladies and envied by men."

It's not that no one talks like this, but would three people thrown together by fate all express themselves so floridly? Neither Beale, Morriss, nor the pamphleteer comes across as a man of affairs struggling to express himself. All are verbose, ornate, Dickensian, and similar to each other.

Is *The Beale Papers* a work of fiction? Legendary cryptographer William Friedman analyzed the Beale ciphers as part of his training in the Signal Intelligence Service. Reportedly Friedman suspected that the text of the solved cipher was written by the pamphlet author himself, basing his conclusion on the style of the writing.

More recently, amateur cryptographer Louis Kruh compared sentence length in the writings of the pamphleteer and Beale. The pamphleteer averages 28.82 words per sentence for his "own" text in *The Beale Papers*. Beale's text (quoted letters plus the text of the cracked cipher) averages 28.75 words per sentence. Not only are these values remarkably close, they are way out of the ballpark for most English text. About fifteen words per sentence is typical.

Kruh's computation was a simple example of *stylometry*, the technique of identifying authors of unknown texts by comparing how often words, letters, or punctuation marks are used. Stylometry has been used to probe authorship questions of alleged Shakespearean works, the *Federalist Papers*, and other literary or historical works.

Stylometry's usefulness and reliability are still being debated. The most you can say is that samples of one author's text are *usually* more similar to each other than to samples of other authors' writing. We thought it would be interesting to apply stylometry to *The Beale Papers*.

Analysis

Most writers show some regularity in their usage. Authors aren't always aware of these regularities. Even when an author is trying to disguise his voice, he is apt to fall back into many of the same habits. Questions about the authorship of *The Beale Papers* are relatively well suited to stylistic analysis. Stylometry requires sizable samples of text (thousands of words) for meaningful results. *The Beale Papers* provides large chunks of text by the anonymous author and by Beale. The texts are first-person, nonfiction (?) accounts of similar subject matter. Changes in a single author's style over years raise further uncertainties. Should *The Beale Papers* be a hoax, it is likely that all the text was written at about the same time.

The Beale Papers purports to collect texts of the anonymous author, Robert Morriss, Thomas Beale, and Thomas Jefferson (the latter because the pamphlet reproduces the Declaration of Independence for reference). The pamphlet's author has nearly 4000 words in his own voice. Beale's two letters to Morriss contain 2234 and 457 words of text. The deciphered message adds 160 words. Morriss's comments come to 865 words.

Beale's letters are quoted verbatim. They are set in a different typeface in the pamphlet. The author makes it clear that these are Beale's words, not his paraphrase.

Although Morriss's story is enclosed in quotation marks, the pamphleteer says that Morriss "gave me the following, which I reduced to writing," and concludes, "Such, in substance, was the statement of Mr. Morriss. . . ." So this is transcribed oral testimony, and they didn't have tape recorders then. You'd expect the pamphleteer's style to color Morriss's text. We'll focus on Beale and the pamphleteer, then.

We tabulated statistics for the complete existing samples of text. For each sample, a word-processor search function counted the total number of words; instances of twenty common, relatively context-free, short words (*a, and, at, but, by, for, from, in, it, no, not, of, or, so, that, the, this, to, which, with*); and five common punctuation marks (apostrophe, comma, dash, period, semicolon). These results were expressed as a count per 10,000 characters to permit comparison between text samples of different sizes. For further comparison, we did the same thing for 10,000-character samples of the writings of Jane Austen, Thomas Jefferson, Edgar Allan Poe, and Mark Twain. The latter statistics were averaged to create representative values for nineteenth-century English usage. The results make a strong case that the same person wrote Beale's letters *and* the 1885 pamphlet.

The first row in the table is the word count, the number of words the author used per 10,000 characters. The greater the number of words per 10,000 characters, the shorter the average word length. The *Beale Papers* author used 1,729 words per 10,000 characters. Thomas Beale used 1,776 words.

These numbers seem fairly close. The question is, then, how close do they have to be to support suspicion that the same person wrote both texts?

You expect a fair coin to come up heads about fifty times out of a hundred tosses. You don't expect heads *exactly* fifty times. That's asking too much of a random statistic. A ballpark estimate of a statistical "scatter" is the *standard error of the mean* (which is

The Beale Papers
(*Usage of common short words and punctuation per 10,000 characters*)

	Author of The Beale Papers (own text: 22,924 char.)	Thomas Beale (letters plus cipher: 16,057 char.)	Match?	Nineteenth-Century Average (computed from Jefferson, Austen, Poe, and Twain)	Shared Idiosyncrasy?
word count	1729	1776	✔	1777	
comma	161	162	✔	133	✔
the	106	99	✔	101	
period	61	64	✔	96	✔
of	62	65	✔	64	
and	61	72	✔	60	
to	65	69	✔	54	✔
a	28	27	✔	40	✔
in	33	41	✔	30	
apostrophe	4	1		30	
it	16	22	✔	23	
that	26	15		16	
for	15	17	✔	14	
semicolon	12	2		14	
but	11	6		12	
dash	1	2	✔	12	✔
with	19	19	✔	11	✔
by	10	9	✔	10	
so	6	6	✔	10	✔
this	16	16	✔	9	✔
or	8	10	✔	9	
at	9	11	✔	8	
from	7	9	✔	8	
which	15	14	✔	7	✔
not	8	7	✔	6	
no	8	2		5	

approximately the square root of the actual count). The square root of 50 is about 7. Most of the time, the number of heads in 100 tosses will be in the range of 43 through 57.

The standard error for the *Beale Papers* author's word count works out to 25 per 10,000 characters. That means that the "real" average value for the pamphleteer is likely to lie within 25 of 1,729: 1,704 through 1,754. These aren't sharp cutoff points, just a rough idea of how much variation to expect in a normal statistical distribution.

The standard error for the Thomas Beale word count is 30. It's bigger because the smaller amount of text creates greater uncertainty. The Beale value is bracketed by the approximate range of 1,736 to 1,806.

These two ranges overlap. That means that the differences are not statistically meaningful. The values are about as close as you'd expect them to be if the two texts were chosen randomly from the same author's writing.

Statistics for all but one of the ten most common words and punctuation marks match up well. The table's fourth column shows a check whenever Beale's values and those of the pamphleteer match reasonably well (when the difference is no greater than the sum of two standard errors). There was a good match in twenty-one of the twenty-six categories overall. This is about what you'd expect for texts by the same author.

One way to illustrate the extent of agreement is to perform the same comparison with the *Beale Papers* author's text and the Declaration of Independence. Obviously, *The Beale Papers* wasn't written by Thomas Jefferson and colleagues in Philadelphia. Using the same twenty-six categories, the pamphleteer's text matches the Declaration of Independence in just ten of them. The average size of the differences is about twice as big as those between the pamphleteer and Beale.

The pamphleteer's and Beale's values for word count, *the, and,* and *of* agree nicely enough, but they are typical of nineteenth-century authors (see fifth column). Beale and the pamphleteer were simply writing like everyone else. Most compelling are those cases where the texts share a quirk. In the sample nineteenth-century texts used for a baseline, commas were used about 133 times per 10,000 characters. The pamphlet author uses far more commas than average (161 per 10,000 characters), *and* Beale shares this eccentricity to almost the same extent (162 per 10,000).

An editor or printer might have imposed some similarities in punctuation. It would be a strange editor who added to, rather than took out, the legion of superfluous commas in *The Beale Papers.*

The pamphleteer and Beale both use far fewer periods than average (61 and 64 times per 10,000 characters vs. an average of around 96). That's another way of saying they use long sentences, as Kruh noted. They both use the word *to* significantly more than average. They *avoid* the article *a* to almost precisely the same degree. They both use *this* and *which* about twice as much as their contemporaries. And they use a mere fraction of the usual nineteenth-century allotment of dashes.

Apostrophes are almost absent from *The Beale Papers*. There are few possessives, and no contractions at all, in Beale's or the pamphleteer's writing. Although the values for apostrophes aren't a good match (4 vs. 1), this difference is trivial next to the fact that the typical value is something like 30 apostrophes per 10,000 characters.

The column at far right shows a check for a shared idiosyncrasy when Beale and the pamphleteer's values match *and* both values differ from the computed nineteenth-century average by at least their standard error.

There are other idiosyncratic similarities not tallied above. A single use is not statistically meaningful, but you can't help notice that Beale and the pamphleteer both manage to use the odd word "systematize" once in their text.

It really looks like the same person wrote the Beale letters and the pamphlet (and Morriss's testimony, for that matter). Once you accept that, the whole story falls apart. It remains possible that the two uncracked ciphers say something. That something isn't likely to lead to a $17 million treasure, though.

Whodunit?

The swell idea that Poe was behind the ciphers has to be ruled out. Poe's usage is significantly different from that of *The Beale Papers*, even on the most common words. Poe uses *the* much more often (145 times per 10,000 characters) than the pamphleteer does; he uses *to* only half as frequently (32 times per 10,000 characters). More to the point, as Beale's contemporary, Poe was long dead when the pamphlet was published. If the pamphleteer and Beale are the same person, that person can't be Edgar Allan Poe.

In the absence of other candidates for the hoaxer, the obvious guess is James B. Ward, the man who applied for the pamphlet copyright. Indeed, many articles on the ciphers attribute the pamphlet to Ward without question (even while accepting the basic story of Beale and the treasure). The pamphleteer explains his anonymity as a ploy "to avoid the multitude of letters with which I should be assailed from all sections of the Union, propounding all sorts of questions, and requiring answers which, if attended to, would absorb my entire time. . . . I have decided upon withdrawing my name from the publication. . . ." The author says that any questions should be addressed to "the gentleman whom I have selected as my agent." He doesn't even say who the agent is (it *was* Ward, as we'll see).

Ward is not a total mystery man. The brother of unsuccessful treasure hunter George L. Hart, Sr., visited Ward, "then at an advanced age," in 1903. According to a 1952 essay that Hart wrote, Ward "confirmed all that is in the pamphlet; and his son, then U.S. Mail transfer clerk at the union station, Lynchburg, added his own confirmation, but in somewhat sad and solemn tones."

We wondered if any sample of Ward's writing existed. The Beale Cypher Association supplied a copy of the brief letter (on feed-store stationery) in which Ward wrote the Librarian of Congress to apply for a copyright. Excluding salutation, closing, and a hand-copied facsimile of the book's title page there are only a scant eighty-eight words of Ward's own text:

> I am informed that to secure the copy wright of a book, all that is necessary, is to send you a copy, written or printed of the title page with one dollar, and you will give the requisite protection. A copy of the book itself, to be sent you when printed. Presuming this to be so, I enclose you one dollar, and the following copy of the title page. Please enter in my name as agent for the author. Trusting to hear from you at your earliest convenience.

Stylometry is an iffy business at best. Ward's letter isn't nearly enough text to work with. But we can't resist noting several hints that our old friend is at work; liberal use of *to, that, with;* no apostrophes; and especially, the abundance of commas, even in this snippet. The seven commas project a rate of a bit over 150 per 10,000 characters. That's more than the nineteenth-century average (133) and close to the pamphleteer (161).

14·

Codes and Texts

Face it: You know only what *they* want you to know. Haven't you ever wondered why the talking stops when you enter the room? Right now big monolithic organizations are talking about you behind your back *in secret code*. Let's expose a few.

Hospital Code Words

It's no joke. People in cardiac wards can drop dead from hearing that the hospital's on fire. Nurses and doctors have evolved a secret argot in order to warn each other of emergencies without panicking patients and visitors. (If you're reading this in a hospital, please skip down to the intriguing article on airline codes.)

According to our sources, the following terms are in widespread use:

"Code Red 123," "Dr. Red 123," or "Dr. Firestone 123" means Room 123 is on fire.

"Code Blue 123" (on a public-address system) means there's an emergency in Room 123. At some hospitals, "Code Red" means the same thing and not necessarily a fire.

"Mr. Strong 123" means the emergency is a patient starting a fight in, or threatening to wreck, Room 123.

Vulnerable to prying eyes, bedside cards and reports demand special circumspection. Prudence demands that physicians use arcane acronyms when they want to make slighting remarks about those entrusted to their care. GOMER (get out of my emergency room, applied to an often homeless malingerer) has virtually entered common parlance. More secure codes include TSTSH (too sick to send home) and FLK (funny-looking kid).

The Airline On-Time Code

A code tells how often specific airline flights are late. That's a useful thing to know—so useful that the airlines are tight-lipped about it. Having a bad code next to a flight amounts to wearing a red letter. If everyone knew about the code, no one would want to book chronically late flights. Chances are that no ticket agent's ever told you about the code.

It's the last digit of the flight code that appears on the computer listings that airline personnel and travel agents call up. Even the pros don't always know what it means, but you can get a travel agent to look it up for you. The code is not in the printed flight schedules. You may be able to get the same computer listings travel agents use by subscribing to an information service.

The on-time code tells the approximate percentage of time a given flight has been on time for the past month. "On time" is defined liberally. It means touching down no later than fifteen minutes past the scheduled time. A flight that's always on time gets a code of 9. That designates any flight that's been on time 90 to 100 percent of the time. If you see a 9, grab it because they're uncommon. A code of 8 means the flight has been on time 80 to 90 percent of the time, 7 designates 70 to 80 percent, and so on, all the way down. Codes of 7 and 8 are typical. The average flight is on time about 80 percent of the time. Ratings as bad as 1 are fairly common at some airports and in some seasons.

Airlines are free to set their scheduled arrival times. When a one-hour flight is late too much, the airline can decide that it's really an hour-and-fifteen-minute flight, and push the scheduled arrival time up fifteen minutes. Then the same flight is officially on time. Of course, no one gets anywhere any sooner than when it was late.

The Christmas Gift Return Code

Surveys claim that over 40 percent of Christmas gifts are returned. Post-Christmas returns and exchanges present opportunities for fraud. Some finer department stores have a secret code to be able to tell if a customer tries to return a "gift" fraudulently.

The problem is this: A crook can walk into a store on December 26 and buy a flashy sweater on sale for $200. He ditches the receipt and takes the sweater to the exchange counter and says it was a gift. The same sweater sold for $400 before Christmas, so he should get $400 credit, right?

The simplest way of dealing with this is for the store to refund only the sale price to people without a receipt. Unfortunately, that means the honest returner, who really did receive a sweater that someone paid $400 for, is out of luck. He gets only a $200 refund or credit, and the store pockets the other $200.

In competitive markets, the big department-store chains usually can't get away with that. Customers expect to get the pre-Christmas price for returned gifts. Some stores use a covert code for telling when an item was purchased and for what price. It's either on the store tag or box. Besides preventing fraud, it also allows the curious to figure out how much someone paid for a gift.

One store that does use a code is Nordstrom, famous for its liberal return policy. The store's PR department claims a customer once returned a set of tires. Nordstrom accepted it despite the fact that they don't sell tires. You might have a harder time pulling a stunt like that now. The current policy is to put not only the price (discreetly scrambled) but the date and salesperson somewhere on the wrapping.

To crack the Nordstrom code, we bought several items on pre-Christmas sale, telling the cashier they were gifts. Then we examined the wrapping for the suspicious numbers.

The Nordstrom code is handwritten on the back of the store tag (the price tag attached to garments with one of those I-shaped pieces of tough plastic you have to snip off at home). The sales clerk tears the printed price off the tag, leaving just the word "Nordstrom" and some printed numbers. Then the clerk writes the code in pen (right in front of you, although you may not know what he or she is doing):

323501212
343234252

Ignore the first digit of the top row. The following digits are the price, without the decimal point, before sales tax is added ($23.50 in this case). The last four digits are the month and day of purchase

(1212 means December 12). The digits on the bottom encode the store and the sales clerk.

Other stores encode a product's wholesale price for year-round use. They take a ten-letter word with no repeated letters (like NACHTMUSIK) and let the letters encode 1234567890. A sticker reading NTK $2.99 means the store paid $1.50. Make some reasonable guesses about markup, and by examining enough stickers, you can crack a store's code. The ten-letter key word is chosen by the merchant and sometimes offers revealing personal insights (it was POLYGAMIST at one store an informant frequented).

Morse Code Beacons

Long after its obsolescence, Morse code finds use for various not-all-that-secret messages. The code in *Mad* magazine's obsessively repetitious "Spy vs. Spy" cartoon spells "BY PROHIAS"—a credit for cartoonist Antonio Prohias. If there's a tall building nearby with a non-periodic beacon on top, get a Morse code chart; it just might be spelling out a banal civic motto programmed years ago as a publicity gimmick. The red light on top of the Capitol Records building in Los Angeles spells out "HOLLYWOOD."

Why Is It Always 10:10 in Watch Ads?

It is eternally ten minutes after ten in the world of watch and clock ads. Stories claim that this marks the exact time that Abraham Lincoln was shot. *Why* a bunch of ad stylists would want to commemorate this particular event in this obscure way is, uh, further than the story goes.

A quick survey of watch ads demonstrated that the 10:10 setting is universal indeed. Cheap little Timexes show the same time as megabuck Rolexes. Mickey Mouse hands match Cartier hands. Coincidence? *We think not.*

Of the first 100 watches and clocks we came across in ads (most of them photographs, but some drawings), 79 were set to 10:10, give or take a couple minutes. Two of the watches reading 10:10 were *digital*. TV commercials as well as print ads conform.

Eight of the 100 watches and clocks were set to 1:50, which looks almost the same. Only 13 clock faces showed a distinctly different time. Many were digital readouts. One was an oddball chronometer with four hands.

There were other correlations. Thirty of 44 visible second hands were set in the range of 31 to 40 seconds past the minute. Eleven were set to roughly 25 seconds after. There was no agreement on whether the ad shoot witching hour was A.M. or P.M., or on the date (of the few watches showing a date, two were set to the first of the month).

The 10:10/1:50 setting is a venerable folkway in the ad industry, said to go back a century. It makes sense to have all the watches or clocks in an ad read the same time. Otherwise, it looks like the watches are broken. Noon or midnight might be the most obvious choices for a standard setting. They're no good because the minute hand is right on top of the hour hand, and both obscure the maker's logo. It's little things like styling of hands that distinguishes one watch from another. The 10:10 setting was thought to be the most practical choice all around. Digital watches are set to 10:10 too, in case they appear in the same spread.

Various witnesses put the time of Lincoln's assassination at 10:10, 10:13, or 10:15 P.M.

The Tootsie Roll Pop Indian

A persistent childhood story claims that if you find a Tootsie Roll Pop wrapper with a picture of an Indian shooting an arrow at a star, you can redeem it for a free bag of candy. The Tootsie Roll Pop wrapper is a rectangle cut from a continuous repeating frieze. Wrapper art depicts children in various poses and apparently has not been changed in a long time. The Indian is a boy in a feather headdress. He is on the right side of the wrapper, below a picture of two girls roller skating and above two girls riding a tricycle.

Indian wrappers aren't exactly rare as hens' teeth. A bag of a dozen Tootsie Roll Pops had three with the Indian. We sent an Indian wrapper with a letter to Tootsie Roll Industries in Chicago. Sure enough, we got a fancy form letter marked "Top Secret." The letter gives a long-winded, derivative legend. It claims that the inventor

> tried everything to get a chewy candy center inside his lollipops but he always failed. Then, one night while the man was asleep, a flash of light appeared in the center of the man's room. The man awoke to find a grand Indian chief smiling at him. The chief told the man that

he would help him make a lollipop with a chewy candy center . . . the chief smiled, walked over to the window where the twinkling of a bright solitary star appeared in the sky. The chief opened the window and reached for his magical bow and arrow. He pointed the arrow directly at the star in the sky and let it fly . . . Then suddenly, there was another flash of light . . . the Indian chief had vanished. . . . the man dashed over to his lollipop shop . . . he grabbed the first round lollipop he could reach and quickly bit into it. A great big smile covered his face because he could taste the chewy candy center that the chief had magically placed in it. . . . But legend has it, that once in a while, the grand chief goes to the man's shop to check and see if the man has continued to keep his promise. The "Indian Wrapper" is supposedly a sign that the grand chief has personally checked that particular lollipop for the chewy candy center.

In other words, you can forget about that free bag, kids.

Beer Labels for Sex

Profound though arcane meaning resides in the labels of various regional beers. So habitual drinkers suppose. Consider the secret of the enigmatic number "33" on the Rolling Rock Beer label. The number appears in quotation marks, with no explanation, on the *back* of the label. Magnified through the green glass of the bottle, it looks mysterious, all right. Theories about its meaning abound.

Theory 1: Prohibition was repealed in 1933. The Rolling Rock brand wasn't introduced until 1939, though.

Theory 2: The copy on the back of the bottle reads "Rolling Rock / From the glass lined tanks of Old Latrobe we tender this premium beer for your enjoyment, as a tribute to your good taste. It comes from the mountain springs to you." That's *thirty-three* words. When they typeset it, they accidentally included the word count.

Theory 3: The ingredients of Rolling Rock ("Water, Malt, Rice, Corn, Hops, Brewer's Yeast") have *thirty-three* letters.

Theory 4: Journalists end a story with "—33—," meaning *the end*. Someone had written the copy for the label and ended it this way. The typesetter took it literally.

None of these theories is convincing. Why would someone include a word or letter count? You don't see "This Bud's for You

4" on Budweiser cans. Even if an obsessive-compulsive typesetter did include it, why wouldn't the beer company demand the number be taken out, at the typesetter's expense?

So many people write to Latrobe Brewing asking about the mystery number that the company has created the Rolling Rock 33 Club. Everyone who inquires is automatically inducted. The club, however, does not appear to hold regular meetings or confer tangible advantages on members. The company's wishy-washy press release mentions the usual theories, endorses none, and calls the word-count idea the "most popular and probable answer to the '33' mystery." We're more inclined to go with the eighteenth amendment date of 1933. Although the Rolling Rock brand didn't come out until several years later, 1933 is the year the revived Latrobe Brewery started producing beer.

It is common knowledge among adolescents that you can trade certain Olympia Beer labels for sex. Peel off the label and look at the back. If it is marked with four dots, it's your red-letter day. Worthless scrap though it may seem, the label can be redeemed for sex. Exactly where and how you redeem labels are not stated.

The Olympia Brewing Company says that, first of all, there has never been such a promotion, and further, it has no idea how the idea started. The markings on the back are a simple industrial code. A typical marking might read:

345 B

. . . .

The color of the ink tells the year the bottle was filled. It's changed each year. The number tells which day of the year the bottle was filled, starting with one for January and running through 365 for December 31. The letter next to it codes the hour. The Olympia factory runs around the clock, so *A* means the hour starting at midnight, *B* is the hour starting at 1:00 A.M., and so on. The dots just tell which of four inspectors was on duty when the bottle was filled. Four-dot labels aren't hard to find.

Computer Software

Secret messages or pictures lurk in the most sedate of office software. Triggered by an undocumented combination of keystrokes or mouse movements, the secret gimmicks lean toward inscrutable humor and pictures of naked women. As programs have gotten bigger and storage space cheaper, simple text messages have given way to color, animation, and stereo sound.

There's not much point in cataloging specific examples here. Although fairly common, most of these tricks have a short shelf life. They vanish or change with each new update of the software. Exceptions are those gimmicks burned into read-only memory (ROM) or in stable segments of the system software.

The ROM chips of the Macintosh SE contain digitized pictures of the (fully clothed) designers. A short machine-language call will reveal the pictures. The following Pascal program will work (but only on a Mac SE with original ROMs):

```
Procedure ShowPictures:

    Inline $4EF9, $0041, $D89A; { jmp $41D89A }



Begin

    ShowPictures;

End.
```

This displays in succession three full-screen snapshots of assembled Apple engineers. There doesn't seem to be any way to save the images, and you have to restart the computer after running the program.

On the Atari ST, ASCII characters 28–31, when displayed side by side, form the head of a pipe-smoking man variously identified as Atari honcho Jack Tramiel, Hugh Hefner, or the Church of the Subgenius's "Bob" Dobbs.

You can check for secret messages in any program by running through the various combinations of the modifier keys: Control, Shift, Alternate, or Escape (IBM PCs and compatibles); Command, Shift, or Option (Macintosh); or similarly named keys on other systems. Many secret features are activated only when the official credit is on the screen. That's the one you get by selecting "About the Program," or some such command. Some computer games display a special screen on Christmas Day only. For instance, some versions of Airborne! showed a Christmas tree instead of a cactus on the game screen on December 25. You can check to see if a game has this feature by setting the clock/calendar to December 25 and starting the game.

One message is so much of a legend that it deserves mention. Until the guys in suits found out about it, the Amiga operating system contained a novel feature indeed. For those who have an early release of the system (up to version 1.2), the instructions are as follows: Load the Amiga "Workbench." Click in the background. Holding down the Shift, Alternate, and one of the function keys produces an undocumented credit in the status bar at the top of the screen.

These credits are ordinary enough as these things go—credits for otherwise uncredited people, some under nicknames. Holding down the Shift, Alternate, and F1 keys produces the message, "System Software: Carl, Neil & Kodiak." Shift, Alternate, and F2 produce, "Graphics Software: Dale, Bart, Jimm & =RJ=." And so on, up to Shift, Alternate, F10, which credits moral support to "Joe Pillow & The Dancing Fools."

If a disk is ejected while one of these three-key combinations is being held down, the status-bar message changes to "The Amiga, Born a Champion." *Reinserting* the disk produces the very brief but startling disclosure, "We made Amiga, they fucked it up."

The message flashes by so quickly that you may not be sure you saw it. You can get around this by running several programs in the background. This slows down the system, leaving the message on the screen long enough to read it. It appears to be impossible to capture the message with a "screen grabber" for printing. The programmers must not have wanted any incriminating hard copy.

The "They" in the message can refer only to Commodore Business Machines. The Amiga was originally supposed to be an Atari computer. That deal fell apart, and Commodore bought the technology. The Amiga people weren't happy with Commodore's version of the Amiga machine.

Commodore management didn't know about the hidden jab until system 1.2 had already shipped. The image-conscious company refused to comment on the messages. (According to our informant, "Questions about the messages are questions that will receive no answer from Commodore.") In version 1.3 of the Amiga system, the message in question was quietly changed. The new message: "Still a Champion."

A 1992 headline in the *New York Post* charged that "MILLIONS OF COMPUTERS CARRY SECRET MESSAGE THAT URGES DEATH TO JEWS IN NEW YORK CITY." They were talking about the Wingdings font packaged with Microsoft Windows. The font is a collection of graphic symbols that can be entered in documents. Someone noticed that the symbols produced by typing "NYC" were a skull and crossbones, a star of David, and a hand making the "thumbs up" gesture. "There's no way it could be a random coincidence," said one computer user in the *Post*. Most people thought otherwise, including Microsoft vice president Brad Silverberg.

Spacecraft

There are secret messages on crafts NASA has sent into interstellar space. It is widely alleged that various people working for NASA and its subcontractors have hidden their initials in spacecraft parts. Best documented is an unauthorized message on the two Voyager spacecraft launched in 1977, the first man-made objects to leave the solar system. These are the same crafts that carry gold plaques bearing pictograms to be read by any alien beings that find them. One Jet Propulsion Laboratory engineer, Bruce Montgomery, sneaked in his own message. It's not on the plaques but on an obscure valve package plate (part number 10073773-1 SN 003) that Montgomery designed. Montgomery revealed (*after* the launch) that he had stamped the mysterious initials, "DEI/FEIF," on the plate.

That's an inside joke at Montgomery's alma mater, Cal Tech. DEI stands for "Dabney Eats It," unofficial motto of an undergraduate residence's food service. FEIF is "Fleming Eats It Faster," an allusion to another dining hall's equally uninspired fare. Another copy of the plate, complete with inscription, is in the Smithsonian's Air and Space Museum.

15·

Graffiti

Urban graffiti isn't as meaningless as it looks. Successive layers of spray paint tell a story that rarely has a happy ending. Lone taggers paint their names or initials for the sport of it. Gang graffiti (below) is mostly about marking territory.

(a) A "piece" or *placa* is a territorial marker, usually the initials or an abbreviation of a gang name. Gang graffiti predates the invention of spray paint and may have its origins in the bus-bench and school-desk carvings of early Hispanic gangs. The angular script harks back to the difficulties of carving round letters. Multicolored illusionistic paintings on subway trains, overpasses, and sides of buildings are often the work of taggers, not gangsters.

(b) Gang members sign their nicknames in smaller letters next to the gang name. Letters after a name are invidious mottoes (CK means "Crip killer"; BK is "Blood killer," etc.).

(c) Other gangs paint over or cross out rival graffiti ("dis marks"). Latino gangs may add *rata* ("rat") or *Y que?* ("What are you going to do about it?").

(d) The penal code for homicide (187) next to a name signifies a person marked for a hit. This brazen custom has provided leads for homicide detectives investigating "random" drive-by shootings. By studying graffiti, police can often determine which gang made the hit and get a membership roster.

(e) After the hit, the victim's homeboys paint a cloud around his name or add R.I.P.

16·

Hidden Pictures

Artists and designers often work alone and unsupervised, yet their handiwork may be seen by millions. Long before Al Hirschfeld teased his first "Nina" out of a comic's comb-over, artists fell victim to the temptation to hide an illicit picture or word in something that will be seen by so many people.

Old Masters

Michelangelo painted his own features, grotesquely distorted, onto the flayed skin of Saint Bartholomew in the Sistine Chapel's *Last Judgment*. Hans Holbein's *Portrait of Two Ambassadors* (National Gallery, London) has a whitish blob hovering at the ambassadors' feet. Viewed from a proper angle on the diagonal, the mysterious form comes together clearly as a human skull. The fame of these Renaissance masterworks has inspired a handful of later artists to hide images in their own work and to devise more inscrutable means of camouflage. The phenomenon has even caused some viewers to see images that may not be there.

No less a figure than Sigmund Freud noted the hidden vulture in Leonardo da Vinci's *The Virgin and Child with St. Anne* in the Louvre. Turn a reproduction of the painting 90 degrees clockwise. The vulture is the outer part of Mary's outfit, a (now very faded) blue cloak. The part of the cloak behind her back looks like the head and beak of a bird of prey. Leonardo wrote of a childhood experience in which a kite (a bird) perched on his cradle. Freud tried to psychoanalyze the artist in retrospect, but mistranslated the type of bird as a vulture. This led one of Freud's followers,

Oskar Pfister, to notice a vulture in the Louvre painting. Pfister wrote that "the vulture, the symbol of motherhood, is perfectly clearly visible. . . . Hardly any observer whom I have confronted with my little find has been able to resist the evidence of this picture-puzzle." Given the faulty translation, even faithful Freudians doubt that it's anything more than a Rorschach blot of a coincidence.

Georges de La Tour's *The Fortune Teller* (Metropolitan Museum, New York) once contained the French scatological epithet "MERDE." Today, all you can see is a half-legible "ME." The museum's conservation staff removed the rest of the offending word. It was present, however, when the museum bought the painting for $675,000 in 1960.

The Fortune Teller shows a young man being robbed by a band of gypsy women while an old woman tells his fortune. La Tour's painstaking attention to detail can be seen in the chain the young man is wearing. Between the links are tiny bars, and inscribed on the bars in minuscule letters are the Latin words "AMOR" ("love") and "FIDES" ("faith" or "trust").

The secret word was on the shawl or collar of the black-haired woman seen in profile directly to the left of the man. The lacy white fabric contains a darker olive and black band. "MERDE" was in the darker band. You can just barely make out the rough capital letters *M* and *E*.

In a letter in *Burlington* magazine (1981), museum staffers John Brealey and Pieter Meyers described the words as "a modern invention done by turning the free brush strokes simulating the decorative design of the collar . . . into letters. The false paint is executed in a coarsely ground black which does not match the dark greenish-grey of the original brush strokes and fills the cracks. The 'R' and the 'D' are additions while the other letters are formed by altering original brush strokes."

Brealey and Meyers were sure that the word was not a seventeenth-century joke of La Tour's because the brush strokes were on top of a layer of varnish. They were a later addition, improvised from a chance resemblance to "ME" in La Tour's brush strokes. The word must have been the work of a restorer with a strange sense of humor. One theory is that the guilty party was a certain Georges Albert Dion Delobre, a restorer known for practical jokes. Brealey noted that restorers sometimes play "malicious tricks."

Self-portraits in Reflections

Various artists have painted tiny self-portraits into reflections depicted in paintings. A circular convex mirror in Jan van Eyck's *Wedding Portrait* (National Gallery, London) reflects two tiny figures, one believed to be the artist. At the time, the depiction of a mirror was a great novelty, and this was surely intended to be seen by anyone who looked carefully. To *conceal* a self-portrait, the artist is more likely to paint it into a reflection on a shiny metal or glass object.

Some still lifes of the Dutch painter Pieter Claesz include a self-portrait in a metal cup or ball. Window, table, and other still-life objects are duly reflected in the polished metal surface. Looking carefully, you can make out the reflection of the entire studio, including the artist himself, who is standing next to an easel. You can't really make out his face. Claesz takes a modicum of artistic license in making the painting on the easel (which ought to be the very painting you're looking at) larger than actual size.

Andrea Solario's *Head of Saint John the Baptist* (Louvre) shows its subject on a silver platter. The dish's trumpet-shaped stand contains a complex maze of highlights, reflections, and reflections of reflections. Discreetly painted into the dish's surface are two reflected self-portraits of Solario.

The self-portraits are so tiny that they are unrecognizable in most reproductions of the painting. They are detailed enough to show a facial likeness. Both are upside-down, situated precisely on the center axis of the dish. One is on the dish's trumpet-shaped neck. The form of the neck distorts this reflection into the shape of an exclamation point. A clearer, less distorted reflection appears on the silver base of the dish, between the two gold rims. This reflection shows a gaunt head with pointed light-colored beard, pursed mouth, shadowed eye sockets, and a dark cap. Nearby are two parallel reddish vertical lines that may represent the sides of an easel.

The Guadalupe Cornea Images

This is nothing compared to the weird reflections said to exist in the *Image of Guadalupe*. Housed in the Basilica of Guadalupe in Mexico City, the image is a traditional depiction of the Madonna painted in Mexico circa 1531 by an unknown hand. The best guess is that it was the work of an Aztec artist who had seen Spanish paintings. A body of legend dating from the mid-sixteenth century claims the image to be a miraculous depiction something like the veil of Veronica or Shroud of Turin. This supernatural reputation has inspired claims that the reflections of people's faces are visible *in the eyes of the Virgin Mary.*

The wet cornea can reflect images. Obviously, it would have to be a fantastically detailed painting to show them. An oculist who examined the painting with an ophthalmoscope was the first to detect a cornea image in 1951. In fact, the pro-cornea images literature invariably cites "prominent artists, theologians, and ophthalmologists in Mexico and the U.S." as saying the images are for real.

The cloth on which the image is painted measures about 66 by 41 inches. The figure is a bit under life size. It's not *totally* beyond the bounds of reason that someone could paint legible images in the space available. The eyes are about one quarter the size of the circular mirror in van Eyck's *Wedding Portrait.*

The usual way of suggesting the reflectivity of the eye (or any surface) is with a highlight, a dab of white paint. Eye highlights are usually just a tiny brush stroke, with no detail. Only when the surface is much larger (for example, a glass bottle in a still life) can you see something—often the familiar distorted window.

The first image was discovered in Mary's right eye (the left eye as you face the picture). The reflected portrait is supposedly that of a bearded man. He was promptly identified as Juan Diego, the man who had a vision of the Virgin Mary commanding him to found the church. Supposedly, the image resembles old paintings of Diego, which depict him with a beard. But the paintings of Diego weren't done from life. Diego was an Aztec, and scholars now say the native Mexicans didn't wear beards in the early sixteenth century. A bearded man of the time would have to be a Spaniard.

Since then, photo and computer experts have joined all those artists and ophthalmologists in studying the images. Examination and enhancement of photographs of the eyes uncovered two other tiny figures dancing in the Virgin's eyes. Over there by the iris, isn't that Juan de Zumárraga, first bishop of Mexico? Yep!

In the early 1980s Aste Tonsmann, who holds a Ph.D. from Cornell, reported that his image processing had revealed nothing less than a microminiature historical tableau of the Guadalupe legend. According to legend, the Virgin gave Diego an armload of out-of-season roses. He wrapped them in cloth and took them to show the bishop in order to prove that his vision was real. When he opened the cloth for the bishop, they found the Image of Guadalupe was miraculously imprinted on the cloth. Tonsmann claimed that the corneas show these principals and bystanders:

- Juan Diego, opening his cloth. This is particularly mind-boggling because the cloth he's opening *is* the Image of Guadalupe we now have, in the eyes of which all of this supposedly exists.
- Bishop Zumárraga, who witnesses the miracle. A single tear runs down his cheek.
- An unidentified young bearded man, dumbfounded, who holds his hand to his chin in wonderment.
- An unidentified Mexican in prayer.
- A black woman, identified as the bishop's maid.
- A family.
- A group of Franciscans, identifiable by their habits.

Tonsmann claimed to find the same reflections in the *other* eye, with suitable shift of perspective.

One thing's for sure. You're not going to see any of this in the original image. The muted icon hangs far above the floor behind thick glass. (This is not an unwarranted precaution: In 1921 an anarchist left a bouquet of flowers containing a stick of dynamite on the altar.)

We examined an enlargement of the Virgin's right eye (left eye as you face the image). Just a crescent of the eye is visible under heavy lids. The right third of the crescent is the white of the eye. The left two thirds comprise mostly the iris and pupil. The reflections are in this part. By consulting published descriptions, we could locate three of them, or at least the dabs of paint that are claimed to represent the reflections.

The claimed image of Juan Diego is the largest. It doesn't require too much imagination to make out the face of a bearded man. But Diego's image is not a reflection or highlight. It appears to be nothing more nor less than the right side of the *iris* of the eye. The weave of the cloth breaks up the paint into a grainy pattern that happens to look something like a face.

To the left of this is a smaller image some identify as the bishop. This is also a modestly striking likeness of a bearded man. It appears to be the left side of the iris, also half-lost in the weave. The dark space between the bishop and Diego is the pupil.

A third visible figure to the far left appears to be the white of the eye. It looks a little like a monkey.

We couldn't find the Franciscans, the maid, the praying Aztec, etc.

The two best reflections are about as clear as the face of the man on the moon, and about as likely to be faces. They're images you can see, if you really want to, in real but ambiguous features of the painting.

Secret Stuff on the $100 Bill

Wavy lines of currency engraving form pictures to the imaginative eye. The U.S. Mint has historically taken the position that there were and would be no hidden images in money. The advent of more powerful and accessible color copiers has caused the Treasury Department to relent somewhat.

Currency engraving reproduces amazingly well on a good office copier. Those who are used to the poor reproduction of photographs and halftones will be surprised to find that photocopies of the engraved portraits on money come out fairly clean. A color copier can pick up the tiny red, blue, and yellow fibers for a trompe l'oeil simulation of currency paper on plain white paper.

In July 1991 the treasury released a redesigned $100 bill with new anticounterfeiting measures. Treasury officials refused to say what those measures were. It was immediately apparent that they included a microfilm strip embedded in the bill.

The strip is invisible in reflected light and won't show up in a photocopy. You can see it easily by holding up the bill to the light. Franklin side up, the microfilm is on the left side of the bill, running vertically. The strip bears the tiny repeated inscription "USA 100," which alternates in normal and upside-down backward form so that it can be read from front or back. Though small (about a millimeter high), the letters are legible without magnification.

There are still plenty of old bills without the strip, and even the new bills presently say, "SERIES 1990." This is not the year the bill was printed, but rather the year of the act authorizing the mint to print the money. Once the new bills are phased in, the micro-film will provide a test of authenticity and a safeguard against such clever counterfeiting techniques as bleaching real bills and printing them with a higher denomination.

Our examination of a crisp new bill revealed another hidden device that's much harder to see. Benjamin Franklin's portrait is framed by an oval consisting of concentric rules, cross-hatching, and white space. Similar, though slightly different, ovals surround the portraits on all U.S. bills. Using a magnifying glass, look at the outermost line of the oval. It turns out not to be a line at all but the repeated words "THE UNITED STATES OF AMERICA."

This is not an embedded film; it's engraved on the face of the bill. The flattened, capital letters are about an eighth of a millime-ter (roughly a hundredth of an inch) high, making the inscription by far the smallest that appears on any U.S. bill. It's so small that some letters are misformed where the paper is irregular.

We copied a new $100 bill on an Océ Library Copier. On the tiny inscription, the toner puddled into a muddy, half-legible mess. The microfilm strip didn't come out at all.

The redesigned bill is good for bar bets. How many times does "The United States of America" appear on a new $100 bill? The answer is twelve (two obvious appearances plus ten times around the oval).

Pop Culture

Al Hirschfeld started hiding "NINA," the name of his daughter, in his *New York Times* drama-page caricatures as a joke after her birth in 1945. The number next to Hirschfeld's signature tells how many times the name appears in the drawing. The secret quickly got out, and people began making a game of it. A weekly pool in the *Times* art department awarded the pot to the first to spot the NINA on the photoengraving plates (an extra challenge because it's backward on the plates). The air force once contacted Hirschfeld about using slides of his drawings to train pilots. Top brass figured that expe-rience spotting hidden text in theatrical caricatures would stand pilots in good stead when it came to spotting munitions factories and machine-gun nests. Hirschfeld, who never intended to put the name in every single drawing for the rest of his career, has likened the NINA business to Frankenstein's monster. Attempts to discontinue the practice have brought puzzled letters from people convinced that the name was in the latest drawing, just hidden particularly well. When the artist once consented to put the name of a daughter's friend ("LIZA") in a *Times* drawing, people sent Hirschfeld flowers and telegrams to congratulate him on the birth of his new daughter. A regulation against hidden text on U.S. postage stamps was waived for Hirschfeld when he was commissioned to design a series of twenty-nine-cent stamps released in 1991.

Claims of phallic images in ads and art are so numerous that it takes something out of the ordinary to get much attention. A case in point is the supposed penis that appears on the packaging of Little Mermaid toys. When Disney released *The Little Mermaid* on videocassette, Michelle Couch of Mesa, Arizona, noted that the illustration of a castle tower on the packaging resembled a penis. She got a Phoenix supermarket chain to pull the video from its shelves. Disney received a handful of complaints, but it was too late to change the design.

The Little Mermaid was heavily merchandised, and the ithyphallic castle appears on many, though not all, of a diverse line of toys, books, apparel, and school gear marketed primarily to girls aged four to ten. There's even a Little Mermaid stencil set to give the budding artist a head start toward creating her own suggestive pictures. The castle in question is yellow and in the upper left of the video label. It's not so much a proper castle as a futuristic assemblage of spindly towers. Two of the towers (both directly below the *r* in *Mermaid* on the video label) are thicker than the others and have rounded heads. That's about it. The theory that the middling resemblance was the intentional work of a renegade Disney artist seems farfetched.

Next to genitalia, devils are the most popular free-association image in unlikely contexts. *Impressions,* an English textbook used in kindergarten and up through the sixth grade, generated controversy in 1990 when certain parents found it to contain a hidden picture of the devil. To see it, you're supposed to photocopy an illustration, hold it upside down, and look at it in a mirror. Seriously.

In 1991 eagle-eyed shoppers noted that veining in Hallmark black and green marbleized wrapping paper formed pictures of Satan, a goat's head, and bats. Debbie Wagner of Norwalk, California, stated, "I knew exactly what it was and got it out of my house. . . ." Wagner got her local Hallmark to ban the wrap. Hallmark denied there was anything wrong with the paper.

We examined the design and can report that there is a fairly recognizable animal-in-cloud monster. The reflected design simulates a split slab of marble. You can see a dwarfish figure with outstretched arms. The oval head has ears, goggle eyes with catlike pupils, eyebrows, a pug nose, and an apelike mouth. Hallmark did not respond to our inquiries about the paper.

Certain collectors prize Fleer's 1989 Bill Ripken baseball card for the fact that the Baltimore Orioles second baseman holds a bat bearing the tiny inscription, "Fuck Face." Sports pages mentioned that there was an obscenity on the card but refused to print it. Baseball-card guides list the card as an error and tactfully render the inscription as "Rick Face." There is a modicum of deniability: With sufficient mental effort, you can read the jot of a *u* as an undotted *i*, and the *F* as a misformed *R* with the loop closed up and a short tail. But no one who sees the card doubts what it *really* says. The words appear on the knob of the bat, just below Ripken's gloved hand. It looks like the bottom of the bat was painted white and the inscription was handwritten in black. It is not entirely clear from the card whether the inscription was physically present on the bat Ripken held, or whether the photo or plate was retouched. The letters appear almost too sharp (compared, say, to the glove brand name—for which Ripken probably earned an endorsement fee). The words' seeming lack of foreshortening hints at a doctored photo.

Fleer wasn't in a position to see the humor in this. Most of its customers are kids, some from pretty strait-laced families. Fleer recalled the shipment, incidentally raising the card's asking price sky high. The card sold for as much as thirty-five dollars when it was brand new. That would have been a bad investment, as the card, in mint condition, sells for about thirty dollars at this writing—provided the inscription is not covered up. Fleer went to the amusing extreme of stamping a black bar over the inscription on most of the recalled cards. These cards are worth only about a quarter, according to dealers. Other cards have the inscription whited out or scribbled out—it's not clear by whom.

Ripken said he didn't know what the bat said; he had been the victim of a practical joke. Others charged that the biggest prankster in the Orioles lineup was Bill Ripken.

IV: Illusion

17·

How to Pull a Rabbit Out of a Hat

The magician's code forbids revealing secrets. Press kits of the top performers make a big deal about legally binding secrecy agreements that cast members must sign. Popular books on magic, the sort sold in any bookstore, are almost always about card and coin tricks. If you want to know how the big illusions you see on TV work, you're out of luck.

Actually, anyone can penetrate the veil of secrecy. A handful of long-established firms (most notably Abbott's Magic Manufacturing Co., Colon, MI 49040; and Louis Tannen, 6 West 32nd Street, New York, NY 10001) manufacture or distribute the lion's share of professional magic equipment in use in the U.S. They accept orders by mail, and they don't check to make sure you're a real magician. Though big illusion equipment may cost thousands of dollars, the firms also market inexpensive "workshop plans" (mechanical drawings) of stage illusions. We sent away for the secrets of some of the most puzzling effects being performed today.

Let's warm up by vanishing the hoariest cliché in the business: pulling a rabbit out of a hat.

Hat Trick

Leisure wear has taken a devastating toll on the rabbit trick. In more genteel times, the stunt was done with a hat borrowed from an audience member—the rabbit itself nicely accommodated in the tails of the performer's cutaway. Today's performer had better bring his own hat, and hiding places on his person are at a premium.

Nevertheless, the classic trick is done pretty much the way it's always been done. It's usually the first thing in the act. That way, the creature's patient and self-effacing nature is not unduly put to the test. The hat *is* empty when first shown. The rabbit is hidden somewhere else. It's either in a special pocket or dark cloth bag concealed in the performer's clothing, somewhere on the set, or (by all odds, the best option) in an assistant's clothing. What makes the rabbit trick practical is a little-known fact of rabbit behavior. Provided it cannot see a way out, a rabbit will not struggle to get out of a dark bag.

As the performer demonstrates the hat to be empty, he manages to turn it so the brim faces the rabbit bag. A bit of misdirection (a bon mot directed to an audience member or arrival of a scantily clad assistant) helps divert curious eyes from the performer as his fingers release snaps or Velcro in the bottom of the bag, causing the rabbit to plop neatly into the hat. The performer may then produce the rabbit at his first convenience.

Watch the performer carefully. You can often spot a telltale bulge. In a business suit or tuxedo jacket, rabbit pockets are most often at the front, about breastbone level, or at the lower front corner. (It's hard to hide a rabbit in a sport shirt.) The rabbit bag may also be connected by a strong nylon string to the performer. A popular arrangement is to tie the cord to one wrist (left in a right-handed performer), run it up that shirt arm, across the shoulders and down the other shirt arm, where it terminates, just outside the sleeve, in a knot securing the bag. The performer has the rabbit bag behind his right hand and must be careful to keep it out of sight. The hat is smartly snapped to scoop up the rabbit. The left hand takes the hat as the rabbit is released into the hat with the right hand. The performer pulls the rabbit out with the left hand and holds it up. While all eyes are on the rabbit, the other hand holds up the hat. Raising both arms makes a suit ride up and causes the nylon string to retract the rabbit bag up the sleeve and safely out of sight for the rest of the show.

It's generally more effective to have the (almost always female) assistant carry the rabbit. The audience's unconscious sexism makes it assume the assistant is there just to look pretty and not to play a crucial role. For another thing, informed opinion judges it easier to outfit a dress than a man's jacket for so-called production work. Hoop skirt–like construction can hold a gown slightly out from the body, leaving ample room for concealed livestock.

Where necessary, a rabbit bag may be hung on a hook on the upstage side of a table or other equipment. This is less effective, in that everyone suspects the rabbit was in the table, and everyone is right. In the variant where the magician produces a rabbit from the jacket of a bona fide audience member, you'll notice that the volunteer stands just in front of an assistant or the break in the curtain. The assistant (the visible one, or an invisible one behind the curtain) hands the rabbit under the volunteer's jacket. The volunteer knows something funny's going on but is too nice or too shy to make a fuss.

Because of all that fur and ears, rabbits can curl into a compact ball, then kick and look really big when held up for inspection. Lifting the rabbit by the ears is now frowned upon. It's much less painful to the little sport to use the skin at the back of the neck. Audience worries about onstage "accidents" are exaggerated. The well-trained conjurer's rabbit uses its litter box as dependably as a cat. *The Bunny Book,* published in 1985 by Magic, Inc., of Chicago, makes the not entirely believable claim that "because of its diet, a rabbit's droppings are not offensive."

The rabbit trick has been around so long that variations and shortcuts are many. One is a "spring rabbit" ($28.50 from Tannen; $50 from Abbott's), a stuffed rabbit pelt that is considerably less demanding than the live article. It folds into a small space a lot more easily, too. Internal springs allow the fake to be manipulated to look like it's alive. According to the Tannen catalog copy, "You'd swear it was alive. . . . [It] has glass eyes that truly resemble the real thing, and is a quality article throughout." Also available from Tannen are spring skunks, raccoons, and foxes.

Why do magicians produce a rabbit, as opposed to anything else you wouldn't expect to find in a hat? The story goes that a British woman claimed some centuries ago that she had been violated by a rabbit. Some time later, she gave birth to a litter of white rabbits. The king ordered an investigation. Under questioning, one of the woman's servants admitted to having procured the rabbits for her. A conjurer took advantage of the topical interest by producing a white rabbit from a silk hat.

18.

Escapes

Harry Houdini is the Elvis of magic. Scarcely less famous years after his death than in life, he has spawned a shadow industry of Houdini imitators. One question that always comes up with Houdini and his followers is whether the stunts are real or faked. The answer is both. Houdini's escapes freely mixed feats of agility with fakery. His contemporary followers do the same—relying, it seems, a bit more on the fakery.

You sometimes hear of Houdini having taken his secrets to the grave with him. Houdini left extensive notes on his escapes and other illusions. At times his writings are vague, evasive, or blatantly false. He held back a few secrets and threw in an occasional whopper. Houdini claimed he could open the Darby handcuffs used by British police without the aid of key or pick. He found they popped open when struck against a hard surface. This amusing claim has been repeated in article after article on Houdini, often with a diagram showing exactly where you're supposed to strike the cuffs. Escape artists who have tried it find it just doesn't work. Most likely, Houdini was pulling someone's leg.

But these are trifles. If there are mysteries about how Houdini operated, they lie in the nit-picking details of where he hid keys and picks. Far from being "lost" to the magic profession, Houdini's methods are known, copied, and (rarely) improved upon by today's performers.

Escapology

There are a few strictly legitimate escapes, done by dint of physical agility, strength, and endurance, with no secret gimmicks of any kind.

A second and larger group of stunts uses legitimate restraints (rope, regulation handcuffs, etc.), but the performer cheats by concealing knives, lock picks, or other hardware on his person or somewhere within reach.

A third group, including many of the most spectacular escapes, are tricked up from the word go. The performer misrepresents what's going on and how dangerous it is. Often there's a secret way to open the restraints.

In his writings Houdini himself commented that there was little correlation between the difficulty of an escape and audience reaction. Stunts that tested his endurance and nerve drew blank reactions, while the audience went nuts over effects depending on cheap gimmicks. You can't blame escape artists for favoring the latter.

The biggest difference between Houdini's act and those of his imitators today is *time*. Houdini would take up to an hour to escape. For a full hour, *nothing visible would be going on.*

Not that Houdini's performances were stone-cold boring. As the minutes passed, the audience grew restive. The appointed time for the stunt to be completed would approach, then pass. Was there enough air in there? People began whispering that maybe the stunt should be called off. Occasionally audience members became hysterical. That is truer theater than most contemporary performers ever attain. Only then would Houdini make his appearance.

TV-generation audiences wouldn't stand for that today. When David Copperfield does an escape on TV, he packs the downtime with frantic visuals, music, and MTV-like cuts lest someone think of changing the channel. Even in stage shows, today's performers work as if the audience was armed with channel changers.

Performers have been able to "fast-forward" escapes because Houdini often required only a fraction of the allotted time to effect his own. He'd get out and stand behind the screen reading a book for half an hour. The theory was that the audience thought they were getting more value for their money when the escape took a long time.

Most escape stunts follow a pattern. One way or another, the performer professes to have "nothing up his sleeve" (in some cases, going so far as to allow a strip search by a local physician). The performer is bound by restraint devices (handcuffs, leg cuffs, rope, chains, etc.; often a combination of those), then put inside something else (a crate, a safe, a coffin, etc.), which is perhaps tied up with rope or chain for good measure. Finally, as a concession to reality, a screen, curtain, or cabinet is placed around the container so you can't see a thing. There are things going on that you're not supposed to see.

Even when the escape is condensed for television, there's the usual stage business with assistants nervously looking at their watches. Finally, free of his bonds, the performer jumps out from behind the screen. The screen is pulled away, revealing the whole setup, still locked tight. It's supposed to look like the performer got out by supernatural means. In Houdini's time there were people who sincerely believed that he dematerialized to perform his act.

Suspense depends on the "penalty for failure." Diverse perils have been incorporated into escape stunts: drowning, suffocation, buzz saws threatening to tear into the performer, a hinged bed of spikes about to snap shut, allegedly wild and vicious animals. Assistants, firefighters, or paramedics are on hand to get the performer out in the nick of time—or gather up the remains. The rarest quality is unpredictability. David Copperfield achieved that in a 1988 TV special. Copperfield was locked in a cabinet and raced against the clock to escape before a "death saw" cut him in two. Ho-hum. Well, of course he's going to beat the deadline by a split second . . . only he didn't. The buzz saw cut him in two. The "escape" was really a sawing-in-two illusion.

Hardware

What's happening behind the screen in an escape stunt? Lock picking, for one thing, and that takes tools. Most escapes require a lock pick, a key, a knife, a saw, or other such devices. Hiding these implements is often the most crucial part of an escape stunt. There are many stories about how or where Houdini concealed tools on his person, with few if any body cavities overlooked. Houdini's notes are vague on this point.

Where an escape artist hides tools depends on how carefully he or she is going to be searched. If no search is to take place, there's no reason not to have them in a pocket. Houdini is known to have worn a secret tool belt underneath his pants in routine performances. Designed for easy access with handcuffs, it carried picking tools on clips that rotated something like a dry cleaner's rack.

It has been alleged that Houdini swallowed keys and regurgitated them at will. This is not quite so incredible in view of Houdini's oral dexterity. In his stage magic act, he "swallowed" needles and then removed them from his mouth, neatly threaded. Penn Gillette does the best-known modern version of this. It's a classic "switch." The performer has the threaded (blunt) needles in his mouth to begin with. He's good at concealing them (for sometimes volunteers are invited to examine his mouth for foreign objects). After displaying them, he disposes of the other needles by pausing for a drink of water and spitting them into the glass.

We'd guess that no one is going to choose to hide small sharp objects in their esophagus or other cavities if there are other practical places to hide them. There are.

In Houdini's notes he mentions hiding tools in concealed pockets on the curtain or screen that is placed to block the audience view. This would be the simplest method for those escapes where the performer isn't totally sealed up and can get to the pocket. The audience members examine the restraints, never the curtain (brought in as an afterthought and above suspicion). Houdini's screen had a framework of metal tubes that could hold not only tools but other objects that might be needed.

But there were escapes where Houdini was strip-searched, then completely enclosed in a bank vault or something. In these cases, the vital key or picking tool was passed to Houdini *after* the strip search. His wife, Bess, would tongue a key from her mouth to his as she kissed him farewell through prison bars; a confederate "volunteer's" handshake would accomplish the same. One picking tool clipped onto a ring during a handshake.

Music is an integral part of escape acts, even if the canned variety replaces the full orchestra Houdini had. It is sometimes necessary to saw, pound, or tear in secret, and the performer works in time to the music.

How to Escape from Handcuffs

The biggest secret about the handcuff escape is this: *The keys to most models of handcuffs are interchangeable.*

The public imagines handcuffs to be like cars or houses, each with a unique key. The escape artist does nothing to discourage this impression. But it's wrong. A key to one set of Peerless handcuffs will work in any other set of that model. It's as if all Toyotas had the same key. Furthermore, many of the most common makes of cuffs can use the same key. A Peerless key will also open a pair of Colt or Smith & Wesson handcuffs, and so on. Remember, handcuffs are normally used only to restrain an *escorted* prisoner on the way to jail. The chance of the prisoner escaping is too slight to justify the expense and bother of unique keys.

Consequently, the escape artist who can hide a key, or several keys, on his person can open most, or nearly all, sets of handcuffs.

It's not always done that way. Often the performer picks or shims the lock. (A pick goes in the key hole; a shim, in the latch.) The relative uniformity of design makes picking and shimming easy, too. As escape artist John Novak says, with commendable frankness, in his manuscript, *A Modern Handcuff Act* (1989), "Being able to open a pair of handcuffs is NOT A BIG DEAL, and *this* is why you must be a showman. You are making a very large mountain out of a relatively small mole hill."

The police who supply the performer handcuffs with great fanfare are in on the performer's secret. It's a Machiavellian bargain. The police know that a single key opens all the cuffs in the precinct and don't want to educate criminals on this point: "By exposing you, they expose themselves," writes Novak.

Houdini challenged his audience to bring handcuffs to the theater. Although he left himself an out with the requirement that they be of a standard make, Houdini evidently did use the offered locks most of the time. He was an expert lock picker who learned to open essentially every handcuff and lock then made in America and Europe. He even learned to deal with locks that hecklers had soaked in water to rust.

It's questionable that it's worth the effort for a modern performer to acquire the encyclopedic knowledge that Houdini had. Houdini's own audiences got tired of the handcuff bit. He eventually dropped it. Today, handcuff escapes are either a throwaway bit or part of a bigger, flashier escape. It's possible, and much easier, to provide one's own cuffs and use a secret key; or to use trick cuffs that open without a key. The average audience member is not going to know real cuffs from well-made trick cuffs imitating a standard model. For this reason, today's escape artists rarely offer such challenges. When they do, they may "randomly" choose a confederate's offered handcuffs. Why not?

How to Escape from a Straitjacket

Houdini got the idea of escaping from a straitjacket after a visit to an insane asylum. If borderline tasteless, the effect remains popular. The Amazing Randi has duplicated Houdini's escape from a straitjacket while suspended upside-down from a rope; Dorothy Dietrich has matched that, *plus* the rope is on fire; Dan Stapleton did it with the rope suspended from a helicopter; Siegfried of Siegfried and Roy escapes from a straitjacket while inside a mechanical dragon's mouth. Legend claims that Buster Keaton learned the secret from Houdini and put it to practical use when the comic was confined in a sanitarium during a bout of the DTs.

Not many viewers realize that this can be one of the hardest of all standard escape stunts. It is when it uses a proper straitjacket with no gimmick. Even when you know how to do it, it takes a lot of work.

The first thing is to tense the arms while the jacket is being put on. The average audience volunteer has little hands-on experience in restraining maniacs and rarely buckles the jacket as tightly as it might be. Once secured, you relax the arms, leaving a bit of slack.

That ruse is the only free help you'll get. The rest of the trick is physically exhausting labor. Rest an elbow on the floor or another support and raise one arm over the head. Then it's possible—but incredibly difficult—for an agile performer to unstrap the buckle by working the fingers through the canvas. The trick takes a lot of practice. Once unstrapped, the jacket is pulled up and off with the aid of the teeth.

Houdini originally performed this escape behind the usual screen. Everyone thought he was faking when he reappeared all sweaty with his hair messed up. Ever since, the trick has usually been performed in full view.

There are also trick straitjackets that slip right off. They look exactly the same; the giveaway is the time required. The fast escapes (requiring about a minute and under, which includes Siegfried in that dragon's mouth and most jacket escapes you'll see on TV) *have* to use gimmicks. The escapes where the performer is suspended from a rope are much more difficult for lack of elbow support and use special jackets, too. The popular jacket marketed by Abbott's Magic (currently, $150 plus postage; specify male suit size when ordering) has a secret retracting strap. The performer grasps a flat piece of metal inside the end of one sleeve. It is attached through a slit to the leather strap. By pulling on it, the performer temporarily shortens the strap for fastening. The assistant is encouraged to fasten the strap tightly, putting a knee on the performer's back for balance. The performer has only to let go of the metal piece to regain several inches of slack. Another feature is that the topmost buckle in back (at the base of the neck) is especially large, which makes it easier to unfasten through canvas. There's a ten-inch gap below it, in the hard-to-reach center of the back, with no buckles at all. Gimmicked jackets are usually made of stretchier fabric than their hospital counterparts.

Dorothy Dietrich's interpretation has the plucky performer suspended in straitjacket from a flaming rope parallel to a second, safety rope. Provided Dietrich gets out of the straitjacket in time, she can climb down the safety rope to the ground. If she fails, she falls like a rock.

The part of the rope that burns is soaked in gasoline. It takes a while for the gasoline to burn off and the fibers to burn through. The time is nearly constant, provided the same type of rope is used. It may be measured using suspended weights matching the performer's weight. The performer and assistants thereby know exactly how much time she has to escape and when they have to rescue her (should it be necessary, and it never is).

The performer is capable of getting out of the jacket almost immediately. She never does. She stalls until the rope is just about to give (using the known average time and perhaps a signal from assistants?). *Then* she throws off the jacket and grabs the safety line. Shortly afterward, the other line burns through and falls flaming to the ground.

Paper Bag Escape

In many escapes, the hard part is not so much getting out as putting things back together so that it's not *obvious* how the performer got out. One of Houdini's most impressive effects was escaping from a paper bag. A paper bag is hard to fake. Audience volunteers examined it. It was just a big paper bag. The volunteers signed their names, or made secret marks, on the bag to make sure it wasn't switched. Houdini got inside, then the top was either folded and sealed with a gummed flap like an envelope, or tied with rope and sealed with wax. The usual screen hid Houdini during the escape. A few minutes later, Houdini emerged, and *the paper bag was still whole, the seals intact*. It was the same bag with the same signatures.

The secret: Once out of audience sight, Houdini cut his way out of the bag with a blade concealed on his person. He cut at the very top of the long bag, just below the seals. Houdini then resealed the bag. He had a duplicate gummed flap or duplicate rope, sealing wax, matches, and a seal. The bag resealed, he concealed all the tools and the original top of the bag. The bag was long enough that no one noticed that it was a couple of inches shorter after the stunt. When asking for the signatures, Houdini told the volunteers to avoid the top of the bag, as it would be sealed.

Jail-Cell Escape

Nothing sounds more impressive than an escape from a jail cell. Handcuffs and straitjackets are temporary restraints and might be gimmicked. Prisons are built to keep people indefinitely, and the performer is using the real thing. Spectacular-sounding escapes have inspired absurd ideas about how they were accomplished (that the performer sawed and replaced bars, or coated his stripped body with oil and slipped between the bars).

Performers escape from jail by *cheating*. They hide, or have passed to them, a pick or the cell key.

It's often with the full cooperation of the police. Police are in the business of keeping criminals in jail. They're under no obligation to keep escape artists behind bars. Doubtless most police stations have better things to do than to play foil to a publicity stunt. But find a police chief who is a magic buff and will agree to play along (with a little honorarium from the performer?) . . . One jailbreak is good for a career's worth of rehashes in programs and press releases.

Typical is the candid advice of a 1955 Abbott manuscript, *Escapes:* "The most efficient way of making an escape from a jail or prison is to have your Advance Agent make all the arrangements.

By making a monetary reimbursement with authorities, it is often possible to have the escape made easy for you. You will find too that these authorities are nearly always pretty fine fellows and if approached in a friendly manner will do much toward making the outcome of your 'break' successful."

Not out of place in this long tradition of abject fraud is David Copperfield's escape from Alcatraz (subject of a TV special). Surrounded by shark-infested waters, Alcatraz had a reputation as the prison no man escaped from. Copperfield's special opened with pictures of Al Capone, Machine Gun Kelly, and other hardened cons who never escaped from the "big house in the bay." These guys were there when Alcatraz was a federal penitentiary. Copperfield escaped from Alcatraz, the National Recreation Area, with the full cooperation of the U.S. Park Service. Maybe he tried the old "monetary reimbursement."

Unlike the old-style publicity stunt, Copperfield's escape was televised. He couldn't just get out; he had to make things interesting along the way. Explosives were set to go off at critical points in his escape route. A Berkeley, California, police officer said that they were real explosives and that Copperfield had a button he could press to deactivate them. We'd guess that the Park Service made awfully sure that the charges didn't go off. Dobermans, supposedly trained to Copperfield's scent, roamed the prison corridors, hungry for meat.

Copperfield used, well, *magic* to get out. No key to that locked door? Copperfield took three coins, joined them magically, and transformed them into a lock pick. Is David going to do something magical to kill the dogs? No, he makes a cat appear. The dogs sic it while Copperfield scrams.

Just as the cops are about to nab Copperfield, he disappears. When the police realize that the wily conjurer has eluded them, they run for their helicopters, incidentally leaving the door to the cellblock wide open. Copperfield, now in police disguise, takes advantage of their laxity to hijack a police helicopter to freedom. Why didn't Machine Gun Kelly think of that?

Buried Alive

Today, as in Houdini's time, the buried-alive stunt never fails to attract publicity. It is, in truth, one of the simplest stunts in the Houdini canon. There were no tricks when Houdini spent an hour buried underground or suspended underwater in a swimming pool. It took nerve, that's all. He was really in the coffin, breathing slowly and steadily, with no secret air source. The coffin is on the large side to provide sufficient air. Undocumented stories of performers dying while performing this trick (a staple of press releases) should perhaps be considered suspect.

The Chinese Water-Torture-Cell Escape

By a certain point in his career, Houdini had escaped from just about everything worth escaping from. We mean *everything*. He escaped from a giant football. He escaped from an embalmed "sea monster" that washed ashore on a Massachusetts beach. The only way to retain interest was for Houdini to invent something new, then escape from it. That's what Houdini did in his most famous stunt, the Chinese Water-Torture-Cell Escape.

The cell is a free invention owing more to then-current stereotypes of Chinese villainy than to any actual device from Chinese history. It is about the size and shape of a phone booth. The front of the cell is clear glass. The cell is filled to the top with water. Assistants handcuffed Houdini and locked his feet in a square stock. This stock then fitted into the open top of the cell, suspending Houdini upside-down in the water. As usual, a screen blocked the audience view after Houdini was in place, lest the audience learn the secrets of his escape. After a tense interval, Houdini appeared, dripping wet and free of his bonds.

Viewed purely as an escape, there is nothing extraordinary beyond the inconvenience of working upside-down and in water. Houdini correctly surmised that the specter of onstage drowning would pull in crowds jaded by mere escapology.

Houdini asked audience members to hold their breath once he was submerged. This way they could judge how long the oxygen-deprived performer had until irreversible brain damage and/or death. Assistants were standing by, ready to smash the glass if necessary and save Houdini.

Houdini never appeared early. He waited until it seemed like something must have gone wrong. The last spectator would gasp for breath; the whole audience would twitch nervously; the assistants would debate whether to do something. Only then would Houdini throw aside the screen.

That's how it was supposed to work, and how it usually did

work. Thanks to the Tony Curtis movie, a lot of people think Houdini died doing this stunt. He didn't, but he did have an excruciating accident performing the trick several weeks before his death.

In Albany on October 11, 1926, Houdini broke his foot when the stock jerked as assistants prepared to lock him into the cell. This much is fact. Many accounts repeat the canard that Houdini was locked inside the cell before he could communicate what had gone wrong: The grim dilemma that Houdini simulated was played out for real. However, there's no mention of that drama in the *Albany Journal's* story the next day, nor in Harry Kellock's authorized Houdini biography of 1928. Houdini stopped the act instantly and asked if there was a doctor in the house. A Dr. Hannock was. He examined Houdini backstage. The doctor told him he had broken his ankle and should go to the hospital. Houdini valiantly insisted on going on with the rest of the show—but *not*, of course, with the demanding torture-cell escape.

Houdini died a few weeks later from a ruptured appendix probably caused by a young fan's playful punch to his abdomen. Ever the trouper, Houdini completed part of a show in Detroit (not the torture-cell segment, though), then collapsed. Houdini died on Halloween in 1926. His body was shipped back to New York City in a metal coffin he used in his act.

19·

The Gun Trick

The gun trick is the illusion where a magician catches a bullet fired directly at him. It has been billed as "the most wonderful feat ever attempted by living man." It is also reputed to be the most dangerous of illusions. It is said to be jinxed; to have caused the death of a dozen performers; to be the one death-defying stunt Houdini was *afraid* to do.

One performer who isn't afraid to do it is Dorothy Dietrich, who is billed as the "Female Houdini." Her avowed goal is to duplicate all of Houdini's feats. With the gun trick, she has done the master one better. In its most basic form, the trick starts with a member of the audience marking the bullet(s) to be used. Another audience member loads the bullet into the gun, takes aim at the performer, and fires. The performer (standing some distance away—often she has not touched the gun or bullet) catches the bullet and demonstrates it to be the same one that was fired.

Curse of the Gun Trick

Now as to this business about a curse. The gun trick's sinister reputation has a germ of basis in fact. Several well-known performers or their assistants were supposed to have been killed onstage performing the trick, and at least one indisputably was. That tragedy prevented others from performing the illusion for some time afterward.

In a biographical sketch of a performer known as Wyman the Wizard, Houdini quoted a description of the gun trick. It appeared in a book called *Threats of God's Judgments,* published in 1631 by the Reverend Thomas Beard. Beard wrote that "in Lorraine a certain man named 'Coulew' . . . would suffer harquebusses or pistols to be shot at him and catch the bullets in his hand without receiving any hurt; but upon a certain time one of his servants being angry at him, hit him such a knock with a pistol (notwithstanding all his great cunning), that he killed him therewith."

So Coulew didn't die *performing* the feat. Anyway, the stunt was wildly popular in the succeeding centuries. Bullets were caught with bare hands, with the teeth, in a plate, in a silk handkerchief, in a bottle, or even, for an extra dash of brio, on the tip of an extended sword.

Then, within a few years, the trick claimed several lives, or so it was alleged. An Indian performing in Britain, Kia Khan Khruse, was rumored to have been killed doing the gun trick in 1818. But there are surviving playbills denying this very rumor. Long after his "death," Kia Khan Khruse was still doing the gun trick—not to mention such other novelties as turning a ball into a toad and changing barley into wheat (evidently a close-up effect).

Approximately contemporary is the tragedy of a certain De Grisy described in Thomas Frost's 1876 *The Lives of the Conjurors* (a source that accepts as fact the false story of Kia Khan Khruse's death, however). As Frost tells it, De Grisy contrived a William Tell–themed illusion in which he shot a marked bullet at an apple on his son's head. In Strasburg the inevitable mix-up occurred, and De Grisy killed his own son. "This horrible event produced temporary insanity in the unhappy conjurer, who recovered his reason only to undergo his trial for homicide, which resulted in his conviction and six months' imprisonment," Frost wrote.

Frost also tells of a performer named De Linsky performing the trick on November 10, 1820, in Arnstadt, Germany, before the prince of Schwartzburg-Sondershauser. Six soldiers aimed and fired at De Linsky's young wife, who was then expecting a child. A moment later, Madame Linsky cried, "Dear husband, I am shot!" and collapsed. She died a day later.

Houdini wrote a historical sketch of the gun trick and thought about performing it. He never did. Given all the things he *did* do, it hardly seems fair to say he was afraid of the stunt. Fellow conjurer Harry Kellar advised Houdini, *"Don't try the bullet-catching trick.* There is always the biggest kind of risk that some dog will 'job' you. And we can't afford to lose Houdini. Harry, listen to your friend Kellar, who loves you as his own son, DON'T DO IT!" The tone implies that Houdini was pretty serious about trying it.

The best documented gun-trick fatality was that of Chung Ling Soo, one of the most renowned magicians of the early twentieth century. For Soo, the trick was not just an act, it was biography. He claimed to have used it to cheat death at the hands of a Boxer firing squad in 1900.

On March 23, 1918, Soo was playing the Wood Green Empire theater in London. At the appointed part of the show, an assistant invited two audience members onstage. They inspected and pronounced genuine two muzzle-loading rifles, gunpowder, and round lead bullets. Besides evoking the turbulent epoch of the Boxer Rebellion, these simple, old-fashioned arms allayed suspicion of trickery. Soo poured some of the gunpowder out and ignited it, demonstrating that it was the real stuff. Two more audience volunteers were permitted to select two bullets and carve their initials or a secret mark on them.

Soo poured the gunpowder into the rifles, tamped it down, and loaded the chosen bullets, all closely observed by the audience members. Then the loaded rifles were given to two of Soo's assistants, garbed as a Boxer firing squad.

Soo marched to the other end of the stage. A female assistant handed him a china plate. Soo held it out from his chest at arm's length. At a signal, the firing squad fired.

Soo collapsed. Some members of the audience began to applaud, then halted as they realized something really was wrong. The assistants rushed to Soo's aid as the curtain was brought down.

One bullet had passed through the performer's right lung. He was rushed to a nearby hospital, where he died early the next morning.

One of the secrets revealed by his death was that Soo was really an American man, William Elsworth Robinson. Robinson had carried on a kind of ethnic *M. Butterfly* deception, even to the point of appearing for press interviews in Chinese costume and eye makeup and speaking Chinese—or something *claimed* to be Chinese—to an interpreter.

For decades after that, the gun trick was all but extinct. When she revived the gun trick at Atlantic City's Resorts International Hotel in 1988, Dietrich again trotted out the story about Houdini being afraid of the stunt. Dietrich modestly claimed that being the first woman to perform the feat would assure her a place in history. She offered a reward—"$10,000 to anyone who can prove the stunt is gimmicked in any way," according to newspaper accounts.

Good luck collecting that $10,000, but *seriously*, no performer in her right mind is going to brave gunfire that isn't gimmicked.

Dietrich is no more believable on her claim of being the first female bullet catcher. A teenage girl name Annie Vernone was performing the gun trick in England in the 1850s. She was assisted by her sister, who was said to be seven.

The first adult woman, maybe? No, the Great Herrmann's widow, Adelaide, continued her husband's act after his death, including his version of the gun trick. On September 5, 1897, at the Chicago Grand Opera House, Adelaide faced a small firing squad and caught *six* simultaneously fired bullets. As souvenirs, she presented audience volunteers with the bullets, still warm from the gun barrels.

There's no reason to think that Vernone and Mrs. Herrmann were the *only* women to perform the trick before Dietrich; they are just particularly celebrated examples.

That said, Dietrich's act has a few nice twists. She uses a .22-caliber rifle mounted head-high on a metal tripod. Thirty feet away, behind a sheet of shatterproof glass, Dietrich dons safety goggles and holds a metal cup in her mouth. The gun is fired directly at Dietrich's face. Dietrich catches the bullet in the metal cup—then falls to the floor, stunned. She gets up, appears dazed for a moment, then recovers, showing the bullet and the hole in the sheet of glass.

The bullet catch appears to lie somewhere in the middle ground between illusion and death-defying stunt. The tightrope artist's act is for real; the sword swallower's usually is, give or take a blunted edge. Fire eaters, glass walkers, and human cannonballs do more or less what they purport to do, under controlled circumstances.

No matter what its muzzle velocity, every bullet fired eventually comes to rest. If the gun was aimed precisely, and you could be at the right place, couldn't it work? That train of thought is what the performer encourages. But Dietrich is standing thirty feet from the gun, and rifles bring down elks from greater distances.

It's an out-and-out trick, of course.

Soo's Method

An inquest was held to determine the exact cause of Soo/Robinson's death. Authorities interviewed cast members and had a forensic expert examine the guns. The secret of the gun trick thereby became a matter of public record. It was published with great fanfare in the newspapers of the time. That exposure, as much as any question about risk or bad taste, is responsible for the gun trick vanishing from performers' repertoires for years afterward. Like many of the best illusions, the gun trick is based on a simple, audacious principle. Reveal the secret, and there isn't much left.

In outline the gun trick works about the way you'd guess. Anyone with a little sense of how stage magic works must suppose that the gun makes a loud bang but doesn't fire a bullet and that the performer makes a show of producing a mouthed, palmed, or otherwise concealed bullet.

A key witness at the Soo inquest was Mrs. Olive Robinson, the magician's widow. She had appeared as a Chinese assistant (Suee Seen) in the act. Mrs. Robinson testified that the audience's marked bullets were switched for pre-marked bullets. The latter were loaded into the guns. She secretly gave her husband the bullets the audience members had marked so that he could produce them at the proper time.

Mrs. Robinson was not privy to all of her husband's secrets, or so she told the authorities. She was aware, of course, that the guns did not fire the bullets loaded into them. She denied knowledge of how the guns were gaffed. Mrs. Robinson said her husband did not allow anyone else to handle the guns, onstage or off. It was he who loaded the rifles, and it was he who cleaned them after the show.

Forensic gun expert Robert Churchill testified on the guns' workings. They were 12-bore single-barrel rifles. As they were loaded from the muzzle, they required a ramrod to tamp down the charge. This ramrod normally fitted into a parallel tube beneath the barrel.

In performing the trick, Soo removed the ramrods and used them, but did not replace them in their tubes. The ramrods were just set aside. Churchill (who, like much of London, had attended Soo's show) said that he had assumed this was done to keep the show moving. His examination of the guns revealed a stronger reason. The ramrod tubes were actually second barrels.

Soo had bored a channel from the percussion caps to the ram-rod tubes. Before each performance, Soo secretly filled the ramrod tubes with a small charge of gunpowder. When the guns were fired, this charge ignited, producing the noise and flash. The guns' main barrels, on the other hand, were sealed off from the percussion cap. The powder in them never ignited in normal operation. The bullets never fired.

No one in the audience was sharp-eyed enough to tell that the explosion came from the ramrod tube and not from the barrel. Everyone's eyes were on Soo, anyway.

On the fatal night, one of the guns performed exactly as Soo intended. The other gun had developed a lethal defect.

After each performance, Soo had to remove the unfired bullets and gunpowder from the main barrels. A muzzle-loading rifle is normally unloaded using a worm screw. Soo didn't do it that way. Instead, he disassembled the gun. He unscrewed the breech plug and extracted the bullets and gunpowder from the base of the barrel.

Why? The unfired bullets had been marked by Soo. Soo's mark-ings wouldn't match the markings the audience volunteers had carved in the openly chosen bullets. They would pass for the cho-sen bullets in a casual inspection, though, and that was all that was necessary. Using a screw to extract the bullets would mess them up, preventing their reuse. The small economy of reusing the marked bullets is apparently why Soo disassembled the guns each night.

This, said Churchill, was the fatal error. The rifles were not made to be disassembled repeatedly—they should have been taken apart only for occasional maintenance. The thread of the breech plug would soon wear down under daily disassembly. Eventually, it fitted so loosely that the gunpowder (a fine pow-der, not the coarse variety Churchill said that he would have used) seeped through the loose threads, forming a channel from the percussion cap to the main barrel. On the night of Soo's death, both the main barrel and ramrod tube ignited. The bullet fired.

Churchill essentially called the trick an accident waiting to hap-pen. The coroner agreed and ruled the death accidental. (Even so, unlikely stories circulated for years that Soo had been murdered, or even that he had chosen this peculiar method for suicide.)

Liquid Bullets

No one today (one hopes) performs the gun trick quite the same way that Soo did. The gun fires a blank charge of powder but no bullet. In its simplest form, no bullet is loaded into the gun. De Linsky's technique was to have the gunmen bite off the bullet and hide it in their mouths when they bit the cartridge before loading (as was the custom with the type of cartridge used).

Normally, the audience suspects blanks. It's almost mandatory that audience volunteers witness bullets being loaded in the gun. Without that, there's not much of an illusion. The bullet loaded into the gun is usually made of wax, colored black. The wax melts instantly upon firing, producing a diffuse spray of droplets harmless to a person standing any distance away. Frost's *Lives of the Conjurors* states that John Henry Anderson, who allowed spectators to load the gun themselves, gave them bullets of an amalgam made of tinfoil and mercury. These looked like lead and felt as heavy. Once again, the bullet was liquidated, and not the performer.

The principal novelty in Dietrich's act, the appearance of the hole in the glass plate, is a separate contraption that works on cue. Producing a palmed bullet in a cup or in one's hand is a cakewalk for any magician worth her salt.

Dietrich does her best to present the gun trick as a daredevil stunt, not an illusion. Besides that $10,000 reward, she feigns shock from the bullet's "impact." Lest anyone get the impression that it *is* humanly possible to do what Dietrich says she's doing, she says, in so many words, Don't try this at home.

The Heckler Undone

The trick can backfire in other ways. Fortunately, the bullet wasn't made that would kill Professor John Henry Anderson, a British performer who died of natural causes in 1874. Anderson (who claimed to have personally invented the gun trick) offered the bold twist of "Bring your own gun." A wise guy once brought an untricked gun and forced his way onstage. Anderson coolly offered to help him load the gun. He was obviously going to switch his tin-mercury bullet for the real one. The heckler insisted on doing it himself—with his own bullet, of course.

Anderson's next actions earn him a prominent place in the

history of show business, or the history of guts, for that matter. He walked to the designated spot and declaimed, "Now, sir, take a good aim at me and fire!"

The volunteer knew he couldn't do that. Anderson shamed him into giving up the gun. The performer pretended to check the firearm to make sure it was loaded, substituting a fake bullet. He then handed the gun to another, more compliant, audience member to finish the stunt.

Anderson told the audience, "Ladies and Gentlemen, the person who has just resumed his seat knew my trick, and foiled it. If he had fired, this, probably, would have been my last appearance before you. But he hadn't sufficient nerve to shoot me!" This exposed the trick, but it didn't matter. The house gave Anderson one of the most heartfelt ovations in the annals of the theater.

20·

Siegfried and Roy's White Tigers

In 1990 illusionists Siegfried and Roy premiered the biggest, most expensive magic act in the history of the world. Staged in a specially built theater at Las Vegas's Mirage Hotel, the show cost twenty-five million dollars to produce—a movie budget for a nightclub act. Breathtaking ticket prices helped defray the costs of such fancy stage business as a fire-breathing mechanical dragon three stories high; elaborate dance numbers with people dressed as robots, evil princesses, and Klingons for no apparent reason; and the Siegfried and Roy theme, sung at each performance by the recorded voice of Michael Jackson—no bootleg taping, please.

German-born illusionists Siegfried Fischbacher (described in the program as the "soft-spoken, introspective" one) and Roy Horn ("the enthusiastic, voluble one") are the foremost exponents of glam magic. Siegfried is the blond. Central to Siegfried and Roy's extravaganza of kitsch are animals. Where other performers shun sharing the stage with animals, Siegfried and Roy revel in it. Their current show includes a python, a vulture, a horse, an elephant, a lion, panthers, and leopards, not to mention the team's trademark, the largest private menagerie of white tigers in the world. At one point in the show, a violet hemisphere rises from the stage. Set like jewels in it are a dozen or so of the blue-eyed tigers.

Years ago, someone presented the illusionists with a pair of white tiger cubs. These cubs became the Adam and Eve of Siegfried and Roy's burgeoning albino dynasty. Snatched from the brink of extinction, and raised at Siegfried and Roy's fabulous Las Vegas home, the tigers are living refutation of spoilsport talk of inbreeding. They are accomplished performers capable of everything short of palming cards.

Three of Siegfried and Roy's large-animal illusions particularly stand out.

- They make an elephant disappear.
- Roy is tied up and sealed in a box, with Siegfried standing on top. Virtually in the blink of an eye, Siegfried changes into Roy, who then opens the box to reveal a black panther.
- A woman is changed into a white tiger (or vice-versa).

You can't judge these tricks by capsule descriptions. The elephant trick is okay. It sounds a lot better than it looks. The quick-change stunt with the panther, on the other hand, is stunning. And for many people, the familiar-sounding woman-into-tiger trick tops anything else in the show.

The latter, Siegfried and Roy's signature stunt, is one of their simplest, *least* special-effect-intensive illusions. By the performers' megalomaniac standards, the tiger trick is small-scale, almost intimate. Many stage illusions involving large animals are performed far upstage so that everyone in the audience has approximately the same view of the illusion. *But there's something happening on the far side of the illusion setup the magicians don't want you to see.* The upstage location also affords easy access to the backdrop. You can probably guess why.

The tiger illusion breaks these rules. The closest audience members are almost close enough to touch the illusion cabinet. Collectively, the audience has nearly a 360-degree view of the illusion.

That's possible because the custom-built theater in Las Vegas has seating in two orchestra-pit-like pockets surrounded by the stage. The woman-into-tiger illusion is done in front of these choice seats. Some people's front view of the illusion is other people's back view.

A glass cabinet descends from the ceiling on cables. Four of the cabinet's six faces—all except the "roof" and "floor"—are of clear glass. The cabinet is decorated on the outside with a metallic spider web that appears to be purely ornamental. This does not obscure the view of the interior. Inside the cabinet is a woman.

The cabinet descends until it is a few feet off the stage. The cabinet proper is prevented from making contact with the stage by some strutlike supports on its underside. You can see people and objects behind the cabinet through the glass. You can look underneath the cabinet and see the feet of people standing behind it.

Roy pulls a cloth cover up over the cabinet, concealing the woman from view. The cloth isn't in place long. A mere instant later, the cloth drops. Inside the cabinet is a massive, snarling white tiger. The woman is gone.

It's spectacular, and it stands up to close and repeated viewing. There's no backdrop anywhere near the illusion. The *Biggest Secrets* research team took the liberty of examining the stage after the show. The portion of the stage used in the woman-into-tiger stunt was translucent with embedded footlights. A semicircular line or crack was visible. It was unclear if this was a trapdoor. But you can see under the cabinet during the tiger illusion. Some audience members are very, very close. The stage is at head level for those nearest it. Funny business with mirrors and trapdoors would be impossible to conceal.

Special Effects

Many of the effects in Siegfried and Roy's show are not too different from those in old-fashioned, damn-the-expense grand opera. Roy's levitation looks neat, and you can't actually see the wires. The trouble is, you can't see things well enough to *not* see the wires. Without that, there isn't too much to be puzzled over. Or take the dragon, a triceratops head with prehensile claws. There's nothing magical about it; it's just something to look at. The illusions using the dragon look puny in comparison. The act's producer, Kenneth Feld, stated that "the advent of breakthrough technology and the creation of a cutting-edge theater built to their exacting specifications have made this show possible." When you think about it, that's not something you'd want to brag about in a magic act.

That's a recurring problem with this kind of show. You can't have, as the program promises, "the mind-boggling special effects of a blockbuster action movie" without diminishing the illusions. Siegfried and Roy use just about every special effect short of computer animation. When anything is possible, the impossible is mundane.

The animals help bring things down to earth. Many an illusion is done with a sylphlike young woman capable of bending or compressing her body with the skill of a contortionist. Siegfried and Roy claim their adult tigers weigh as much as 600 pounds. That's like doing an illusion with Refrigerator Perry. Tigers and panthers are large, intractable flesh eaters. Like most cats, they are independent and not the easiest things to train. A person wouldn't want to be crammed up against one in some secret compartment when a trapdoor snapped shut on its tail.

You can downplay the danger and say these tigers are big pussy-cats, raised like pets from day one. Okay, but accidents happen. A Siberian tiger mauled Doug Henning onstage during a Christmas Eve show in Lake Tahoe. The tiger charged the audience. Henning gallantly stopped it, then the berserk cat reared on its hind legs and (reportedly) tossed the diminutive Henning fifteen feet across the stage. It jumped on Henning's chest, breaking two ribs and closing its jaws on his head. Henning woke up in a hospital to find Bob Hope cracking jokes at his bedside. Hope had been in the audience. *No* animal is going to be as dependable or intelligent as a human assistant.

Essentially everything Siegfried and Roy do with animals may be explained accepting these two premises: (1) The animals do not have to *do* much of anything to effect the illusions. They are docile props. (2) The animals are tame enough to allow themselves to be closed up in tight spaces without getting riled.

The ingenuity rests with the human performers (and in the design of their equipment).

Making an Elephant Disappear

Let's start with the elephant trick. The garden-variety large-animal appearance/disappearance involves hiding the animal behind a backdrop. That's how Siegfried and Roy make their elephant disappear. Consequently, the elephant illusion is done far upstage.

Roy rides the elephant across the stage to convince everyone that it's a real elephant. It is. Roy and elephant halt at a point upstage center, near a backdrop. Assistants assemble a large cloth screen around the elephant. In short order the screen is opened to reveal Roy, but not the elephant. At this moment of dramatic triumph, the music swells and the lights blaze up. The blinding lights (some aimed at the audience's retinas) keep you from seeing the black cloth screen that is concealing the elephant. Curtains close, and the action moves elsewhere, *fast*.

Metamorphosis

Let's detail the quick-change trick with the panther. The illusion's impact is founded on a seemingly irrelevant fact you probably note only unconsciously: Siegfried and Roy are wearing distinctly different costumes.

A large chest is brought on stage. Roy gets in a sack, and Siegfried ties it up. The sack is locked in the chest. Siegfried climbs up on top of the chest and drapes a curtain over the chest and his body. Just his head shows above the curtain. On a count of three, he ducks under the curtain for a moment, then again, then again—suddenly, *Roy's* head bobs up instead of Siegfried's.

Roy throws down the curtain. Siegfried is nowhere to be seen. Roy is now wearing Siegfried's outfit. Even if you don't consciously notice this, it adds to the sense that Siegfried has "magically" changed into Roy. You don't have much time to ponder, for Roy quickly opens up the chest. Inside is a huge black panther. Siegfried is gone, the sack empty. You barely have a moment for this to sink in before Siegfried appears from the opposite end of the stage.

Siegfried and Roy did not invent this trick. It is known as Metamorphosis or the substitution-trunk illusion. Only the panther is Siegfried and Roy's own touch. Doug Henning performs the trick with his wife and no panther; in fact, most of the big names perform it from time to time, and none of these guys invented it. It was really invented by (again) Houdini.

Houdini, in turn, drew on a tradition of manacled escapes from seemingly impermeable trunks. That isn't the part that bowls people over here. It's the darned-near instantaneous change. You see the one performer's face, then he's gone in a split-second. That was Houdini's, or rather the Houdinis' innovation, for Harry performed it with his wife, Bess. Even the now-usual business about counting from one to three dates back to the Houdinis' act in the first decade of the twentieth century.

Metamorphosis is explained in many magic manuscripts and books. John Novak's comprehensive *Metamorphosis*, available from magic suppliers, runs through all the common variations, including Siegfried and Roy's version with the panther.

Metamorphosis is built for speed, not scrutiny. Chest, sack, and other restraints have secret openings. You never see them properly offered for inspection.

As usually performed, the illusion takes about three minutes.

Performer A is bound in trick handcuffs that snap off in an instant. The audience is none the wiser. The instant he's in the sack, the cuffs come off. The bag is either already open at the bottom or secured only with snaps or Velcro. It doesn't much matter that the *top* of the bag is tied. The instant the chest is shut, the performer pulls the bag up over his head. The chest has a secret panel. It's either on the top or the side, and it swings inward.

Traditionally the cabinet is offered to audience volunteers for inspection. When that is done, the trapdoor must be well hidden. The chest is often made of wood planks braced with metal or wood. Cracks between planks conceal the trapdoor hinge and the door's opposite edge. The other two edges of the door are hidden beneath (and not attached to) the crosspieces. The trapdoor may be opened with a key, or else it's held in place with the same type of magnets used to hold a refrigerator door shut. A handle for opening the trapdoor from the inside would be suspicious. So the performer may use air holes in the trunk as finger holds to swing the panel.

None of that's necessary here. Siegfried and Roy don't offer their metamorphosis cabinet for inspection. Whatever the design, the bound performer is out seconds after the cloth is draped around the trunk.

Performer A now climbs up on top of the chest behind Performer B. He keeps under the cloth, but places his hands just behind Performer B's, so that they're also supporting the curtain frame. Just before the count of three, Performer B drops down. Performer A ducks his head out above the curtain. This typically occurs about two minutes and fifteen seconds after the stunt begins.

In the garden-variety Metamorphosis, Performer B immediately scrambles inside the chest—for the standard denouement is for Performer A to find B tied up inside the chest. Meanwhile Performer A tosses down the curtain. He takes care that it falls across the front of the chest, buying a few seconds' more cover for Performer B. Performer A jumps down and takes a bow.

Etiquette demands that an audience applaud a bowing performer—especially one who has just done something amazing. Once the audience starts applauding, they're likely to continue for ten or fifteen seconds, especially if the performer milks the audience with further bows. Etiquette likewise decrees that the gracious performer must halt what he's doing until the applause dies down.

Performer A flouts the niceties a wee bit. He's in a hurry.

Before the applause quite dies, he pulls away the curtain to fully expose the chest. The rope, chains, and/or padlocks didn't restrict access to the secret panel, but they do now slow down A as he tries to open the trunk. Performer A throws open the chest and unties the sack. Inside is Performer B, bound in handcuffs. We're now three minutes into the stunt.

B has had 45 seconds to get inside the chest, close the panel, pull the sack over himself, and snap on the cuffs. That's not how the audience remembers it, though. They saw B "instantly" change into A. Many will assume the illusion was complete at that instant. The audience scarcely recalls applauding a good ten seconds (that's second nature), nor the time A took struggling with locks and chains. If anything, spectators take away the conviction that A was in such a big rush he didn't have time to accept a full round of applause.

In the Siegfried and Roy variation, Siegfried is not in the trunk, but a panther is. The panther was in there all along. The audience doesn't see inside the chest at the beginning.

Roy is locked in the chest with the unseen panther, and has to wriggle out of his bonds without disturbing the big cat. No problem there. He's obviously on good terms with the cat. Besides getting out of the bag, Roy has to change costumes. The change (involving quick-change artists' peel-off clothes with the second costume worn underneath) adds only a few more seconds to the standard metamorphosis routine. It is customary to place the discarded clothes in the sack so that they won't be visible.

Roy performs the switch with Siegfried. Instead of getting inside the chest, though, Siegfried takes advantage of the cover to steal off into the backdrop. Everyone's looking at Roy by this point. Roy opens the chest to show the cat to the audience. Meanwhile, Siegfried does what is known in the trade as a runaround. He runs around the theater, out of sight of the audience, so that he can appear at the opposite end of the stage or in the audience.

The Lion's Bride

As a premise, transforming a woman into a tiger is not new, either. A history of gender politics could well be written around the many illusions of the past century where a caged woman is changed into a snarling cat. The standard illusion is known by such names as the Lion's Bride and Girl to Lion. Many performers still use it, and in fact, Siegfried and Roy presented a conventional woman-into-cat illusion before they came up with the much-improved model they now use.

In the classic Lion's Bride the performer displays a cage with chrome bars on a wheeled stand. The front door of the cage opens out. A female assistant gets in, allowing the performer to lock her in. The magician drapes a cloth over the cage, concealing the woman. He rotates the covered cage once to demonstrate that there is no connection to the backdrop. Then he whisks the cloth off. Inside the cage is a lion. The woman is gone.

Backdrop

False back to cage is trimmed in same material as backdrop, set with half-bars. To audience, it looks exactly like they're seeing through the cage bars. (One bar removed here for clarity.)

10 inches of crawlspace ingeniously carved out of beveled table top and bottom of cage. That's adequate for an agile, slender woman.

Trap doors
Secret compartment

The illusion turns on two secrets. The first is that the cat is already in the cage when it's brought out. You don't see the cat because it's sequestered behind a false back to the cage. The false back is trimmed or painted to match the backdrop (often black) and set with half-bars duplicating the cage's real bars. The audience thinks they're seeing *through* the cage. They're really seeing only to the false back. This is the Achilles' heel of the illusion. The performer must take care that no person or object is positioned behind the cage from the audience's perspective.

The false back is collapsible. A hinge allows it to fold forward and down into a recess in the floor of the cage. Thus the false back may be folded flat into the cage floor.

The second secret of the cage is that there is a pair of trapdoors in the recessed part of the cage floor. The trapdoors open up and out like shutters. They lead to a secret compartment for the woman to hide in.

Not only is the audience unaware that this hiding space exists, but they would very likely reject this explanation if offered. The secret compartment is concealed according to several standard tricks of illusion design.

You're supposed to think that the cage and its stand are separate, that the cage has been placed on the stand for better visibility. Actually, they're all of one piece. The cage doesn't come off the table top. The secret compartment is partly in the top of the stand and partly in the base of the cage.

The top of the stand is not flat. It's beveled. The outer edges angle up toward the cage. The cage bars do not extend all the way down to the floor of the cage. A frame at the bottom adds a bit more space. And the floor is a bit higher than the top of the frame. The design in Paul Osborne's *Girl to Lion* manuscript provides 10 inches of crawl space. About four inches of that are from the tabletop proper, another two from the bevel, and four inches from the bottom of the cage.

Once the cloth is in place over the cage, the woman opens the trapdoors, crawls inside the cavity, and makes sure the trapdoors close over her.

Under cover of adjusting the cloth or rotating the cage, the performer unlocks two bolt releases mounted on bars on the right and left sides of the cage. These releases hold up the false back. The back is mounted at a slight forward angle, or has a spring hinge, or both, so that releasing the catches causes the back to fall forward to the floor.

A foam-rubber cushion muffles the noise as the false back slams flush with the cage floor. The cat is then free to roam throughout the cage. Oddly, according to Osborne, the falling trap spooks some cats into staying in back. Rubbing meat on the front bars before the performance usually remedies this.

As the magician or assistants wheel the caged cat offstage, it's good practice to let the audience see someone or something behind the cage, through the bars. They'll go home convinced the illusion wasn't done with a false back.

Lady or the Tiger?

Anyone who's seen Siegfried and Roy's glass-cabinet version of the trick will grant it's a great improvement. There *can't* be a false back. People see the glass cabinet from all sides.

Yet the illusion owes something to the older trick, for the woman, and the tiger, are successively concealed in a secret compartment of a cabinet that looks way too thin to have a secret compartment.

The cabinet design employs several tricks that are all the more ingenious for being things the average person never notices.

As we've established, a slim woman can hide in a scant ten-inch-thick space. There's a photograph of Roy standing next to the glass cabinet in the program of the Las Vegas show. By our measurements, the maximum thickness of the bottom of the cabinet is about 17 percent of the height of Roy (who's striking a spread-legged pose). If Roy is six feet tall and stands a couple of inches shorter as posed, that would make the cabinet bottom about 12 inches thick. That's a little bigger than a tiger's head, which is about what you'd expect.

No one goes away thinking the cabinet is thick enough to conceal a tiger. We're so used to boxes, furniture, rooms, and buildings being rectilinear that it's easy to be fooled. When you see a reasonably cube-shaped cabinet, you assume that all the angles are right angles, all the lines straight. The bottom of the cabinet is lens-shaped in the photograph. The edges you see are several inches thinner than the middle is. Because the cabinet is so wide, a nearly imperceptible angle can add several inches of depth.

Another trick: The outer edges of the cabinet are black with a contrasting reflective band in the middle. This design, used in many illusion cabinets, makes the edges look thinner than they are. It's the same principle as a heavy person wearing vertical stripes to look thinner.

At first glance the cabinet looks symmetrical. It's tough to compare top and bottom directly because the bunched-up curtain hides

Weird spidery decoration leads the eye *up*, away from suspicious bottom. Glitter and glass blind audience, make it hard to see dark parts of cabinet.

You're supposed to think that the top and bottom are the same thickness and that both are as narrow as this reflective strip. Not.

Trap doors

Lens-shaped bottom is more spacious than it looks, judging from the edges.

Curtain

The cat: 600 pounds of finicky, but it knows how to fit in a tight space.

the bottom. Given the approximate symmetry, it's easy to carry away the impression that top and bottom must be exactly the same. If you stop and think about it, this is an uncalled-for assumption. The point is, you never stop and think about it. The illusion is over, the cabinet out of sight, before you can scrutinize it. And you're sure the cabinet was too thin to hide a tiger; it was practically all glass.

The spidery decoration is another red herring. As the novel, nonrectilinear element, it looks suspicious. The center of the "web" directs wandering eyes up, away from the bottom.

Even with the see-through design, the background is important. Like its predecessor, the illusion is brightly lighted and performed against dark surroundings. All the things you're supposed to see—the snow white tiger, the narrow reflective bands on the cabinet top, the metallic spider web—blaze away in the noonday glare of floodlights. Things you're not supposed to pay attention to are dark or black. To the audience's eyes, the exact shape and size of the cabinet bottom can be hard to make out against the surroundings.

Other than that, the trick is similar to the older effects. As soon as the curtain covers the glass sides, the woman lifts a trapdoor and gets into an empty compartment carved out of the relatively spacious cabinet. She pulls the trapdoor shut. Most likely, she can release a catch from inside her compartment to open (and then close) another trapdoor, the one imprisoning the tiger. For all their bulk, cats are good at rolling their bodies into a compact ball. It would not take much training to get a tiger crammed into a small compartment to leap up and pace around once it was released. Brushed and fluffed, tail whisking, the tiger fills the entire cubicle.

Appearances in suspended glass cabinets are popular of late. David Copperfield has opened recent shows by appearing inside an empty glass cabinet. This is the same trick without the tiger.

Talented as the tigers may be, they haven't got the knack of lip-synching. Their gut-wrenching roars, a dramatic way of emphasizing the supposed danger, don't match the movements of the tigers' mouths. The same goes for all the other animal noises. They're on a tape that is replayed at every show.

21·

Is Stage Hypnotism for Real?

At the beginning of her nightclub act, hypnotist Pat Collins solemnly promises she won't make audience volunteers bark like a dog. She doesn't. She *does* hypnotize female subjects into believing that their breasts are growing to the size of watermelons, and males into believing that their penis is missing. With shticks like that, many people don't take nightclub hypnotism seriously. Others do. Is nightclub hypnotism for real? Or is it just a bunch of extroverts kidding around?

Collins, like the Amazing Kreskin and other practitioners of stage hypnotism, takes pains to emphasize that what she's doing is real. Collins explains that she became interested in hypnotism when she was cured of hysterical paralysis by a hypnotist as a teen. Aside from her show-business career, Collins offers classes and therapy for treatment of overeating, substance abuse, and other problems.

To emphasize the reality of the hypnotic state, all stage hypnotists have subjects demonstrate immunity to pain or feats of endurance. In the uncanny "rigidity test," a standing subject is given the suggestion that his body is becoming rigid. The subject is then placed like a log on the backs of two chairs, one placed under the shoulder and the other under the ankle.

Pat Collins's Act

Pat Collins's stage setting consists of six chairs. Behind this is the Pat Collins Trio, introduced without intentional sarcasm as "the hippest band in show business." Band members double as prop masters in stunts that require assistance.

Collins asked for subjects from the audience. The six chairs were filled almost immediately. If the night we observed was typical, you would have to have a seat near the front to be selected as a subject. However, Collins offered to hypnotize people in the audience as well as the onstage volunteers.

In Pat Collins's TV shows, the induction of hypnosis is edited out. A voice-over explains that this is to prevent the possibility of anyone becoming hypnotized at home. In the stage show Collins has the onstage volunteers (plus anyone in the audience who wants to be hypnotized as well) fixate on an object in the room—any object. Collins instructs the volunteers to close their eyes and raise their right arms. The right arm, she intones, is to become rigid. On this particular night, two of the six volunteers were sent back to their seats with a mere gesture from Collins. Collins chose replacement subjects from those people in the audience who had been following the arm-rigidity suggestions.

The group of subjects selected and put under, Collins had them stand up individually (by telling them their seat was getting hot, for instance) and tell the audience their occupations. This group included a female weight-training coach, a tile layer, a male exotic dancer, and an unemployed woman. The subjects generally seem to be attractive young people.

Collins asked each subject if they thought they were hypnotized. Of the six, two said yes, one said no, and two weren't sure. Collins commented that people often don't realize they are "under."

To demonstrate that the subjects really were under, she had them raise their right arms in the air again and make them rigid. Collins produced a disposable lighter and ran the flame quickly up and down near the upper part of each subject's arm. She told the subjects they would feel nothing and the only effect would be the singeing of the hair on their arms.

The main part of the act used such stock suggestions as having subjects pretend they are watching a funny movie; pretending they are nude; pretending the audience is nude; and acting drunk after consuming an imaginary drink. Other suggestions included acting out a soap opera, growing breasts, a stolen finger, a stolen male member ("thing" in Pat Collins's lingo), reading *Playboy* or *Play-girl*, and imitating inanimate objects such as vibrators. The show concluded with the rigidity test (the standard one, not a naughty version).

Stage vs. Clinical Hypnotism

As this suggests, there is a world of difference between nightclub hypnotists and clinical hypnotists. A whole raft of people use hypnosis, some with credentials and some without: psychoanalysts, medical doctors, psychologists, weight-loss and quit-smoking clinic personnel, nightclub performers. The various groups of hypnotists aren't always too crazy about each other.

Hypnotism is a debatable subject. There are those who doubt that hypnotism—of any kind—exists. Even in a clinical setting, it's difficult to demonstrate that someone is really under and not just being compliant to the suggestions of a therapist or researcher.

Here we're interested in the nightclub act and how, as a practical matter, its practitioners put on a show night after night. The secrets of stage hypnotism are to be found in manuscripts and books sold through magic retailers. Written by performers for a closed circle of fellow performers, this is stage hypnotism's professional literature.

In no literature we examined did the author come right out and say that hypnotism is bunk. On the contrary, the writers of stage-hypnotism literature all seem to believe in a genuine phenomenon of hypnosis, in the possibility of inducing this phenomenon on-stage, and in the likelihood that some of their stage subjects are at least lightly hypnotized.

By the same token, all the writers countenance, and describe candidly, thoroughgoing deceptions that wouldn't be necessary if things were as pat as the more gullible audience members believe. They mention use of audience plants, hoaxes with prepared props, and physical tests of hypnosis that will work on any willing subject. It sounds like getting people to play along is the core of the stage act, and any real hypnosis, mere lagniappe.

The main secret of stage hypnotism is that the performer selects only the best subjects from a large group of volunteers. In this case, "best" means the most cooperative, outgoing, and funny people;

natural hams who will play along, enjoy themselves, and not do anything to spoil the show. A performer playing to houses of several hundred people will usually narrow down the volunteers to half a dozen.

The tests performed at the start of the show help the performer to choose. Some dignified souls won't even bother to hold their hands up. They're out. Others will hold it up, but at an angle. The performer wants people who hold their arms straight up, as per instructions. People who follow orders during the tests are most likely to follow orders throughout the show.

The stage hypnotist has two points in her favor. People normally don't volunteer in the first place unless they want to be hypnotized and take part in the show. It's best to avoid people unwillingly "volunteered" by friends. Second, it takes a nervy subject to do anything that might ruin the show. The stage hypnotist exploits this pressure. A subject might tell friends he really wasn't hypnotized after the show. Not many would denounce the hypnotist as a fraud in front of an audience.

The only subject the performer has to fear is the rare heckler smart enough to go along with all the suggestions just so he can get onstage and goof off. Learning to spot and avoid hecklers is an important part of a performer's psychological expertise. "Such subjects have a habit of pretending to be asleep while you are watching them, and then while your back is turned open their eyes and poke fun at you," warns Ormond McGill in his *Encyclopedia of Genuine Stage Hypnotism* (1947). McGill's advice will be familiar to any teacher: "Whenever a laugh comes in your show for no apparent reason, be on your guard that someone is faking, and spot that trouble-maker as soon as possible . . ."

Shills, Chloroform, and Choke Holds

Shills have been part of some professional stage hypnotists' acts. A performer billing himself as Professor Leonidas wrote in a classic 1901 book, *Stage Hypnotism*, "You get as many good subjects as possible from the audience and what you can't do with them you can and will do with your trained subjects." McGill opines that "the use of confederates in the audience still has its place to a limited extent in the modern hypnotic act to be sure, but in the acting as 'starters' for the other subjects."

Other deceptions psych the subject into thinking he really is in an alternate state of consciousness. McGill suggests seating subjects in a chair with damp armrests wired to the backstage power supply. Turning on the juice creates "psychological anticipation."

Hypnotists often give suggestions of odors or tastes. The subject is told his fingertips will taste sweet as sugar. This can be faked by coating objects with saccharine. The subject is given some excuse to touch or handle the coated objects earlier in the act. This gets just enough saccharine on the fingertips to facilitate the fingertip suggestion later on. It's easy to imagine that this would make an uncertain subject a true believer. Itching powder has been used to complement the suggestion, "You're itching all over."

There was a time when the recalcitrant subject was considered fair game for just about anything. Would you believe covert use of chloroform? McGill tells how to rig up a device to spray chloroform on the hapless subject. A bottle of chloroform is secreted in a hip pocket, and a tube runs down the arm of the suit. Squeezing a rubber bulb (in another pocket) spritzes the subject, who gets just enough of a dose to cause light-headedness. Easy does it: McGill warns against drenching the subject in liquid. "You will find this method will greatly assist you in hypnotizing the most stubborn cases." The hypnotist is advised to burn Oriental incense to mask the chemical's scent.

The infamous "bulldog method" of Bill Larson was a Vulcan death grip applied to the neck. The two carotid arteries just below the Adam's apple supply blood to the brain. Modest pressure on them causes quick loss of consciousness. Today, use of this technique—by police or rape victims—is controversial. McGill calls it "one of the most cherished secrets of stage Hypnotists." He writes:

You will find that he will suddenly **go limp.** Catch this moment and shout loudly, **"Sleep," and let him drop to the floor in a heap.** Step aside to give the audience a chance to see the "hypnotized" man on the floor. . . .

After that demonstration you will find that subject will be most docile and willing to follow whatever whispered instructions you care to give. It also serves to impress the other subjects on the stage to the end that they'd better co-operate along with you—or else.

McGill warns not to do this to people with heart problems (did his hecklers fill out medical histories?).

Lest there be any doubt, the more progressive hypnotists have sworn off chloroform and choke holds. Pat Collins doesn't use any of this stuff. But she does use the butane-lighter test. That is scarcely less deceptive. Try it yourself. Since heat travels upward, the hot part of the flame is above its center, not to the sides. When the arm is vertical, it is hard to burn it with a small flame.

Rigidity Test

The rigidity test also is not that difficult, hypnotized or not. Two chairs face each other, their backs about five feet apart. A cushion is placed on the back of each so that the subject will be comfortable. According to the literature, the hypnotist chooses the "best" subject for the rigidity test. (But not in Collins's show: She let an audience member choose. However, the audience member is likely to choose the biggest ham of the lot, who often is the best choice.)

The performer instructs the subject to stand feet together, arms at his side. She gives suggestions of stiffness. On a count of three, usually, the subject, she says, will go completely rigid.

One person holds the subject by the shoulders, another by the ankles, and another by the small of the back. They tilt him over and carry him to the chairs. The subject's shoulder blades—not his head or neck—goes on one chair. The legs should contact the other chair a little above the ankles. Collins provides a "modesty band" to cinch in the dress of female subjects.

The performer doesn't leave the subject in this position long. Ten seconds is enough for the audience to get the idea. The subject is lifted off the chair and back into an upright position.

Some professional hypnotists place a rock on the subject's chest and break it with a sledgehammer. That's asking rather a lot of a volunteer subject. There is a trick to it. According to Professor Leonidas's *Stage Hypnotism,* one of his accomplices was always the subject. A folded piece of carpet was first placed on the subject's chest. The rock was a flat slab, so it wouldn't roll off. It was sandstone, which breaks easily. The inertia of the sandstone protects the subject. The rock crumbles before the force of the blow is transmitted.

V: Performance

22·

Blue Movies
of the Famous

A struggling unknown makes a pornographic movie, later becomes
famous, and is haunted forevermore by surviving prints of the film.
It *has* happened, a number of times. Yet an ample measure of
skepticism is called for in evaluating such claims. Titillating stories
involving a famous person are often repeated whether true or not,
and names are supplied with little justification. Generations too
young to remember Clara Bow's movies know her as the actress
who had sex with the entire USC football team. It's what Bow is
best known for today. Saying that she *didn't* do it is like saying that
Homer didn't write the *Iliad* or the *Odyssey*—and also, he had
perfect 20-20 vision. But it's not true. The tale is now acknowledged to be false.

No porn-film rumor is more dogged than the one about Joan
Crawford. Although the first impulse is to credit it to the general
wave of post–*Mommie Dearest* Crawford bashing, the rumor was
current in Crawford's lifetime, long before she was generally held
to be a despicable person. The story often claims that Crawford or
MGM managed to buy up all the embarrassing prints and destroy
them. Almost as old as the story are debunkings of it. Bob Thomas's
1978 biography, *Joan Crawford,* tells it this way: In 1935 a man
claiming to have a print of the film phoned Crawford, and told her
to pay up or else. Crawford referred him to MGM head Louis B.
Mayer. Mayer and MGM attorney Robert Rubin viewed the film.
They concluded that the woman in it *wasn't* Crawford.

Thomas gives no source for this information. *Playboy* writer
Arthur Knight went so far as to search the archives of the Kinsey

Institute (which has a large collection of erotica) for the Crawford film. Knight concluded that there is no such movie, or very probably not, anyway.

We had no luck, either. Anyone trying to locate early porn films of celebrities hears repeatedly that friends of friends have seen the Crawford film or a still from it. Contacting the friends of friends never turned up the film or still itself. Conceivably someone looking like Joan Crawford did do a porno film way back when, but even the look-alike film does not seem to be in general circulation.

To draw the line somewhere, let's consider only those claims backed by the film or videotape itself.

Let's also take the Supreme Court view that a pornographic film is one intended to titillate and without redeeming social value, by the standards of the time. This produces a sliding threshold of pornography whereby old stag films may actually be less explicit than "serious" R-rated films today. The first big star to achieve notoriety for an explicit film was Hedy Lamarr, who came to fame in a Czech-produced art film, Gustav Machaty's *Ecstasy* (1933). At the time, the film's nude scenes were such hot stuff that Lamarr's parents walked out at the premiere and the actress's first husband, millionaire arms dealer Fritz Mandl, tried to buy and destroy every print of the film. However, *Ecstasy* was made with serious intent and taste.

Harder to classify is some footage of Jayne Mansfield taking a bubble bath (outtakes?), and certain clips attributed, not too convincingly, to Marilyn Monroe. *The Misfits* was filmed with a scene in which Monroe exposes her breasts to Clark Gable and the camera. Monroe tried unsuccessfully to convince director John Huston to use the scene in the European release. Likewise, Natalie Wood filmed nude scenes for *Splendor in the Grass,* but they were never used. Presumably this footage still exists somewhere. But sexy outtakes from a legitimate project are not the same thing as a pornographic film, either.

Closer to the mark was the whole string of British sexploitation numbers Joan Collins churned out in the 1970s and early 1980s. *The Stud, Homework, Nutcracker Sweet,* and *The Bitch* are more explicit, in an absolute sense, than *Ecstasy,* and have no pretense to artistic merit. One critical opinion of *The Stud:* "a cheap sex show." Still, films had become much more explicit in general in the four decades since *Ecstasy,* leaving the Collins films in the limbo of very, very soft porn. Besides, Collins was already a well-known fading starlet when she made *The Stud,* and she doesn't try to hush up the fact that she made these films.

Today there is perhaps nothing so explicit that it could not appear in a regular, nonpornographic movie. Madonna must wince when she thinks of her role in *A Certain Sacrifice* (1981). It's an *awful* movie where she plays a woman who gets raped and smeared with blood. But no, *A Certain Sacrifice* isn't a pornographic film; it's a bottom-of-the-barrel exploitation number. The average person understands pornographic films to be those produced to be shown in seedy theaters, rented out for bachelor parties, or rented in so-called adult sections of video stores. Some of today's biggest stars have made them.

Did Barbra Streisand Make a Porn Film?

When Barbra Streisand filmed the legitimate 1970 comedy *The Owl and the Pussycat,* she did a nude scene on the condition that she have a right to veto its use if she didn't like it. She didn't like it. Streisand and the filmmakers struck a compromise. They used the scene but had it "fogged"—the detail was obscured in the printing. Years later, someone got hold of stills from the shoot— unfogged, of course—and sold them to a sleazy men's magazine called *High Society.* Streisand successfully sued the magazine. This has tended to create an impression of her as having a conservative view of film nudity. Despite this, stories tell of a pornographic film Streisand made before she became famous.

A tape clip exists that contains about fifteen minutes' worth of grainy black-and-white footage of a nubile, prominently nosed woman looking uncannily like a younger Streisand having sex with a man (who resembles no one famous). This clip is light-years more explicit than the coy films mentioned above. Extended and monotonous footage shows the actress fellating and copulating with her boyfriend from almost every angle, and the actor exposing the actress's vagina for a camera lens that seems to be just inches away.

It's hard to reconstruct the circumstances under which the film was made. The tape has no credits or copyright notice, and its origin is lost in a farrago of repeated duplication. The clip has been shown on sex-oriented cable-TV shows, and the off-air tapes have been passed from collector to collector. Whoever put together one compilation video in circulation clearly wants you to think that it's Barbra Streisand in the footage. The tape cuts several times between a still publicity photo of Streisand and the porn footage. The porn footage proper doesn't look professional enough to have been commercial erotica. It looks like a home movie that a friend shot (only it's a lot longer and more graphic than you would expect from someone playing around with a camera).

Is it Streisand? A tape with credits gives the fact-conscious investigator something to go on. The cast may not have used their real names, but someone associated with the film may be around to say whether it was or wasn't Streisand. Here there are no such clues.

The quality of the tape we saw is comparable to that of an old 8-millimeter home movie transferred from film to videotape. The actress's face is not visible all the time, partly because of the filmmaker's obsession with other parts of her body. At its best, the image quality of the facial close-up shots is comparable to a head shot in a newspaper. While it's not the sharpest film ever shot, you can't say that it could be anyone. It's someone who looks like Streisand, and actresses with noses that could be mistaken for hers are not common in blue movies.

The woman appears to be in her late teens or early twenties. A photograph of Streisand at the age of 18 has been published in biographies. It's an unflattering shot of her rehearsing for her nightclub act. She looks much less polished than the Barbra of today: She's chubby, has long stringy hair, and there's a trace of acne or some skin problem. The woman in the film is on the chubby side, has long hair, and appears to have bad skin—or is it the tape? She looks reasonably similar to the Streisand photo.

Streisand's career took off in 1963, the year she turned 21. In a publicity photo from the mid-1960s, a then thoroughly glamorized Streisand appears to have a slight mole or blemish under her lip on the right side, and two even smaller marks above her right breast. No such distinguishing marks were visible in the film clip. The grainy tape might not show such detail, though, and other clear still photos of Streisand don't show the marks.

The tape we saw had a rock soundtrack that was apparently added later. There was no voice to compare with Streisand's.

Resemblance, however great, proves nothing. It is possible that someone noticed a coincidental resemblance between Streisand and a prominent-nosed porn actress and then (innocently, maliciously, or just as a joke) passed the clip off as film of Streisand. It is barely conceivable, taking a somewhat paranoid stance, that someone produced the film as a hoax, hiring a Streisand look-alike, and intentionally making the tape amateurish and grainy to simulate authenticity.

We screened the clip for a group of three viewers. Two said they believed the actress was Streisand. The third was less certain but felt it might be her.

That leaves only Streisand and the uncredited people who made the film knowing the truth of the matter. Our letter to Streisand, asking her to confirm or deny her participation in the film, brought no response.

Chuck Connors's Blue Movie?

Another erotic clip in circulation is attributed to Chuck Connors. You'd have a tough time guessing that from the tape copy we saw. The tape was many generations removed from the original print.

This clip shows two sailors in a park, who shed their uniforms and have sex. There are no facial close-ups. Only one shot would likely suggest Chuck Connors to a viewer who had not been clued in as to who it was supposed to be. For a few seconds, the blond man is on his back, his face visible. He looks vaguely Chuck Connors–esque there. The alleged Streisand clip is more compelling because the resemblance holds up from various angles.

In the absence of any information about where the tape came from, you can't do much more than shrug and say maybe it is Connors, and maybe it isn't. Connors didn't reply to our inquiries, either.

The Rob Lowe Sex Tapes

The best-known amateur erotic film of recent times is Rob Lowe's. Shortly after the Lowe sex-tape scandal hit the press, bootleg copies were reportedly being sold for as much as $5,000. *Screw* magazine publisher Al Goldstein said he paid $15,000 for his copy. Goldstein has since defrayed this cost by hawking copies via mail order.

Lowe picked up some women in an Atlanta nightclub on the

night of July 17, 1988, and made a private video. The tape shows Lowe having sex with two mystery women (identified as Justin and Jennifer). Another man (Mark) watches and also has sex with the women. Brief clips of the tape were shown on tabloid TV shows, the participants' writhing bodies censored with a large black rectangle. Both video and audio quality are poor. It's hard to hear most of the dialogue. Lowe asks one woman, "Is it hot in here or is it just me?"

The tape was clearly made with the knowledge and consent of all. At one point in the tape Lowe says, "Look at this when you're done, and see what you look like." However, the mother of one of the participants initiated a suit against Lowe, charging that the actor "used his celebrity status as an inducement to get females to engage in sexual intercourse, sodomy, and multiple party sexual activity for his immediate sexual gratification, and for the purpose of making pornographic films of these activities."

The whole thing gets kind of confusing because Jan Parsons, on whose behalf the suit was brought, isn't in the version of the tape that's widely available. She was underage. It remains difficult to say who was the most culpable. While Lowe was in the bathroom, Parsons and a friend swiped the videocassette from the camera and left. According to Lowe, they also helped themselves to some excess cash he had lying in his wallet. The two women paid to have the cassette duplicated, and were not so traumatized by the matter to preclude telling friends that they had met Rob Lowe. According to a neighbor's affidavit, Parsons invited people to see the tape and said she was going to use it to blackmail Lowe for $2 million.

(As of this writing, the tape is available, as part of a *Midnight Blue* episode, from Media Ranch, P.O. Box 432, Old Chelsea Station, New York, NY 10011.)

Sylvester Stallone in *A Party at Kitty and Stud's*

Not all porn movies involving now-famous people are amateur efforts. Most denialproof is the professional blue movie with screen credits.

Forget the story about Woody Allen "discovering" Sylvester Stallone. True, Allen cast the then-unknown actor as a subway terrorist in *Bananas* (1971). But Stallone had already achieved star billing the previous year for his role in the XXX-rated sleazefest, *A*

Party at Kitty and Stud's. In 1985, the year that *Rocky IV* and *Rambo II* came out, the porno film's money-hungry yet legally justified owners rereleased *Party* on video, to Stallone's considerable mortification. The distributors retitled the video *The Italian Stallion.*

The plot: Kitty (Henrietta Holm) and Stud (Stallone) are hormone-crazed Aquarian Age hipsters who can barely stand to be apart. The camera finds homebound Kitty pining for Stud: "Oo, I wish Stud'd hurry up and get home. He's so animalistic. I love getting him mad. It gets me so horny." This cuts to Stud running home through the snow. He trips—one of several gaffes that probably wasn't in the script. Retakes cost *money.*

Once Stud gets home, the mod couple hit the green paisley sheets (which match the green paisley wallpaper). A typical line for Stallone's character: "Be careful, you bit me last time." When Kitty isn't keeping him busy, Stud has a mirror where he can see beautiful lesbians "making it."

Stud goes to a poker game. Kitty practically goes nuts being separated from him. When transcendental meditation fails to take her mind off sex, she takes off all her clothes and dances around the house. Finally she gets a grip on herself and sets out some wine and marijuana to get Stud "in the mood" when he returns. "Stud says a girl hasn't completed her education until she knows how to really lick a good joint. He's so far out!"

When Stud does get home, he's angry, either because he lost all his money or he passed up a chance to have sex with a woman in the street. He slams his fist into glass and cuts himself. Definitely for specialized tastes is the following shot, a mind-numbing 48-second close-up of Kitty licking obviously fake blood from Stallone's hand and getting it all over her face.

The couple have sex again; Stud gets mad again and whips Kitty with his belt; they have sex again to make up; and then Kitty and Stud throw a party where all the guests have sex with each other, some in front of a fun-house mirror.

The players in *Party* actually seem to be playing themselves, actors and actresses so insanely desperate for exposure that they're willing to appear in a movie like *A Party at Kitty and Stud's.* Stallone's character talks about moving to Hollywood and wanting to be famous someday. One of the actresses speaks volumes when she says, "Hell, he told me this was going to be an art movie."

A *Party at Kitty and Stud's* was directed by Morton Lewis from an original screenplay by Milton Lewis. Stallone reportedly earned two hundred dollars, plus nothing of the gross.

(Available from JEF Films, 143 Hickory Hill Circle, Osterville, MA 02655; [508] 428-7198.)

In Search of Coppola's 3-D Porn Opus

Long before *The Godfather*, even before *Dementia 13*, Francis Ford Coppola directed at least two porno films. One is in 3-D.

Coppola's first film was *Tonight for Sure*. Shot before the twenty-two-year-old Coppola graduated from UCLA, *Tonight for Sure* was released by Premier Pictures Company in 1961. *Tonight for Sure* is no mere student film. Nor is it an art film that happens to include nudity. It's your basic early 1960s stag-party number, a movie that exists solely to show women's breasts and buttocks (though no sex). Coppola directed a cast of guaranteed nonprofessionals, plus a few real burlesque performers. Most of the latter have just one name (Electra, Exotica, etc.). Exotica's name is misspelled in the credits.

Like *Apocalypse Now*, *Tonight for Sure* is practically all flashbacks introduced by voice-over narration. Unlike *Apocalypse Now*, *Tonight for Sure* uses that technique to recycle footage of massively endowed naked women from an unfinished pornographic western. *Tonight for Sure* is two movies stitched together. One is a dirty western about a cowboy who keeps having hallucinations of nude women. The cowboy looks at a cactus, and it turns into an attractive woman with large breasts. He looks at a herd of cows' rear ends, and they turn into the shapely rear ends of naked women. The other movie is about a prude (who's really a sex fiend) plotting to stamp out "indecent feminine exposure." He's so obsessed with getting rid of a pinup photo studio near his apartment that he keeps nude photos in his apartment for study purposes. He keeps trying to spy on the nude photo sessions, resorting to telescopes, bombs, tunneling into the photographer's studio, and other Peeping Tom antics that would earn him a jail sentence if this were real life, rather than an alternate Russ Meyer universe.

All of the above is incorporated in *Tonight for Sure* via a frame story about the Peeping Tom and a "friend" of the sex-crazed cowboy. The pair meet at a burlesque house and plant a device to turn off the lights at midnight. That way, the customers won't be able to see the strippers. While waiting for this to happen, the conspirators order round after round of drinks and swap stories. The friend of the cowboy sets up the western footage. It would make a lot more sense if the man in the nightclub *was* the cowboy, flashing back to his own past, but he's not. He's not even in the western footage, and the actor in the western footage does not appear in the main, nonflashback story line.

By midnight the two men are so smashed they get up on the stage to cavort with the strippers. Just then, the lights go out. A decency league shows up to picket the burlesque house, and pandemonium erupts.

Peter Cowie's *Coppola* (1990) says that Coppola had shot a risqué short feature, *The Peeper*, to cash in on the booming market for soft porn. This became the voyeur story line. Coppola hooked up with people who had money and smutty cowboy footage. They decided to join the two films, undeterred by the fact that they had nothing in common besides frontal nudity. Coppola shot the frame story about the burlesque house. He told Cowie, "Sixty to seventy percent of it was not my work, but I was so eager for recognition that I shot the credit sequence and printed 'directed by Francis Ford Coppola' up on the screen!"

Coppola is too modest. The credit says, "Produced and Directed by Francis Ford Coppola," the writing is credited to Coppola and another guy (Jerry Shaffer), and, by our timing, Coppola's frame story and *Peeper* footage make up fully 78 percent of the movie. Even during the fourteen minutes of non-Coppola western footage, it's clear that the voice-over narration, delivered by the actor in the frame story, was written for the combined movie. Coppola's father, Carmen, gets screen credit for the film's music. This consists mainly of jazzy bumps and grinds every time a nude woman is on the screen.

Tonight for Sure is intended to be funny. A typical joke for which Coppola took cowriting credit: "By the corral, you can just sit for hours and smell the wind, watch the cows. Sometimes you watch the wind and smell the cows. It all depends on which way the breeze is blowing." The movie *is* pretty funny due to the amazingly bad acting of the bit players. Don't miss the parking attendant and waitress's lame reaction shots, or the "spectacular fire dance of Electra," a strange woman jiggling in the midst of some red strips of fabric flapping in a wind machine's exhaust. (Available from Video Yesteryear, Box C-137, Sandy Hook, CT 06482.)

Coppola entered yet another sexy dimension with *Bellboy and the Playgirls,* released by Screen Rite Picture Company in 1962. Once again the movie isn't entirely Coppola's, but, yes, *all* the 3-D parts are. *Bellboy* started life as a 1958 black-and-white German film, *Mit Eva fing die Sünde.* Coppola was hired to repackage it by shooting new material, including 3-D color footage of *Playboy* centerfold June Wilkinson. Wilkinson receives star billing in the repackaged film. The title character is a hotel employee who spies on buxom guests through keyholes. When he spies on Wilkinson, she busts right off the screen for lucky viewers wearing polarized glasses. It would have taken a hard-hearted continuity checker indeed to point out the lack of stereoscopic vision from a keyhole.

Reportedly, only eight 3-D prints were made. *Bellboy* played many adult theaters, not always in 3-D. The film was released for home video by Sony Video Communications, which recently dropped it from its catalog, leaving the film without a video distributor.

Critic R. M. Hayes wrote of *Bellboy and the Playgirls,* "It is pointless to really criticize this thing; it was made for the sixties 'raincoat' crowd and intended only as a fast buck for grind-houses . . ."

23.

Ingmar Bergman's Soap Commercials

Many people have a crummy job they leave off their résumés. Some waited on tables. Some sold encyclopedias. Some *only sold their souls*. Yes, there is a small corpus of bad television and commercials made by first-rate "serious" writers and directors during their lean years and now calculatedly omitted from lists of credits. Though disavowed, and often not shown since television was young, these early efforts are preserved in unforgiving celluloid or videotape. We sought out copies of these forgotten gems of TV's vast wasteland.

Bergman Pitches Soap

During the 1951 Swedish Film Industry strike, Ingmar Bergman was hard-up for cash and directed nine commercials for Bris ("Breeze"), a Swedish brand of deodorant soap. Like all Swedish commercials, they were shown in movie theaters before the feature, not on TV. Never seen in the U.S., most of the Bergman soap commercials are preserved in the archive of the Swedish Film Institute, in Stockholm.

Bergman was not an unknown when he took the commercial work. By 1951 he had several feature films under his belt. He wasn't well-known overseas—*Smiles of a Summer Night* was several years in the future—but he was a respected working director in Swedish theater and film.

Sweat doesn't smell. That's Bergman's message in the Bris commercials. Bris was Sweden's first deodorant soap, and Bergman was charged with explaining the concept of deodorant soap to the Swedish public. All nine commercials feature a sales pitch that translates as, "Sweat doesn't smell, it's the skin bacteria which do it, when they come into contact with your sweat. . . . Bris kills bacteria! No bacteria, no smell!" Bergman didn't write that. An ad agency did and required that it be incorporated in each commerical. Otherwise, Bergman had creative control. He wrote everything else and directed.

While every bit as mercenary as the foregoing suggests, the commercials are identifiably Bergman's. A kind of horrible self-parody produces close-ups (of someone's hands holding soap), infrequent cuts, and pans (between attractive nude women lathering up and white-coated, hard-sell-spouting male "experts"). All nine Bergman commercials involve a movie or performance within the commercial. Bergman used the same device, *later,* in *The Seventh Seal, The Magician, Through a Glass Darkly,* and *Hour of the Wolf.*

Most grotesque are those commercials in which Bergman essays a cinematic explanation of the phenomenon of perspiration. It was evidently Bergman, and Bergman alone, who created Brisman, the superhero mascot of Bris soap. A commercial titled "The Magic Show" finds Brisman wrestling with a bacterium. That's right, someone was paid to dress up as a microbe. In a 1988 article on the Bris commercials in the film journal *Chaplin,* Bergman scholar Maaret Koskinen stops just short of branding as derivative Wood Allen's talking sperm cell in *Everything You Always Wanted to Know About Sex.*

Another commercial ("The Magic Theater") starts with a young woman finishing a set of tennis and heading for the showers. In the pseudoscientific tradition of 1950s commercials, a narrator reveals what is happening on "the human skin, greatly magnified." An actor dressed as a bacterium chases an anthropomorphized drop of perspiration. His goal is to catch it and create odor. Two extremely silly-looking actors fight it out until subdued by soap lather (not another actor—balloons).

When Bad Sitcoms Happen to Good Writers

Neil Simon and Gore Vidal are the rare exceptions—respected writers who can look back on their forays into prime-time American television without being completely aghast. Most are not so lucky.

Many genre writers have written for television. Some of the results are more predictable than others. Jim Thompson, American hard-boiled novelist beloved of French intellectuals, wrote episodes of *Combat* and *Mackenzie's Raiders*. It's fairly well-known among science-fiction fans that Harlan Ellison wrote a *Star Trek*. Not so well known is that he also penned an episode of the somewhat science-fictional *Flying Nun*. Ellison had the presence of mind to use a pseudonym (Cordwainer Bird) on his episode, which is no better than a *Flying Nun* ought to be. "You Can't Get There from Here" is *The Flying Nun*'s homage to *Gilligan's Island*. Sister Bertrille (Sally Field) is stranded on a desert island with playboy Carlos Ramirez (Alejandro Rey).

More surprising is the relatively prolific bad TV career of Stephen Sondheim. Long before his Broadway successes, Sondheim wrote or cowrote about a dozen scripts for *Topper,* one of TV's earliest fantasy sitcoms. Banker Cosmo Topper (Leo G. Carroll) lives in a house populated by ghosts that only he can see. The series is theoretically in syndication but is rarely shown. We tracked the scripts to the Wisconsin Center for Film and Theater Research, in Madison, to which Sondheim donated them.

The most tantalizing find among the Sondheim scripts occurs in an episode titled "Preparations for Europe." Topper's wife, Henrietta (Lee Patrick), enters a breakfast cereal's jingle contest to win a trip to Europe. What are the jingle-contest entries but lost and unheralded Sondheim lyrics?

The contest requires Henrietta to complete a jingle beginning, "Everyone loves Individual Oats . . ." Her entries include

Everyone loves Individual Oats
They're just like music with beautiful notes.
. . . / It's the cereal on which the whole family dotes.
. . . / The person who eats them gloats.
. . . / It's the cereal everyone votes—for.

The latter entry, which wins the contest, prefigures Sondheim's mastery of internal rhyme.

Joseph Heller's *McHale's Navy* Episode

In 1962, the year after *Catch-22* was published, Joseph Heller wrote an episode of *McHale's Navy*. Aired originally on ABC on

November 1, 1962—and still running in syndication—"PT 73 Where Are You?" was written by Heller and produced and directed by Edward J. Montagne. Montagne confirmed for us that the screen-credited "Joe Heller" is indeed *the* Joseph Heller. *Catch-22* did not become a best-seller until its paperback publication in late 1962, and Heller presumably needed the money. Montagne said he had not heard of Heller or *Catch-22* at the time he assigned the script. He was sold entirely on the merit of Heller's pitch: McHale's men lose the PT boat. "I liked the idea," Montagne told us. "It was funny."

Is the Heller *McHale's Navy* episode discernibly better than the average *McHale's Navy* episode? An employee at one of the few stations showing *McHale's Navy* reruns was good enough to send us a tape of the Heller episode. Here's the plot.

Captain Binghamton (Joe Flynn) orders Commander McHale (Ernest Borgnine) and his men to New Caledonia for a week's leave. But one of the men has lost the PT 73 on a date with an island woman. McHale sends two sailors to find the boat. Meanwhile, McHale's men drape camouflage nets over a pile of junk to simulate the missing boat. Binghamton shows up for a surprise inspection. Admiring the camouflage job, he looks under the nets and discovers the boat is missing. Binghamton asks McHale where his boat is. McHale says he lost it. Binghamton gets upset, cancels the leave, and prepares to court-martial McHale. While Ensign Parker (Tim Conway) assists Binghamton with the court-martial papers, McHale's men steal the PT boat of sycophantic Lieutenant Carpenter (Bob Hastings). They paint over its identification number with "PT 73." McHale tells Binghamton that the PT 73 has been found. That gets McHale off the hook, but Binghamton orders Carpenter to New Caledonia instead of McHale. Carpenter reports that he has lost *his* boat. Binghamton gets upset.

They find the real PT 73. Now McHale has two PT 73s. McHale's men hide the real PT 73 and repaint it with the identification number of Carpenter's boat. An anonymous phone call leads Carpenter's men to this boat. Thus Carpenter has McHale's boat and McHale has Carpenter's. Carpenter boasts to Binghamton that his boat is always ready for combat. Binghamton finds McHale's cache of beer inside the torpedo tube and blames Carpenter. McHale gets to go on the leave after all. En route to New Caledonia in Carpenter's boat, Gruber (Carl Ballantine) realizes he has forgotten to stock the boat with beer, and McHale yells at him.

Heller's episode falls in the so-called Taratupa period of *McHale's Navy*, usually judged more successful than the late or Voltafiore period. Going by the laugh track, there are 130 humorous lines or sight gags in the Heller episode. This compares with 126 laughs in a control episode not written by Heller. A typical line that Heller evidently wrote: "I'd never last on submarine duty—I like to sleep with the windows open!" Ironically, *Catch-22*'s early critics faulted its plotting as being "of the type which television comedians blame on their 'writers' " (*Daedalus*, Winter 1963).

24·

The Wasteland

The Truth About Lassie

You might think that because Lassie is a fictional dog whose original TV show has long been off the air, there is, at this point in time, no Lassie. You'd be wrong. There is no Timmy right now, but there will always be a Lassie as long as dog shows, conventions, state fairs, and rodeos are willing to shell out as much as $7,500 for Lassie to appear.

Lassie is, strictly speaking, a literary character, the canine protagonist of Eric Knight's 1940 novel, *Lassie Come Home*. Lassie as a real dog dates from the 1943 movie with Elizabeth Taylor. That means Lassie has been around five decades, or 350 dog years. Everyone knows that Lassie has been played by quite a few different dogs. This is not the only secret of TV's enduring canine. The dog you see is the combined product of fake fur, bleach, and eugenics.

Rudd Weatherwax trained the first Lassie, a brainy male known offstage as Pal. Pal had a white streak running between the eyes and up the forehead. As Pal grew old, Weatherwax had a problem. He needed another dog with the same white streak to take over.

Subsequent Lassies are the result of a *Boys from Brazil* mass-breeding scheme. Pal's genes were doled out to dozens of likely bitches with the hope of producing more of his remunerative kind. The Weatherwax family has bred and raised over 3,000 collies just to get the seven reasonably intelligent and pliable specimens, *with* the trademark shock of white, that have assumed the role of Lassie. All the Lassies have been male. Behind each Lassie that you see are an average of some four hundred rejects. At this writing, the present (seventh) Lassie is a lineal descendant of the others. The trademark honey blond color is not natural for a collie. Lassie is bleached.

The late Rudd Weatherwax was a feisty sort with little patience for Lassie detractors. These included embittered individuals within the show-dog world who hated Lassie because she wasn't perfect. The white streak is considered undesirable for the breed. As far as some people are concerned, collies like that should be put to sleep. In 1989 Rudd Weatherwax's son Bob recalled, "The collie people at the dog shows would always tell us, 'You know, you have a flawed collie; he would never win any awards.' One day my father . . . reached into his pocket and held up some money. 'You go ahead and collect the blue ribbons,' he said. 'I'll keep collecting these ribbons.' " It's this in-your-face attitude that makes Lassie so special.

There are, and always have been, doubles and stunt dogs. The actual number of Lassies, broadly interpreted, is indeterminate and considerably larger than seven. The stand-ins are often castoffs of the Lassie breeding program, genetic near misses who didn't quite have what it takes. A current stunt dog named Roxy has the white streak, but one of his paws is dark rather than white. Roxy wears a socklike prosthesis of white fur for the camera.

The Pillsbury Doughboy

Much of the food in Pillsbury Doughboy commercials is inedible. That's not a critique of Hungry Man Butter Tastin' Biscuits; the food is actually made of synthetic goop. It has to be fake to look real.

The Doughboy has been created both by stop-action animation (like Gumby, with an actual posable Doughboy action figure) and by computer animation. Unlike other animated characters, the Doughboy plays with food. He touches baked goods, tests cake with a toothpick, and tosses a pizza. That poses special challenges. Real food does not last long under hot lights. Baked goods dry out and collapse, icing melts. While Poppin' Fresh sneaks a bite of cake—mere seconds on your TV screen, but sometimes hours in the studio, getting everything perfect—you ought to see the cake disintegrate before your eyes.

Whenever possible, the commercial makers simply superimpose the Doughboy on a shot of food. They can't do that when he interacts with the food. Then someone has to dent the touched baked goods in the studio. So they use fake food, glued to the cookie sheet so that no one moves it accidentally.

The fakes raise problems of their own. Several years back, the government cracked down on use of deceptive stand-ins in food ads. The crackdown has made life difficult for Poppin' Fresh and his human helpers. Government requirements say the body-double edibles can't look bigger or more appetizing than real Pillsbury products. According to Doughboy commercial stylist Carol Peterson, photos of the fake food used in the commercials are routinely sent to Pillsbury's legal department for comparison with photos of the corresponding edible stuff.

Is Jerry Lewis on Drugs for the Labor Day Telethon?

There is a widespread belief that Jerry Lewis uses drugs to stay alert for his Labor Day telethon. "To get through his grueling round-the-clock muscular dystrophy telethon last September, Lewis had a doctor friend inject painkilling Xylocaine into his back," claimed a writer for *People* magazine in 1978. Such reports may have fueled the legend. But this was for back pain, and the legend refers to stimulants.

Certain drugs cause speech disturbances. Consider the following statements from past telethons: "The romantic ballad will never be dead as long as this man's music is in demand." And: "Mel Torme's talent goes from the galaxy to the universe and back." These are not made-up quotes. Jerry Lewis actually said them.

We wrote Lewis, politely putting the question to him. He promptly replied that he does *not* take drugs. Lewis wrote (this is not an edited statement; the ellipses are in the letter): "On the last telethon that I did for the Muscular Dystrophy Association . . . I made a statement which could have been interpreted as taking 'drugs' to stay awake. Since I am violently opposed to drugs and pills of any kind I'd like to set the matter straight!! During the telethon . . . actually the last 12 hours . . . I take vitamin pills and a vitamin B-12 shot . . . this does keep my energy up . . . and helps to keep me awake."

Vitamin B-12 is sometimes claimed to enhance athletic endurance or cure memory loss. *Consumer Reports* (1989) noted that "some physicians give B12 injections to patients as a placebo, to alleviate what the doctor feels are psychosomatic symptoms."

How Award Shows Keep the Winners Secret

With all the media attention and even all the money riding on bets, you have to wonder how Price Waterhouse manages to keep Academy Award winners a secret. For it's not just Mr. Waterhouse counting all the ballots himself in his locked office one night. It takes a team of about eight employees to count the nearly 5,000 multicategory ballots. Then someone in a print shop has to print up the winners' names for the envelopes. If just one of these people were to tell one other person who wasn't as trustworthy as they thought, the secret could get out quickly.

Advance information could fetch high prices. One year Chevy Chase brazenly tried to bribe Price Waterhouse's Daniel R. Lyle. Chase flashed a $1,000 bill and told Lyle he wanted just one winner's name to use in his monologue. He didn't get it.

According to Price Waterhouse, the ballots are "derandomized" as they are apportioned to the counters. They make sure that the counters get nonrepresentative samples of the total vote. Otherwise, each counter (who has more than 600 of the total 5,000 ballots) would be able to project many of the winners. Each counter sits in his or her own room and isn't allowed to talk to the other counters.

To avoid print-shop leaks, Price Waterhouse prints up cards with the names of *all* the nominees. Shortly before the telecast, someone from the accounting firm puts the right cards in the envelopes. Two complete sets of cards in envelopes are made up, and two executives from the firm take them to the theater in separate cars (in case one is delayed).

Other televised award shows use similar techniques. The downside of printing up all the nominee's names is that a losing name may get in the envelope. It's not happened (yet) for the Oscars, but it has on other award shows. At the 1990 Soul Train Music Awards, presenter Young M.C. announced the winner for best urban contemporary single to be Karyn White. White *was* nominated, and her name *was* in the envelope, but she wasn't the winner. It was Janet Jackson. Price Waterhouse corrected the error too late to make even the tape-delayed telecasts. Fortunately, or unfortunately, depending on how you want to look at it, neither White nor Jackson was there to gush, act gracious, or claw a coveted award out of the other's hands. A similar flub gave *The Young and the Restless* an undeserved 1986 Daytime Emmy for writing.

25.

Backward Messages
on Records

Hidden illicit messages are almost as old as the recording medium. A bootleg tape of a classic Metropolitan Opera production of *Madame Butterfly* has Geraldine Farrar singing, "He's had a highball!" instead of *"Sì, per la vita!"* to an inebriated Enrico Caruso. You won't hear this on the legitimate release, though (Victor DM 110).

If you listen carefully to the Who's "Who Are You?" (1978), you can hear Roger Daltry singing, "Who the fuck are you?" behind the title words. It's so subtle that it's more or less an inside joke. But the program director's dilemma of whether or how to play a popular song incorporating the seven words you can't say on the air is often a serious one. A semi-audible word in Alice in Chains's "Man in the Box" (*Facelift* album) is *spit* when played on the radio, but *shit* on the album. The "spit" remix is a "radio edit" produced expressly for airplay on more conservative stations.

In recent years, the issue of secret messages on records has taken a darker turn. Widespread allegations charge that backward messages on rock albums have driven listeners to desperate acts. It's hard to know what to believe. LPs could be turned backward with a steady finger, but that was rarely satisfactory. There's no low-tech way of reversing a cassette or CD.

For this investigation, we purchased new CDs of a number of albums alleged to have backward or otherwise concealed messages. The CD player was hooked to an audio digitizer, which fed the music into a computer. There, software allowed the music to be edited, reversed, amplified, split into stereo tracks, and otherwise manipulated to uncover any messages.

Speaking generally, there are two kinds of "backward messages." True backward messages are created in the recording studio. The performer records the message normally, reverses it with suitable equipment, then mixes the reversed track into the master tape. Such messages make no sense to the listener on the record. They can be reversed to recover the message in intelligible form.

Then there are coincidental reversals. Reversing *any* speech may *happen* to produce gibberish sounding something like a word or phrase. Musician Mark Mothersbaugh reported that when the phrase "Jesus loves you" is played backward, it comes out "we smell sausage." Of course, this is pure coincidence. Most of the time, these coincidental reversals are easy to distinguish from engineered messages. In these coincidental cases, a clear lyric becomes a muddled, oddly intoned "message" when reversed.

There's no simple way of telling what a word or phrase will sound like when reversed. The reversal does not necessarily sound like the backward phonetic spelling. Even the number of perceived syllables may change.

Suicide Suits

Fueling the secret-message controversy is a series of lawsuits filed against record companies and artists by parents of teen suicides. The first suicide linked to a rock record was that of 19-year-old John McCollum of Indio, California. In 1984 he killed himself after drinking and listening to *Blizzard of Ozz*, an album by heavy metal's middle-aged bad boy, Ozzy Osbourne. One of the songs on the album is called "Suicide Solution." McCollum's father filed suit against Osbourne and his record company, claiming that the song's morbid content had driven his son to suicide.

Two days before Christmas 1985, 17-year-old Raymond Belknap of Reno and his friend James Vance, 19, locked themselves in Belknap's bedroom for an afternoon-long binge of beer, marijuana, and heavy metal. The day ended with the boys going to a nearby church playground's merry-go-round and shooting themselves with a sawed-off shotgun. Belknap died instantly; Vance blew off half his face but survived. Interviewed by police the following day, Vance could offer as a reason only that "life sucks."

The two boys had been listening to a Judas Priest album, *Stained Class*. Vance's mother read about the pending Ozzy Osbourne suit. Subsequently the boys' families filed suit for millions in damages, not against a beer company, a drug dealer, or a gun shop but against Judas Priest and CBS Records.

At first (though not, apparently, until some time after the tragedy) James Vance spoke of being "mesmerized" by suicidal themes in the music. He cited the song "Beyond the Realms of Death." Vance was talking about the album's lyrics, the words anyone could hear.

Then in 1988 the California District Court of Appeals dismissed the aforementioned Ozzy Osbourne suit, citing the First Amendment. Seeing the handwriting on the wall, the Vance and Belknap parents and attorneys did some quick thinking. A few months later, they announced that it was not the audible lyrics but hidden "subliminal" messages that had caused the suicide attemps.

A subliminal stimulus is one that is perceived only by the unconscious mind. Usually, the term is applied to a stimulus of very brief duration or (in the case of sound) low volume. That such a thing is possible can be demonstrated in carefully designed laboratory experiments. But the reality of subliminals pales beside the mythology that has grown up around them. It is charged that backward messages can be unscrambled by the unconscious mind; that the unconscious mind is highly suggestible; that messages that would be ignored by the conscious mind are taken literally by the unconscious, even when the message is to commit suicide. There's no believable evidence for these charges.

The 1990 trial in Reno was a media circus, complete with members of Judas Priest, groupies, subliminal junk-science expert extraordinaire Wilson Bryan Key, and the national press. Rob Halford of Judas Priest and CBS Records insisted that they had no intention whatsoever of exterminating their markets. The judge agreed, ruling against the suit.

Despite the ruling, rockers and record companies have become popular deep-pocket targets for families of suicides. Within weeks of the Judas Priest trial, alleged subliminal messages on Ozzy Osbourne's "Suicide Solution" were blamed for the shooting suicides of Georgia teens Michael Waller (1985) and Harold Hamilton (1988). Waller, depressed over a D.W.I. arrest, shot himself after a beer bash; Hamilton had a history of drug and alcohol problems. Once again the families were perspicacious enough to recognize the real problem as the Ozzy Osbourne tapes. As of this writing, similar suits have been filed in at least five states.

The allegedly lethal records from the McCollum and Vance/

Belknap suits are available from CBS Records as part of the "Nice Price" discount line. Here's what we found.

"Better by You, Better than Me"
Judas Priest, *Stained Glass*

The claimed subliminal messages at issue in the trial were the lyrics "Do it. Do it. . . ." on the track "Better by You, Better than Me" and "numerous" instances of backward prosuicide sayings such as "commit suicide" and "try suicide" throughout the album.

The repeating "Do it" message was not a reversal. It was held to be subliminal by virtue of being barely audible. That it was; in a poll taken by a Reno newspaper, only 2 of 12 courtroom witnesses said they could hear it in the amplified and doctored clip played in court as proof of the message's existence. We couldn't hear it, either. A defense expert said the "Do it" chant was only the amplified breathing of one of the singers and sounds from the guitar.

Not only couldn't we find numerous backward suicide mottoes, we couldn't find even one. We reversed the entire tracks of "Better by You, Better than Me" and "Beyond the Realms of Death" and listened carefully. We really tried to hear the claimed phrases—if only to be able to say, "Aha, here's what they're talking about." But no dice. The closest approach was something that sounded like "Sousa." This is on the reversed version of "Beyond the Realms of Death" and resulted from the word *understand* being played backward. We also heard syllables that sounded something like "try." They never preceded anything that sounded even remotely like "suicide." There was nothing that would qualify as a proper backward message.

"Love Bites"
Judas Priest, *Defenders of the Faith*

Testifying in Reno, Rob Halford said that once, and only once, did he put a reversed message on a record. It was not on the album the boys had been playing, but rather on the song, "Love Bites," on the *Defenders of the Faith* album. Halford stated that the message consisted of the words "In the dead of the night, love bites."

The message is well concealed. Most bona fide reversed speech is unmistakable. On casual listening—even on a metalhead's repeated listening—you're not likely to notice the reversed speech in

"Love Bites." It starts at approximately 2 minutes and 56 seconds into the track and ends about 8 seconds later. All you hear is some incoherent stuff in the background. Digitize this and reverse it, and you still have to listen carefully to hear anything. A guttural voice says the first part. The only words we could distinctly make out were "of the night." A pause follows and then another voice yells, "Love bites!"

"Suicide Solution"
Ozzy Osbourne, *Blizzard of Ozz*

As was brought out repeatedly in legal proceedings, the song is actually antisuicide, written in memory of the alcohol and drug overdose of AC/DC's Bon Scott. The issue is hidden messages. According to documents filed by plaintiffs, a forward subliminal message occurs during a 47-second bridge in "Suicide Solution." The 27-second message is alleged to be, "All right now people, you really know what it's about. You've got it. Why try? Why try? Take the gun and try it. Try it. Shoot. Shoot. Shoot. Go on." Another message supposedly occurs at the end of the song.

It was also charged, in a deposition by Martin Hall of the Institute for Bio-Acoustic Research of Eugene, Oregon, that the record contains "pure hemi-sync tones" that were said to cause the brain to process information at a "higher-than-normal" rate.

Huh? We were unable to find "hemi-sync" in any dictionary, in the indexes to *Biological* or *Psychological Abstracts*, or even in the *New Grove Dictionary of Music and Musicians*. McCollum family attorney Thomas T. Anderson described it as an 11-kilohertz hum that makes listeners more susceptible to suggestions in the lyrics. The hum seemed to be from the bass guitar and is supposedly heard only in live performances or when wearing stereo headphones.

Anyone who listens to "Suicide Solution" will find that the claimed message is not concealed at all. It is an integral part of the song, a little softer than the rest of the lyrics but understandable to anyone who's paying attention. It runs from 2:01 to 2:29 on the counter. The wording alleged in court is a little wrong. We made it out to be, "[uncertain word, sounds like "Aye"] now people [echoes a few times], you really know what it's about. Uh, uh, uh. You got it. Why try? [echoes] Take the gun and [inaudible]. Shoot [the word sounds electronically modified and is actually closer to "suit"—we guess it has to be "shoot"]. Shoot. Shoot. Shoot. Shoot. Shoot. [Laugh] Oh." This is not a subliminal message.

The message said to be near the end apparently refers to a similar vocal segment from 3:08 to 3:25. This, too, is hardly concealed, though at least you can say that it is hard to make out some of the words: "Take me away. Oh oh tomorrow. It never gives me pleasure." The next part is difficult to make out and sounds like, "No pleasure nobody no pleasure nothing."

In the course of this investigation, repeated listening to *Blizzard of Ozz* failed to inspire the slightest inclinations toward suicide—or the purchase of other Ozzy Osbourne albums.

"Dinner Bell"
They Might Be Giants, *Apollo 18*

Several They Might Be Giants songs have been purported to have backward vocals. DJs propagated the story that "Ana Ng" (*Lincoln* album) means something backward. Close listening to the track discloses no evidence of any engineered reversal. When played backward, the words "Ana Ng" produce something sounding like "I'm a Cadillac"—not a lot like it, but *something* like it. It seems unlikely that this was intentional. In the song, Ana Ng appears to be a woman on the other side of the earth (China?), which would account for an unusual name.

"Dinner Bell," on the *Apollo 18* album, contains an almost unintelligible stanza that appears to have been recorded using the *Twin Peaks* dwarf technique. A person can listen to his own voice played backwards and learn to imitate it phonetically. A tape is made of the person imitating his speech, and then *that* tape is played backward. The result is eerie but understandable speech (which was used for a little person's dialogue in a dream sequence on *Twin Peaks*). The "Dinner Bell" stanza is a recitation of body parts (shoulder, bicep . . .) running for ten seconds that begins about one minute into the track. It is oddly intoned, with some words run together. The accompanying music is not reversed and presumably was recorded separately.

"I'm the Magnificent"
Special Ed, *Youngest in Charge*

"I'm the Magnificent" has two clearly reversed sequences. They're only samplings of the regular forward lyrics: "Record is a smash I can still survive 'cause I'm the man of steel on the wheel that you're steering."

"Detour Through Your Mind"
B-52s, *Bouncing Off the Satellites*

Near the end of "Detour Through Your Mind" you'll hear a longish stretch of scrambled speech, concealed somewhat by the music. Playing it in reverse, you recover a legitimate backward message. Fred Schneider's voice says, "I buried my parakeet in the backyard. No, no, you're playing the record backward. Watch out, you might ruin your needle."

Bob "Bobcat" Goldthwait, *Meat Bob*

Bob Goldthwait is apparently the first to put a backward message on a comedy album. *Meat Bob* was recorded live at a comedy club. Some of the material makes light of Tipper Gore and congressional hearings on record lyrics. The message is at the very end of the recording. Bob closes his act to loud applause and cheering. Partially drowned out by the ovation is some unintelligible mumbling—recognizably Goldthwait's voice, but actually backward. Since the applause is forward, it's not apparent that the mumbling is reversed. The last part sounds a little like "nipple." As the applause dies out, an emcee says, "Bob Goldthwait."

Played backward, the message becomes, "Obey your parents, be nice, don't eat snacks, and go to church. Um, give money to Jerry Falwell. Bye."

George Bush (speeches c. 1990)

In 1990 paranormal investigator C. B. Scott Jones played recent speeches by President Bush, Secretary of State James A. Baker III, and Secretary of Defense Richard B. Cheney in reverse as part of a study investigating a theory that people's hidden thoughts are somehow encoded backward in their normal speech. Jones claimed that the word *Simone* kept popping up in the reversed speeches. Jones wrote Defense Secretary Dick Cheney to ask if it was a code word. His letter stated, "I mention this situation in case it is a code word that would not be in the national interest to be known. If the word means nothing special to you, this is a non-event, just another mystery in a new technology we are developing."

Jones was an aide of Rhode Island's somewhat nutty Senator Claiborne Pell. Pell was the only U.S. senator to keep a full-time paranormal investigator on his payroll. Chairman of the Senate Foreign Relations Committee, Pell admitted that Jones's theory "sounds wacky." He told the *Providence Journal-Bulletin* that Jones was "motivated by patriotic reasons." Pell expressed concern that the possible top-secret code word was accessible to any malcontent with a tape recorder. Pell was up for reelection at the time the Jones letter was made public and conceded that the timing of the letter "certainly isn't helpful." (He was reelected.)

The most likely explanation for a reversed "Simone" popping up in administration speeches is that some repeated word or phrase (or part of a word or phrase) produces "Simone" when reversed. The speeches Jones used pertained to the developing Persian Gulf crisis. We taped "Persian Gulf," "Saddam Hussein," and "Dan Quayle," then reversed them. Nothing sounded much like "Simone." We reversed the code word *Simone*. It sounded something like "no mees."

Then Eugene Emery of the *Journal-Bulletin* reported that the word was *enormous*. Evidently, Jones's "Simone" was with an accent on the *e:* "Si-mo-*nee.*" *That* pronunciation reverses to something resembling "enormous." Conversely, reversing "enormous" produces Si-mo-*nee.*

26·

Subliminal Shots

A subliminal shot is a video or film image too brief to be seen consciously. No sci-fi fantasy, real subliminals have been hidden in well-known TV shows and movies. They're there for anyone with a freeze-frame on their VCR to find.

Subliminals are easy to produce. They may occupy a single frame of film or videotape, in which case the secret image flashes by in $1/24$ or $1/30$ of a second. That's too fleeting for most people to notice under normal circumstances, although it's not impossible for sharp-eyed viewers to spot the edit. Visibility depends on how much the inserted frame contrasts with the surrounding frames and whether the viewer is cued to expect the subliminal (he usually isn't, of course). Longer shots may span several frames but may be difficult to perceive or interpret for various reasons. Most of the known subliminals have been discovered by people who noticed something on a tape, then step-framed to the image.

Subliminal shots don't appear to violate any federal law. The big three American TV networks voluntarily ban subliminal advertising but not subliminal images per se. Most genuine subliminals are not ads. Many are just jokes. Peter Hays's 1990 book, *Movie Anecdotes*, says that Disney animators once put a single frame of a nude woman in a film. Sharp-eyed Disney caught it. "If that gal had any clothes, I wouldn't have paid any attention to her," he said. Hays doesn't say what film it was.

Biggest Secrets obtained tapes of TV shows and movies alleged to contain subliminal shots and examined them by freeze-framing.

Mad Max

Directors of horror and action movies have long experimented with subliminal shots. The effect on the audience, if any, is hard to gauge. Director George Miller used ultrabrief images in *Mad Max*. (This is the first of the *Mad Max* movies, not to be confused with the bigger-budget and better-known *Mad Max Beyond Thunderdome*.) The subliminal shots occur in the climactic scene where Max is chasing the head of the biker gang on a narrow road. A truck heading in their direction appears out of nowhere. The biker is trapped between Max's car and the truck. As cycle and truck approach, action cuts quickly between close-ups of the doomed biker's face and the oncoming truck. This much you realize, but the crash is jarring for reasons that are easily missed. Before you realize what's happening, the biker plows into the truck.

Mad Max was shot in Australia. The Australian press exposed and commented on Miller's secret. Miller (who was trained as a physician) reportedly used a special prosthesis for the biker's facial close-ups, showing his eyes opening unnaturally wide.

The biker, who is wearing goggles, takes them off as the truck approaches, turning his head squarely to the camera. The next few frames show his eyes opening wide. There is white all around the irises. Finally, you see the whole conjunctiva. It's obvious in freeze-frame that no one could open his eyes that wide. There's a quick cut to the oncoming truck, then another cut back to the biker's face. This time there's an exaggerated close-up that shows just the eyes and bridge of nose. The eyeballs are almost bare, the skin around them pulled back. These close-ups recall the grotesque mask that Max and his wife play with earlier.

The same technique is used at least one other time earlier in the film. When the Night Rider crashes, there's a more understated brief shot of a wide-open eye.

Anguish

The 1987 horror flick *Anguish* came with a warning: Viewers "will be subjected to subliminal messages and a state of brief hypnosis"—and should leave the theater if they, uh, feel themselves going berserk. This sounds like your basic publicity gimmick. Are there really subliminal messages in *Anguish?*

At the time of its release, parties associated with the film gave interviews on the alleged subliminal messages, stopping short of saying exactly what they were. Spectrafilm's Terri Johnson defended the warning in matter-of-fact terms: "Of course, some people watch the film without even noticing the subliminal messages, and they're fine. Others don't react so well—it depends on the person."

The publicity apparently refers to a sequence at about midpoint in the film. The mother hypnotizes the son (Michael Lerner)—and maybe the audience—by waving a point of light back and forth. The point of light explodes into a fast-paced succession of images: the son running, snails, birds, the mother, a whirling hypnotic spiral. This builds to a shot of the son superimposed on the hypnotic spiral, and spinning rapidly. Stepping through these frames reveals distorted images of the son's face. (An "anamorphic lens" maker gets screen credit at the end.) For a split second, the son metamorphoses into a ghoulish skull-like face.

The Young Ones

The Young Ones is a British situation comedy that has been rerun on cable in the U.S. The show's directors must have really liked the concept of subliminal images because they included them in a number of episodes.

In "Cash," the subliminal occurs just after Neil serves snow to his roommates and says, "It's risotto, Mike." There's a brief shot of a skier in a yellow and red outfit. What's more, the headgear visibly reads Carrera, so this might be considered a subliminal ad. The shot of the skier is three frames (one clear, the other two double exposures blending the skier and the main action) and lasts ⅒ second in all.

"Sick" has two subliminals, a shot of a frog (cut into a shot of Rik standing over a pile of manure) and another of a person leaping or falling.

Midway through "Bambi," after they get back from the laundry, Rik says, "You know what they say, dirty pants, clean body." Cut into a shot of Mike's face is a noticeable but unexplained 6-frame (⅕ second) clip from the credits of a western. You see a western town with three bodies lying in the dust. Superimposed in red are the titles:

Made at

Pinewood Studios, London, England

The End

Released throughout the United Kingdom

by

WARNER PATHE DISTRIBUTION LTD.

Max Headroom

The first episode of ABC's *Max Headroom* series, which is *about* subliminal advertising, has a subliminal image. The plot centers on "bleepverts," subliminal ads that a company called Zik Zak is sneaking into Channel XXIII's programming. You're shown several bleepverts, which consist of off-center pictures of an Asian man's face and hands and the words "Zik Zak" and "KNOW FUTURE."

Freeze-framing reveals a brief image of the name "FRED RAIMONDI" printed diagonally across the screen. Raimondi must have put together the bleepvert and decided to give himself a plug. He is listed as visual effects editor in the show's credits.

ALF

The most publicized subliminal shot of recent years was in NBC's Saturday morning cartoon version of *ALF* (not the live-action show that is also rerun). In 1988 viewer Ken Sobel of Long Island taped the cartoon and claimed to find a subliminal image of the Statue of Liberty in the cartoon. A Big Brotherish attempt to implant patriotism in American youth? Sobel wasn't sure, but he told the FCC about the image.

The animation in *ALF* is pretty good. *ALF* contains a number of clever fleeting images, some perceptible without freeze-framing. In the first-season opening sequence, cats look at menus in a diner. One cat turns, briefly sweeping its menu past the camera. The screen shows a picture of a cat's face on the menu—taking up most of the screen—for a few frames. That's just long enough to see it, if you're paying attention, but perhaps not long enough for cat lovers to appreciate the bugged-out eyes and bulging tongue of a clearly dead cat.

Another feline image occurs in the "John Henry" episode. A

robot is about to capture Gordon. Gordon seizes the wrong remote control and changes the channel on the TV rather than switching the robot off. The brief image on the TV is a throwaway you can't really see except by freeze-framing: It's a fat Garfield the cat, who has passed out in front of an open refrigerator containing wine bottles, one spilling its contents. One of Garfield's normally bulging eyeballs is missing, leaving a pink socket. Taped on the side of the refrigerator is a note saying, "I ♥ ALF."

Like most cartoon fare, *ALF* is violent enough to offer at least one good explosion per episode. Stepping frame by frame through the typical *ALF* explosion reveals a number of single-frame, though often unremarkable, images. There is frequently some effort to show the explosion accurately (broken glass and other fragments are shown in perspective). There are also single frames of geometric patterns: stars, circles, and curlicues; sometimes a blank frame. Episodes copyrighted in 1988 have a different opening sequence in which Gordon tosses a bomb toward the camera. The bomb explodes with a boom and clouds of smoke. Stepping through the explosion reveals frames with images of musical instruments (tuba, saxophone, mandolin, drum, French horn, and trumpet). The joke must be that when Gordon throws the bomb at the camera, it's actually going into an imaginary orchestra pit. Hence the explosion of musical instruments (a few of them bent or broken).

The Statue of Liberty image occurs in "Phantom Pilot," the first episode of the series. It has a copyright date of 1987, suggesting that Sobel was watching a rerun. For all the brouhaha, the episode is still being rerun with the subliminal (on televangelist Pat Robertson's Family Channel, yet).

The subliminal shot is in a space-war scene. When the phantom pilot cuts the cable holding the bad guys' spaceship, it falls away, out of control, into the path of some hovering ships. The last dialogue heard before the subliminal is delivered by the bad guys. One says, "Throw her in reverse." The other counters, "We don't have reverse, sir; budgetary cutbacks." The action cuts to the oncoming wasp-shaped craft, followed by the explosion.

A single frame shows a cartoon picture of the Statue of Liberty in front of a waving American flag against a blue background. Superimposed on the image is the slanted word "AMERICA" in red letters. The eyes of the statue appear slightly Asian.

This is followed by a number of other single- or multiple-frame images. One is of spiral streamers and confetti against a black background. There is an extreme close-up of someone's face (one of the bad guys? or someone in the ship they just crashed into?). Other frames show broken glass, a dial, and finally the growing cloud of smoke and fire (which you do see in normal viewing).

The Statue of Liberty frame lasts a mere ⅟₃₀ second and is easy to miss even if you know where it is. In repeated viewings at normal speed, knowing *exactly* where the image is, it was frequently possible to perceive the word "AMERICA." It was difficult or impossible to see the Statue of Liberty or the flag except by freeze-framing.

The FCC tried to find out where the subliminal image came from. The production company for the series, DIC Enterprises of Burbank, California, said they didn't know. Then an FCC official was quoted as saying the show's director had claimed the subliminal frame was put there to enhance the explosion effect somehow. DIC denied that. Finally, the show's director, Richard Raynis, said the subliminal was the work of the Japanese animators. Like most American animated shows, *ALF* was drawn in Asia from storyboards. Raynis had not called for the Statue of Liberty frame; the animators had put it in as a joke. Raynis had seen the image in the finished drawings and didn't think it was worth taking out.

It turned out that a firm called Studio Korumi, located outside Tokyo, was responsible. President Yasumi Ishida told a *TV Guide* correspondent, "I don't know if the Americans would understand, but sometimes we like to play around." According to Ishida, it is a custom for Japanese animators to throw single-frame images into cartoons as jokes. *ALF* was being drawn for the American market, so they threw in the most hyper-American image they could think of.

VI: Ritual

27.

The Boy Scouts

The Boy Scouts promise members a taste of self-sufficiency, patriotism, leadership, and respect for native cultures. They also give them a taste of shameless deception and humiliating ritual. The secrets of scouting are to be found not in the watered-down manuals given to scouts, but in the huge body of literature for scout leader/den mother eyes only. The Boy Scouts of America (BSA) organization publishes a price list of manuals and pamphlets for scout leaders and camp counselors (available by writing to P.O. Box 909, Pineville, NC 28134). Like the Pentagon, the Boy Scouts have several levels of classified information. The highest level of security ("restricted item, must be ordered directly from your local council") applies mainly to honor certificates and official scout ID. The specter of rogue scouts obtaining illicit Eagle Scout credentials is taken *very* seriously, it seems. Though much of the literature proper offered in the price list is described as "restricted, for council use only," we were able to obtain a wide selection of information by posing as a new scout troop. We thereby got the official lowdown on scouting's secret initiations and—rudest shock of all—methods for cheating in starting a scout campfire.

Humiliating Ordeals

Boys will be boys. Not every childish prank occurring at scout camp takes place with the approval of the scouting organization. Nonetheless, the standard literature of scouting describes enough humiliating ritual to give scouts a general idea of what they can get away with.

No one seems to disapprove of the well-known snipe hunt. (Older scouts propose a snipe hunt at a remote site and tell newcomers to hold a bag as they flush the quarry out of the underbrush. Then they go back to camp and see how long it takes the rubes to realize the origin of the expression "left holding the bag.") On approximately the same level is the prank of putting the hand of a sleeping person in lukewarm water. It's supposed to cause him (or her) to wet the bed. The medical status of this is dicey. Just to be on the safe side, scouts should keep their hands tucked well under the covers.

Less generally known is the cruel initiation of the Royal Order of Siam. In this the scout leader tells uninitiated scouts a story about how Baden-Powell, founder of all scoutdom, learned a special ceremony from the king of Siam. The leader has the scouts pray to three Siamese gods: Ahwa, god of the sky; Tanas, god of the wind; and Siam, god of the earth. The whole point of this is to get the scouts to stand around and repeat, "Ahwa, Tanas, Siam" and see how long it takes them to realize that this sounds like "Aw, what an ass I am." Once they catch the drift, they're members in good standing. Some troops issue membership cards, which don't count for much in the real world.

These rituals are horseplay. Not so, the solemn Ordeal of the Order of the Arrow, the pinnacle of secret initiations for scouts. The order is a junior fraternal lodge offered at Boy Scout camps. In the spirit of democracy, all the boys at camp, not just order members, get to vote on who should be inducted. Up to 5 percent of the campers may be inducted per season. Only the chosen few learn what the ordeal is.

Candidates for the Order of the Arrow are instructed in lore loosely based on legends of the Lenni-Lenape or Delaware tribe (this because the order began in 1915 at a scout camp near Philadelphia). The complex Native American–inspired ritual has long been a point of contention with scout leaders and parents. As early as 1925, it was found necessary for the order to insist that its mention of the Indian deity Manitou should not be construed as an attempt to undermine the Christian faith. By 1948 Arrowmen had tacked a pluralistic disclaimer on their quasi–Lenni-Lenape prayers: "Pray you now in reverent silence, each in your own fashion."

Those chosen for the order are led through the woods one evening to a campfire. Around it are order members in Native

American costume. Strict authenticity is not a requirement, to judge by the photos in the BSA's official *History of the Order of the Arrow*. Hollywood-inspired Plains Indian war bonnets coexist with totem poles.

The ordeal proper consists of four parts. The candidate has to spend the night in the woods; he has to spend a day at hard labor; he has to go 24 hours with very little food; he has to spend 24 hours without saying a word. The last three penances are served concurrently. The term of the fast is often abbreviated to allow a big dinner for new members at the end of the second day.

To outsiders, the visible benefit of initiation is that the newly minted Arrowman is eligible to select from a dizzying profusion of custom Order of the Arrow patches, sashes, neckerchief slides, bolo ties, tie tacks, belt buckles, rings, and key fobs.

Playing with Fire

Fact: It is almost impossible to start a fire by rubbing two sticks together. Today's scout leaders often resort to cheap tricks and messy chemicals to impress their charges.

It was naturalist and author Ernest Thompson Seton, chief scout of the Boy Scouts from 1910 to 1915, who started the business about rubbing two sticks together. Seton advocated the use of the Native American bow and drill and wildwood materials. Tinder should be a field-mouse nest, not crumpled newspaper. The tenth edition of the *Boy Scout Handbook* devotes three pages to techniques for starting fires without matches. Small wonder that innocent campers assume that their campfires have been started using these rough-and-ready methods.

For the real story, check out the BSA-distributed *Creative Campfires* by Douglas R. Bowen (1974). It lists ten ways of starting a campfire. Most are cheats. Even more of an eye-opener is a book originally written for YMCA camp counselors, Allan A. Macfarlan's *Camp Fire & Council Ring Programs* (1951). This disarmingly cynical treatise quickly segues from poetry to calculating schemes for duping campers. "Before we even begin to lay a fire, let us determine to use whenever possible only dead trees, trees blown down by the wind, or those blasted by lightning," Macfarlan starts out. "These dead trees will burn even more brightly than fresh-cut timber, and as we sit entranced before the fire's fountain of iridescent flames, we should realize that the trees are sharing with us the beauty of things they have stored in their hearts. . . . The forest and its fire-child are our friends."

Two paragraphs later, Macfarlan gets real: "Should there be no one skilled in building a fire which must blossom into flame immediately when it is lighted, then, and only then, may dry newspaper rolled into little balls about two inches in diameter be shamefully concealed in the center of the wildwood material. This is better than having the awful fiasco of a council fire which will not burn instantly when a light is applied to it." This is only the beginning. Macfarlan countenances the covert use of kerosene, slow-burning fuses, and sulfuric acid—where absolutely necessary. (Now *napalm*, that's definitely out of the question.)

Let's look at a few of these quick and dirty methods for starting the modern campfire.

The concealed candle. Both Boy Scout and YMCA leaders employ this method, as simple as it is fraudulent. Set a candle into the center of the prescribed "log-cabin" arrangement of wood and kindling. Light the candle and balance over it a flat tin can such as tuna comes in. Make sure the flame is invisible from all angles. Attach a long string to the can and conceal it (ideally, by putting it in a pipe and burying it). Pile kindling on top of the can. Bring on the campers. Build up anticipation by calling on the Wind of the East, the Wind of the West, etc., etc. At the right moment, pull the can off by tugging on the string.

Medicine-breath fire. A camper got up as a medicine man kneels before the fire and raises his hands to the sky. He blows on the fire and miraculously brings it to life. The secret is a slow-burning fuse hidden among the logs. It's made by soaking a thick soft string in a concentrated saltpeter solution and letting it dry. Six inches of this fuse will smolder for about 9 minutes with virtually no smoke. The fuse is lighted, and then the campers are led to the council site and seated around the logs. The medicine man puts on a mock Native American rite until the fire starts. The logs are arranged so that he alone has a view of the fuse's progress and can synchronize his actions accordingly. Blowing on the fuse helps ignite the kindling. The latter is shredded timber bark or, for that added frisson, the traditional field-mouse nest, doped with chemical oxidants.

Matches and sandpaper. If there is a *special hell* just for scout leaders, might not the seventh circle be reserved for those who start campfires with a fistful of matches? That's how this Boy Scout technique works. Drill dozens of holes in a flat piece of board. Stand a wood kitchen match upright in each hole. Carefully balance another board, covered with sandpaper, on the match heads. Tugging on the upper board with an attached string sets the matches on fire.

An alternate implementation uses an upside-down T-shaped piece of wood made by nailing a short length of two-by-four perpendicularly in the center of another piece of wood. The sandpaper is glued to the center projection. A nail protrudes from the base a few inches from the sandpaper surface. Make a "big match" by bundling together several dozen kitchen matches with rubber bands. Impale the big match on the nail and tie fishing line to it. Pulling on the line causes the big match to pivot on the nail and scratch the sandpaper, bursting into ill-gotten flame. Just to be safe, douse the kindling with lighter fluid, too.

Magic fire. Scrounge around the forest for some sulfuric acid. Pour 1½ ounces of acid in a small bottle. Tie the bottle securely to the center of a stick, and support the stick a few inches above ground with two upright forked sticks—as if the bottle were on a spit for roasting. A string is tied around the neck of the bottle. Place directly beneath the bottle a paper plate containing 2 tablespoons of potassium chlorate and 2 tablespoons of sugar mixed together. Around this, carefully build a log cabin of pine or spruce sticks doused with kerosene. Make sure no one can see the science project. After all are seated, pull the string, which spills acid on the dry chemicals and starts a fire. WARNING: Scaling up the amounts of chemicals will create an antipersonnel device.

Electrical ignition. Creative Campfires incites technology-minded scout leaders to cannibalize a retractable ballpoint pen for its spring. Cut off a few match heads and cram them into the spring's coils. Run wires from the two ends of the spring to a 6- or 12-volt dry cell. Completing the circuit on cue heats up the spring like a toaster coil, thus, igniting the match heads. Scout leaders have also reported success in igniting steel wool with a battery.

Extreme though the above measures may be, they all encourage belief that the fire has been started in authentic fashion. With a couple of pyrotechnic effects, suspension of disbelief is scarcely possible.

The fireball. A fine wire (or pulley arrangement) runs from a nearby tree to a stake in the center of the kindling. Threaded on the wire is a wooden spool that has been covered with cotton or gauze soaked in melted wax. The leader asks the Great Spirit to light the campfire. An assistant, concealed in the tree, lights the spool and lets it slide down the wire to the waiting kindling.

The flaming-arrow method. All right-thinking scout leaders ban this now-discredited method, which can easily become the *Hindenburg* disaster of campfires. A hidden firebug shoots an arrow ablaze with kerosene-soaked cloth at the pile of logs. The fire starts wherever the payload hits. According to the YMCA book, it once hit a camp director.

28·

The Equator-Crossing Ritual

The equator-crossing ritual is the secret initiation of the sea, a ceremony performed when sailors cross the equator for the first time. It is a long-entrenched, worldwide custom that occurs in the navy, marines, and merchant marine alike—services reluctant to reveal its secrets for publication. Nothing in the equator-crossing ritual will boost these services' reputations for military readiness or workplace safety. Every once in a while an outraged sailor tries to blow the whistle when he gets to shore. The service downplays the ceremony as harmless horseplay, likens it to fraternity hazing, and then officially, once and for all, bans the equator-crossing ritual. And nothing changes.

Or almost nothing. Women now serve on navy and merchant-marine ships. Complaints of sexual harassment on the *Golden Bear*, a merchant-marine training ship, triggered a 1989 investigation by the National Maritime Administration. Although the abuses cited were almost mild compared to some reports, the federal investigators recommended a ban on the equator-crossing ritual and "any further irresponsible and violent behavior." The maritime academy had already banned it. An academy spokesman said, almost wistfully, that the ritual had been a custom "as long as there have been sailors at sea."

History

That's not literally true, but the ritual has been around at least four centuries. French navigator and scholar Jean Parmentier recorded a semireligious rite observed when crossing the equator on a trip to

Sumatra (1529). By the end of the sixteenth century, several voyagers had written of a boisterous ceremony that resembles the present one in many particulars. Many famous travelers have witnessed or taken part in the equator-crossing rite. Charles Darwin wrote of the *Beagle's* ceremony in his diary (omitting it from his official account of the voyage). Mark Twain mentions it only as a near-extinct custom in *Following the Equator*—actually, reports of the ritual's death were greatly exaggerated long before Twain's time. King Edward VIII was initiated in 1920; Franklin D. Roosevelt, in 1936; Queen Elizabeth II watched a ceremony in 1953. Columnists of the 1950s took glee in the belated discovery that Senator Joseph McCarthy's famous war injury was suffered not in combat but in equator-crossing hijinks.

Photographs of the equator-crossing ritual exist. German-born photojournalist John Gutmann took one in 1933. His photo shows a carnival scene of costumed revelers. A standing man, barefoot and shirtless, his face blackened, receives a scroll from a seated man in a top hat and funny glasses. Next to the man in the hat is another man dressed as King Neptune. Behind this group are two men, one in drag, both with their faces painted black. Two of our (U.S. Navy) informants had photographs of the ritual too. They had snapped the shots openly and were allowed to keep them. They knew of others who had videos of the rite.

The official position on the equator-crossing ritual has been equivocal. Though the rite has been outlawed many times, by many different bodies, every now and then some nostalgic admiral gets the service to publish an official version. In 1946 British taxpayers unknowingly financed the British Admiralty's publication of *Crossing the Line*, a how-to pamphlet for hazing British sailors. The pamphlet cites "the obvious necessity to foster an awareness of the old traditions in the minds of the rising generation."

Biggest Secrets canvassed several former navy men who had been through the ritual for their stories. The following are the more common and standardized elements of the U.S. Navy equator-crossing ritual.

Wogs and Shells

A sailor who has never crossed the equator before is called a "wog," short for "polliwog." Those who have been initiated on previous crossings are "shellbacks" or "shells." As the ship nears the equator, word gets out that some sort of awful ordeal is in store. Meanwhile, shellbacks are busy with secret tasks (making costumes, a throne, and torture implements; stocking up on rotten food).

The day before the ship crosses the equator is declared Polliwog Day. This is the wogs' chance to vent their grievances against the shellbacks. Mostly, wogs throw rotten food at the shellbacks. Polliwog Day ends with a traditional mock mutiny. The wogs revolt, storm the captain's quarters, and tie him up. The rebels order the ship to be turned away from the equator (which is actually done, briefly, at least in some cases).

Sooner or later, shellbacks regain control of the ship. They put the ship back on course. And then there's hell to pay. The captain orders a roll call on the quarterdeck. Mutiny is a serious business, he says; the guilty parties must be punished.

They are soon interrupted by the appearance of a shellback made up as Davy Jones, the keeper of lost ships. Jones and other ritual personages may make grand entrances. The sometimes incredible *Crossing the Line* suggests decor worthy of a Polynesian restaurant: green floodlights, a "water curtain" produced by punching holes in a navy hose, and a sound system with microphones concealed in conch shells.

There's a catechism where Davy Jones asks the captain the name of the ship and its course. Jones then announces that King Neptune himself must judge the mutineers. The captain intercedes for the hapless wogs. He assures Davy Jones that his own punishments will be cruel and unusual enough—there's no cause for the more dreadful penalties that Neptune would dispense. But Davy Jones has heard quite enough from bleeding-heart captains and sets the time for Neptune to appear the following day. Jones hands out summonses to each wog, detailing his crimes and sometimes specifying the costume he must wear. The summonses are official-looking documents produced in a print shop.

On the morning of the equator crossing, two breakfasts are served. Shellbacks dine on chow about as good as it gets in the navy: pancakes, eggs, and sausage. Wogs get the same food secretly poisoned with loads of Tabasco sauce, salt, pepper, etc.

After breakfast, wogs are ordered to appear for inspection. A "beauty contest" selects the most beautiful wog. The lucky winner is crowned "Queen Wog" and presides over the equator ritual in drag. Selected wogs may be required to dress as "cigarette girls" or animals (sea gulls, dogs, horses). One of the complainants in the 1989 investigation testified to midshipmen defecating in her hat. When she elected not to wear the hat for inspection, she received demerits for appearing out of uniform. The humor of equator crossing is rarely of the Algonquin Round Table variety.

The wogs must follow any ridiculous orders given by shellbacks. The cigarette girls have to offer lighted cigarettes, and most are required to dance or sing songs to entertain the shellbacks. Special horror is reserved for those wogs who happen to outrank shellbacks. A high-ranking wog may be ordered to scramble up the ladders again and again to check for the invisible line of 0°00″ latitude.

Whenever a shell asks a wog what he is, he has to answer, "I am a slimy polliwog." Failure to respond properly is greeted with a slap from a cutoff piece of fire hose.

Trial and Punishment

King Neptune and his court arrive in such lavish style as can be improvised. The elevator on aircraft carriers is sometimes used. Assuming he's been initiated, the captain usually has the honor of playing Neptune. He wears a tin crown and a beard of frayed rope and sits on a throne. A suitable flag of Neptune, or sometimes the Jolly Roger, is displayed. King Neptune comments on the fine ship and its cargo of landlubbers.

Highest-ranking shells play Amphitrite, the king's consort, and the aforementioned Davy Jones. Other traditional shellback roles are the Royal Baby, the Royal Barber, the Royal Doctor, the Royal Dentist, and the Devil. Shells who aren't assigned specific roles wear pirate costumes.

The wogs change clothes for their trial—the reason being that it gets messy. Older published sources say wogs wore T-shirts and pants turned inside-out. Our informants wore specially made T-shirts, each printed with an embarrassing nickname held to fit the wog's personality.

The wogs are herded into a long line and must crawl on hands and knees, noses to the deck, which has been plastered with the appalling leftovers of their over-seasoned breakfast.

The first wog to stand trial is brought before King Neptune,

Amphitrite, and Davy Jones. Neptune reads the charges. These consist of complaints about personality, discipline, or conduct during Polliwog Day. An all-shellback judge and jury find each wog guilty as charged. Common penalties are lashes from the cut fire hose; unpleasant duties, such as cleaning up the prodigious mess created by the equator-crossing ritual; and time in the stocks, specially constructed for the occasion. Sometimes Neptune or the Devil has an electrified trident/pitchfork to jab wogs. It's actually hooked up to the ship's power. Or, wogs may be required to sit in an electrified chair.

The wogs then endure abuse from a line of costumed tormentors. The Royal Baby is the fattest, grossest shellback available, his abdomen slathered with Crisco. The wog is required to kiss the Baby's protruding gut and/or to suck an item (raw oyster, maraschino cherry, etc.) from his navel. The Baby grabs the wog's head and rolls it against his belly, covering the wog with grease.

The Royal Barber then dirties the wog's face with a "lather" reportedly made of such variable ingredients as flour/water paste, grease, soot, and/or tar. The barber "shaves" the wog with mock movements of a wooden sword (not removing much of the mess), then switches to real implements, taking care to shave off half the wog's mustache and just enough of his hair so that the victim will subsequently have to be shaved bald in order to approximate a human being by the time the ship gets into port.

The wog's appointment with the Royal Dentist finds the latter filling a cavity with a foul-tasting compound (a squirt gun is sometimes used). The doctor dispenses bitter "medicine." Among the many ingredients dentist and doctor prescribe are seawater, coffee, salt, quinine, and gentian blue (a blue dye that's hard to remove from skin).

U.S. ships have inflatable escape chutes similar to those on airliners. Navy regulations say these chutes are to be opened only for drills, maintenance, and emergencies. During the ritual, shellbacks open a chute, fill it with a putrefying mass of rotten food, then shove the wogs down it.

The ritual traditionally ends with a baptism. Old accounts mention a canvas sail, filled with water, for baptizing the wogs. Our sources report that this custom has been replaced by that of turning high-pressure fire hoses on the wogs. The effect—wogs slipping, falling, sliding, and clawing at railings to avoid being cast overboard—is held to be comic. Our informants believed that the risk of being thrown overboard was real.

At the end of the gauntlet, shellbacks may again ask wogs what they are. Those who give the formerly correct "I am a slimy polliwog" endure the punishment again. The right answer at this point is "I am a shellback." Once the unfortunate says that, he's released.

After every wog has been initiated, there's a big "shellback dinner" of steak with all the trimmings. There the ritual ends. But this is only part of the general free-for-all that is the day of crossing. The equator crossing is an excuse for a daylong binge of beer or liquor drinking—many seamen were soon falling-down drunk—as well as for any abuse or harassment the shellbacks care to dispense.

In the 1989 investigation by the National Maritime Administration, sailors complained of "mock sodomy." Wogs were required to simulate anal intercourse and to perform "fellatio" of a shellback who had a piece of fire hose protruding from his fly. According to our sources, real sodomy is sometimes part of the ritual, despite the AIDS epidemic. Two male informants said they were subjected to unprotected anal intercourse by senior officers during the rite. They said that many others received the same treatment.

Why do generations of sailors put up with this? Isolation is a factor, obviously. The ceremony takes place in the middle of the ocean. The superiors to whom one might complain are shellbacks.

What keeps any hazing tradition alive is the promise of vengeance. The equator-crossing ceremony recognizes this unappealing fact of human nature by awarding each initiate a certificate. The scrap of paper is the owner's ticket to shellback status of future voyages. With considerable variation, the certificate reads (this text from the U.S. Naval Academy's *Naval Customs, Traditions, and Usage*):

In Latitude 00-00 and Longitude _____

All Mermaids, Sea Serpents, Whales, Sharks, Porpoises, Dolphins, Skates, Eels, Suckers, Lobsters, Crabs, Polliwogs, and other living things of the sea,

_____

has been found worthy to be numbered as one of our trusty shell-backs, has been gathered to our fold and duly initiated into the solemn mysteries of the ancient order of the deep.

29.

Organized Crime

Like the Shriners and Elks and Knights of Columbus, organized crime has secret initiations, revealed only to those who swear never to reveal them to outsiders, on pain of dreadful retribution. Unlike the usual men's club, the mob plays for keeps. Dreadful retribution is how they earn their living.

The police have often made it a priority to ferret out the secrets of mob initiations. The feeling has been that exposing the rituals is a kind of psychological warfare that will damage the organizations involved. Unfortunately, the mob seems to be made of sterner stuff than that. But thanks to informants and hidden recorders, we do know, in surprising detail, what goes on in Triad and Cosa Nostra initiations.

Cosa Nostra

It is estimated that there are at present only about 2,000 "made" (initiated) members of the Cosa Nostra. You wouldn't guess it from their prevalence in movies and on TV, or from the degree of their influence. Like the old Communist party, the Cosa Nostra is an elite that controls a much larger empire of nonmembers. Members are bound by *omerta*, the code of silence. Even the name of the organization betrays nothing. "Mafia" can be translated as "beautiful," and "La Cosa Nostra" is evasive Italian for "this thing of ours."

The organization may have its roots in late-eighteenth-century Sicily. It was then a guerrilla group trying to drive the occupying

French from Italian soil. "Mafia" is sometimes held to be an acronym for "*Morte alla Francia Italia anela!*" ("Death to the French is Italy's cry!") By the late nineteenth century it was well established as a protection racket in western Sicily. Mussolini's police state vowed to eradicate the Mafia in Italy, and nearly succeeded. Ironically, Allied forces used Mafia collaborators during the invasion of fascist Italy and may have helped reestablish the organization in Italy after the war.

The Cosa Nostra initiation is almost an obligatory device of Mafiosi fiction. Various versions of the initiation appear in oral accounts, fiction, and nonfiction. They agree mainly in the use of knives. One version cited in older sources has the candidate enter a dark room. The lights are switched on, and he sees that members are holding an assortment of knives to all parts of his body. Someone yells, "Death to all traitors!" The candidate is forced to kneel and hold a stiletto to his heart. He vows to stab himself rather than betray his brothers in the Mafia.

The definitive exposé of the Mafia initiation took place on October 29, 1989, when the FBI secretly tape-recorded an initiation in Medford, Massachusetts. This quashed any remaining speculation that earlier stool-pigeon stories were fabricated for the police. It also confirmed that the traditional blood-mixing ritual was still practiced. Raymond J. Patriarca, identified as don of a New England family, unknowingly presided over the bugged initiation of four new members. The parties involved took the pledge to secrecy seriously. One person on the tape boasts, "Only the fucking ghosts know what really took place over here today."

The initiation goes like this. The candidate repeats an Italian oath that translates, "I swear not to divulge this secret and to obey, with love and the code of silence." Then members cut the index finger of the candidate's right hand—the trigger finger—with a knife. A few drops of blood are mixed with the blood of the member sponsoring him. A card bearing the image of the particular family's patron saint is moistened with the blood, then burned in the new member's hand. The candidate promises, "As burns this saint, so will burn my soul. I enter alive into this organization and leave it dead."

The FBI tape records specific protocol for approaching other Mafiosi. According to a voice on the tape identified as Joseph Russo, family members never reveal their membership to anyone without a proper introduction by a mutually known member. Just in case you're wondering, people with "Mafia Staff Car" bumper stickers *aren't* in the organization. The currently accepted recognition sign: Family members introduce another "made" member as a *friend of ours.* Kissing is strictly for the movies. "Years ago we used to kiss each other," new initiates are told on the tape. "Now we try to stop it because . . . we stand out."

The Triad Society

Scarcely known to the average American, Triad societies probably have more members in the U.S. than the Cosa Nostra. Parallels between the Chinese Triad and the Cosa Nostra are many. Like its Sicilian counterpart, the Triad organization had a political and relatively idealistic phase as an underground organization vowing to overthrow colonial rule—in this case, to get the Europeans out of China and restore the Ming dynasty. Over the years, that goal was put on the back burner. Like the Cosa Nostra, the Triad was suppressed in its homeland, even as it was being carried around the world through waves of immigration. A popular conception of a monolithic Triad organization is as much a myth as that of a unified Mafia. Triad societies share traditions but often find themselves battling each other for turf.

No one in the organization calls it the Triad. It goes by such names as Hung Mun ("Hung League"), Sam Hop Wui ("Three United Association"), and Tin Tei Wui ("Heaven and Earth Association"). Chinese nonmembers sometimes call it Hak Sh'e Wui ("Black Society Association"), which has a sinister connotation. The English name refers to the society emblem, a triangle whose three sides represent heaven, earth, and man. Each individual society has its own name as well.

As recently as 1960, H.W.E. Heath, the Hong Kong commissioner of police, could estimate that *one in six* residents of Hong Kong were Triad members. These membership figures are possible because a wide membership is recruited, some by coercion. Only a minority become actively engaged in criminal activities. Anyone initiated is technically a member for life, and (rare among fraternal orders) women are admitted as well as men.

In the U.S. the Triad is strongest in New York City, San Francisco, Los Angeles, and Houston. In some U.S. cities Vietnamese and other non-Chinese are widely recruited. According to testimony at the 1991 Senate hearings on Asian organized crime, a Triad power struggle for control of the San Francisco Bay area resulted in the murder of at least five members of the warring Wah Ching and Wo Hop To societies. (The Wo Hop To Society won.) Among the more creative forms of extortion detailed before the Senate was hawking concert tickets. Wo Hop To members called on merchants in Oakland's Chinatown, ostensibly selling tickets to a concert by sultry songstress Amy Yip (a.k.a. "the Madonna of Hong Kong"). Although the ticket prices were high, most were swayed by the Wo Hop To members' assurances that anyone who passed up Ms. Yip's performance might well regret it for the rest of her life, however long that would be.

Perhaps no secret society of any kind has a more pomp-and-circumstance-laden initiation than the Triad. Initiates swear to keep the ritual secret on pain of death by "myriads of swords." From time to time members have squealed to the police, usually in return for leniency. In the 1950s the Hong Kong police made a concentrated effort to uncover information on the society's initiations and secret signs. They checked information obtained from informants against each other and against seized documents. This effort culminated in 1957, when the police went so far as to stage an initiation and film it. The film was said to be supervised by four Triad members. Even so, the people in the film were actors who concealed their faces lest the society not hold imitation to be the sincerest form of flattery.

Certain similarities between the Triad and Cosa Nostra initiations are so remarkable that you have to wonder who copied from whom. As in the Cosa Nostra, Triad initiates have their fingers cut and their blood mixed; they burn paper images.

The classic Triad initiation lasted three days and nights. It is still common for candidates to return three nights after their initiation for additional ceremonies. The full-blown initiation entails lengthy poetic formulas; dozens of symbolic flags, signs, foods, utensils, incense, and regalia; the teaching of secret hand signs, numbers, and even paper-folding techniques. The Hong Kong police report is itself a heavy volume. In outline the initiation goes as follows.

Candidates enter the lodge through an eastern entrance. The lodge is decorated with flags and banners. Candidates pass under three temporary arches, bringing them to the Heaven and Earth Circle.

Made of bamboo, it looks like a hula hoop, except that red paper "teeth," nine on the top and twelve on the bottom, are pasted on it. As two members hold the hoop, the candidate kneels on his right knee and climbs through, left leg first. This recalls the escape of the monks from the Siu Lam Monastery through a jagged hole. It symbolizes the candidate's rebirth as a society member.

Next comes the Fiery Pit. Members set afire a quantity of joss paper on the floor, and the candidates have to step their way through the flames.

The candidates end up in front of an altar, surrounded by members. The initiate swears to 36 oaths. All are in the form, "I won't do X, or else I'll suffer horrible punishment Y." Frequently mentioned punishments are "death by five thunderbolts" and (more believably) being "killed by myriads of knives." Oaths No. 5 and 35 protect the secrecy of the society:

> 5. I shall not disclose the secrets of the Hung family, not even to my parents, brothers, or wife. I shall never disclose the secrets for money. I will be killed by myriads of swords if I do so. . . .

> 35. I must never reveal Hung secrets or signs when speaking to outsiders. If I do so I will be killed by myriads of swords.

Others frankly anticipate business dealings of a paralegitimate slant: "I shall never betray my sworn brothers. If, through a misunderstanding, I have caused the arrest of one of my brothers I must release him immediately" (No. 6). "If I have wrongly taken a sworn brother's case or property during a robbery, I must return them" (No. 17). "If it comes to my knowledge that the Government is seeking any of my sworn brothers who have come from other provinces or from overseas, I shall immediately inform him in order that he may make his escape" (No. 21). "I must not disclose the address where my sworn brothers keep their wealth" (No. 29). "If any of my sworn brothers has committed a big offense I must not inform on them to the Government for the purposes of obtaining a reward." Furthermore, initiates must swear to keep their hands off the wives, concubines, and small children of other members (Nos. 9 and 32). This isn't the Rotary Club.

A yellow sheet of paper containing these 36 oaths and the names, birth dates, and addresses of the candidates is burned, and the ashes are dissolved in a bowl containing wine, sugar, and cinnabar (a toxic red pigment containing mercury).

A member decapitates a live rooster, and candidates are warned, "After joining the Hung family remain loyal and faithful. The treacherous will die like this cock." Blood from the rooster drips into the wine mixture.

The candidates kneel and hold their left hands up—right hands for female candidates. The Incense Master, a high-ranking member, takes a needle threaded with red silk and pricks the middle finger of each candidate's raised hand, drawing blood. As he does so, another member holds the bowl of wine, poison, and rooster blood. The Incense Master says to each candidate, "The silver brings blood from the finger. Do not reveal our secrets to others. If any secrets are disclosed, blood will be shed from the five holes of your body."

The candidate repeats this, presumably while making a mental tally of orifices. Then the Incense Master dips the candidate's bleeding finger in the wine mixture. He bends the hand backward and has the candidate suck the blood from the finger. The candidate is to say, "It is sweet." Then the candidate stands up, and the Incense Master repeats the process with each candidate. Each candidate then receives a small bowl of the wine mixture and sips from it.

There is a secret code number for each rank of membership. For the rank-and-file member, the number is 49. The significance of this is that 4 times 9 is 36, the number of oaths the members take.

Many verbal signs or recognition phrases have been recorded. "My mother's vagina has teeth" refers to the symbolic rebirth in passing through the Heaven and Earth Circle.

30·

Tales from the Crypt

The Crypt Above Marilyn Monroe's

Urban legend tells of a man who was so enamored of Marilyn Monroe that he bought the empty crypt above hers. Eventually the man died and was placed in the crypt. A few friends lingered at the funeral until everyone else had left. Then they honored the dead man's last request. They turned the body face down, on top of Monroe for eternity.

Is there anything to this? All we could learn is that the crypt above Monroe's *is* occupied, by a male decedent, who was interred after Monroe. Monroe's grave is nothing fancy, a wall crypt identical to its neighbors except for having her name on it. The grave is in the Corridor of Memories section of Westwood Memorial Cemetery, a small park now surrounded by tall buildings in western Los Angeles. For years ex-husband Joe DiMaggio had fresh roses put on the crypt. There are still enough Monroe fans out there that the grave nearly always has fresh flowers. The body was interred with an expensive necklace, and on at least one occasion, robbers tried to break into the crypt. According to cemetery spokesmen, the actress's remains are sealed safely behind two feet of concrete.

The crypt above Monroe's bears the name Richard F. Poncher and the inscription, "To the man who gave us everything and more. You're one in a million, 'Freddie.' " Unfortunately, we couldn't trace things any further than that. Poncher didn't get an obituary in the local papers. He was born in 1905 and died in 1986—so that's when this stunt would have happened, *if* it happened.

Space Shuttle Death Video

There is a small body of purportedly suppressed films or videotapes of famous people's deaths. Take, for instance, the rumor that NASA has a never-released videotape of the *Challenger* space-shuttle crew in the moments before they died. In its way, the story sounds reasonable. Astronauts shoot hours of video, most of which is now considered too mundane to make the news. If NASA *did* have a video of the *Challenger* crew's death, wouldn't they have to keep it under wraps?

Any video from the *Challenger* would be brief. The shuttle exploded just 73 seconds after lift-off.

Biggest Secrets asked William Robbins, audio-visual manager of public affairs for NASA, about the video. Robbins would have been one of the first to see it and decide what to do with it, *if* it existed. But Robbins insisted convincingly that there never was any such footage. The *Challenger* was still in the "launch configuration" at the time of the explosion. That means, by regulation, that all cameras were stowed.

Ground control had audio and computer data links only—plus, of course, the TV coverage of the launch from the ground. NASA staffers watching the flight-data monitors were not immediately aware of the explosion. The computer screens filled with S's. That was the symbol for "static" and didn't necessarily mean there was anything wrong with the spacecraft. TV viewers heard NASA communicator Steve Nesbitt continue to read routine data even after they had seen the explosion. Nesbitt was looking at the computers, not the TV.

There is not even an audio record of the explosion, at least such as you could recognize it. The last transmission from the *Challenger* is Francis Scobee saying, "Roger, go with throttle up." This, a routine remark about the engines reaching full power, shows that Scobee was unaware of anything being wrong at 70 seconds after lift-off. There were then only three more seconds until the explosion. The crew may have never known what hit them. Ground-based shots show an orange glow on the center of the orbiter bursting upward and engulfing the craft in well under a second.

JFK's Macabre Home Movie

Elusive—but very likely real—is a secret home movie that prefigures President Kennedy's death and was made just two months before his assassination. The John F. Kennedy Presidential Library in Boston periodically receives inquiries about it. Archivist Allan B. Goodrich told us he had heard about the film, but it was not and had never been in the library.

There is a whole assortment of prophetic acts or statements Kennedy made foreshadowing his death—some true, some fabricated, many somewhere in between. (While attending an official to-do at Arlington National Cemetery on Armistice Day, 1963, the president supposedly told Congressman Hale Boggs, "This is one of the really beautiful places on earth. I could stay here forever.") Kennedy spoke of death, *his* death, a number of times. Ralph G. Martin's 1983 biography, *A Hero for Our Time*, quotes Senator George Smathers of Florida: "I don't know why it was," Smathers said, "but death became kind of an obsession with Jack. 'How do you want to die?' he asked me. 'Would you prefer drowning? Would you prefer strangling? Or hanging? Which way would you rather go?' All that sort of stuff. He talked about that a *lot*. We must have gone through that routine more than a dozen times." Kennedy's own answer: a plane crash because it's quick.

This same strain of morbidity reportedly led Kennedy to stage his own death for an amateur film. The death film is described in *A Hero for Our Time*: "Suddenly Kennedy clutched his chest and fell flat on the ground. . . . [Red] Fay stumbled and fell directly on the president's body. Just then, a gush of red surged from the President's mouth covering his sport shirt. It was a grisly kind of humor," Martin wrote.

There are discrepancies in accounts of the movie. Martin does not give a source for his information and further says that "the date of this home movie was Labor Day weekend, 1963." That date appears to be wrong, as news coverage said that the Kennedys spent Labor Day in Hyannis. The Newport trip, in the company of the Fays, took place the weekend of September 21–22.

But there can be little doubt that some kind of movie was made. Some press actually observed part of the film making, from a great distance, through binoculars. The film was mentioned in contemporary AP and UPI stories, but not as a movie of Kennedy being killed. The wire-service stories mentioned clowning around, and it was Red Fay (under secretary of the navy and JFK crony from his PT-boat days) who was trodden underfoot. For instance, a *New York Times* headline of September 22, 1963, declared, "KENNEDY ACTS ROLE OF THE STRAIGHT MAN TO AIDE'S CLOWNING." In a UPI story dated the previous day and printed in the *Times*, a reporter wrote:

> At the end of the cruise, Under Secretary of the Navy Paul B. Fay, Jr. stretched prone on the dock of Hammersmith Farm, clowning with Mr. Kennedy for the benefit of a Government photographer. Mr. Fay, his wife, and the Countess Crespi, a friend of the Kennedy family, were guests aboard the yacht.
>
> After the Honey Fitz berthed at the dock in front of the estate of Mrs. Kennedy's parents, Mr. and Mrs. Hugh Auchincloss, Mr. Fay scampered down the dock, lay down across the narrow walkway and smiled up at the President.
>
> Mr. Kennedy laughingly put his foot on Mr. Fay's stomach. As a Navy motion-picture photographer filmed the scene the President walked over Mr. Fay and into a convertible for a brief motor trip to the Auchincloss home . . .

All the *Times* made of this was that Kennedy's back wasn't bothering him anymore.

Given that JFK's brain is missing, it's not too surprising that a little old home movie got lost in the shuffle. Many of the people who were in the film are still around. The photographer, Robert L. Knudsen, is still around to talk about it. He insisted that Kennedy was the film's writer/director/producer: "He just called me over one day and said they wanted to have some fun and shoot a movie." There were about four other couples. The film was intended to be a comedy. The movie was shot with dialogue, and the death sequence was shot several times to get it right. The plot goes like this.

President Kennedy is seen getting off his yacht, the *Honey Fitz*. He walks down a long pier. Suddenly he grabs his chest and falls to the ground. Countess Crespi and son blandly step over the fallen leader of the free world. Ditto for Jackie. Finally Red Fay trips over Kennedy and falls on him. Blood spills from Kennedy's mouth, staining his shirt red.

Even a cinematic death of the president was thought too distressing for public consumption, so they evidently put out the story that Fay was the victim. If the administration was antsy about the film to begin with, its misgivings must have multiplied after Kennedy's real death. Had the film not been suppressed, we would almost surely be plagued with lists of eerie parallels between JFK's real and fictional deaths (both recorded in a home movie; both with Jackie at his side; Newport film shot more than once/Kennedy shot more than once?; etc., etc., etc.).

The Plot to Clone Saddam Hussein

No human being has ever been cloned. Saddam Hussein contemplated having himself cloned, though, and may still intend to go through with the plan.

Hussein is evidently pinning his hopes on cryonics, the movement that freezes people after their deaths in the hope that future medical science may be able to bring them back to life. Keeping a body frozen in perpetuity is expensive. In recent years cryonics organizations have introduced cheaper alternatives. Some people's heads—only their heads—have been frozen. Supporters reason that by the time the reanimation is possible, it will be a cinch to clone a new body from cells in the head. At present prices, freezing a head cost $45,000, vs. $125,000 for a complete body. (Freezing a *pet* can run $16,000.)

But for a relative pittance, it's possible to freeze tissue samples. Semen is frozen, thawed, and used successfully for artificial insemination all the time. Cloning a body from the genetic material in frozen cells is still cyberpunk territory, but perhaps less far-fetched than reanimating a frozen corpse. It has been alleged that Malcolm Forbes and Halston secretly had cell samples frozen before their deaths for cloning purposes and that Michael Jackson and Muhammad Ali plan to have tissue samples, or maybe their whole bodies, frozen. But celebrity-cloning rumors have been impossible to pin down—until the Hussein story came along.

According to American Cryonics Society president Dr. Avi Ben-Abraham, Iraqi representatives contacted the society in the summer of 1990. Ben-Abraham did not speak with Hussein personally, but he said he had no reason to doubt that the representatives were who they said they were. The Iraqis wanted information about freezing Hussein's semen and tissue samples for future cloning. Ben-Abraham gave them the information they asked for. There was no reason not to at the time. Ben-Abraham did not freeze any Hussein tissue and doesn't know if the Iraqis did or will.

Gruesome Practices

Most people have heard the usual round of grisly stories about funeral homes: how the ashes returned are not necessarily those of the loved one; how workers pocket jewelry; how the serene and lifelike body may be lacking vital organs in demand by medical schools. Do these things really happen? A perusal of recent court cases shows that the answer is *sometimes*.

In 1990 highway workers found a container of human ashes on the median of the Glendale Freeway in southern California. Cremation ashes aren't like cigarette ashes. They're a fine gravel often likened to cat litter. A label identified the peculiar find as the remains of Susan Lescoe, a Las Vegas woman. This information came as a rude awakening to Lescoe's family, who were under the distinct impression that Lescoe's ashes were in the tasteful and expensive marble niche they had purchased at Forest Lawn Memorial Park. They had held a funeral and everything. Their curiosity whetted, the family decided to open the niche at Forest Lawn. Inside were *somebody's* ashes. Ashes are normally labeled with the name of the deceased. These had no label. Lescoe's family filed a lawsuit. Forest Lawn denied all wrongdoing. They insisted that the unlabeled ashes were Lescoe's and that the ashes labeled as hers were somebody else's (but not a Forest Lawn customer's).

In 1989 David Sconce, who ran the respected and long-established Lamb Funeral Home in Pasadena, California, pleaded guilty to 21 charges of corpse mishandling. Currently awaiting trial on charges that he attempted to arrange the murder of a prosecutor and his grandparents, Sconce was cleared in 1991 of an earlier charge of poisoning a rival mortician with an extract from a toxic shrub.

Ash commingling was Sconce's undoing. After his own crematory burned down, Sconce (a Bible school football coach) began sending corpses out to a nearby ceramics kiln. Word got around that Sconce's funeral home was cremating more than one body at once. Economy of scale is sound business practice, but it would be an exacting chore to separate one person's ashes from another's once they had been mixed. It appeared to the court that families were getting not the 100 percent pure mortal remains of their own relative, but rather a mélange of the funeral home's recent customers. The prosecution claimed that Sconce's home stored ashes in 55-gallon drums and dispensed them as needed.

Investigation revealed other irregularities. Sconce reportedly used screwdrivers and pliers to extract gold fillings from death-clenched jaws, clearing more than $5,000 a month this way. Any cosmetic downside to such brute-force extractions was invisible. Lips are always closed for presentation.

Eyelids are closed, too. In an apparent conflict of interest, Sconce also operated an eye and organ bank. In a further conflict of interest, funeral-home staff forged signatures of decedents' next of kin on organ-donation forms for eyes and hearts, according to testimony. In order to maximize the synergy, the address of Scone's Coastal International Eye and Tissue Bank was the same as that of the funeral home itself.

Court papers claimed that Carolina Biological Supply Co. had purchased organs from about a *thousand* human bodies from Sconce's funeral homes in the period between 1980 and 1987. Carolina Biological is a well-known and reputable firm supplying dissection material for high school and college biology classes. We obtained a copy of their 1987–1988 catalog, which touted preserved human remains for all budgets. A human sciatic nerve could be had for a mere $13.12, while $320.00 would have bought a complete human digestive system. A testis cost $70.44. Despite the plethora of reasonably priced internal organs, no complete bodies were for sale—which may have something to do with the fact that funeral homes are expected to leave relatives something to look at.

No one supposes that the above cases are typical of the mortuary profession. But on the other hand, reason demands that the proportion of funeral-home abuses that are ever prosecuted is awfully small. There are few scenarios so unthinkably ghoulish that they have not, at some point, been established as fact, in court, under the presumption of innocence until proven guilty.

Index

About the Author

Book Publications

Big Secrets (William Morrow, 1983)
The Recursive Universe (William Morrow, 1984)
Bigger Secrets (Houghton Mifflin, 1986)
Labyrinths of Reason (Doubleday, 1988)
The Ultimate (Doubleday, 1990)
Prisoner's Dilemma (Doubleday, 1991)
Biggest Secrets (William Morrow, 1993)
Carl Sagan: A Life in the Cosmos (Henry Holt, 1999)

Reviews and Publicity

William Poundstone's three Secrets books have received extensive print and broadcast publicity, including the David Letterman show, CBS Morning News, Cable News Network, Book TV, the Larry King show, Entertainment Tonight, Inside Edition, MTV News, the Regis Philbin show, and hundreds of radio talk shows.

The Recursive Universe, about computer simulation and the laws of physics, received a front-page notice in the *Los Angeles Times Book Review.* "The work is a tour de force in every area it touches, and it touches some of the most important and deepest thinking of the 20th century. This highly original and creative work provides a new way of looking at familiar facts. . . . Poundstone's book is a science writer's ideal, satisfying to both specialist and amateur."

Labyrinths of Reason explores the role of paradox in science. *Publishers Weekly* wrote, "In a dazzling tour de force Poundstone (*The Recursive Universe*) leads us through a series of paradoxes that move from Sherlock Holmes's puzzles to time travel, from dismembered brains in vats to multiple worlds, from the libraries of Atlantis to black holes. Eminently accessible, this delightful, rapid-fire entertainment will appeal to readers of Douglas Hofstadter's *Gödel, Escher, Bach*." Hofstadter himself praised *Labyrinths of Reason* as "a sparkling and highly original approach to the deep mysteries of common sense, evidence, knowledge, and truth. Poundstone is superb at converting philosophical debates into wonderfully clear and stimulating mind-benders. Anyone interested in how minds reflect reality—from beginners to professionals—will get a big kick out of this book."

Prisoner's Dilemma, an account of mathematician John von Neumann's game theory and its effect on public policy, was on the *San Francisco Chronicle* bestseller list for two months. It has been published in Britain, Germany, France, Spain, and Japan. The *Coast Book Review* called it "an absolute, mind-blowing page-turner. . . . *Prisoner's Dilemma* is the latest title from one of the best science/contemporary thought writers we have in the English language.

Carl Sagan: A Life in the Cosmos (Henry Hot, 1999) was praised in the *New York Times, The New Yorker, Scientific American, Nature, Entertainment Weekly,* and the *Washington Post* as a compelling and balanced treatment of the private life of one of America's most visible scientists. Biologist Lynn Margulis wrote: "Poundstone's scintillating tale of the intellectually precocious but emotionally crippled Brooklyn boy who become the greatest science spokesman in history sparkles with originality. . . . As Carl's first wife, I authentically testify to Poundstone's competence, responsibility, veracity and scientific insight." *Carl Sagan* was a selection of the Book of the Month Club and was featured on CSPAN's Book TV.

Other Publications

Poundstone has written for *The Economist, Esquire, Harper's,* the *Journal of Men's Studies,* the *Los Angeles Times,* the *New York Times Book Review, Penthouse, Spy,* and many other publications.

He is cofounder of, and regular contributor to, *The Keeler News,* a bimonthly publication devoted to eccentric American novelist Harry Stephen Keeler.

Visual Art Exhibitions

"1998 Exhibition of Southern California Artists." Los Angeles Municipal Art Gallery. July 15–August 23, 1998.

"Human [Realist/Abstract]." Circle Elephant Art, Los Angeles. July 7–30, 2000.

"New Digital Emblems." Web project for California Museum of Photography, 2000.

"Doom Arbor," "Denied,"etc. Web projects for UbuWeb, 2000.

"New Photography." Circle Elephant Art, Los Angeles. December 1–24, 2000.

Television

"Secrets Revealed" (produced by Dave Bell Associates; aired on ABC, February 1994). Writer. Based on the *Secrets* books.

"More Secrets Revealed" (produced by Dave Bell Associates; aired on ABC, May 1995). Writer and coproducer. Based on the *Secrets* books.

"Identity Crisis" (pilot for game show, 1996, in development with Time Warner Telepictures and Bogorad-Wyler Entertainment). Creator, producer, and writer.